The Y2K Survival Guide

Getting to, Getting Through, and Getting Past the Year 2000 Problem

Bruce F. Webster

ISBN 0-13-021496-5

Prentice Hall PTR
Upper Saddle River, New Jersey 07458
http://www.phptr.com

Editorial/production supervision: *Joanne Anzalone*
Cover design director: *Jerry Votta*
Cover design: *Scott Weiss*
Manufacturing manager: *Alexis R. Heydt*
Acquisitions editor: *Jeffrey Pepper*
Marketing manager: *Dan Rush*
Editorial assistant: *Linda Ramagnano*

To my children—
Chase Vivian Ochs (and Frank)
Aaron Vivian
Jacqueline Webster
Heather Vivian
Bethan Webster
Jennifer Burton Schiewbert (and Dean)
Wesley Vivian
Jon Webster
Crystal Vivian
and Emily "Pooker" Webster—
to whom the next century belongs

May your generation be wiser than ours
Or at least, plan ahead a bit better

Contents

Chapter 2
How We Got Here, or, All Our Sins Remembered   29

Chapter 3
The Roadblocks to Fixing Y2K   55

Chapter 4

Myths, Facts, and Opinions About Y2K 83

Chapter 5

Chapter 6

Contents   xi

Chapter 9

Chapter 10

Chapter 11

EPILOGUE
THE ENDLESS MILLENNIAL SUMMER?   381

Chapter A
Testimony Before Congress   385

Chapter B

Chapter C

Appendix D

Introduction: The Winter of Our Disconnect

There is a common logical fallacy, called the *fallacy of false dilemmas*. In its most common form, someone presents a false choice between two alternatives without acknowledging or allowing that there might be any number of other alternatives outside of the two given. For example, someone might claim that you face two choices—get a college education or flip burgers for the rest of your life—ignoring a wide variety of other paths through life. A second, even more common one is the *strawman fallacy*, so-called because it consists of presenting a weak or implausible ("strawman") version of an argument and then demolishing it.

Unfortunately, these two have been combined in much of what has passed for reporting and pronouncements on the Year 2000 (or Y2K) technology issue. Typically, an article or report presents two alternatives: the end of the world as we know it, with planes (and missiles!) falling out of the sky, cars and elevators coming to a halt, and your VCR and refrigerator going on the blink...or not a big deal at all, a non-event with most things fixed. The first alternative (the strawman) is debunked or, at least, ridiculed—usually with an armed survivalist or two thrown in for "color"—and so the implicit and sometimes explicit conclusion is that the other alternative—no

The Y2K Survivial Guide

big deal—is what will happen, and so there is nothing to worry about.

Wrong.

The plausible consequences of the Y2K problem encompass far more than these two alternatives. Indeed, as you'll see later in this book, I would argue that the *likely* consequences include neither; it will not be the collapse of civilization, but neither will it be a stroll in the park. Service and supply disruptions, if they happen, will tend to be short-lived, but the economic consequences will last longer.

Beyond that, though, is this simple fact: the exact consequences are difficult to predict. We lack sufficient accurate and reliable information about how various organizations—corporations, government agencies, utility companies, and others— are doing in tracking down and fixing their Y2 problems. We have even less information about how Y2K is being dealt with outside of the United States. All this is happening within the context of a global economic meltdown and any number of regional political crises. And the very nature of complex systems means that we can't predict or anticipate how they will respond to all these factors.

But guess what? Life is like that. It is full of uncertainties and unexpected developments. Hurricanes, floods, earthquakes, and other disasters come upon us no matter how much we would prefer otherwise. Likewise, we can face job setbacks and unemployment regardless of the overall strength of the economy. Problems in our personal lives—health, relationships, finances—can hit us at any time. However much we may want things to continue as they are, they can change in an instant, irrevocably.

The Year 2000 problem is more predicable than most life events—if not in consequences, then in timing. As such, we have the chance to track its development, to make appropriate preparation, and to deal with whatever may come. In so doing, we can prepare for other surprises that life may hold and in general reduce worries or a sense of helplessness.

This book is about getting to, getting through, and getting past the Year 2000. It has three major goals:

Give you a reliable and balanced looked at the origin, history, and status of the Y2K problem;

Lay out a method for helping you and your family to plan and prepare for not only Y2K but just about any type of setback in a manner adjusted to your goals, needs, and circumstances;

Outline a broad range of possible Y2K scenarios to give you a better understanding of what is and isn't likely to happen.

We tend to fear what we don't understand and aren't prepared to handle. The overall goal of this book is to replace that fear with confidence. That will not only help you in your own life, but it will help reduce the potential for Y2K consequences driven by fear and panic. The more prepared and calm we are about Y2K, the less impact it will have.

Above all, we need to maintain some perspective. In February of 1998, I was a guest speaker at the Middle East Year 2000 Conference in Beirut, Lebanon. One of my presentations outlined the nature and extent of the Y2K problem and detailed some of the potential consequences. Afterward, a high official of the Bank of Lebanon came up to me and said in so many words, "What's the big deal? We've been living with far worse than that for the last 25 years." So much of what has been detailed as "awful" Y2K consequences is a way of life for the rest of the world—and life for them goes on each day.

Regardless of what happens, life will go on for us as well. And even if it gets a bit tougher than we expected or hoped for, so what? Many of our parents and grandparents went through the Great Depression and World War II; it is highly unlikely that what we face rivals either, much less both. But whatever we face, I believe we can do it with the same dignity, courage, honor, and perseverance that set the standard by which we shall be judged. We have a work to do; let's get it done and move on to the next millennium.

Bruce F. Webster
Irving, Texas
October, 1998

Acknowledgments

I'm grateful to Carole McClendon of Waterside Productions for all her help and support in bringing this book into existence. She has been involved in every book I've written in the past ten years, and I appreciate her experience, judgment, and professionalism; most of all, I value her friendship.

Much responsibility for this book and many thanks go to Tony Gibson, president and owner of Object Systems Group (www.osgcorp.com). Tony was outstanding in his support of my taking the time to write this and letting me continue my involvement in the Washington DC Year 2000 (WDCY2K) group and other Y2K activities.

Of course, I almost certainly wouldn't have written this book were it not for Carol Teasley at Fannie Mae, who drafted me into the war on Y2K (they say that misery loves company). Carol runs one of the finest Y2K remediation projects in the whole world, one of the few Fortune 100 efforts that will be complete a full year ahead of time. About 20 percent of U.S. homeowners, not to mention Fannie Mae shareholders and upper management, have a lot for which to thank her.

Almost as responsible is Linda Vance, a key member of Fannie Mae's Y2K effort, who came up with the idea for a DC-region Y2K group in a staff meeting one day, then looked at me and said, "And, Bruce, I think you're the one to do it." Next is Helen Drew, my partner-in-crime and co-chair of the Washington D.C. Year 2000 group. While I may have more of the visibility, Helen is the power behind the throne and the true reason why the WDCY2K meetings run so smoothly month after month. I'm also grateful for my professional and personal association with the rest of the Fannie Mae Y2K team, including Linda Eatmon, Rich Valus, Diana Truby, Carol Schreiber, and the many members of the Fannie Mae Y2K Contingency Planning Team, to whom mortgage- and shareholders may also end up owing much to before this is all done.

And, of course, I need to thank the general membership, participants, and rowdies of the Washington D.C. Year 2000 group. Some 1600 strong, they represent the largely unsung heroes of the Year 2000 effort, the ones who have been working on this problem, day in and day out, for months or years, while trying to get everyone else to take the problem seriously. There are too many WDCY2K members to thank individually, but y'all know who you are.

I need to thank Jeffrey Pepper of Prentice Hall for being willing to publish this book under challenging circumstances; as with Y2K repair efforts, the deadlines for Y2K books are tight and, ultimately, immovable. Likewise, I appreciate Jim Markham's input as development editor and Joanne Anzalone's work as production editor. All moved heaven and earth to get this book out on time; all made this book better than it would have been otherwise.

Finally, and always, I'm thankful for the ever-constant love, support, encouragement, and understanding of my eternal sweetheart Sandra, who had to run things on her own for weeks after our move to Texas while I traveled and wrote. And I'm grateful for our conglomerate of offspring—Chase and

Frank, Aaron, Jacqui, Heather, Bethan, Wesley, Jon, Crystal, and Emily—scattered across three continents and twelve time zones. It is to our children that this book is dedicated.

Bruce F. Webster (bwebster@bfwa.com)
Chief Technical Officer
Object Systems Group
Irving, Texas
October 1998

Disclaimer

This book is to educate you. It is not intended as formal legal, financial, medical, nutritional, educational, employment, or investment advice; for that, you should seek the services of a certified and qualified professional. Use at your own risk. Your mileage may vary.

PART I

HOW WE GOT TO THE YEAR 2000

Setting the Stage: 1600 to 1999

Amici, diem perdidi. (Friends, I have lost a day.)
—Titus Vespasianus

Some four hundred years ago, an unknown inventor of great skill and vision constructed an exceedingly clever device to predict the relative positions of the sun and the planets for centuries to come. It worked by rotating an arm along the outside of a large stone wheel. The arm "read" bumps and notches on the wheel and used that information to adjust the replica of the solar system in the middle of the wheel. The arm could move forwards and backwards, so that you could select any given year.

However, since there was room for just so many notches and bumps along the outside of the wheel, the inventor had to set bounds on the years that could be represented, had to pick a start date and an end. The starting date—1600—was likely selected because of the epoch when the document was created. As for the end date—ah, there's the rub. Was it convenience? Religious beliefs? The human proclivity for round numbers and tidy endings? We don't know. What we do know is that because of a conscious engineering decision, this device, whose function has spanned a dozen generations and the rise and fall of nations and empires, cannot see past 1999. For the first time in its life of nearly half a millennium, it will only be able to look back, not ahead.

This instrument represents the oldest known variant of the Year 2000 problem. To the artisan who made it, the year 2000 must have seemed terribly remote, the end of a millennium barely half over. Indeed, she or he probably doubted the mechanism would last that long. And now the date has come. Centuries have ticked off like clockwork, the earth spinning on its axis as it revolves around the sun. Time moves on, as time always does.

This time, though, we have built a clockwork that spans the globe and reaches its tendrils out into space. It is an evolving system that touches every aspect of life. To paraphrase [Haldane], it is not only more complex than we imagine, it is more complex than we can imagine. And at millions of points throughout this system, we have created time faults that will trip over the year 2000 and its poor relations. Time will move on, but the resulting timequake and its aftershocks will be felt worldwide for months and years to come.

How did we come to this pass, this crisis that was at once avoidable and yet somehow inevitable? How did we reach the year 2000?

One day at a time.

A Brief Primer on the Year 2000 (Y2K) Problem

A little neglect may breed a great mischief.
—Benjamin Franklin

Our situation is ironic yet somehow appropriate. Having anticipated for so long our entry into the twenty-first century and the third millennium, we're about to trip on the threshold and stumble—not stride—through the door. And we have no one to blame but ourselves. The Year 2000 (or Y2K) problem, also known extravagantly as "the millennium bug" (it's a mere century bug), has emerged from our own civilization and choices. Indeed, it is an entirely human manifestation—not completely natural, such as an earthquake or a hurricane, or intensified by human acts, such as the 1998 floods in Mainland China, but caused solely by that which we have created.

Through all the coverage of Y2K, questions have been raised about how real this problem is, what caused it, how we are going to fix it, and what kind of progress we are making. Our goal for this chapter is to answer those questions in clear and relevant terms. Chapter 2, "How We Got There, or, All Our Sins Remembered," will focus on how we got into this mess, Chapter 3, "The Roadblocks of Fixing Y2K," will explain why there aren't any miracle solutions, and Chapter 4,

"Myths, Facts, and Opinions About Y2K," will debunk some common Y2K misunderstandings, But first, let's tackle some basic computer concepts and terminology.

What Does It All Mean?

Discussing the Y2K problem requires using some basic terminology, most of which you hear (and possibly use) on a regular basis. Even so, let's take a minute to go over some brief, simplistic, but sufficient explanations for four key concepts: hardware, software, data, and embedded control. Much of the confused reporting and misperceptions around Y2K stem from a lack of understanding of these elements and how they relate to one another and to us.

Hardware

Hardware is something you can touch. Hardware includes chips of all sorts, the circuit boards they reside on along with other electronic components, wiring, slots, cables, cases, covers, displays, keyboards, keypads, disk drives, and so on. Your personal computer is hardware, as are workstations, servers, minicomputers, and mainframes.

For that matter, though most people don't use the word as such, hardware includes pagers, cellular and digital phones, telecommunications equipment (including phones), cars, consumer electronics, appliances, nuclear power plants, offshore oil platforms, and just about anything else that has chips in it.

Hardware is physical. Hardware is small and getting smaller. Hardware is cheap and getting cheaper. Hardware is fast and getting faster. And hardware (at least, most hardware) runs software.

Software

Software is less tangible. Put simply, software tells hardware what to do. It can take a variety of forms: microcode, embedded right within individual chips; low-level software stored in read-only memory (ROMs), such as the basic input/output system (BIOS) found in most PCs; operating systems, such as Windows, MacOS, UNIX, and VMS; custom applications, such as those developed with an organization for its own use; commercial applications, ranging from games and word processors to large, complex programs for mainframes; utilities, such as virus scanners; development environments used to create software itself, such as Borland C++, Visual Basic, or the Java Development Kit (JDK); and hundreds of other forms.

Software is a bit like music. Music is a set of notes and/or data, interpreted by the appropriate device (or human). You can create music on various instruments. You can write down or print out music. You can store music on tapes, records, and disks. You can transmit music over radio, TV, phones, cables, and the Internet. But none of those things is the music itself. The music has its impact, its effect when it is played and listened to.

In much the same way, software is a set of instructions, interpreted by the appropriate device, usually a processor chip of some sort (the central processing unit, or CPU, of a computer or embedded control system), but sometimes a specialized device. Software can be created, stored, copied, and transmitted in different ways and on different media—but it only has its impact when it is actually executed. Software, as noted above, can be embedded in chips; it can be stored on tapes, floppy and hard disks, CD-ROMs, and other media; and it can be transmitted via phone lines, cables, and over the airwaves.

What is important to realize is how utterly pervasive software is in our world. It surrounds us in ways of which we are largely unaware. And the foundation of the Year 2000 problem is how that software chooses to represent and manipulate time-related data.

Data

Data is information: logical values (true/false), numbers, dates, names, addresses, text, tables, images, sounds, video, animations, and so on. It's a bit more tangible and general than software in that it doesn't have to be interpreted by hardware in order to be data. For example, data may exist in human-understandable forms (printouts, screen images, sounds) and have value independent of hardware or software. You use software to manipulate data when you type into a word processor, fill numbers in a spreadsheet, load Web pages over the Internet with a browser, or play the latest shoot-'em-up game.

The fundamental unit of data in computers is a **bit** (**bi**nary digi**t**). A bit has two possible values: 0 or 1. You cannot get any simpler than that, and those two states are very easy to represent, detect, and manipulate with electronic circuitry, which is why computers ended up based on them. These happen to be the only two digits available to you in base-2, or **binary**, math (as opposed to the base-10, or **decimal**, values represented by the digits 0…9).

Collections of bits are gathered into a **byte**, which today is almost universally defined as 8 bits. A single 8-bit byte can represent a total of $2^8 = 256$ values. The ASCII character set, the most common one used in computers, defines its entire set of alphabetic characters, punctuation marks, decimal digits, control codes, and special characters as a range of values, 0…255, and so uses 1 byte per character. Thus, the text string

"Webster, Emily: 11/29/85" would be stored as 24 bytes of data. Other kinds of data—numbers, records, images, sounds—would be encoded in other ways, but they are all bytes and bits at the core.

Information that is represented at the lowest level using discrete numeric values is called **digital**. This contrasts with **analog** information, which is stored or transmitted as continuous physical, magnetic, or electromagnetic manifestations. For example, the grooves in a vinyl record and the tape in a cassette contain analog information, while the microscopic bits on a compact disk contain digital information. The two forms of information are frequently converted back and forth, using A-to-D (analog-to-digital) and D-to-A (digital-to-analog) converters.

Hardware often receives information in analog form, converting it to digital. Software manipulates data, taking in what it needs, what it can get, and/or what it is given, and then takes actions and produces output based on the results. This is the fundamental model of software development: bringing together the necessary data and instructions to create the desired result. In many cases, the digital output is then converted back to analog, particularly if it's for human consumption: light, sound, and so on.

All software is itself ultimately data. That concept was one of the great insights in the early days of computer science. Data becomes software when something decides to interpret a chunk of information as a list of instructions. When software executes, it is usually in the context of having been manipulated by other software, such as when an operating system loads and runs an application. Even at the lowest level, all a central processing unit (CPU) is doing is fetching small pieces of data and moving and combining them in particular ways based on the bit patterns in other small chunks of data.

Embedded Control Systems

An **embedded control system** (ECS) is the functional equivalent of a computer, usually embedded inside of something else. It can range from a tiny specialized chip within a wristwatch to a dedicated workstation on board an aircraft carrier. ECSs are also found in manufacturing equipment; sensors and other monitoring devices; chemical and food processing plants; mining, oil, and gas extraction sites; scientific, lab, and medical equipment; ships, satellites, planes, trucks, and cars; radar and other air traffic systems; building environment control and security systems; household appliances; consumer electronics; and so on.

An ECS comprises hardware, software, and data; indeed, the boundaries between the three are often fuzzy. The hardware is typically one or more processing chips along with other supporting chips and circuitry, sensors, input/output (I/O) device, and interfaces with other systems or devices. The software is most often in read-only memory (ROM) or electronically programmable ROM (EPROM); software in the former can be updated only by physically replacing the ROM chip(s), while that in the latter can have new software loaded into it without having to be removed. Data typically comes from various I/O ports, sensors, and other interfaces. As noted, some ECSs are actually full-blown personal computers (PCs) or workstations. Some may have been "repackaged," but many are just off-the-shelf systems running dedicated software, often with specialized cards and devices attached.

ECSs typically carry out one or more of five key functions:

- metering: measuring, sensing, or otherwise monitoring other systems, sensors, controls, or devices, and then taking action when certain events occur;

- scheduling: taking specific actions at specific times or when certain periods of time have elapsed;

- maintenance: allowing remote examination, trouble-shooting, and correction of devices, or signaling the need for maintenance to occur;

- data crunching: providing raw horsepower to carry out intensive calculations for "less intelligent" devices and systems;

- interfacing: delivering information to humans and/or other systems, and allowing it to interact with the ECS and other systems it might control or communicate with.

Again, it's hard to convey how pervasive software has become in our world. I travel to work each day in a car that probably has a dozen or more embedded control systems, each running its own software. I wear a digital watch, a two-way pager, and a digital mobile phone—all with embedded systems and software. I carry in my briefcase a laptop that, while battered, somewhat old, and a bit flaky, still contains all by itself more memory (RAM), more hard disk space, more software, and likely more computing power than existed on the entire campus of my alma mater when I was an undergraduate computer science student back in the mid-1970s. There are hundreds of millions of computers and tens of billions of embedded control systems worldwide—and all function because of the software that tell them what to do and when to do it. And that is what has opened the door for the Year 2000 (Y2K) problem.

What Is the Year 2000 Problem?

It's quite simple, really. Think about the forms you might fill out in the course of a year: school registration, driver's license, tax filings, and so on. In most cases, when you write a date in those forms, you likely do it as "11/29/85" or "29/11/85" or "11 Nov. 85." Until recently, your checks likely came with "19" preprinted in the date field. You knew what the dates meant, and so did most other people.

Software can and often does operate in the same way. In much of the software written over the past 50 years, dates were (and are) represented in data using just two digits for years: "67" instead of "1967," "95" instead of "1995," and so on. In the instructions that deal with dates, the "19" is assumed, and the calculations and operations are carried out accordingly.

The problems start when software using this format encounters or calculates a date involving the year 2000 or beyond. Such a date will be represented as "00," "01," and so on. It's as though your car had a two-digit odometer: after you had gone 99 miles, it would roll back to 00 and start over. Of course, your car probably wouldn't care, since most cars don't do calculations or carry out operations based on the actual odometer, but you might get confused trying to figure out exactly how far you had come. In the same way, much of the software currently in use can get confused when dealing with a year—"00"—that can be interpreted in two or more ways.

Some software using the two-digit date format will presume that "00" means "2000." Such software is most likely doing what is known as *windowing*, which means the fundamental problem has been postponed, not eliminated. We'll talk more about how this works later on.

Other software has code that presumes that all years are in the 1900s and so will interpret "00" as "1900." This may cause any number of problems. If the software is calculating elapsed time between dates, then it will interpret the interval from 12/31/99 to 01/01/00 as nearly a full century instead of a single day—and the interval will be negative (going back in time) instead of positive (going forward). This can result in inaccurate, unexpected, or nonsensical results. It can even cause the software to "crash," that is, to have an error that halts that particular program. Likewise, if the software were putting data into chronological order, that is, sorting by the dates, then all the dates in 2000 would be placed before all the dates ranging from 1901 to 1999.

Some software uses "00" in the year field to signal some special condition. In other words, a date with the year set to "00" represents neither "1900" nor "2000," but something entirely different—perhaps the end of a set of dated records, or a date that occurs every year. In such a case, to suddenly deal with lots of dates with a year of "00" can again cause unexpected, erratic, and incorrect results or may cause the program to crash.

Finally, there is software that never expects to have a year of "00" at all. Again, such software is likely to behave in unexpected ways, particularly in embedded control systems. A friend tested her camcorder for Y2K compliance by setting its date and time ahead to just before midnight on December 31, 1999, and then started taping. When the camcorder's internal clock hit midnight, it ejected the tape—and froze in the eject mode. Nothing she could do—including resetting the date—would make the camcorder work again. She finally had to send it back to the factory to be repaired. Less amusing are some of the stories that have come out of chemical factories and utility

plants about unexpected and possibly destructive consequences of Y2K problems in embedded control systems.

The Actual Extent of Y2K Problems

The bulk of software in use today either doesn't use dates at
all, already uses a four-digit representation for years, or uses a
two-digit representation with windowing. Capers Jones, chairman of Software Productivity Research, estimates that roughly
two-thirds of all software systems and applications have no
Y2K problems,[1] while probably more than 99 percent of all
embedded control systems are unaffected.

Such Y2K-ready software is, in theory, unaffected by the
Y2K problem. However, it can be impacted anyway. It may
receive data from software that isn't Y2K compliant, and so it
has to determine, for example, whether a given date is "1900"
or "2000." Even if it doesn't receive data with dates, it may
receive the results of calculations made by noncompliant software—and those calculations may be erroneous or corrupted.
Or it may depend upon noncompliant software in order to
run at all, and if that other software crashes, then the compliant software may not be able to run anyway.

Most of the software that does have Y2K problems only has
them in a tiny fraction of the actual program source code. For
example, a mainframe-based COBOL program that has one
million lines of instructions may only have 1–2 percent of its
lines that need to be changed to make it Y2K compliant. On
the other hand, that's still 10,000–20,000 lines of code that
have to be found, interpreted, and corrected.

Where Y2K Problems Occur

It is a common misconception that the problem occurs only
or primarily in old COBOL programs running on large main-

frame computers. While such programs probably have the greatest percentage of Y2K problems, they are not alone. Every type of software environment—minicomputers, client/server systems, workstations, personal computers, and the myriad of embedded control systems—has examples of Y2K problems. Note that commercial programs as recent as Windows 95, Internet Explorer 4.0, and JavaScript have Y2K issues. The problem can also show up in every other type of software: ROM-based software (such as in embedded control systems), operating systems, utilities, development tools, applications of all kinds, macros, scripts, and configuration files.

The problem doesn't just involve the software—it also involves any stored, displayed, or printed information. Data files, spreadsheets, databases, reports, and other stored information may have two-digit dates in them. These seldom cause problems in and of themselves, but they can trigger errors in the software that uses them. Likewise, software with Y2K problems can cause "data pollution" by storing invalid or erroneous values into these information sources.

How Widespread Is the Y2K Problem?

It's hard to get accurate numbers—indeed, it's hard for the average Fortune 500 corporation to determine just how many applications it has. But it has been estimated that there are roughly 36,000,000 software applications in the United States and, as already noted, about a third of them—12,000,000—have some form of Y2K problem.[2] For the entire world, you can roughly triple those numbers—about 100,000,000 applications, of which about 36,000,000 have some potential Y2K problem.

Remember that it appears there are somewhere from 10 billion to over 40 billion embedded control systems worldwide. Estimates of the percentage of ECSs with Y2K problems varies from 0.2 percent to 1 percent, though some feel even that's too high. But even if we take an ultraconservative estimate of 0.01 percent—saying that only one out of every 10,000 embedded systems has a Y2K problem—we are still looking at a potential of 1–4 million failures. And, of course, we face the far more serious challenge of how to locate, evaluate, and test those 10–40 billion ECSs in order to find those 1–4 million defective ones, and then how to replace those that need to be. Plus, it is not always obvious which ECSs might be affected. Rep. Steve Horn (R-CA), Chairman of the House Subcommittee on Government Management, Information, and Technology, reported a meeting he held in Louisiana at which the mayor of Baton Rouge reported finding a Y2K problem in the mechanism controlling ladders on the city's fire trucks.[3]

More significantly is that the ECSs that have a greater impact on our daily lives appear to have a higher probability of Y2K problems. Actual evaluations done in specific instances—an oil supertanker, an oil refinery, off-shore oil platforms, critical medical systems in a health care chain—have resulted in Y2K problem rates of 3 percent to 18 percent.

Our Response to Date

Consider this parable. There was a man who inherited a professional farm just after the fall harvests were gathered in. The silos were full, and the grains sold well. As fall slipped into winter, those in charge of the farm told the man that the fields would need to be prepared and replanted in the spring. But the man wanted to make some improvements to the farm equipment and to look at some new ways of farming, and he said that they would worry about tilling and sowing later. As spring arrived, the farm workers reminded the new owner—a bit more urgently—that the planting needed to be done, but the man looked around and saw other farms that hadn't planted yet, and so he told them that the money would go to other projects first and to pay off some debts, and they would still have to wait a while. As spring left and summer came, the farm hands—with great intensity—pointed out the need to till and plant now. The man let them start some trial plantings but wanted them to stay focused on other priorities, such as repainting the barn and looking at some new hybrid seeds. Finally, at the end of summer, the man realized that some other farms had planted months earlier and had crops that were well along. He ordered a crash program of preparation and planting, buying expensive farm equipment and the best fertilizers, hiring lots of new farm hands, and seeking advice from agricultural experts, most of whom told him he should have planted back in early spring. The crops were sown at last. But fall was in the air by the time the stalks were starting to shoot up, and the first frosts came while the grain was still unripe. Only a meager crop of poor quality was harvested before winter set in, bringing the season to an end.

Now, here's a shorter one. A man bought a set of bungee cords, and he stored them in the trunk of his car, looking for the right chance to use them while he read the best books on the subject. One day, he came to a bridge spanning a lovely gorge with a breathtaking view. So he got out the cords, carefully attached them to his ankles and to the bridge, put on a helmet and pads, and soared off the side of the bridge. He smashed at full velocity into the rocky ground below, the extra 40 feet of bungee cord piling up on his broken and bleeding body.

In short, we would be in great shape if this were 1994 or even 1996. But since I'm writing this early in the fall of 1998—and you're most likely reading it in 1999—we're in serious trouble. Many businesses, agencies, and organizations showed enough foresight to get started on Y2K repairs early and to devote the proper planning and resources to it, but far too many—by several indications, the majority—have started late or have not given it sufficient emphasis.

Status of the U.S. Federal Government

While the Social Security Administration got off to an early start, the rest of the government hasn't been doing so well. There are three basic sources of information: the Office of Management and Budget's quarterly report; a series of reports from the General Accounting Office; and a quarterly "report card" issued by Rep. Steve Horn, Chairman of the House Sub-committee on Government Management, Information, and Technology. These sources don't always agree, but they do give you a general sense of things. See Resources (in the back of the book) for how to get this information yourself.

The following lists are from Chairman Horn's quarterly report card released on September 9, 1998. The ratings reflect only how these departments and agencies are doing with their own internal systems, not the status of any sectors, industries, or organizations that they oversee or regulate.

- **Departments/agencies doing well** [A]: Social Security Administration, National Science Foundation, Small Business Administration.

- **Departments/agencies doing moderately well** [B+, B, B-]: General Services Administration,

Department of Commerce, Environmental Protection Agency, Department of Veteran's Affairs, Federal Emergency Management Agency.

- **Departments/agencies scraping by** [C+,C,C-]: NASA, Department of Agriculture, Department of Housing and Urban Development.

- **Departments/agencies in trouble** [D+,D,D-]: Department of the Treasury (including the IRS), Department of Transportation (including the FAA), Office of Personnel Management, Department of Defense, Department of Labor, Department of the Interior, Nuclear Regulatory Commission.

- **Departments/agencies in serious trouble** [F]: Department of Health and Human Services, Department of Energy, Department of State, Department of Justice, Department of Education, Agency for International Development.

Horn's overall grade for the Federal Government was a D— an improvement over the "F" of the June 1998 report card, but, as Horn noted, "This is not a grade you take home to your parents; and it is definitely not a grade to take back to the voters and taxpayers."[4]

There are three agencies and one department whose names keep bubbling to the top as having significant problems with their Y2K repairs that could have serious repercussions. These are the Federal Aviation Administration (FAA), responsible for air traffic control in the United States; the Internal Revenue Service (IRS), upon which the U.S. government depends for the money to operate; the Health Care Financial Administration (HCFA), which makes the majority of Medicare/Medicaid payments to hospitals, HMO, and other health care organizations. Likewise, the Department of Defense, including both the Pentagon itself and the U.S. armed forces worldwide, appears to have significant struggles.

Almost as serious are the changes from the previous report card to this one. Five of the departments and agencies improved their grades, but ten of them had their grades decline. That trend could be a result of more accurate and/or honest reporting, but it's still not encouraging.

Status of U.S. Industry

Consider the following reports.

- An analysis of corporate 10-Q and 10-E filings (summer 1998) by the 250 largest public companies in the United States showed that about half failed to disclose Y2K status as required by the Security Exchange Commission (SEC). Of those that did, the majority indicated that they were still in the inventory/assessment phase, which represents about 10 percent of the total effort required by a typical corporation to reach Y2K readiness.[5]

- This agrees with the spring 1998 survey of ten of the largest power producers in the United States done by the Senate Special Committee on the Year 2000 Technology Problem: 80 percent were still in the inventory/assessment phase.[6] Likewise, the committee did a survey of 32 transportation companies in the summer of 1998; half of the compa-

nies refused to respond, and of the other half that
did, a third were still in assessment and none had
completed any Y2K contingency plans.[7]

• Based on progress through mid-1998, Capers
  Jones of Software Productivity Research estimated
  that up to 75 percent of U.S. enterprises (including corporations, small businesses, military installations, and federal, state, and urban governments)
  will face significant to severe Y2K problems.[8]

Major corporations, after a slow start, are devoting major
resources to fixing Y2K. Of greater concern are the small-to-
medium enterprises (SMEs), including both small businesses
and local governments. Surveys indicate that the majority of such
firms had not started Y2K repair efforts by September 1998.

Status of the Rest of the World

While the United States may be behind, the rest of the world
is even worse. Here's a brief report card as of September 1998:

• Europe is focused on conversion to the Euro
  currency and has spent little real time on Y2K.
  This is due both to the political pressures surrounding Euro conversion and to a general lack
  of belief in Europe that the Y2K problem is real
  and affects European systems. The irony is that
  many European systems won't even be ready
  for the Euro trading, which is scheduled to start
  on January 1, 1999. Additional pressure to get
  the Euro conversion done is likely to push back
  Y2K repairs even more.

- Russia has some awareness but lacks financial resources and political focus. The fall 1998 turmoil will only make things worse.

- Asia, especially Japan, is dealing with a recession—possibly sliding into depression. Firms and governments are worried more about making payroll than dealing with Y2K.

- Africa, South America, and the rest of the developing nations are far behind. A survey done in mid-1998 by the World Bank indicated a significant lack of awareness and effort in these countries.

- The greatest public awareness—frankly greater than in the United States throughout much of 1998—is in the British Commonwealth: Britain, Scotland, Canada, New Zealand, and Australia.

In short, the rest of the world is anywhere from 6 to 18 months behind U.S. efforts on Y2K.

Is There a Solution for Year 2000 Problems?

Yes. Modify the programs or devices to work properly, or replace them with ones that do. That's it.

It's not rocket science; it's barely computer science. Many businesses, government organizations, and other organizations have made their repairs; many more will complete their efforts well before problems arise, and a fair number will hurry to complete their repairs once problems do appear.

The Y2K Remediation Process

For a given organization, the entire Y2K **remediation** process consists of several steps, some of which must be repeated at various points. These are:

- **Inventory**: Tracking down every application, utility, operating system, software package, embedded control system, and any other potentially affected system within your organization.

- **Assessment**: Determining which of the above actually have Y2K problems.

- **Repair**: Fixing, upgrading, replacing, or retiring the affected systems.

- **Testing**: Making sure that all your systems (including the ones you didn't modify) work in a time-shifted environment.

- **Reintegration**: Hooking all the modified and unmodified systems back together to make sure they still work with one another correctly, as well as with all the various external systems with which they interact.

- **Contingency planning**: Determining what your critical business functions are, what they depend upon (internally and externally), what risks you face due to Y2K, and how to cope with them should they come to pass.

Note, by the way, that this set of activities has to be applied (as much as you can) to your external dependencies as well: customers, suppliers, service providers, agencies, utilities, markets, and so on.

A somewhat longer discussion of this is given at the start of Chapter 3.

Repairing Y2K Problems

There are three basic approaches to the Y2K problem itself. The first is called **date expansion**. In it, you convert all dates and date-manipulation instructions in the program, as well as any data files or databases, to use four-digit years ("1998," "1999," "2000," etc.). It is the most general solution and it takes care of the problem for the next eight thousand years. However, it is also the most time consuming and expensive.

The second is called **windowing** (mentioned before). You continue to use two-digit years, but you define a **pivot year**, such as "50." You then modify your code to interpret all years below the pivot as starting with "20" (e.g., "2000" through "2049"). You interpret those from the pivot year and up as starting with "19" (e.g., "1950" through "1999"). The disadvantages are (1) you are limited to a span of 100 years; (2) one program's choice of a pivot year (say, "50") may differ from another program's choice (such as "40"), causing data exchange problems; and (3), you've merely postponed the day of reckoning for a few decades.

The third approach comprises a set of clever solutions that have limited application and usually only apply to specific computer languages and environments. These are often touted in the press as "squashing the millennium bug" and get news coverage for a week or two. But then the hype dies down because in the end such solutions only impact a small part of the overall Y2K remediation effort; in many cases, the solution brings along its own set of problems.

Challenges

Our first and foremost obstacle is time. As noted, the best solution for Y2K is to have started working on it in 1994. Unfortunately, we're now almost through 1998, and many corporations and government agencies are still in the inventory and assessment phases. Even many that are in the repair phase are in trouble, because these first three phases only account for about 40 percent of the overall effort. Testing and integration account for 50 percent or more of your resources and time in Y2K remediation, yet that is where most organizations appear to be skimping. Virtually every organization that has completed or is close to completing its Y2K remediation has found that the actual time and cost involved greatly exceeded the initial estimates. This means that many organizations that feel that they are on schedule now are likely in for a rude awakening as the time to Y2K grows shorter—hence the "bungee jumping" parable above.

Compounding all this is a long-known truth in the software industry: You cannot compress a software development project beyond a certain point, even (or especially) by adding more people to it.[9] Put another way: It doesn't matter how many farm hands, tractors, or fancy chemicals you have, you cannot plant wheat in August and harvest a decent crop in October. Yet far too many organizations think that they can speed up their Y2K remediation efforts by throwing money and staff at it.

Next is the "circle of death" problem. Even if you get every last internal system and device within your organization Y2K compliant, you typically have a large number of direct and indirect dependencies upon other organizations: customers, suppliers, service providers, and so on. If they aren't Y2K compliant, then your organization may suffer anyway. And even if every last one of them is sufficiently Y2K compliant, they have yet other organizations upon which they depend, and so on.

Then there's the issue of complexity. We have spent the past 50 years constructing an intricate, planetwide network—technical, informational, economic, logistical, social, even political—that contains highly complex interconnections, and that we don't (and cannot) fully comprehend nor control. In many cases, we become aware of these interconnections only as failures occur, for example, noting the ripple effect of the UPS strike in 1997 or the Galaxy IV satellite failure in 1998. We will almost certainly overlook key dependencies and influences until Y2K events flush them out—at which point we will have to respond after the fact. We reacted in various ways to the UPS strike and Galaxy IV failure, but those were isolated incidents and readily bounded, adapted, or solved. What will happen if we face a hundred equivalent problems simultaneously?

What Are the Likely Consequences of Y2K?

This is a good question and one that we'll spend much of this book addressing. As of this writing, we still lack a lot of information, and we obviously lack experience. Also, much depends upon the degree of mobilization and effort, not just in the United States but around the world. Part III, "The Winter of Our Disconnect: Getting Through," presents a range of possible scenarios along with relative probabilities.

What will likely be hardest hit is the entire worldwide production, refining/processing, manufacturing, assembly, and logistics systems upon which our economy—and the world's—depend. The pervasive use of billions of embedded control systems almost guarantees a certain level of failure in these areas. The recent sight of General Motors shutting down most of its North American operations, laying off nearly 200,000 workers, and losing over $2 billion because of a strike at one key supply plant, is a harbinger of what Y2K could cause on a national and global scale.

Because of this, a majority of people heavily involved in and knowledgeable about the Y2K problem feel that the United States will most likely go through a recession as a consequence of Y2K, due not just to problems here in the United States but elsewhere. The recession will be more severe worldwide and may even be a depression in certain regions (such as Asia). However, many of those same people predict a post-Y2K economic boom analogous to the post-World War II reconstruction boom. Time will tell.

Did I mention the lawsuits? Legal firms are already training lawyers on both sides of Y2K liability issues (in some cases, within the same law firm). This may be the biggest cost of all and could even delay or dampen the post-Y2K boom.

Impact on Economic Sectors

The Cutter Consortium did a study for the International Finance Corporation (of the World Bank).[10] They identified the following sectors as having key vulnerabilities to the Y2K problem:

- Financial services

- Utility/power industry

- Telecommunications

- Manufacturing

- Industrial and consumer services

- Social services (health care and education)

- Food and agribusiness

- Chemicals and petrochemicals

- Hotels and tourism

- Transportation

In addition, they identified a number of "niche" sectors tied to this list, including mining, cement and construction materials, textiles, timber, pulp, paper, motor vehicles and parts, oil refining, fertilizers and agricultural chemicals.

Here's a good place to introduce a term that we'll use time and again: **infrastructure**. It literally means "understructure" or "substructure," and it refers to the fundamental things we need in place in order to conduct our daily lives, including business: power; water; transportation (especially roads, rails, etc.); telecommunications and broadcast media; municipal services, such as garbage and sewage; and so on. Where you draw the line depends upon your point of view. Telecom firms see the power grid as infrastructure; the power companies see telecom as infrastructure; Internet service providers (ISPs) see both as infrastructure; and regular businesses count on all three, as well as any number of other services (e.g., water and transportation). The term is quite handy in Y2K discussions, because what it often means is "all the things I take for granted will just be there"— and those are the very things that might have the greatest impact on you should they be disrupted somehow.

Time of Impact

Y2K problems have already started cropping up. As mentioned, programs have different "time horizons," that is, the time span that they look ahead. Mortgage companies had to deal with some Y2K problems back in 1969; Social Security ran into them in 1989; and the Information Technology Association of America reported a survey that indicated that about half of major corporations in America had already experienced some form of Y2K difficulty.

The year 1999 will see an increased number of Y2K problems. Many programs in business and government use a one-year time horizon; if unrepaired, they could experience problems starting on January 1, 1999. Some 44 states start their fiscal year on April 1 and so would have problems then. The federal government starts its fiscal year in October, which could flush out more unrepaired errors. Still, many computer programs and most embedded control systems have no "look ahead" and so would not start to experience Y2K problems until January 1, 2000. The actual problems may not show up for hours, days, or even weeks.

Much of the impact of Y2K will come from an effort to anticipate or avoid problems. Many firms may stockpile key parts in late 1999 and then place few orders in early 2000. Various operations (processing, manufacturing, transportation) may be curtailed or shut down to avoid Y2K consequences and liability. And it's still unclear what the social, economic, and political impact of all this will be, both in the United States and worldwide.

So, What Should We Do?

Part II, "The Coming Fall: Getting Ready," will talk about that in detail, but here's the bottom line: Don't panic. Resist the "survivalist" urge and urgings; they solve nothing and compound the problem. Don't buy guns, cash all your stocks, withdraw your savings, and move to South Dakota unless you already had a really good reason for doing so, and maybe not even then. It's really cold in South Dakota, and the last place you probably want to be is out in the countryside with a lot of other folks armed with guns and waiting for Armageddon.

Instead, acknowledge the reality of the problem and learn more about it. Demand accountability and accurate information from those organizations upon which you depend, starting with the U.S. government and your own employer. Focus on solving as many problems as you can in your own circle of influence, starting with your own life and family, but including your community. Build social cohesion. Do the same sensible personal preparation as you would if you knew a hurricane or earthquake were coming.

And, of course, read the rest of this book.

2

How We Got Here, or, All Our Sins Remembered

Indeed, when asked why so many IT [information technology] projects go wrong in spite of all we know, one could simply cite the seven deadly sins: avarice, sloth, envy, gluttony, wrath, lust, and pride. It is as good an answer as any and more accurate than most.

—Testimony given before the Subcommittee on Government Management, Information, and Technology, June 22, 1998[1]

Many explanations for the root causes of the Year 2000 problem have appeared in the media or been offered by commentators. Most are overly simple, woefully incomplete, or significantly inaccurate. In the end, the real issue is not why we used two-digit years in the first place, but rather why it took so long to begin to fix a software problem known, documented, and discussed for decades. The story is worth knowing, in part so that you understand how we got here, but mostly because years from now our grandchildren are going to ask us how we got ourselves into this mess.

For the Want of Two Digits

This part most reports on Y2K have gotten right: The root of the problem dates back to the start of software, some 50 years ago. It's hard for people to grasp that they are walking around with $50 digital watches that have more processing power and storage than some of those earliest computers, which took up entire rooms and cost millions of dollars. Computing and storage resources were scarce and expensive, and the earliest software developers were forced to use all their wiles to shoehorn in every last bit of data.

The practice of using only two digits to represent the year began as soon as software using dates appeared. It was an effort to conserve space in memory, on storage media such as tapes, disks, and punched cards, and in screen displays and printed reports. Indeed, there were many early programs that used only a single digit ("3," "4") to indicate the year by its last digit. But such programs were constrained to a single decade; the two-digit format ("53," "54") was far more powerful and flexible by comparison.

There were few compelling reasons to use more than two digits. Some programs had to look ahead or behind into other centuries, or deal with time spans of more than 100 years, but they were a small percentage of those being developed and used. Most software dealt just with the current date and the recent past; if it looked ahead at all, it was seldom more than a year. And since 2000 was still so far away, it was hard to believe that these programs could possibly still be in use at century's end.

In the meantime, hardware costs were slow to drop relative to other expenses. Even 25 years from the start—halfway through the computer era, in the mid-1970s—adding a megabyte of RAM to an IBM 360/65 mainframe still cost around $250,000. By comparison, my aging laptop has 40 megabytes of RAM in it. The IBM 360/65 couldn't have held 40 megabytes—each megabyte was something larger than a shoebox—but even if it could, the upgrade would have cost $10 million in 1975 dollars, or something on the order of $30–40 million in current dollars. There were similar price issues about hard disk storage, where it was even available; many systems relied heavily upon magnetic tapes and punched cards, which were likewise constrained.

The issue occurs in everyday life outside of computers. Case in point: The next time you fill out a (paper) form of some kind, note how much space is given in which to write each piece of information requested (name, address, and so on). Whoever designed that form had to make decisions about how much space to allow for each field. If you happen to have a longer-than-normal last name or a particularly complicated address, you might have run out of room. My wife and I often run into this with any form requesting us to list some or all of our children; most such forms are not set up to handle nine children, since that is so unusual.

When developing software, you may face the same trade-off. This is known as a *bounding issue*: How much space to allocate for a given range of values. For numeric values, these often fall around power-of-two (2^n or 2-to-the-nth-power) values because of the underlying binary representation that we discussed back in Chapter 1. This is why, when using programs, you often run into values with ranges of $-128...127$, $0...255$, $-32768...32767$, $0...65535$, and so on, though that's less common (or more hidden) now than it used to be.[2]

If the value is going to be displayed or stored as alphanumeric characters, then the issue tends to be length: How many characters in a name or address, how many digits in a number, and so on. Again, given the scarcity of data storage resources and the decades that remained until four digits would be required, bounding the representation of years to two digits made a lot of sense.

Because of all these factors, the use of two-digit years was almost universal through the first 20 to 30 years of the computer era. It became part of various software and data standards and so was mandated for use in certain situations. As new software was created, more often than not it used the two-digit format because of those standards, because it was created with tools and systems that used two digits, because it had to exchange information with existing programs that used the two-digit format, or just because that's what the developers were used to. In short, the original practice made tremendous sense, both technically and economically, and was often required or compelled.

And then the information revolution really hit.

Moore's Law

The most important thing you can understand about hardware is Moore's law. Moore's law, covered by Gordon Moore, co-founder of Intel, states that the price/performance level of hardware doubles every 18 months. In other words, every 18 months, you can get hardware that does twice as much for the same price, or hardware that does the same work for half the price.

Table 2-1 shows of Moore's law as applied to personal computers[3] over a 20-year span. The real impact lies in the acronyms. A kilobyte (1 KB) is 1024 bytes.[4] A megabyte (MB) is 1024 KB or 1,048,576 bytes. A gigabyte (GB) is 1024 MB, or 1,073,741,824 bytes.[5] These, obviously, all measure information storage in the computer's main memory or on various media (floppy disks, hard disks, Zip disks, CD-ROMs). A different unit, the megahertz (MHz), stands for one million

YEAR:	1978	1982	1986	1990	1994	1998
System	North Star HORIZON	IBM PC	No-name IBM XT clone	Excel	Gateway P5-R	Dell Dimension XPS
CPU	8-bit Z-80	8-bit 8088	16-bit 80286	16-bit 80386	32-bit Pentium 90 (w/FPU)	32-bit Pentium II (w/MMX, FPU)
Clock speed	4 MHz	4.33 MHz	6 or 8 MHz (switchable)	20Mhz	90 MHz	450 MHz
Memory (RAM)	16 KB	64 KB	512 KB	1 MB	16 MB (with 256-KB cache)	256 MB (with 512 KB cache)
Storage (disk)	90-KB floppy	160-KB floppy	1.2-MB floppy, 20-MB hard	200MB hard, 1.2 MB floppy, 360 KB Floopy	540 MB hard, 1.4 MB floppy, 2x CD-ROM	16.8 GB hard, 100 MB zip, 1.4 MB floppy, 4.8x DVD-ROM
Display	ADM-3A Terminal (80 x 24 text)	80x25 text or 320 x 200 x 4 colors graphics	80 x 25 text and 640 x 350 monochrome graphics	640x200x4 color graphics	640 x 480 x 256 color graphics (2- MB video RAM)	1024 x 768 x 256 color graphics with 3-D acceleration (8- MB video RAM) and real-time video playback (DVD)
Cost	$2755	$3020— $3720	$2560	$2999	$3495	$3273

Table 2-1

33

clock cycles per second and is a measure of how fast the CPU is cranking through the steps required for each instruction. Note that the costs given are what the prices were *at that time*. When you adjust for inflation, the prices above reflect a steady decline; the 1998 Dell system costs roughly $1100 in 1978 dollars, while the North Star HORIZON cost roughly $8000 in 1998 dollars. So, after 20 years of personal computer evolution, a third of the original cost will buy you at least 1000 times the computing power, 16,000 times the memory, and nearly 200,000 times the storage space. Similar changes have gone on in the workstation, minicomputer, and mainframe markets. And every time it looks as though Moore's law may be running out of steam, another technological breakthrough hits, and progress continues apace.

All Our Systems Remembered

Moore's law applied over time has also created a spectrum of computer systems. Fifty, even 40 years ago, pretty much all you had were **mainframe computers**, which started out the size of rooms and gradually shrank.[6] At some point, though, the size stabilized a bit, and the focus was on increased speed and capabilities.

In the meantime, a new generation of systems—**minicomputers**—continued the shrinking trend and became the second tier of computers. These would support multiple users in a division or office, usually through terminals. As with mainframes, the size stabilized, and the systems grew in power.

Then at that point in the mid-70s that we keep coming back to, the **microprocessor** went commercial, fitting processing power that used to take up one or more circuit boards into a single chip. This introduced three new categories of systems. The first category, **workstations**, was in essence a minicomputer set up for a single user. They were controversial—the idea of dedicating an entire computer to just one user seemed a scandalous waste of resources. But the payoff was often worth it, and they became heavily used in engineering and scientific disciplines.

The second category, **personal computers**, was even more controversial, with many pundits and business leaders stating for years that they would never be more than a fad. Indeed, the original PCs were build-it-yourself kits for hobbyists; Bill Gates and Paul Allen of Microsoft got their start with a BASIC interpreter that ran on such systems. But the Commodore Pet pioneered the idea of a preassembled PC intended for non-technical users at home; the Apple II (from Steve Wozniak and Steve Jobs) offered color graphics and a simple design that set the home market on fire; the IBM PC, from the company whose name was synonymous with mainframes, legitimized the use of PCs in business; and the Apple Macintosh set the standards for user interfaces that permeate the entire computer market today. The two major developments of the past ten years have been the advent of mobile computing—battery-operated laptops, notebooks, and now hand-held devices—and the advent of the sub-$2000 and now sub-$1000 PC.[7]

The third category, **embedded control systems**, represented the flip side of Moore's law: Every 18 months, you could get the same processing power at half the price—and sometimes in half the space. This meant that manual and/or analog controls for various systems could now be enhanced or even replaced with microprocessor-based control systems.

As time went on, minicomputers—at least, by that name—went away, squeezed between the centralized power of mainframes and the desktop power of workstations and PCs. However, that middle category reestablished itself with two general categories of systems. **Mid-range systems** are, in effect, main-

frames shrunk to minicomputer size and are used much as
mainframes were (and are). **Servers** fill the role minicomputers
once had, but with PCs, workstations, and networking systems hooked up to them. For a while many observers predicted mainframes might go away, but the pendulum toward
spreading computer power and information out to users' desks
has started to swing back toward centralization, and mainframes have become hot again.

Even as actual computers—PCs, workstations, servers, mid-
range systems, and mainframes—continue to push the leading
edge of information technology, the trailing edge of IT—
which has grown cheap, tiny, and very well known—finds its
way into literally millions, if not billions, of places. There are
probably dozens of ECSs in the typical modern home, located
in appliances, security alarms, heating/AC systems, and consumer electronics. Every passenger seat in a Boeing 777 aircraft has the equivalent of a Pentium-based PC running all its
functions (on-demand video, etc.). There can be hundreds in
an office building, a chemical processing plant, a supertanker,
a manufacturing facility, or an off-shore oil platform. Estimates of the total number of ECSs worldwide range from 10
billion to 40 billion, with billions more being manufactured
and put into use each year.

And they all run software.

Speeding in Tongues

It is hard to overemphasize the pervasiveness of software.
Even just 25 years ago, halfway through the current computer
era, software was largely confined to mainframes and minicomputers, plus some early (and primitive) embedded systems. With the "intelligence" explosion mentioned above,

software began to find its way into more and more areas of life. We are now building and shipping more computers and ECSs per day than were built and shipped in the entire decade of the 1970s. The rate at which we build them continues to increase.

It's important to understand, at least on a high level, how software is created. In its most basic format,[8] software is binary data, composed entirely of the electromagnetic equivalent of 0s and 1s. In this form, it's known by various names, such as **object code**, **machine language**, or **executable code**. It's data that can be directly interpreted as instructions by a given chip, such as a processor (e.g., Pentium II, PowerPC, SPARC). While it is possible to directly create and edit object code, it's tedious, difficult, and very error prone for a system of any complexity. It is very common, however, to create and edit programs written in a human-readable form of machine language called **assembly language**. The commands are then translated to binary data form (machine language) using a program called an **assembler**. Each processor and processor family has its own assembly/machine language, so that the assembly language for an Intel Pentium processor is quite different than that for a Motorola PowerPC processor, but it's just a more expanded version of that for its predecessor, the Intel 80486. Since there was now a distinction between the source of the program and the executable code, the program as written in assembly language became known as *source code*, and the act of translation was known as **assembling the program**.

However, even assembly language development can be tedious, and, as noted, the actual language is different for each type of processor. So **high-level languages** (HLLs) were created to make software both easier to write and portable across different processors. Some of the earliest HLLs included FORTRAN (FORmula TRANslation language), COBOL (Common Business-Oriented Language), and Lisp. Each instruction in an HLL does the work of several (or sometimes dozens) of assembly language instructions. Also, a program written in HLL can be run on computers and other hardware using different processors. This is done one of two ways. For some languages, the HLL source code is translated into either assembly language[9] or executable code via a program known as a **compiler**; the act is known as **compiling the program**. For other languages, the HLL source code is never translated into executable code; instead, a program known as an **interpreter** reads in the HLL source code one statement at a time and interprets it, carrying out the instruction. Many variations on these two approaches exist, including one in which the HLL is compiled into a processor-independent pseudomachine code (or **p-code**); a p-code interpreter (sometimes called a **virtual machine**) specific for the local processor then interprets the p-code. Most HLLs can use any or all of these approaches, but they tend to use just one. So, for instance, FORTRAN, COBOL, Pascal, C, and C++ are usually compiled, Lisp and BASIC are usually interpreted, and Java usually uses a p-code implementation.

Creating new high-level programming languages has been a favorite pastime of computer scientists, researchers, and hackers almost as long as computers have been among us. The result: There are some 500 different HLLs in use today, though 20 or so, along with the various assembly languages, account for the majority of the software in use.[10] Most new HLLs occupy small niches and are just curiosities, though every five to ten years, one becomes a "breakout hit"; the most recent example is Java, developed at Sun Microsystems just a few years ago.

Another key point is that there are numerous dialects of HLLs due to time, environments, and vendors. While there are standards for most major languages, few implementations are identical to one another. Just as English evolves—changing syntax and usage, discarding old words, adding new ones or borrowing them from other languages—so most HLLs have changed over time. In much the same way, the implementation of a given HLL on a mainframe may be subtly (or not-so-subtly) different from a PC implementation. Finally, most major vendors of software development tools cannot resist putting nonstandard, but desirable, features into the language to entice developers. If the developer comes to depend upon those features unique to a given implementation, then she or he is locked into that vendor. Thus, there have been scores of COBOL variants over the past five decades—and lots of software written in all of them. The same is true for most other major HLLs.

Few developers create programs in assembly or high-level languages from scratch. They almost always use what are known as software **libraries**. These are collections of prewritten (and usually precompiled) software that provide some useful function, so that the developer doesn't have to reinvent and reimplement what has already been solved. Such libraries may deal with data manipulation (sorting and searching), mathematical calculations, representing certain types of information, providing a standard user interface, allowing access to system functions, and so on. They may be developed in-house, purchased from a third-party software firm, included in development environment, or provided by the host operating system.

Then there are the so-called **fourth-generation languages** (4GLs). These languages are environments set up to allow rapid development of applications (usually for business) without having to deal with HLLs, assembly language, or machine language (the other three generations). They are often touted as replacing the other levels of programming languages, as well as the software developers themselves; in reality, they form only a small fraction of both new and existing applications. Perhaps the most popular example of a 4GL is PowerBuilder.

In addition to all these are various **scripting** and **macro languages**. These are specific to a given application, operating system, or environment. They allow you to write **scripts** or **macros**, sequences of commands that are commonly repeated. Systems that allow scripts include most environments that have a command-line interface, such as MS-DOS, UNIX, and others. Various applications allow you to write macros, including word processors such as Microsoft Word and WordPerfect, and spreadsheets such as Lotus 1-2-3 and Excel.

Again, this explanation is simple, but you don't need to understand all the details of, variations on, and exceptions to what's just been said. What you do need to know is that the Y2K problem isn't confined to software written in a few languages, but that it runs the full gamut from machine code to scripts and macros.

Code Bloat, Code Bloat, Code Bloat

Even as Moore's law was making processing hardware smaller, faster, and cheaper, software was following a sort-of inverse Moore's law: It was getting larger, more complex, and more demanding of resources as time went on. A Digital VAX/11-780 minicomputer back in 1980 could support 30 users on terminals with just 1 MB of RAM; the VMS operating system only took up 400 KB of that. When the Turbo Pascal development environment for personal computers first came out in 1984, the entire environment—text editor, compiler, and supporting tools—took up 40 KB of disk space.

Now we have operating systems and applications that consume tens or hundreds of megabytes of disk space—all to support one person. The Windows NT 5.0 operating system, due out sometime in the next few years from Microsoft, is said to be over 20 million lines of code by itself. The META Group estimates that by the year 2000, a personal computer will have to have 128 MB of memory just to load Microsoft Office 2000 running under Windows.[11]

Various factors account for this. First has been the move from a text-based interface to a graphical user interface (GUI). Consider just the difference in the memory required to represent a snapshot of the screen. The classic text-based screen was 24 or 25 lines of 80 alphanumeric (8-bit) characters. That means that a entire screen took up 2000 bytes, or just a touch under 2 KB. By contrast, most systems sold currently offer a typical screen resolution of 1024 x 768 **pixels** (**picture elements**, i.e., individual dots on the display), each of which uses 8 to 32 bits (1 to 4 bytes). That means that a single screen snapshot uses somewhere from 768 KB to 3 MB—or over a thousand times the memory required for the old text-based display. With multiple overlapping windows, the need for memory increases.

But that's not all. We are no longer content with static text or even static images. We want animation—not Pacman images chasing each other around the screen, but full, smooth 3-D animation that looks ever more lifelike. We want sound—not just little beeps, but stereo CD-quality sound in real time. We want video—not just a jerky sequence of images, but smooth, TV-quality video running in real time off of a DVD drive or, eventually, over the Internet. All these demands soak up and exhaust processor bandwidth, memory, disk storage, and network throughput as fast or faster than Moore's law can increase them. And the software to support them grows ever larger and more complex.

There is also an ever-driving demand for more functionality in software. "Feature wars" are a cornerstone of competition between vendors, even when the new features slow performance and decrease stability. The irony is that many users don't particularly want or care about most features—they would be happy with a word processor at the level of functionality that existed 10 to 15 years ago. But then there are features that are indeed critical or that provide a true competitive edge; those lead to software that is ever larger and more complex.

On top of that, software is increasingly interconnected. This is true within individual PCs and workstations. You can embed spreadsheets within word processing documents, or have browsers launch and use various document translation utilities. It's also true within computer networks. An application running on a PC or workstation (the **client**) may interact with a transaction processor (**middleware**) running on a mid-range system somewhere, which in turn interacts with a distributed database running on various servers (hence the term **client/server architecture**). In the meantime, all these systems depend upon the underlying network hardware and software—which itself may be a melange of various systems, standards, and protocols—to allow them to "talk" with one another.

At least one more factor leads to software bloat: Moore's law itself. If you are designing software to run within 640 KB of memory on a 4.77-MHz 8088 CPU (the old IBM PC standard), you craft your code with care, reducing every unneeded byte or clock cycle. If, however, you are designing software for a 300-MHz Pentium II with 32 MB of RAM, you may get sloppy with both memory and processing power. It becomes a variant of Parkinson's law:[12] Software tends to expand to consume the hardware resources available.

The Perils of Adequacy

As software becomes larger and more complex, it also becomes more difficult to understand, to test, and to modify without introducing defects. This is why so many software projects, particularly those above a given size, are late and over budget; some fail altogether. It also becomes a factor in the persistence of Y2K problems. First, as programs grow in size, they become less comprehensible; it's harder for any one person (or even a group of people) to understand all that it does and how it does it. If there are sections still using two-digit years, it may be that no one knows.

Second, as software becomes more complex, it becomes less stable in the face of changes. The more complex the software, the greater the risk of introducing new defects when you modify it, even (or especially) when removing existing defects. Organizations learn to leave such systems alone except when it is absolutely necessary.

Third, as a rule old software never dies, it just becomes **legacy code**. There are major corporations and government agencies using software that is 30 to 40 years old. Few, if any, of those programs were intended to be running at the end of the century. But it was easier to continue to extend, patch, and use the existing program, which works, than to pay the money to write new programs. And the more complex the software, the more likely it is to be kept around, because it's a lot harder to rewrite or replace.

These three factors combine to this end: The software that is hardest to understand, hardest to modify, and most likely to have Y2K problems is also the software that tends to stick

around. In some cases, such legacy code becomes interconnected and intermingled with newer software, corrupting it
with the old, bad habits, if you will.

The Resistance of Vision

As the information revolution took root in the early 1980s,
the excuses for using two-digit years began to vanish. Memory,
disk space, and other data resources, continuing a steady drop
in price and increase in capacity, ceased in most cases to be a
reasonable constraint. By 1986—a little more than ten years
after the 1MB upgrade for the IBM mainframe cost
$250,000—you could buy a 1MB upgrade for a Macintosh
computer for $799.

More importantly, the year 2000 itself began to be foreseeable. We were learning just how well old technology could
entrench itself and resist being replaced. After all, we were then
using programs and systems that had been around for 15–30
years and could have reasonably assumed that much of the software created in the 1980s would still be around and in use in
2000. To top it off, an article was published in 1984 in *Computerworld*, one of the major information technology weeklies, calling attention to the year 2000 problem.[13] Many of us in the
software engineering field remember discussing Y2K in the mid-
80s (myself included). So the awareness was out there.

Here, then, was the opportunity to set things right. A gradual, systematic approach to phasing out two-digit years in
existing software and data, along with new practices and standards recommending or requiring four-digit years, spread out
over 15 years, would have solved the problem at a fraction of
what Y2K will end up costing us.[14] The old reasons no longer
held water; the millennium was not that far over the horizon.

And here is where we fell down.

Make no mistake: The failure was not universal. A few organizations, some vendors, and many software engineers began to consciously plan for dealing with 2000 and beyond. New software was created to be Y2K compliant; old software was either updated or retired. Some corporations and government agencies, such the Social Security Agency, encountered Y2K problems early, recognized the problems for what they were, and started work. More articles began to appear, starting with Peter de Jager's well-known piece published in 1993.[15]

However, the vast majority of organizations and vendors, and probably the majority of software engineers and developers, continued with business as usual through the 1980s and into the 1990s. For that matter, far too many businesses (and governments) continued with business as usual all the way into 1997 or even 1998. This, in spite of all that was being written, all that we knew, and the self-evident nature of the problem itself. And so we come back to the question: Why did we not solve the problem sooner?

All Our Sins Remembered

It was popular for a while to say that Y2K is not a technical problem, it's a management problem. But while there are both technical and management aspects to the challenge of Y2K, it is at its root a human problem. Indeed, the most significant and universal challenges in information technology are human; hence the statement at the start of this chapter about the seven deadly sins being at the root of IT failures. Let's look how each "sin" has, in its own way, contributed to the Y2K problem over the past 50 years.

AVARICE

That's "greed," as in "greed is good," the proclaimed business mantra of the 1980s and the unspoken one of most other decades. This is among the principal factors behind the Y2K mess. How? Time and again, when the issues of Y2K were raised within an corporation, those higher up said, "How much will this cost? Nonsense. We're not spending that on maintenance and repairs, expanded memory and more disk space, all to support the same functionality. We want new development, new applications, new systems." Governments and agencies have done much the same, funding new projects or continuing old ones while ignoring the threat to the well-being of those they are supposed to serve. In too many cases, the response was the same: "We'll worry about Y2K next year."

Unfortunately, we ran out of years.

Understand that this is not a critique of capitalism or the free market per se. I think we're about to see the free market operating on a scale and with an intensity seldom if ever witnessed before. A large—and possibly tremendous—gap is going to open up between those businesses that are ready for Y2K and those that are not, and the former will feast upon the latter, directly and indirectly. The same dynamics will apply to governments; in both cases, we may see massive, perhaps unprecedented, transfers of wealth. To quote a colleague, Dr. Jerry Pournelle, "Think of it as evolution in action." Those organizations with foresight, wisdom, and competent personnel will fare far better than those without.

These consequences are instead an indictment against short-sighted financial and political management that sacrifices long-term benefits for short-term payback and popularity. This isn't like a natural disaster, arising and impacting in a matter of minutes, hours, or even days. We've known about this for years. It will be fascinating to hear some of the explanations from CEOs and government leaders as to why they waited so long in the face of a well-defined, easily-proved problem with a fixed deadline.

SLOTH

Not all the blame lies at the feet of upper management. I belong to a profession—software development—that aspires to be considered an engineering discipline, but which does little to earn that distinction. The simple, regrettable truth is that many software developers are not very good at what they do, and many of the ones that are good are also lazy and sloppy. How else can one explain Y2K "issues" (as Microsoft calls them) in commercial software as recent as Windows 95, Internet Explorer 4.0, or (to spread the shame around) JavaScript?

All these were developed in the past few years, almost within spitting distance of the millennium, as it were. What kind of "software engineer" could or would write code using two-digit years at all, much less two-digit years that don't know how to get past 1999 correctly? It's a bit like a general contractor locating a building smack in the middle of a dry river bed and then being surprised when it's flooded in the first heavy rain.

It doesn't even matter whether the developers had heard or read anything about Y2K; the problem itself is obvious after a minute's reflection. Indeed, it was obvious decades ago. The only explanations are sloth and/or incompetence, and neither reflects well on the profession and its practitioners. Stupidity is not normally considered a deadly sin, but it may well be in this case.

ENVY

For all the talk of leadership and vision, organizations tend to mimic one another, especially in terms of information technology. This leads to what those in the trenches often call "management by *Business Week*." The folks at the top see an article in a leading business publication about some great results that XYZ Corp has gotten with a particular technology or implementation. They pass the article down the food chain with a note attached saying, "Why aren't we doing this?" Even when the basic idea is a good one, the glowing results for XYZ described in the article are often overly optimistic and lead to unrealistic expectations on the part of upper management. Mind you, I'm not saying that the CEOs, CIOs, or project managers quoted in the article are exaggerating, much less being dishonest. But I have read a few articles about projects that I'm familiar with, and the…disconnect…is often breathtaking.

The flip side is that if they can't find an article about the work other organizations are doing in a particular area, they feel that it must not be worthwhile. And if there's an article casting doubt on a particular issue or technology, then it become anathema, and any attempt to consider it is done at significant political peril. That's why many of the earlier, less informed articles about Y2K—particularly those that dismissed it as a minor problem being overly hyped by consultants to rake in big bucks—had such a damaging effect.

The resulting reluctance on the part of specific organizations to address the problem was itself a factor in other organizations avoiding it—after all, they reasoned, if it were a real threat, more organizations would be doing something about it. The situation became a self-fulfilling and self-reinforcing cycle, broken only by the leadership of those organizations that actually thought for themselves and did the brief research required to understand how real the threat is.

GLUTTONY

Paul Strassmann, in his seminal work *The Business Value of Computers*, concluded that there was little correlation between money spent on information technology (IT) by an organization and the return on investment. This was no surprise to those who labor in that field and who have seen for years the self-defeating practices that characterize it, particularly when it comes to purchasing or developing IT for deployment. Many corporate and government IT organizations, like gluttons, find themselves slow, bloated, short of breath, with clogged arteries and high medical bills.

The roots are the same: a deliberate choice to consume, not for fitness or health or to fuel the body, but because of self-gratification and as an expression of self-importance. Too many managers, business and technical, seek to build empires by pushing new projects when a cleaned-up version of an old one, or one managed by a peer (i.e., competitor), would do as well or perhaps better. The result: a bloated IT infrastructure, expensive to maintain, difficult to modify, and full of overlapping, redundant, and often incompatible solutions.

The Y2K impact is threefold. First, instead of spending the time and money to clean up and improve older applications, and thus removing Y2K problems, such firms develop new applications instead—never really retiring the older ones and possibly perpetuating Y2K problems. Second, the ever-growing costs for maintenance of the bloated infrastructure soaks up more and more of the IT budget, leading to delays in addressing Y2K. Third, the very size of the infrastructure slows down and increases the costs of Y2K remediation, given the challenges of counting, assessing, and tracking so many systems.

Now many of my colleagues are going to protest, clamoring about how they have been choked by budget cuts year after

year, and many times that is the case. But even in such organizations, the budget wars come out of high-level managers
fighting over pet projects and who gets how much. Even in
such environments, the bloat continues.

WRATH

We like to pride ourselves that we're responsible adults and
that we seek the greatest good for our organization—corporate, government, or educational—and those around us. The
not-so-pretty truth is that grown people in positions of
responsibility and power often act in amazingly petty and self-
consumed ways. At times, such people are willing to see others
within their organization stumble or even fail out of spite,
regardless of the potential impact on the organization itself.

Those emotions can be especially intense when information
technology is involved. Large budget dollars are often at stake,
both for IT itself and for business initiatives driven by IT. The
perennial disconnect between business and IT—business
wants the impossible, tomorrow, while IT can *never* deliver
anything on time and budget—merely intensifies things. And
business sees time and money spent on infrastructure as at best
marking time and at worst a waste.

Introducing an organizational Y2K effort into this environment of high feelings and intense rivalries can be a tremendous
challenge, even with the clear backing of the chief executive,
but especially without it. The person in charge has to make
hard choices and unpleasant decisions about where to spend
resources, and any number of peers (or, tougher yet, superiors)
may be profoundly displeased at having their special oxen
gored, much less being told what they have to do instead. Such
organizational politics have hindered any number of Y2K
efforts, but self-destructive anger is nothing new to humanity.

LUST

OK, I couldn't think of anything.

Except this: During the period of time when the United States (and the world) could have most benefited from strong leadership from its Commander-in-Chief on Y2K, that is, late 1997 through most of 1998, he was otherwise distracted with other matters directly related to this human weakness and was profoundly silent on the Y2K issue.

As of this writing, President Clinton has made exactly one speech on Y2K, given in a nontelevised setting on a weekday morning. That lack of leadership has led much of America and most of the world to take Y2K far more lightly than we all should. After all—if the President doesn't see fit to address it even a fraction of the times he addresses other issues, such as education and Social Security, how important could it be?

PRIDE

This is often cited as the primal sin, the root of all the sins mentioned. It is the intersection of self-interest and self-importance. And it is the foundation of our problem with the year 2000.

There's nothing particularly tragic or noble about the pride that got us into this mess. It's just stupid. We knew about the problem long ago. We could have fixed it, or at least started to, any time in the past 20 years. For that matter, a lot of people did just that. They chose to engineer, or reengineer, software intelligently. They looked ahead and asked, "What if...?" They initiated long-term plans to track down and eliminate problems. They designed systems to function not just long after they left their jobs, but after they left this world. In short, they did what responsible adult humans do when faced with, well, responsibility.

But far too many did not. They caused the problem, leaving others to clean up after them. They ignored the problem or denied it when it was brought to their attention, absolutely refusing to believe that such a problem could exist. They avoided it, wanting someone else to dirty their hands. They made conscious, deliberate decisions to focus on other priorities, hoping someone else would come up with a quick fix—cheap grace, if you will—that would spare them having to do all the intricate, time-consuming, mind-numbing tasks that a full-blown Y2K remediation effort requires. And in making all these choices founded on arrogance and selfishness—the essence of pride—they squandered for all of us the one absolutely nonrenewable, nonrecoverable resource in all this: time.

The Greeks, as always, had a word for it: *ate*, the point of no return, that fullness of pride reached just before destruction. Oedipus reached it when, in spite of the accumulating evidence and the cautions of the chorus, he pushed ahead through patricide, into incest, and finally to self-immolation. We likewise have brought ourselves to a brink in spite of our own evidences and choruses. We have done so through decades of short-sightedness and self-deception in our development and deployment of information technology. And now we find ourselves moving, inexorably, toward the chasm on the road ahead known as the Year 2000 crisis.

Anxiety has begun to set in through the private and public sectors as the true scope and difficulty of the Y2K problem—with its roots in all the sins related—become apparent. For the first time in the half-century of the computer era, these organizations will realize what it means to face a problem that is inexorable with a deadline that is unmovable. This time, the difficulties cannot be finessed, buried, reorganized away, or dragged out until they're finally fixed.

What remains to be seen is whether we make it across the chasm or fall in. Chapter 3 explores why building the real bridge to the twenty-first century won't be easy.

3

The Roadblocks to Fixing Y2K

Man errs as long as he strives.

—Goethe

It's just two digits, right? How hard could it be to fix?

Plenty, as it turns out. A wide array of factors have combined to make what seems a simple problem into the greatest technology challenge faced to date by humanity, and one, as noted, entirely of our own making. Since it's likely you work for and/or depend upon a lot of organizations—government, business, community—that have to deal with Y2K remediation (a fancy term for fixing things), this chapter will briefly review how that's done and then discuss general categories of roadblocks that can slow down remediation efforts. The point is to help you get a sense of how those organizations are doing with regard to Y2K. We'll talk later in the book about how to respond to such problems if you see them.

How to Fix Y2K Problems

As briefly discussed in Chapter 1, the remediation largely consists of six steps: inventory, assessment, repair, testing, reintegration, and contingency planning. Let's look at each of these in a bit more detail.

Inventory: How Many Systems Are There?

We've talked in the last two chapters about the scope and range of hardware and software, and how it's all over the place. Well, during inventory you track down all the hardware, software, affected documents, databases, and embedded systems that you have or have to care about. This is not an easy task, and you're usually dealing with an ever-shifting (and usually ever-growing) list. Most large organizations find that they have far more systems than they ever expected, often with strange and unexpected interdependencies.

Assessment: How Bad Is It?

Here's where you determine where the Y2K problems are. There are two fundamental approaches: examination and actual testing. Numerous commercial tools exist that will go out and scan source code for areas of date reference and manipulation, producing reports telling where to find them. Others will scan data files, databases, and various documents for two-digit years. Yet others, more highly specialized, can scan object code and find certain kinds of data references. And there are several tools out that will scan desktop systems, home or office, for Y2K problems. Some of these tools are surprisingly good, given what they have to work with, but there are still problems you may miss.

On top of that, it can be very challenging to assess the Y2K status of embedded control systems. Unless you produce them yourself, you usually don't have the source code for the software driving the system and so have to rely upon direct testing. But that carries its own challenges. First, it may be hard to actually

manipulate the date. Second, because it's embedded and interacting with other systems, you may have to test all of them
simultaneously—and then figure out where the problem is if
one occurs. Third, problems don't necessarily show up immediately, so you may need to let things run for awhile. (The IRS did
a Y2K test of the phone equipment—private branch exchanges,
or PBXs—that it uses in its offices. The PBX system ran fine for
three days, and then crashed.) Fourth, you may have to take a
processing or manufacturing system off-line in order to do the
testing, but that may be expensive or even infeasible.

Repair: What Do We Do with the Problems?

Having found the problems, you have four choices. First, if
the impact is insignificant or if you have an easy workaround,
you can **ignore** the system and its problems. Second, you can
repair the software—usually by modifying the source code
and recompiling the program. Third, you can **replace** the system, buying or building a new one. Fourth, you can **retire** the
system, that is, stop using it but without explicitly replacing it.
Each choice has its set of costs, risks, and trade-offs, and for
complex systems you can actually apply different choices to
different components—repair some, replace others, and so on.
But in the end, it does boil down to these four choices.

Testing: Does It Work Now?

Y2K testing is very important, and it can be very difficult.
The challenges are myriad. First, you have to define what you
mean by "Y2K compliant." The essence is simple—the system
continues to work correctly as time passes—but the details can
be complicated. Second, you have to determine how to verify
Y2K compliance, that is, what set of tests you can put the software through to make sure it's going to work correctly. Third,

you have to create the environment for Y2K testing. It's very risky to play around with dates on the computers you use day in and day out, so you may need a separate set of test systems. Fourth, you may need to do **data aging**, that is, create test data that represents what your software would be working with under Y2K conditions. Finally, you need the staff (and time) to actually carry out the tests and verify the results. All these factors explain why testing is often 40–70 percent of the entire Y2K remediation effort.

Integration: Will Everything Work Together?

It's not enough to fix a single program, platform, or embedded system. You then have to reconnect it to all the other systems with which it interacts and see if they get along well. This can be (and, ideally, should be) done to some extent during testing. But unless you can recreate the entire production environment, there will always be a gap between the test setting and real life. There is the challenge of coordinating systems that have been repaired with those that have not, or which have been repaired using a different solution—four digit expansion versus windowing, or windowing with a different pivot year. In some cases, you may not be able to put repaired software into production until other systems have likewise been repaired or upgraded. And you need to ensure that the Y2K repairs haven't adversely affected how the systems work here and now.

Contingency Planning: What If Things Still Don't Work?

Even if you complete all your Y2K repair efforts—and especially if you don't—you need to plan for two major contingencies: What if some of your (repaired) systems turn out to still have Y2K bugs. What if external organizations with which you deal have Y2K-related problems? The former is straightforward. Since you have control over your own systems, you should have a good idea as to what effort was put into make them Y2K compliant, and you can anticipate and deal with lingering problems.

The latter issue—Y2K problems among external organizations—is more critical and entails greater risk. Suppose you have ten companies that you depend upon to be able to conduct business. What are the chances that all ten will not only do a great job with their own Y2K efforts, but that all the companies they depend upon are in great shape, and so on? So, what are you going to do if they're not? That's the essence of contingency planning.

What Keeps Us from Fixing Y2K Problems More Quickly

Now that you have a general idea of what it takes to carry out Y2K remediation within an organization, let's talk about why so many organizations have been so slow to start the repairs and why their efforts may take a lot longer than they think.

Understanding the Problem

One of the biggest challenges of the Year 2000 problem is taking it seriously. By the time you read this, most people, particularly those in power in government and business, will likely be taking it quite seriously. But that will represent a major shift in attitude, and one coming rather late in the day, in spite of all that has been known about this problem for decades and all that has been written in the last several years.

Three roadblocks in particular fall into this category. The first is underestimating the seriousness of the Y2K issue. The Y2K problem itself seems so simple and so silly that it's hard for many people to understand just how devastating it could be. Specific instances are hard to come by, especially since many organizations are reluctant to release information about potential or discovered Y2K problems due to legal concerns (see the section below about dealing with lawyers). However, the information that has come out—specific anecdotes, surveys, evaluations of key systems—has consistently shown the reality and potential consequences of the problem. And the Y2K controversy differs from most popular scientific disputes—such as global warming—in that there are few ideological overtures, the reality of the problem is trivial to prove, the consequences are sure and soon, and it is the most technical, informed, and involved practitioners who are most worried.

The second roadblock is underestimating the scope of the Y2K issue. The popular image in the media and among decision makers up until early 1998 was that the problem existed in old mainframes running even older COBOL programs. It was a curiosity for most people and a problem for only a few. However, as Y2K pioneering organizations actually set about doing their assessment, they found that Y2K problems showed up across the full spectrum of computer systems—mainframes, mid-range systems, servers, workstations, PCs, and embedded control systems—in a variety of languages and across the decades up to and including just-developed software. The challenge wasn't that there were lots and lots of Y2K problems in a specific system or application; it was that there were a small number of Y2K problems scattered among a vast number of systems, and there were few, if any, ways of determining ahead of time which had problems and which didn't.

The third roadblock is underestimating the difficulties of the Y2K issue. Again, we're back to the question, how hard can it be? Well, it's not that the issue is rocket science; it isn't. Instead, it's hard, complex, tedious work that's difficult and time consuming to carry out and test thoroughly, as any organization that has gone through an entire Y2K remediation effort (and there aren't many) will tell you. But there's only one way to do the work, and that's to do the work. Industry and society must realize that the federal government isn't going to solve their Y2K problems—indeed, the government will be hard-pressed to solve its own—and that no other organization, vendor, or individual, least of all Bill Gates, will come riding up with a miracle solution.

Far too many government agencies, corporations, and other organizations have fallen into these traps and have been slow in starting their Y2K efforts. Unfortunately, they—and those who depend upon them—will suffer the consequences.

Working Together

The operative word here is "politics." This doesn't refer (just) to those problems associated with government agencies and leadership. It has to do with issues of power, cooperation, and interpersonal relationships within the context of an organization or other coordinated effort. You would assume that with an issue this significant that political issues would get set aside, but it was human factors that got us into this mess in the first place, so they're not likely to get us out.

The single biggest political obstacle to solving Y2K problems has been a lack of leadership. It is hard to overstate what this has cost us in terms of getting people to take this problem seriously and to mobilize appropriately. The two greatest failures of leadership in Y2K to date have been on the part of

President Bill Clinton and CEO Bill Gates of Microsoft. Senator Daniel Moynihan (D-NY) urged President Clinton back in 1996 to focus on the Y2K problem; that started a steady stream of public and private requests that the president give the subject the airing it deserved so that the nation would take it seriously. Even when the president appointed a Y2K "czar," John Koskinen, the announcement was buried behind several others. The president, along with Vice-President Gore and Koskinen, did finally give a public speech on the subject at the National Academy of Sciences in May 1998, but that remains to date his only such statement of any substance.

Even less comprehensible has been Bill Gates' initial public dismissals of the problem, followed by a belated and half-hearted acknowledgment of Y2K problems in Microsoft's own products, including "minor issues" in software as recent as Windows 95 and Internet Explorer 4.0. The irony is that Gates could not only have a tremendous impact on having the nation—indeed, the entire world—take the Y2K problem seriously, but he could also burnish his own image, which has suffered from his collisions with the U.S. Justice Department on anti-trust issues.

Lack of leadership is also an issue within organizations. The responsibility for Y2K leadership lies with the CEO or agency director, not with the CIO (Chief Information Officer) or some IT manager. Without that leadership, the organization will be far less likely to take the threat and the remediation efforts seriously. And that leadership must go hand-in-hand with strong support for the person in charge of Y2K remediation.

Another pair of political roadblocks are assuming that others in an organization understand the Y2K issue and that they want whoever is in charge of Y2K to succeed in their efforts. In fact, the less someone understands or believes the seriousness of Y2K, the more likely they are to resist it, since they will see it as interfering with, draining resources from, or even threatening their own projects and goals. Even someone who does grasp the problem may be calculating enough in their organizational politics to see it as an effort to undermine someone they oppose or feel threatened by.

Yet another political roadblock for the internal Y2K manager is lacking the power to make the hard decisions. The seriousness of Y2K can require diversion of resources, postponement or cancellation of other projects, adoption or deferment of new technologies, and other choices that can cause a lot of howling. But—especially at this late date—if that power isn't there, the tasks just won't get done in time. Instead, time and other resources are lost; the Y2K work doesn't get done or done in time.

Managing the Process

Y2K is actually far more of a management challenge than a technical one, so many management issues have delayed or slowed down Y2K remediation efforts. For starters, there's the simple fact that most information technology (IT) organizations lack what is known as **engineering maturity**. This refers to the ability to estimate with acceptable accuracy the time, money, and resources required for a given IT project and then deliver that project with acceptable quality within those parameters. As a result, most IT projects are late and over budget, and many fail to deliver the desired benefits or simply fail altogether. The larger and more complex the system being built, the more likely that it will be seriously late or never be delivered at all.

To take such organizations and charge them with assessing every system, doing repairs and testing on all that have Y2K problems, and then reintegrating all of them is an act of faith unlikely to be rewarded with miracles. Even in organizations with high maturity, Y2K efforts have almost universally taken longer and cost more than originally estimated. Some common errors include not having clear, centralized ownership of the problem, taking too long to make decisions, wasting time on unnecessary tasks, or omitting critical tasks from the project plan.

A major roadblock for many organizations is the decision to create (or purchase) new software that is Y2K compliant to replace the software that isn't. Again, IT organizations with high maturity have a better chance of accomplishing this, but those with low maturity run the risk of having neither the old system repaired nor the new system in place in time. Organizations choosing to buy replacement software from outside developers or commercial software vendors face the same problem but have even less control and supervision over the project.

Any IT organization, mature or not, faces the challenge of dealing with infrastructure requirements and constraints. "Infrastructure" here refers to all the hardware, software, and supporting information technologies already in place within the organization. For example, critical operations or applications may depend upon older hardware and/or software that is not Y2K compliant. Efforts to migrate to a newer (and compliant) environment may cause any number of problems, ranging from having to recompile existing software to having subtle (or not-so-subtle) problems in interacting with other parts of the infrastructure.

Finally, many organizations have not paid enough attention to establishing realistic contingency plans. They assume that they'll get all their work done, they won't have any Y2K (or other) defects left in their systems, and that all the external interfaces, suppliers, partners, customers, and so on they depend upon will all be there and working just fine.

Finding the People

This has been a major Y2K concern all along. This is due both to the general shortage of IT workers—the ITAA estimates that the United States has roughly a –10 percent "unemployment" rate in IT—and the decline in numbers of computer science graduates (a 40 percent drop in BSCS degrees awarded annually from 1985 to 1994) and the number of high school students planning to go into IT. On top of that, only a percentage of existing IT workers are really talented at what they do; many of the rest are decent and skilled, but far too many are mediocre or worse.[1]

The good news is that staffing seems to have been less of a problem to date than anticipated. The bad news is that this may be because the vast majority of organizations are actually quite a ways behind on Y2K work. It will be interesting to see what the start of 1999 brings.

While the massive staffing shortages anticipated still haven't materialized—beyond what we've all been living with for some years—plenty of organizations have been hampered by other issues. The single biggest problem is one that has been well documented in the literature for nearly 25 years: Beyond a certain point, you can't shrink the time required for an IT project by adding more people, and if the project is already late and in progress, adding more people can actually make it later.[2]

And while major shortages may not be here yet, spot shortages can be just as difficult for an organization. The ever-increasing demand for IT workers has caused serious wage inflation in the IT marketplace, which can make it very hard to keep within a budget or simply to keep someone. That, in turn, can cause hiring managers to run into organizational roadblocks in procurement and hiring due to salary or consulting fee standards or ceilings that haven't kept pace with wage inflation. Given the short time frame remaining for Y2K solutions, delays in hiring that might be acceptable or tolerable in normal circumstances can be very damaging.

Another set of staffing challenges deal with getting the right people working on the right projects. Often, the people available lack familiarity or skill with the technologies, subject matter, and applications involved. This slows down their rate of work and increases the probability that they will miss existing defects or introduce new ones. In addition, many IT personnel don't want to work on Y2K projects. They see it as a dead end, doing maintenance on old systems while new technologies pass them by. Beyond that, there's the simple fact that organizations face an ongoing need for IT personnel outside of the Y2K arena. In many cases, non-Y2K work in IT has been scaled back or even stopped, but for some organizations, that's not an option.

Many government organizations face additional problems hiring and keeping staff. First, they have a hard time competing with private industry salaries for IT personnel, so they not only have a hard time hiring new staff, but also many of their existing staff have left to pursue more lucrative work in the private sector. Second, they are often required to meet certain equal opportunity/affirmative action goals in their hiring. Unfortunately, and for reasons not understood, minorities and women are underrepresented in the IT field; indeed, the percentage of female graduates in computer science has declined over the past ten years. Third, and salaries aside, a lot of IT personnel have no desire to work for the government. This is due to a number of factors, including a general libertarian/

independent streak among many software developers, and a perception that government projects (military and intelligence agencies aside) are even more uninteresting and "trailing edge" than those found in the private sector.

Getting Outside Help

Because of the staffing problems described, many firms have looked at other options. They may **outsource** their Y2K remediation effort, that is, turn it over entirely to an outside firm. In some cases, this outsourcing is being done **off-shore**, that is, overseas, typically by firms in India, Europe, Russia, or other parts of the world. This approach may be useful or even essential, especially for assessment of large quantities of source code, but it carries with it its own roadblocks if repair and testing are also involved. Such firms seldom have **domain expertise** specific to the hiring organization. For example, if the company in question is in telecommunications, their systems will have lots of code very specific to the issues, standards, and presumptions found in telecommunications in general and to the company in particular. However, the developers and testers in the outsource firm—the ones actually modifying and verifying the software—won't necessarily have that expertise and so may inadvertently introduce or fail to catch errors specific to telecommunications. At the same time, there is a degree of risk in depending upon an outside firm to accomplish the job in time, especially if that firm has multiple customers with competing priorities. The more remote the firm is, the harder it can be to effectively supervise what is being done, and if things are truly falling behind, the hiring organization may find out too late to recover.

Another response to staffing issues, or issues of Y2K expertise, is to bring in Y2K consultants. Consultants are a lot like grains of salt: A few can really improve things, but too many can be unpleasant or even disastrous. Part of the question lies with how the consultants are being used. If they are providing advice on how to organize and run some aspect of the firm's Y2K effort, or if they are accomplishing tasks assigned to them, then they can be very worthwhile. Indeed, the roadblock here may be failing to listen to them. Back in 1997, at an early meeting of the WDCY2K group, I was listening to a knowledgeable Y2K consultant talk about his efforts. Someone asked him if most of his clients were in assessment; without missing a beat, he replied, "No, most of my clients are in denial." I suspect those same clients now wish they had followed his counsel. On the other hand, if the consultants wish to bring in large numbers of people to do the actual Y2K repairs and testing, then the hiring organization may run into the same problems as with outsourcing, though to a lesser extent.

Finally, there are many software tools available for Y2K assessment, repair, testing, and project management. Organizations tend to fall into one of two traps: They ignore the tools altogether, or they rely upon them too heavily. Automated tools are essential for assessment, and they can be extremely useful for automated testing. But they are not a substitute for all the other tasks involved, nor can they be 100 percent reliable because of the sheer complexity of the systems involved.

Dealing with Legacy Systems

As you may recall, the term "legacy" refers to software and hardware systems that have been in use for a long time. The term, as commonly used, carries with it a certain aura of "We'd really like to get rid of this, but we depend upon it too much and just haven't had the money/time/mandate to do so yet." The truth is, even modestly effective technology tends to entrench itself and become legacy, resisting our efforts to rip it out and replace it. Indeed, this is a major cause of the Year 2000 problem in the first place: systems still in use that their creators and users thought would (and should) have been retired long ago.

There are some Y2K roadblocks specific to legacy systems. The most direct roadblock comes from dealing with computers, operating systems, tools, commercial applications, and/or embedded systems that are no longer produced and supported. The manufacturer may have discontinued the entire product line, and the organization finds it difficult to switch to a different product line. This has been a challenge at the FAA, which has relied for decades upon obsolete mainframes that IBM no longer supports. It may be that the manufacturer itself has disappeared. When a major oil company did a Y2K assessment of an oil refinery, they identified 92 critical embedded control systems—and could not find the vendors for 20 of them.

Or it may be that the manufacturer has newer versions of the tools or systems, and the organization hasn't had the resources or incentive to upgrade. This problem can be more complicated to solve that it may appear. For example, the organization may have to upgrade the operating system for a particular hardware platform. That, in turn, may require that the applications used on that platform be recompiled using a newer version of the compiler for whatever programming language in which they were written. But that, in turn, may require changes to the source code that have nothing to do with Y2K, and that may, in turn, impact data files and interfaces with other systems that the applications use.

As noted back in Chapter 2, there are some 500 programming languages in use today, though 20 or so account for the majority of software. However, many military and intelligence agencies have made extensive use of obscure and custom technologies—specialized hardware, operating systems, and programming languages—and they face a major challenge finding anyone who's familiar with them.

Finding the Problems

Inventory and assessment, as noted here and in Chapter 1, are the first two phases of a Y2K remediation effort. They are easy to start, hard to complete, and absolutely essential to any Y2K effort. Indeed, a significant roadblock is to underestimate the need for a thorough inventory and assessment. One major power company, contacted by the Senate Special Committee on the Year 2000 problem, responded that it didn't know how many millions of lines of source code it had, nor how many embedded control systems, and that it felt that it was not "cost effective" to gather that information. The problem is, if you don't know what you have, how can you know what is Y2K compliant and what isn't?

A major roadblock faced during inventory and assessment efforts is the inability to locate the original source code for the software in question. Many organizations have major and minor software systems for which they have no source code, only the executable (object, machine) code. Needless to say, this makes it very hard to assess and repair the software. Imagine trying to do significant troubleshooting and repair work on your car without any manuals—or spare parts. It's a bit like that.

Even when source code does exist in some form, it may be very difficult to build a new executable version of the program. Suppose the firm has a program written in Pascal and compiled using a development system that's not Y2K compliant, for example, it inserted noncompliant date-manipulation routines into the program. So they find a Pascal development system (compiler, libraries, etc.) that is Y2K compliant. But that Pascal compiler has some differences in syntax and library routines. So they make the changes to the source code, not just to remove Y2K problems, but to be compatible with the development environment. But that now forces changes to how certain information (including nondate information) is represented in the data files used by the program. So now they have to write a program to convert all their existing data files to an updated format—and so on, and so forth.

The problem can actually get far more complicated than this, with various interactions and incompatibilities between compilers, libraries, data files and databases, utilities, operating systems, and even hardware platforms. Even when they have the source code, many organizations may not have rebuilt a given application from it for years—and when they try, they may find that they can't without significant effort.

Another common roadblock is to not take the time to assess, directly or indirectly, commercial software purchased from third-party vendors, but instead to simply take the vendors' word that the software is Y2K compliant. Major corporations running separate Y2K test environments have discovered Y2K problems in allegedly compliant software packages from major vendors. But many other organizations haven't done such testing and may face some unpleasant surprises later on.

Though it's less of a problem now, many organizations were overlooking Y2K issues in embedded or dedicated systems. Publicity on this topic through 1998 has focused attention on what may end up being the single greatest Y2K threat and impact. But given the sheer number of embedded systems in the world today—numbered in the billions—and the various challenges in actually assessing embedded systems for Y2K problems, this effort should have started years ago. If you do the math, you'll find that we just don't have time to get to them all, so we can only hope that the organizations involved are focusing on those systems likely to have the greatest impact should they fail.

Inventory and assessment have to also consider end-user applications, which, again, are commonly overlooked. These are application developed and used by workers at their PCs and workstations. They can run from full-blown applications developed using assembly or high-level languages to applications built upon fourth-generation languages to complicated macros and scripts, either running within an application (such as a spreadsheet or database program) or performing some function within the operating system.

Last, and probably least, firms may overlook Y2K problems with fixed displays, printed forms, and operating procedures. These aren't likely to be critical, but they can cause confusion among customers and employees.

Fixing the Problems

Many factors have hindered the actual work of doing Y2K repairs. The most obvious is missing or incomplete source code, or roadblocks to doing a complete "build" of a given program. It's hard to repair what you cannot modify and recompile.

Even when the source code is complete and able to be compiled, it may still be poorly written and poorly documented. Most people are not aware how much the quality of the source code, or its underlying architecture and design, can vary. Imagine the differences between a junior-high essay and, say, Faulkner. Now imagine having junior-high level writing filling up dozens of volumes—and you have to read through it and correct it without changing the meaning or content.

Then there's the issue of software stability. Anytime you modify an existing, functioning program, you run the risk of introducing new errors; industry studies have indicated that 7% to 10% of defects repaired introduced a new defect,[3] though that will vary based on the complexity and quality of the program, as well as the developer's skills and familiarity with the program itself.

Programs tend to become both more stable and more brittle with time; more stable, because existing defects are more likely to have been uncovered; more brittle, because the fixes and improvements tend to be "quick and dirty" modifications, rather than carefully thought out enhancements. At the same time, the software is running within an environment (operating system, computer, supporting software) that may be undergoing updating and modifications as well. To go into such a program and make wholesale changes can destabilize it in any number of ways and drag out the process of Y2K repair.

Another potential roadblock is the impact of Y2K modifications on performance and resource requirements. A common complaint about older, larger software systems is that they are often barely fast enough to accomplish their required tasks, usually because they're being asked to do more work and process more data than was ever envisioned. The Y2K changes, particularly if they are made in areas of the software that are performance bottlenecks anyway, can slow the software down below the acceptable level.

In a similar fashion, databases and data files for these applications may have grown far larger than ever expected; it's not unusual for a large corporation to have thousands of separate databases running on hundreds of servers. If the Y2K changes involve expanding years from two digits to four, the sudden expansion in size of the files and databases can require buying new servers (or adding more storage to existing ones). It can also slow down the response time when data is read from or written to these databases, as well as the time required to transfer large amounts of this data over networks.

Verifying the Fixes

The experience we have to date from Y2K projects that have neared completion indicates that testing the repaired software requires somewhere from 40 percent to 70 percent of the overall time and resources allocated to Y2K remediation. This becomes an immediate touchstone for the likelihood of a Y2K project being on schedule: If the project is allocating only 10–30 percent of its overall time to testing (three to seven months of a two-year effort), then it is likely to go several months over its schedule or be insufficiently tested when it goes back into regular use.

Of course, there is the simple problem that the organization may not know how to test the software. That is, there may not be an existing test plan or other documentation to verify that the program still behaves correctly now that it's been repaired. This is especially true when you have large, complex systems that have been in use, largely unmodified, for years.

Even when test plans do exist, appropriate test data may need to be created. To test the software to see if it will work correctly in the future (e.g., in 2000 and beyond), you need test data that has been "aged" appropriately. In other words, the data has to have future dates in it and has to be internally correct. With that created, you also need some way of knowing what the correct results are for that set of data. None of this is as easy as it may appear.

The problems may go deeper than that. Far too many information technology (IT) departments—those responsible for developing and maintaining software within an organization—do not do a good job of quality assurance (QA) under the best of circumstances, and good QA practices are critical for Y2K work.

Especially critical is the need for rigorous configuration management (CM). This is an industry term for keeping very careful track of all the different versions of all the various files involved: source code, object code, libraries, tools, scripts, data files, and so on. Without good CM, it's easy to lose track of what has been assessed, what's been modified, and which set of files you need to rebuild a particular piece of software.

In all this is the need to define what it means within your organization for a system to be "Y2K compliant," that is, how it has to behave under various Y2K circumstances. Again, this may seem obvious, but there is no standard definition (though there are a lot of similar ones).

Finally, there is the challenge of creating an environment in which to carry out your Y2K testing. Some organizations do this using the same computer systems with which they do their daily work. That carries two risks: impacting or disrupting current daily operations, and not being able to have sufficient time available to accomplish the testing. Other organizations set up separate test environments, in some cases buying desktop systems, servers, and even mainframes to be used just for Y2K testing. The risk here is the time (and money) it may cost to do that.

Making It All Work

Once software has been assessed, repaired, and tested, it often must be put back into production, that is, daily use. Unfortunately, there are any number of roadblocks encountered there. The first is when the organization has failed to establish a process for replacing the existing version of the software with the Y2K-compliant version. Since the repair and testing process may take months, changes—improvements and repairs—may have been made in the original. These need to somehow be made in the Y2K-compliant version, which may then have to go through testing again.

A related challenge is trying to integrate Y2K-compliant systems with other systems that are not yet compliant. For example, suppose you have two programs, A and B, that both use two-digit dates that they interpret as 1900 through 1999 and that exchange data with each other. Now suppose you repair and test A and put it back into production. If you changed A to use four-digit dates, its date format is now incompatible with B. Even if you create a conversion routine to translate dates between the two (often called a **bridge**), program A can still generate dates—such as "2000"—that program B cannot or won't interpret correctly. Similar problems can exist if A uses windowing and B doesn't, or even if B uses windowing with a different pivot year than A, and so on and so forth.

In short, those doing integration face a dilemma: Either wait until everything has been repaired and tested and put it all into production at the same time, or put compliant systems back into production as they become compliant. Either approach has difficulties and challenges. On top of all this are all the data files and databases that may have to have dates within them converted (to four digits, to a given two-digit windowing standard, or even to some special date format). There may also be date format issues in screens, reports, and forms, namely that these might still be using two-digit nonwindowed years, while the software producing or interacting with them does.

The greatest danger with integration is not software crashing because of a compliance mismatch. It is the silent corruption of data. If the integration isn't done and checked carefully, you may have your data files and databases slowly (or not so slowly) filled with erroneous values and results. For example, if there is a windowing mismatch between two programs that share the same database, then a value that one program interprets as 1945 might be interpreted as 2045 by the other—and so the two programs may arrive at very different conclusions about how to handle related data.

Finally, as you put your Y2K-compliant software back into production, you may flush out previously unknown Y2K problems in third-party and custom systems and hardware. This can complicate your efforts, slow down full integration, and increase your budget. A good thing to keep in mind: Almost anything that goes wrong in your Y2K remediation effort will slip your schedule and increase your budget.

Planning for Problems

Many organizations have overlooked the need for contingency planning altogether. Their attitude is they will of course get all their systems completed on time, and that their systems will work fine, therefore they have no need of contingency plans. This ignores both the general history of software development projects over the past 50 years and the specific problems of most Y2K remediation efforts to date.

Furthermore, it overlooks the most critical aspect of Y2K contingency planning: external dependencies. Many firms have existing business continuity plans, which are useful as starting points. But there are usually two major problems with those plans. First, they tend to deal only with major infrastructure issues: fire, flood, blizzard, power outage, and so on. Second, they tend to presume just one event at a time.

A more serious roadblock may be determining the organization's external dependencies. A good starting place is the accounts payable records: everyone that receives money from the organization. Next are the accounts receivable records: everyone that pays money to the organization. The former dependencies will determine whether you continue to receive the supplies and services the organization requires to function; the latter, whether the organization will have the money it requires to pay the former.

The biggest challenge, though, is tracking down the nonobvious dependencies. These can be several steps removed: suppliers to the suppliers to the suppliers to the organization. Or they can be indirect influences: Changes in the interest rate may impact certain purchasing decisions, which in turn may hurt or help the organization.

Dealing with Lawyers and Customers

Some of the greatest roadblocks to dealing with Y2K have been legal and market issues. For example, suppose Foo Corporation decides to let it be known that the Foo Widget is not Y2K compliant, but a new version coming out will be. This seems to be a direct, honest solution. Unfortunately, it can have a lot of nasty consequences for Foo:

- The Bar Company quickly lets it be known that the Bar Widget is already Y2K compliant. This may or may not be true, and Bar may or may not know that their widget really *is* compliant, but the results are likely to be the same: Sales of Foo Widgets drop off. Foo's market share and net income decline.

- Foo's stock price also goes down, triggering a class-action shareholder lawsuit filed by one of the many law firms that specialize in such suits. They claim that the officers of Foo Corporation should have foreseen this problem

- Foo hurries and rushes the Y2K-compliant Foo Widget to market. Because their income has been hurt by the decline in sales, they charge for replacing noncompliant widgets with compliant ones. Another class-action lawsuit is filed against Foo for charging their customers to fix a known defect that was Foo's fault in the first place.

- In the meantime, Acme, Inc., whose Acme Gizmo has a Foo Widget integrated within it, faces an impact on its own sales because the Gizmo is noncompliant due to the Widget. Gizmo faces most or all of the same consequences that Foo faces.

Now let's construct a different scenario. Foo has made no public announcement on the Y2K status of its Widget. Acme, however, discovers the Foo Widget isn't compliant and switches over to the Bar Widget. This information is distributed to Acme's customers to alert them to the need of a repair or replacement due to the Foo Widget's noncompliance. Foo now suffers the consequences above and sues Acme for damages to its business, stock prices, and so on.

Yet another scenario. Foo starts late on its Y2K effort and remains noncommittal about the Y2K status of its widgets; perhaps it doesn't really know. The Y2K-compliant version of the Foo Widget isn't done before the widgets out in the field start failing. One such widget is used in a critical transportation control system. A crash occurs, and many people are killed or injured. The Foo Corporation and its officers and directors are named in both civil and criminal charges rising out of the fact that it was their component that failed. Foo's attempt to defend itself is undercut by one simple truth: The Y2K problem has been known for 20–30 years, has been publicized heavily in the trade press since 1993, and yet Foo still delayed its Y2K remediation effort until 1997.

I'm sure actual lawyers out there could construct any number of additional (and perhaps more realistic) scenarios. This is just a small taste of the potential legal consequences of going public with Y2K compliance.

Most organizations will not divulge such information, at least in any meaningful and specific detail, unless they are sure that it is (a) safe and (b) beneficial. At the same time, many organizations may face liability for failing to disclose Y2K problems with the organization and/or its products in a timely manner so that others can adjust appropriately.

Yes, Y2K Remediation Is Hard

Here's what may be a sobering thought: The list of problems is far from complete and comprehensive. First, far more roadblocks specific to Y2K efforts exist, as do far more details about the ones given here. Second, the process above is subject to all the various pitfalls and danger inherent to the development and deployment of information technology—and those do fill many books. Those of us who have been involved in a full-blown Y2K remediation effort from start to finish know all the myriad challenges that pop up daily, even when the effort is well-funded, well-supported, and led by highly competent people. Unfortunately, that doesn't describe the majority of Y2K projects.

Having made it through these three chapters, you should have a better idea of what the Year 2000 problem entails, how it came to pass, and why we haven't fixed it yet. The next chapter covers the most prevalent myths and most important facts about Y2K, as well as a few personal opinions, before you move on to looking at how you should personally prepare for coming events.

Myths, Facts, and Opinions About Y2K

Let's get the single most common misconception out of the way right up front. The year 2000 is not the first year of the twenty-first century or the third millennium; the year 2001 is. The span A.D. 1 to A.D. 100 makes up the first century; A.D. 101–200 makes up the second century; and so on; while A.D. 1 to A.D. 1000 makes up the first millennium, and A.D. 1001 to A.D. 2000 makes up the second millennium. Of course, the vast majority of people couldn't care less about such niceties and made all their plans for New Year's Eve blowouts for the end of 1999. After all, that's when every date—after a thousand years of starting with "1"—will now start with "2," which is the big shift. Frankly, and despite a personal inclination to pick nits, my sentiment for years has been to agree with the rough wisdom of the masses: Let's just concede that the first century and the first millennium were both a year short and kick everything off in the year 2000.[1]

But now the purists may help us save face. Many of the extensive and extravagant plans for New Year's Eve 1999, some booked years in advance, may well be cancelled, disrupted, marred, or put on hold by the Year 2000 problems that we'll discuss in this book. So let's just postpone it all a year and have the big blowout on New Year's Eve 2000. It really *will* be the century/millennium shift, we'll have had a year to get things straightened out, and—God willing—we'll have a lot to celebrate. Besides, if you act quickly, you can reserve one of those special locations that are tied up for New Year's Eve 1999. It's a bit like being near the end of a long line waiting to get in somewhere—and having them open the doors at the back of the line, not the front. A guilty pleasure, and a bit unfair to those who planned ahead, but a pleasure nonetheless.

The Top Ten Myths of Y2K

That said, let's look at the top ten myths concerning the Year 2000 issue. These myths live on, in spite of having been debunked time and again, and they have been repeated by periodicals that should have taken the time to learn better.[2] Unfortunately, these myths have led many organizations to not take Y2K seriously and to delay responding to it.

Myth 1:
Y2K will cause planes to fall out of the sky, elevators and cars to stop working, ATMs and credit cards to stop working, and VCRs to go on the blink

This comes first because an amazing number of articles and news reports on Y2K start off with this litany of potential consequences, all of which are either wrong, out of date, or irrelevant. By so doing, such articles discredit the very real and likely consequences of Y2K in many other areas.

As I said before, I know of no credible Y2K analyst who has ever asserted that airplanes would "fall out of the sky" because of Y2K problems. Air transportation is one of the most heavily regulated industries, especially in the United States, because hundreds of thousands of lives are potentially at risk each day. The liability consequences of even a single plane crashing are enormous. If there is any question at all about an airplane's readiness to fly or the ability of the Federal Aviation Association to handle its flight, that flight will be cancelled and the plane grounded.

Elevators and cars always seem to appear in popular news stories on Y2K as well. I know of only one second-hand source that asserts that problems cropped up with a Y2K test of elevators. That particular problem has likely been fixed by now, and given how frequently elevators are mentioned in these news reports, one hopes that all the rest will be tested and dealt with between now and the end of 1999. As for cars, even less evidence exists of any meaningful Y2K problems. Occasional reports crop up, but they tend to fall apart when you push back to the source.

As for automatic teller machines (ATMs), there did indeed appear to be problems with them early on. Senator Robert Bennett, Chairman of the Senate Special Committee on the Year 2000 Technical Problem as well as of the Senate Subcommittee on Financial Services and Technology, stated in a WDCY2K meeting in March of 1998 that less than 20 percent of ATMs were Y2K compliant. In much the same way, many early problems existed with credit cards that were issued with a post-1999 expiration date. But both concerns appears to be what author David Brin calls a "self-defeating prophecy"—that is, by having attention called to it, the problem will be dealt with and go away.

Finally, I'm puzzled why VCRs are mentioned at all. Older VCRs don't care about the year at all; indeed, you have no way of setting the year. Newer VCRs do care about the year (because of VCR+™ programming), but I have seen no reports that any such VCRs stumble over the year 2000. You can easily test yours, I tested mine; it appears to use windowing (see Chapter 1 for an explanation), since it handles years from 1993 to 2092.

Myth 2:
The Y2K problem has been greatly exaggerated by consultants in order to make money

This was the other great myth found in media coverage of Y2K up until mid-1998. It's starting to vanish, but it lives on in the general public. And the truth is that a lot of firms have sprung up to offer various services and products associated with Y2K remediation and have made a lot of money.

However, the general myth collapses when examined from any number of angles. First, the reality of Y2K problems has been well-documented time and again in a variety of settings and industries, despite the reluctance by many of the major players in those industries. One has only to read the long list of reports and testimonies issued by the U.S. General Accounting Office on the subject—an organization that is not anxious to see the federal government spend more money—to see how seriously they take the problem and how well established they find it to be.[3]

Second, if the problem were exaggerated, then you would expect the estimates of costs required to carry out Y2K remediation to go down as the "real" nature of the problem was discovered. Instead, just the opposite has happened with virtually every major organization that has progressed in its Y2K efforts. For example, the U.S. federal government's estimate of its total costs on Y2K remediation has doubled from 1996 to 1998 and now stands at about $6 billion. Many outside analysts feel that this is still too low.

Third, many of the more vocal and visible "alarmists" on Y2K have made little (if any) significant money for doing so. In many cases, they have even taken damage to their personal and/or professional reputations for being so outspoken and out in front on this subject.

Fourth, major financial firms—savvy with both money and technology—have been the leaders on Y2K remediation, spending in some cases hundreds of millions of dollars to fix the problem. You can rest assured that they didn't do this because some consultant scared them with exaggerated stories. The problems they found were real and pervasive.

Finally, there is a large number of competent, bright IT professionals who work on this issue full time in their respective organizations, know it intimately, and are seriously concerned. It is those who are most involved and most technically competent who are most worried. A good reference is the pair of surveys released by the Washington D.C. Year 2000 group in 1998.[4] Both surveys yielded the same results. Two-thirds of the members responding felt there will be at best an economic slowdown; one-third felt there will be at least a strong recession and regional infrastructure failures; a tenth foresaw a second Great Depression or worse. Even when the votes from those who might stand to profit from such concerns—vendors, consultants, and lawyers—were factored out, the results remained largely the same. Indeed, the vendors were more conservative than the overall group on their predictions, while the consultants pretty much mirrored the group as a whole.

Myth 3:
Y2K alarmists have no basis for their predictions

I cannot summarize it any better than this quote from a letter to the *Wall Street Journal*: "They raise the specter of airplane crashes, loss of phone service, traffic lights going out, banks losing all records—without ever pretending to suggest how any of these catastrophes might have anything to do with the year 2000."[5]

This statement is wrong on several counts. The FAA's Year 2000 problems are well documented and still a matter of some dispute, with the GAO questioning the FAA's claim of tremendous progress in a short period of time.[6] The real specter raised is not of plane crashes, but of severely curtailed air traffic due to a combination of factors, including Y2K problems in air traffic control systems and airport operations, as well as deliberate grounding of flights by airlines to avoid liability. Again, as noted above, I know of no credible Y2K analyst who has claimed that planes would fall from the sky, yet it appears frequently in newspaper and magazine articles.

Likewise, Y2K-based phone problems are well documented. Art Gross, the former CIO of the Internal Revenue Service, has publicly voiced his serious concern about the IRS's private branch exchange (PBX) systems,[7] and other telecom issues can be readily located. Senior officers in multinational corporations have stated that they have serious questions about telecom access—simple dial tone—to countries outside of Europe and North America based on what the telecom companies have told them.

One direct citation about traffic signals comes from one of the GAO reports, but Y2K problems with embedded systems have already been well documented; the CIO of GM (hardly a fear-mongering consultant out for big bucks) called its impact on their worldwide manufacturing facilities "catastrophic" in a recent *Fortune* article.[8] Traffic lights may be the least of our problems.

Again, I know of no credible Y2K analyst who has predicted that banks would lose "all records." The likely danger is not loss, but silent errors being introduced through miscalculation, as well as limitations or inability to function due to incomplete repairs. Such errors are nothing new or unique to Y2K; that merely increases the likelihood.

The point of this is not proof of the specific items above; it's that the evidence is there and the mechanisms are well known, both on a general and a specific level. Indeed, in two years of explaining Y2K to individuals and groups, I've found that the greater the technical depth and breadth of a given individual, the more readily they grasp the plausibility, reality, and significance of the Y2K problem.

The same letter referenced above goes on to claim that "[t]here is no believable scenario whereby a twenty-first century date or a zero date could crash a program." This assertion is not only false, but breathtakingly so. Plenty of programs—and operating systems, and computers, and embedded control systems—have already crashed, frozen, or otherwise ceased to operate when faced with a zero date, either in the course of normal operations or under Y2K test conditions. Such an assertion reflects little understanding of the realities of software and what can happen when a completely unexpected value is introduced into a set of calculations, particularly at a lower level of operations.

Myth 4:
Y2K problems only happen in old COBOL programs running on older mainframe computers

This is one of the older myths, and one that is quickly going by the wayside. But it's still worth mentioning here. What is true is that old COBOL programs running on old mainframe computers are more likely than most other software to have Y2K problems. Unfortunately, Y2K problems are found just about anywhere that dates are used, including commercial applications, computers, and embedded control systems that are being sold in 1998.

Myth 5:
Y2K problems only happen in software or devices that care about the year and that are doing certain year-based calculations

The truth behind this myth is that Y2K problems only happen in software that is somehow keeping track of the year, is using two digits to do so, and will mishandle a year of "00." Unfortunately, that truth is often extrapolated to unsupportable or inaccurate generalizations, such as that Y2K problems only impact systems that care about the current year and that are doing before/after or elapsed time calculations.[9]

Y2K problems start with the most basic of data operations: testing for a given value. Some developers created programs in which they do an explicit check of the value of the year (e.g., IF YEAR == "00") and take action accordingly. In some number of programs, a year value of "00" is considered to be one that would never be reached and so was used as a flag, that is, a data value that indicates ("flags") some special action to be taken. For example, it might be considered a "wild card," so that a date with a year of "00" stood for a recurring date in every year, as opposed to a date in a specific year. Or it might be used to indicate the last date in a list of dates, so that the software would work its way through a list of dates (or records with dates) until it hit one with a year of "00."

The next basic operation is comparing two dates and determining which date is earlier. This is used to test for certain conditions (e.g., the date a certain law or regulation went into effect) or to sort a set of data records by the date (e.g., sorting employees by date of hire). In such cases, a later date (2000 or "00") may be wrongly interpreted as being before an earlier date (such as 1975 or '75). Almost as basic is calculating the time elapsed between two points in time. This is the source of what most people think of as "the" Y2K error: trying to determine the years elapsed from, say, 1965 ("65") to 2000 ("00") and getting –65 years instead of 35.

This is where the myth begins to break down. Programs and embedded control systems that would not appear to care about the year can still have Y2K problems when dealing with elapsed time. This is because they use time manipulation software, sometimes in conjunction with real-time clock (RTC) hardware, that has been developed by others, is part of the operating system and/or hardware platform, or is purchased "off the shelf." Such software (and hardware) is intended to be as general purpose as possible and so is usually designed using a year value in case the application using it needs to keep track of the year. But even when the application doesn't "care" about the year, the software it's using does. And if the year format in use is two digits, this will open the door to all the usual Y2K errors. This is why Rep. Steve Horn (R-CA) could report that the city of Baton Rouge found a Y2K problem in the mechanisms that extend the ladders on their fire trucks.[10]

Beyond that, there are more complex date-related calculations. These include determining leap year (2000 is, though 1900 and 2100 aren't); determining day of the week of a given date (January 1, 1900 is a Sunday, while January 1, 2000 is a Saturday); determining whether a given date is a business day; determining elapsed business days between two dates, which has to take into account weekends, leap years, and holidays (many of which are calculated); determining key business process dates (when a given action is automatically initiated); warehousing and inventory control; calculating interest, finance charges, and penalties; and so on.

Myth 6:
Only a small fraction of all computer programs are affected, and they can easily be identified

This myth is partly false, partly irrelevant. If we set aside embedded control systems for a minute and just focus on "regular" software (applications, operating systems, utilities, and so on), we find estimates that as many as one-third of such programs have Y2K problems of one sort or another.[11] This isn't surprising when you realize that dates are among the most common types of information found in programs and data files.

But even the exact percentage is irrelevant, because the work involved remains the same. There is no means other than inspection to tell whether a program contains date information and is using it in a potentially erroneous way. Suppose I lock you in a room with a thousand crates and tell you that roughly 33 percent or 10 percent or even just 3 percent of them have time bombs in them. Most of them will only do limited damage, but a few of them might be strong enough to destroy everything. How many of the crates will you search? Only a small fraction?

As far as identifying those affected, there are good procedures and tools for finding most uses of dates in programs written in relatively common programming languages, such as COBOL, C, and so on. That ignores the Babel of niche and custom languages (many of which are used in military and government intelligence systems), the lack of available source code for many older applications, and the regrettable obscurity and perversity used by many "creative" software programmers to entertain themselves. Even with the tools, you're playing the odds. If you're back in that same room with the crates and the bombs, and I give you an explosive detector that is 90 percent guaranteed to detect a bomb in a crate, how many crates will you leave unopened?

Embedded control systems are a different story, though even there the percentages can be misleading. The most commonly quoted estimates are from 0.01 percent (1 of every 10,000) to 1 percent (1 out of 100) of ECSs have Y2K problems. That really is a tiny fraction, and some argue that the percentage is even smaller. Unfortunately, several issues make this situation more serious than that with regular software. First, because of the nature of embedded control systems, there is seldom a way to quickly "scan" them to assess them for Y2K problems, partly because they're embedded, but mostly because you usually don't have the source code—and even the executable code is locked up in a ROM (read-only memory) chip somewhere. Second, apparently "identical" models of a given embedded control system can actually have different behaviors depending upon which chips and software were used to build each ECS unit and how that ECS is wired up to the devices that it controls. Third, it appears that there is a rough correlation between the critical nature of a given ECS and its likelihood to use dates and so potentially have Y2K problems. So while the overall estimates of ECSs affected run from 0.01 percent to 1 percent, actual surveys done in key areas (oil platforms, supertankers, critical medical systems) show Y2K problem rates of 3 percent to 18 percent. Fourth, with some 1 to 10 billion ECSs worldwide, the law of large number comes into play. Even if we pick conservative estimates—just 1 billion ECSs with a 0.01 percent error rate—we end up with 100,000 ECSs with Y2K problems in a world where a single ECS failure can shut down a processing plant, a supertanker—or a critical life-support system.

Myth 7:
Bill Gates (or someone else) will come up with a solution.

It's amazing how often this gets stated, even by people who one would expect to be better educated on Y2K. Leaving aside for the moment the fact that Microsoft is principally known for delivering software that is (a) late and (b) buggy, this myth is based on a profound misunderstanding of the nature of the problem. It is probably to be expected; information technology engineering is not an easy discipline to understand. But this myth overlooks two important facts.

First, *we already know how to solve the Y2K problem.* The problem isn't technology, it's time and scope. Here's a simple, rough analogy. We know how to send astronauts to the moon; we did it 30 years ago.[12] So if the president asked NASA to send a small team of astronauts to the moon and back safely, they could do it, given enough time and money. If the president said they had to get the astronauts there and back by the end of 1999, NASA almost certainly couldn't do it; if they did, it would only be with high risks. Finally, if the president said that NASA had to send 10,000 people to the moon and back by the end of 1999, they just couldn't do it. It's not a lack of zeal or technical brilliance or even resources. They just could not design, build, and launch that many ships in that period of time.

Second, *there is no "silver bullet" for Y2K.* In other words, there is no one solution that will magically make the problem go away. As noted back in Chapters 1 and 3, Y2K remediation is a lengthy, complex process that involves many steps. There are "breakthrough solutions" that appear for the code repair phase from time to time, usually getting significant press coverage and then fading away. Many of them are real solutions for certain types of Y2K problems and/or in certain environments and languages. But they are limited to those special circumstances. To use another simple, rough, and somewhat silly analogy, it's as if we had to convert all gasoline-powered internal combustion engines to diesel fuel. Someone might come up with a clever solution for Ford V-6 and V-8 engines—but that doesn't address all the other car and truck engines, not to mention generators, lawn mowers, water pumps, and so on. And few if any of the so-called breakthrough solutions address the single largest problem: embedded control systems.

Myth 8:
Hiring more people will help speed up late Y2K repair projects.

This myth doesn't impact just Y2K projects; it is endemic throughout software development organizations. It makes a certain amount of sense at first glance—if a project that's underway and running late will take six more months to finish with 10 developers, then it should take just three months to finish with 20 developers. After all, either way you're looking at 60 "staff-months" of work. But by that same argument, the project should only take two months to finish with 30 developers, one month to finish with 60 developers, one week to finish with 240 developers, and a mere one day to finish with 1880 developers.

At some point here, you realize that the presumption that time and staff are interchangeable breaks down. After all, creating new software or modifying existing software, isn't like filling sandbags. It's an intensely creative, complex, and intricate effort with many phases. Many aspects are noncompressible; others cannot easily be divvied up and farmed out, and even when they can, the additional communication and coordination required can slow efforts down.

What you probably didn't realize is that the effort to speed up the late project likely broke down at the very first step, that is, trying to cut the remaining time left to three months by doubling the number of developers. In fact—and this is so counterintuitive that you can be forgiven for not believing it—adding ten more developers to the original ten will likely cause the project to take *more* than six months to finish, not less.

This principle is known as **Brooks' law**: Adding personnel to a late software development project makes it later. It is just one—but perhaps the best known—of many key insights on software engineering detailed over 20 years ago by Frederick P. Brooks in *The Mythical Man-Month*,[13] a classic that stands as the Bible of IT because it is universally known, often quoted, occasionally read, and rarely heeded. In the two decades since *Mythical Man-Month* came out, many managers have shipwrecked their information technology (IT) projects on Brooks' law, chasing after the mirage of getting a late project back on schedule by increasing the staff.

In short, efforts to draft or train programmers to help out Y2K projects that are running late are likely not to have much impact and may in the end make things worse.

Myth 9:
Y2K is a technical problem

As noted above, we know how to fix Y2K, just as we know how to get to the moon. This is not a problem in search of a technical solution. Because of that, technical solutions buy us only a little bit. Unfortunately, many people view it as a technical problem and so keep waiting for some great technical breakthrough (see myth 5). The truth is, the only real technical issue—the cost and availability of memory and disk storage—was resolved well over a decade ago. It was even applied broadly, which is one major reason why (by Capers Jones' estimate) two-thirds of all software has no Y2K problems, the other major reason being that a lot of software just doesn't use dates.

Y2K is very much a management problem. For an organization of any size, it is an amazingly comprehensive, tedious, mind-numbing project that requires someone who can keep track of a vast number of details, making sure nothing important falls through the cracks, motivating (and retaining) the Y2K staff through a thankless, uninteresting effort, and dealing with reluctant internal and external partners—all in the face of an immovable deadline.

Above all, Y2K is a human problem, that is, founded upon human frailties and tendencies. As laid out in Chapter 2, once the technical issues were resolved, human issues predominated in keeping the Y2K problem from being fixed years ago. They still predominate; note how many of the roadblocks in Chapter 3 are just reflections of such issues.

Myth 10:
Civilization as we know it will collapse.

One can argue that this is a matter of opinion rather than an established myth, but I'll stand by this assertion. Had Y2K hit us before, say, mid-1998, this could well have been a consequence. But enough momentum and progress have now been established here in the United States on Y2K repairs in both government and business. The state of Y2K repairs and awareness by the end of 1999 will, in my opinion, be more than enough to forestall the extreme consequences predicted by some parties.

Make no mistake: It could still be a nasty blow economically, with a level of unemployment and economic contraction unseen since the Great Depression. Many of our assumptions and the day-to-day details we take for granted may shift, evolve, or disappear. But that depression, not to mention two world wars and any number of smaller ones, failed to end Western civilization or even come close. Barring an extreme scenario (e.g., a nuclear exchange with rogue forces somewhere in the former Soviet Union), we'll get through whatever we need to get through, pick ourselves up, and go on from there.

In fact, the global complex systems built on technological, market, and social factors that have made us vulnerable to Y2K are the same systems that will eventually get us past the Y2K consequences.

The Five Most Important Facts To Know About Y2K

Some of these are just the flip side of the myths above, but they are still important to know and realize. If you have doubts or questions about any of these, it would be

Fact 1:
Y2K is real

This may seem a redundant and obvious assertion, especially after all that has been covered in these first four chapters, but I have heard too many otherwise intelligent and informed people question the very existence of Y2K, calling it a hoax or, at least, a horribly overblown problem.[14] Indeed, listening to them, I wonder if they don't on some level welcome Y2K, hoping it will either prove that things are not as complex and dependent upon information technology as they appear to be, or that things will become less complex and dependent as a result.

Listen carefully: Y2K is real. I spent 18 months involved with the Y2K remediation effort of a Fortune 50 corporation. The problems they found and fixed were very real problems; left unchecked, they would have brought the corporation to its knees. The same is true for the Y2K problems they found in various operating systems, development tools, utilities, database programs, and other third-party software. Fortunately for that corporation, they started relatively early and had an outstanding person in charge who did whatever it took to see that the Y2K repairs went forward.

The last nine months of that time I was assigned the responsibility for setting up and guiding the corporation's Y2K contingency planning effort. The information that crossed my desk or screen daily, the interviews I had with people at all levels of the corporation, and the analysis of the corporation's marketplace and external dependencies brought home all the vast complexities of the Y2K problem.

Fact 2:
We will not get everything fixed in time

This is relatively easy to prove based just on the numbers of embedded control systems, the roadblocks to assessing and repairing them, and the progress actually made to date. But we won't even get all our regular computer systems repaired before Y2K problems crop up. Too many organizations have started too late and are moving too slow. Many of them don't realize it. Like the bungee jumper described back in Chapter 1, they are sure that their Y2K remediation effort will start to slow down as they approach the end of 1999; and, like the bungee jumper, they are in for an unpleasant surprise.

The situation will be much worse overseas, especially in developing countries. Various estimates have been made about this country or that region being some number of months behind the United States in awareness and Y2K efforts. Given how late so many of our own organizations are, that does not bode well. But it's actually worse than that. For reasons that have been debated for years, most other countries outside of the United States are slower and less adept at developing software. Exceptions and counterexamples do exist, most notably India, and there was a time when it appeared that the United States might be losing its edge, but that time has passed.[15]

But we cannot sit back and gloat, or even feel satisfied. Our economy, our expectations in daily life are founded heavily upon food, materials, and goods imported from the rest of the world. We are, as someone has put it, the market of last resort, the country willing to buy up whatever any other country has to export. We will feel the impact of Y2K problems in other countries, and vice versa.

Fact 3:
Y2K problems will have consequences we do not expect

We live and work within a global net of complex systems:[16] social, economic, informational, technological, logistical, political. These systems constantly adapt to existing circumstances, changing or reinforcing themselves as appropriate. We do not and cannot comprehend these systems fully, nor can we control them. Their behavior is emergent and dynamic, not deterministic and static. The 1990s have been a decade of education on the nature of these complex systems. As problems or issues have cropped up, we have found how interconnected things have become and have been taught the law of unexpected and *n*th-order consequences.

As a simple example, when the Galaxy IV satellite drifted off in mid-1998 due to a minor malfunction, most people were not surprised when pager service across the United States went away. A lot of people were surprised, though, that they couldn't buy gasoline using credit cards at certain service stations, because those stations used two-way satellite communications for rapid authorization of purchases. National Public Radio found itself using phone lines and the Internet to broadcast its feed to radio stations around the country. And hospitals found themselves scrambling to cope with the loss of pager contact with doctors and nurses.

As a more complex example, we have watched what started as a currency crisis in a small Southeast Asian country—Indonesia—ripple and reverberate around the world, plunging Asia into recession (if not depression) and impacting Russia, Europe, and even the United States.

As Y2K events begin to occur, they will reveal—often in real time—unknown and unanticipated aspects and interconnections of these systems. It's why efforts to predict firm scenarios of Y2K consequences are likely to be wrong, and why Part III of this book takes the approach of listing a series of escalating scenarios with indicators of each. Whatever happens, though, we're likely to be surprised.

Fact 4:
Y2K events will be distributed, overlapping and interacting

Y2K events will not occur just on the weekend of January 1-2, 2000, and then be done with. Minor Y2K events have already occurred in nearly half of Fortune 500 corporations; in some cases, they led the organization to take Y2K seriously. More Y2K events will occur in 1999 as more systems "look ahead" to 2000. The rate will start to rise rapidly towards the end of 1999, will peak somewhere around the Y2K crossover, then taper off over a period of days, weeks, and even months. The consequences will last far longer.

At the same time, Y2K events by and large will not be isolated, occurring as a series of discrete events that can be handled individually. Instead, they will overlap each other, especially right at the end of 1999 and start of 2000. Efforts to cope with one event may be hindered—or possibly even helped—by the consequences of another event. And the events themselves may intensify, cancel out, or transform their respective consequences. If you've ever seen what happens when several people jump into a small pool at roughly the same time, you may get a good mental image of what the interactions may do. And if you've ever tried to *swim* in a pool under those conditions, you may get a sense of what coping with those interactions may be like.

Fact 5:
Self-reliance, social cohesion, and leadership are the most important factors in getting through Y2K

Human factors predominate in the history and causes of the Y2K problem, as well as the stumbling blocks in resolving it. It shouldn't be a surprise, then, that human factors—in particular, self-reliance, social cohesion, and leadership—are the more critical components in dealing with Y2K. These three factors will be the central themes of Part II, but they are worth looking at for a few minutes here.

Self-reliance does not mean building yourself an armed compound somewhere out in the Badlands. It means, simply, taking responsibility for what happens to you and seeking, as far as possible, to solve your own problems with regards to Y2K. It also means not waiting or expecting the government to come "do something" for you. The government—local, state, and federal—has enough problems of its own, and in any case will not likely be in a position to deal with the Y2K problems of the entire population of the United States.

Social cohesion means recognizing that you depend upon a myriad of other people, not just in your community but across the United States and around the world, for most of what you enjoy, use, and live off of on a day-to-day basis. In other words, you're part of a complex system, and the best overall Y2K solution—the best way to ride out the storm—is to seek to entrench yourself in that system and help hold it together.

Leadership means offering trustworthy information, counsel, and example with the end of encouraging others to line up toward a common goal that serves the group. Part of that example includes personal sacrifice and integrity, while the act of being a leader requires shared risk and mutual loyalty. These factors are all critical to help overcome and counteract the human factors that impede Y2K repairs and that could intensify—in the wrong way—the impact of Y2K events.

Three Personal Opinions about Y2K

One can argue that much of this book comprises my personal opinions about Y2K. That may be, but most of that opinion is shared by those who have been working longest and hardest in the Y2K arena, as I've tried to show in the endnotes and as you can see if you read the books and Web sites given later in the book. What I'm giving here are three conclusions I've reached that aren't widely discussed in media reports on Y2K. Take them for what they're worth.

Opinion 1:
January 1, 2000, will be anticlimactic, at least in the United States

This doesn't mean "anticlimactic" as in "having little or no impact" (such as in scenario levels 0 through 2 given in Chapter 14). What it does mean is that by the time we reach December 31, 1999, several things will have happened. First, as I've said in many forums, if you think you were tired of hearing about El Niño, just wait—you will be absolutely sick of hearing about Y2K by late 1999. Second, I think we will finally have the national leadership and mobilization we need to fix the problems we can in the time remaining and to prepare to ride out the ones we cannot. Third, we should have a solid idea at that point as to what is going to happen, at least in the United States, and probably for a good part of the rest of the world. Finally, that New Year's Eve will definitely not be "business as usual." Corporations and government agencies at all levels will have Y2K "SWAT" teams in place for that weekend. Travel will likely be at a minimum, either out of necessity (due to FAA problems and airlines' concern over liability) or out of concern by the general populace. The majority of that populace will likely be at home, hunkered down, and prepared.

The upshot is that we won't have the scenarios you see in the media of an unsuspecting public, business community, and government finding itself in the midst of a series of Y2K failures.

Opinion 2:
At least one (non-U.S.) government, probably in a developing country, will collapse or be overthrown because of Y2K

Unlike the scenario painted above for the United States, I believe there will be one or more countries that are so unprepared for Y2K that the government will collapse or be overthrown by opposition forces, an angry populace, or an ambitious neighboring regime. Surveys done in the summer of 1998 showed a profound lack of Y2K awareness at all levels in a variety of developing countries in Latin America, Africa, and Central and Southeast Asia. One can argue—wrongly in many cases—that the daily lives of the general populace would not be impacted by typical Y2K failures, but that could be irrelevant in any case. The continued functioning of the government of such countries does depend upon enterprises that depend upon technology: internal and external finances, power utilities, water, telecommunications, transportation, and especially the military. Significant breakdowns in several of these sectors could disrupt the functioning of the government to the point of leaving it vulnerable to internal or external forces. If the global financial crisis we currently (October 1998) face continues, it will only undermine the governments further.

The flip side is that we may see some ongoing military conflicts between countries die down because the aggressor countries can no longer support or sustain the military operations due both to Y2K disruptions back home and to a forced demobilization because of Y2K problems in military systems and equipment.

Opinion 3:
Y2K—or some direct consequences thereof—will be a (or possibly the) major factor in the 2000 U.S. Presidential and Congressional races

The actual impact and whom it favors will depend in part on what happens between now and the end of 1999. There was a growing drumbeat of concern and criticism for nearly two years over President Clinton's and Vice-President Gore's profound silence on the issue of the Year 2000 problem, which they finally broke in a single set of addresses (along with John Koskinen, Chairman of the President's Council on Year 2000 Conversion, who has been far more vocal and visible) in May, 1998, before the National Academy of Sciences. However, it was in the morning and was not televised (except in delay broadcast on C-SPAN) and so was probably seen by less than 1 percent of the U.S. population. As such, it seemed less an opportunity to truly inform the nation than an effort to put down a marker that could be later referred to should criticisms arise.

Koskinen was appointed in February 1998. Most of his work has been behind the scenes and has focused on two tasks. First and foremost, he has been working to ensure that the various federal agencies and departments are on track—as much as they can be—to have their critical Y2K work done in time. Second, his council has organized a set of working groups focused on different key areas: energy (oil and gas), water, transportation, financial services, and so on. These groups have representatives from both the appropriate federal agencies and departments, as well as from the corresponding industries.

It's unclear at what point the current administration plans to seriously address Year 2000 issues with the general public. Koskinen, while doing a tough and necessary job, is largely invisible; it's doubtful that more than 1 to 2 percent of the populace could name him, much less recognize him by sight. Congress, in the meantime, has been taking the lead on publicizing Y2K issues, particularly with Senators Robert Bennett (R-UT) and Christopher Dodd (D-CT), Chairman and Ranking Minority Member, respectively, of the Senate Special Committee on the Year 2000 Technology Problem, and Rep. Connie Morella (R-MD) and Rep. Steve Horn (R-CA), who jointly chair the House Year 2000 Task Force. Other committees in both chambers have held Y2K-related hearings on an ever-increasing basis. But, again, these hearings don't have much visibility to the general public, though they do generate a steady stream of small news reports.

My best guess is that the administration will start a full public awareness effort, with talks by the president and/or vice-president, no sooner than after the November 1998 elections and likely not until early in 1999.[17] Some comments from administration officials indicate that they may be currently thinking of a date closer to August 1999—which, in my opinion, will greatly intensify Y2K-related turmoil through the rest of the year.

The real question, though, is what will be the state of the Union in 2000, and what impact will that have on the campaigns? On a strictly Y2K-related basis, my opinion is that the Republicans will argue for a change due to the economic impact of Y2K (which typically hurts the party in power, e.g., George Bush in 1992) and the fact that the Clinton/Gore administration had eight years to deal with Y2K and wasted most of them. The administration's response is likely to be to put Vice-President Gore in charge of Y2K mobilization and recovery sometime late in 1999, then have him campaign in 2000 on themes of continuity and stability (e.g., "Let him finish the job he started"). In both cases, the parties will campaign to provide a Congress to support the new president. In either case, the more serious the Y2K consequences in the United States, the more it will impact the elections.

However, it may well be that Y2K is a triggering event for other serious events: a global depression, possibly spreading into the United States; serious political upheavals in Europe, Russia, or Asia; or even eruption of a limited war somewhere in the world that we don't start but we end up getting dragged into. And somewhere in here I expect one or two major events that are unexpected and unpredicted and so have even more impact.

In my opinion, all these events together—direct, indirect, and unexpected—will have a tremendous and perhaps deciding impact on the 2000 campaign and its election.

Summary

This has been a long, detailed discussion of the nature, causes, and challenges of the Year 2000 problem. I hope you've stayed through this for at least two reasons. First, dealing effectively with the Y2K situation requires understanding these factors. You need to understand these details in order to sort through the tremendous volume of Y2K information you're going to face as you go through the year 1999. A lot of that information will be irrelevant, misleading, or downright wrong—and if you act upon it, you could cause unnecessary grief for yourself.

Second, knowledge and understanding help to build confidence and reduce fear and anxiety. That, in fact, will be the theme of Chapter 6: Education is a critical aspect of preparation, not just for actual preparation, but for peace of mind.

PART II

THE COMING FALL: GETTING READY

Setting the Stage: December 1998 to November 1999

It is better to deal with problems before they arise.
— Fortune cookie slip in the author's possession

At this point, you have read Part I. You know what the nature of the Year 2000 problem is. You know how we got into this mess in the first place. You know why many Y2K remediation projects won't finish in time. And you know enough to separate myth from fact.

Now, what are you going to do about it?

This section of the book is about doing. It's about determining what's important to you and then planning accordingly. But if you merely read through this book and then shelve it, you will have accomplished nothing.

This section is about action. It's about getting ready. It's about making decisions, some of them tough, some of them potentially costly, one way or the other.

You'll need a pencil and paper to start. But before you get through this section, you'll need more. You'll need a checkbook (and pen). You'll need files and financial records. You'll need to use a phone, a car, maybe a calculator. You'll need to talk with the people with whom you live and share your life. You will need to knock on your neighbors' doors, talk to people in your congregation, contact your local government.

It is indeed better to deal with problems before they arise—and the problems are starting to arise even as you read this.

It's time to get to work.

5

Understanding What's Important

Never let things that matter most be at the mercy of things that matter least.

—Goethe

A common guideline given for Year 2000 preparation is to approach it as if you were preparing for an earthquake, hurricane, or other natural disaster. That's a good first thought, but it can be misleading. Earthquakes and hurricanes cause physical damage and offer physical dangers unlike anything most people will face as a result of Y2K. On the other hand, Y2K confronts us with events and circumstances quite different from such events. Because of that, it is important to determine up front what is important to you, what your true priorities and principles are, and then see how they apply to various areas of your life.

This chapter, then, frames the structure for Part II. It discusses those challenges unique to Y2K preparation. It outlines an approach to help cope with those challenges. And then it touches on each of the areas of personal and family preparedness that will make up the balance of Part II.

The Three Challenges of Y2K Preparation

In the spring of 1998, I was asked to participate in a conference on Y2K contingency planning for the various U.S. intelligence agencies. Since several presentations were being made on how to do such planning, I focused instead on those factors that make planning for Y2K so difficult. I came up with three: complexity, humanity, and simultaneity. These three keep showing up as organizations ranging from national governments to small businesses seek to prepare for Y2K events. And they apply for your plans as well.

Enmeshed in Complexity

The area of study known as **complexity** has grown from an obscure subject pursued by a few to a major touchstone used to help analyze much of the world, natural and man-made, that we live in today. Time and scope do not permit an extended discussion here, but a brief overview is important, since complexity is a major factor in understanding Y2K and its implications.

Among other things, complexity deals with the emergence of complex, sophisticated, goal-seeking behavior of a system as a consequence of sets of simple rules followed by individual components (or **agents**) within the system. For example, individual ants do not understand or think of goals for the entire ant colony, and they follow simple and strict rules based on their caste and the circumstances at hand. Yet the colony as a whole adapts itself to events and circumstances as they arise.

Organizations such as the ant colony are known as **complex adaptive systems** (*cas*). The same principles apply in a variety of settings: biological, sociological, technological, organizational, and so on. Most particularly, they appear to apply in the vast, complex, and interrelated network of systems that we have created for ourselves, comprising technology, economics, telecommunications, finance, sociology, politics, logistics, and many other factors. No one person or group understands or controls even a fraction of what actually exists currently in our world, any more than a single ant understands or controls an ant colony.

A key characteristic of a complex adaptive system is that its behavior is **emergent**, as opposed to being deterministic. Efforts to control or predict the system from outside usually fail; it adapts and continues to seek that behavior that emerges from it. Consider, for example, the never-ending revisions to the U.S. federal tax code, which are constantly met by ever-new and creative ways to find loopholes and reduce tax liabilities.

Beyond that, such systems are **dynamic**, as opposed to being static. They transform themselves over time, sometimes in small ways, occasionally in medium ways, and on rare occasions in major ways. The transformations do not necessarily require major influences, just the right ones at the right time. Consider, for example, the collapse of the Soviet Union. It had endured for decades through wars, famine, and prolonged political and economic conflict, including 45 years of nuclear confrontation. But it fell apart in a matter of months, not because of any major event but because of the (accurate) realization of its member states that Gorbachev would not send in military force to keep them in the USSR. More recently, we have seen a currency problem in a small Southeast Asian country—Indonesia—ripple and reverberate worldwide over a period of months, causing a global financial crisis of a scope unseen for many years.

This, then, is the context in which Y2K events will occur. Small or isolated events can have large or broadly distributed consequences. True, most events within a complex adaptive system tend to be dampened out. But because we are so far behind in so many settings in dealing with Y2K, the sheer number of Y2K events will have some significant impacts. And because these systems are dynamic, it would be very hard to predict now what exactly those consequences would be even if we knew exactly what Y2K events will happen—which we don't.

So the first challenge to Y2K planning is that we don't know now what exactly will happen, and in many cases we won't know what's going to happen, and what the consequences will be, until it does happen. Because we don't and cannot fully understand the complex systems that surround us, Y2K events will reveal to us—in real time—unknown and unanticipated aspects of those systems, and we'll have to respond in real time as well.

The Hazards of Humanity

Chapter 2 discussed at length the degree to which the Y2K problem has its roots in human nature and human frailties. Chapter 3 likewise talked about how many of those same factors hinder Y2K repair efforts. Those factors likewise act as barriers to effective Y2K planning. People who avoid dealing with Y2K, who cannot or won't understand its seriousness, or who are focused instead on short-term issues and gratification aren't going to support or assist Y2K planning.

Beyond that, issues of self-justification can come into play. Suppose Acme Corp has made a series of bad decisions regarding Y2K out of skepticism, incompetence, and/or poor planning. If you now ask Acme about its Y2K status, the corporation is not likely to respond by saying, in effect, "Well, we really blew it in dealing with this issue, so we're quite a ways behind." Instead, it's likely to resist giving you the accurate information you might need for your planning because such information would reflect poorly upon Acme's prior efforts.

An entirely different set of human factors make Y2K planning hard to do. Sociology and psychology, both individual and mass, are major components of the complex systems in which we live; a week or two of observing the stock markets make that clear. Human anticipation of and reaction to Y2K events, then, may in and of themselves be major factors in the consequences of those events, even if the events themselves never occur or are relatively mild. Thus, if a single bank in some small town in the United States runs out of money as nervous depositors withdraw cash, such news could trigger a mass run on banks nationwide and could even ripple across the globe. This is why social cohesion (see Chapter 12) is such a critical factor in Y2K preparation; without it, these mass reactions could make relatively mild Y2K events far worse than they need to be.

The ultimate expression of this tendency is what has been labeled **millennial fever**, that is, individual and group reaction to the end of one millennium and the start of another.[1] The primary source of this is millennial expectations rooted in the Christian religion, with anticipation of the end of the world as we know it and the start of a millennial era.[2] But there are also "New Age" expectations, not to mention the sense of uncertainty and irrevocability associated with leaving behind forever any calendar year beginning with "1." These factors alone would likely have been enough to trigger some unusual reactions from individuals and groups (especially within Western society), but the Y2K problem is acting as a tremendous amplifier. It not only provides a visible, well-documented potential mechanism for the anticipated collapse of civilization, it also adds the ironic twist of modern technology containing the seeds of its own destruction, a common theme of

literature and popular entertainment since Mary Woll-
stonecraft Shelley's *Frankenstein*. The soil, if you will, has been
well tilled and prepared for the idea of a technological disaster
of some sort. It you dovetail that with the emotional, psychological, and religious issues surrounding the transition to a
new millennium, you have the recipe for intense reactions at
every step of the way.

A Downpour, Not a Drip

The last of the three challenges to Y2K planning has to do
with simultaneity. Most personal preparedness and business
continuity planning tends to focus on dealing with a single
event (power outage) or class of event (earthquake).

However, the consequences of Y2K promise to be quite different. For starters, Y2K events will not all be compressed into
the weekend of January 1-2, 2000. They have already started,
though in small, insolated incidences. They will continue to
pick up through 1999 and at some point will reach a threshold
that makes them visible to the media and, thus, to the public.
The frequency of events will gradually increase and then peak
sharply at the end of 1999 and start of 2000.

Single or grouped Y2K events—or anticipation of such—
may start a causal chain not directly related to the events
themselves. For example, suppose it becomes known a major
manufacturer has plans in place to focus on production of its
most critical (that is, popular and profitable) products in case
Y2K problems force it to choose. Their customers might react
by stockpiling those products not on its "most critical" list.
That, in turn, may cause a shortage—and jump in price—of
some key materials or goods those products require. That, in
turn, may impact other manufacturers that depend upon those
key materials.

In much the same way, interactions between overlapping Y2K events will tend to intensify impact rather than dampen it. As a simple (if extreme) example, losing both power and telephone service is worse than losing just one or the other. For starters, you cannot call the power company (or anyone else) to find out what the status of repairs is, and you cannot turn on the TV to find out more details about the phone outage.

Primary Y2K events—that is, actual failures—will drop back down to a low level soon after the start of 2000, but could still crop up for weeks or months. Secondary events are likely to reverberate for some time. The effects of these events will resonate for months or years.

Step 1: Examining Your Assumptions

In the light of Y2K and the challenges it presents, as well as continuing uncertainties about what the actual events and their impact will be, what should you do? How can you prepare for a crisis with so many unknowns at all levels, from the global impact down to how things will actually turn out in your neighborhood?

First off, don't panic. Regardless of how serious you think the Y2K situation is, panic will only make things worse. Panic is the opposite of careful, methodical planning, and this kind of planning is just what you need.

The planning needs to start with your fundamental assumptions about what's important and go from there. This is important for two reasons. First, your situation is your situation—not anyone else's—and you have to decide what you need to, and can, protect and maintain. That will shape the plans you make.

Second, all the challenges of Y2K planning mentioned above make it hard to predict what will happen, especially on your personal level. Whatever you plan for, you are likely to be faced with events that you had not anticipated. In that case, you need to be able to make decisions quickly about how to handle the situation—and that should be consistent with your priorities.

Determining Priorities

This may seem at first a funny way to start emergency planning, but it is critical. You need to examine your life and your beliefs about what's important. Consider, for example, the following list of possible priorities:

- Current living quarters, neighborhood, geographic area

- Career or profession

- Your personal well-being

- Various assets (savings, investments, possessions)

- The well-being of your spouse/partner

- The well-being of your children or other dependents

- Adherence to certain religious or philosophical beliefs or standards

- Standard of living, including diet, clothing, transportation

- The well-being of relatives, friends, neighbors, co-workers

- Level of income, or some sizable fraction thereof

This is a brief list, and many of the items given could be broken down into more specific priorities.

ACTION. Add other items that you can think of to the list above, or break apart some of the complex ones (such as "standard of living"), and then **stack rank** them in order of importance. "Stack rank" is a management buzzword that means that you don't get to cheat and state that any two of the above are equally important; you have to pick one or the other as being more important, however slightly. Talk this over with those important to you and with whom you share your life. Have them do the same exercise; note where the differences are. Work until you agree upon the list and its priorities.

OUTCOME. The list becomes your touchstone. As you face difficult decisions in this effort—which course to take, where to spend resources—use this list to guide your choices. Often it won't be an either/or choice; instead, it may be an issue of whether you've done what you need to for the first number of items on the list, and if so, you can then focus on the next item down. Also, the list may change over time; as you face hard decisions or think about consequences, you may change the order of the list, add new items or even drop old ones from consideration.

Reviewing Commitments

Life is full of commitments that you have made or make on a regular basis. Some have to do with relationships; others, with employment; still others, with mutual benefits. The nature of those commitments range from a simple promise to stay in touch to complex legal and financial agreements. But they all have this in common: some other entity, be that the love of your life, a corporation, or the U.S. federal government, expects you to keep the commitment(s) you've made to them. If you don't, there is a price to pay, ranging from wistful disappointment from others to repossession, interest, penalties, and time in prison. If one throws religion into the mix, the stakes can become even higher.

Because of the range of potential Y2K events and their impact on your life, you could find yourself unable to fully or even partially meet some of those commitments, and so face the consequences. The next step, then, in your preparation is to examine your life and look for all the commitments you've made, explicitly and implicitly. We're not just talking about interpersonal relationships, though you shouldn't discount them; indeed, they may be the most important in the end. Ultimately, you need to examine every financial, legal, and ethical commitment you have. These may put constraints on your plans and options; at the very least, they imply a limiting of choices and dedication of resources, be that money, time, or something else. So you need to be very clear about each commitment, what it entails, and how Y2K might hinder you from keeping it. You then need to see how you can renegotiate or resolve that commitment or understand the consequences of breaking it.

The other side of this issue involves those commitments made to you: What are they, what do you count on them for, and how might Y2K impact them? This is important to determine. Your ability to keep yours may depend heavily on whether others keep the ones made to you. In addition it is your responsibility to document any obligations to you—from stocks and bonds, loans, borrowed tools, to all financial income, insurance and medical records. As an example, you don't want to have to investigate whether you are covered by insurance in an emergency if the Year 2000 problem does effect communications. So know the commitments others have to you. Keep good records handy. In short, be prepared.

ACTION. Much of Part II involves looking at different types of commitments, particularly financial and legal ones, and determining a plan of action. But for right now, get out a pencil and paper. Start listing as many of your commitments as you can think of. For each one, write down the nature of the commitment (for example, "credit card"), the person or entity to whom you're committed ("First Universe Bancorp"), and a simple description of the commitment ("make minimum monthly payment"). Then note whether the commitment is one you wish to terminate or reduce and how you would do so ("pay off balance"). Don't get too bogged down in details; that comes later. For now, work fast and keep things light; the idea is to get an idea of your commitments.

Having done so, determine how important each commitment is to you. This isn't a stack ranking; ideally, all commitments should be kept or fulfilled. But if there are too many—if you are overcommitted—you may find yourself unable to keep many or most of them under Y2K circumstances. And those of you who are counting on some great technological collapse to wipe out your debts and tax obligations are likely to get a very unpleasant surprise; those entities to whom you owe money will make preserving that information their highest Y2K priority.

Now make a list of commitments made to you. Again list the nature of the commitment ("employment"), the committed person or entity ("Acme Corp"), and a simple description of what you count on from the commitment ("paycheck, health benefits"). And, again, don't get bogged down; just do what comes off the top of your head for a few minutes. Some of these will be reciprocal agreements to your commitments: "job↔employment," "spouse↔spouse," and so on.

Finally, match up the two lists by noting which commitments to you help you keep each of your commitments to others; for example, "employment" helps you meet your "credit card" commitment.

OUTCOME. This list becomes your second touchstone in your Y2K planning. As you look at choices and options, examine just how they help you keep your commitments or possibly hinder you from doing so. At the same time, consider how Y2K events could cause commitments to you to be broken, and the consequences that would have.

The ultimate goal is to narrow down your list of commitments to those you can keep or that you can be sure are met if you are unable to do so. You can do this by fulfilling commitments (paying off your credit card), ending it by agreement with the other party involved, or redefining it to something you can meet. At the same time, the list of commitments on which you count forms the basis of your contingency planning. For each one, you need to ask, "What if this is broken or not completely kept?" Try to reduce or at least understand and document commitments to you.

There are two cautions for this exercise. First, some might interpret this to mean that commitments are something to be avoided, particularly in trying circumstances. On the contrary, commitments can be a tremendous resource, especially in trying circumstances. Second, taken to an extreme, this can devolve into survivalism, that is, attempting to be 100 percent self-sufficient somewhere out in the backcountry. That may be your choice, but it is, in my opinion, counterproductive and ultimately a dead end, both personally and socially. Besides, I suspect you'll end up looking rather foolish.

The upshot is that in order to effectively prepare for Y2K, you will not only want to fulfill and end some commitments, you will want to make new ones. What is needed is not mutual isolation; it is social cohesion; a weight that would snap several individual sticks can be supported by all of them together.

Determining Relevant (and Irrelevant) Y2K Events

This is the last set of assumptions you need to examine, and ones that will change as time goes on. Consider the range of scenarios given in Chapter 14 and the types of Y2K events associated with each. If you think that we'll have something along the lines of a level 2 scenario, your preparations are likely to be quite different than if you think we'll have a level 8 scenario. As time goes on, as events unfold, and as more information becomes available, your estimate may change in one direction or the other, again shaping your plans. The mix of Y2K events may not (and almost certainly won't) exactly match those spelled out for each scenario level in Chapter 14. Finally, given the set of all likely or possible Y2K events, you only care about some number of them.

This step, then, requires you to determine those events that are relevant so that you can prepare appropriately. If you ride a bike and telecommute to work, you probably won't care much about the cost of gasoline and the availability of car parts, but you will be very concerned about power and telephone service. If you live in New England, you will be far more concerned about heating issues than if you live in Florida. If you live in

New York City, you will be more concerned about water (and power and heat) than if you live out in the countryside.

ACTION: Go to Chapter 14 and choose a scenario level, either at random or based on what you think might happen. Examine the list of associated Y2K events. Using a pencil (or pen, if you want—hey, it's your book), put a check mark beside those you see that would impact you and for which you can make some kind of preparation.

OUTCOME: At this point, you will likely either be relieved that you have less to worry about than you thought, or concerned that you have more. But in either case, you'll likely have more peace of mind. Uncertainty and vague anxieties exhaust you far more than a clear list of likely events; the monster we cannot see, lurking free in shadows, terrifies us more than the same creature under bright lights and strapped down on an examination table. Your task is to dissect the Y2K monster, assess its real threats, dismiss the irrelevant ones, and take appropriate actions.

Step 2: Mapping Out Your Strategy

Now that you have a sense of priorities, your commitments to others (and vice versa), and the set of Y2K events that you care about, you can start to map out your strategy. This comprises three steps: identifying risks; looking for opportunities; and establishing principles. You'll apply these steps for each area covered in the remaining chapters of Part II; for now, let's look at what they mean.

Identifying Risks and Corresponding Mitigation

Given your priorities and commitments, along with the relevant Y2K events, you need to determine what risks you may face, and then figure out how to **mitigate** or reduce those risks. You'll want to identify each risk; give your estimate of how likely it is to affect you; how serious the impact would be should it do so; what your mitigation strategies might be; and additional issues.

Suppose, for example, that one of the Y2K events that concerns you is a possible Y2K impact on your local water company. Perhaps news has gotten out that they're behind, or that they have concerns about receiving the chemicals required for water purification.[3] You might do the following analysis:

- Risk: Danger of tap water being improperly or insufficiently purified

- Probability: Medium (based on news reports)

- Impact: Little on toilets, gardening; some on bathing, washing clothes and dishes; high on drinking

- Mitigation: Store a week's worth of drinking water in five gallon bottles (one per person per day) and/or water purification system for prolonged needs

- Issues: Storage location for water; any problems using tap water for bathing, washing

This exercise doesn't have to be formal; that is, you don't have to type this up, or set up index cards. But it is worth going through because it forces you to think about what's really probable and what isn't. As you'll rapidly discover, most risks lead to trade-offs, a combination of the risk's probability, its impact, and the issues surrounding any mitigation effort. Storing a few days' water for one person is easy; storing a month's worth of water for a large family would be difficult.

Looking for Opportunities

It may seem strange to be looking for opportunities in the midst of crisis, but they're there. Not in the sense of exploiting the misfortunes of others, but in taking advantage of opportunities through preparedness to help yourself and your friends and relations. Also in the sense of having your own life shaken up: questioning assumptions, having things you count on become uncertain, and being forced to look at paths different from those you had chosen. And finally in the sense of using Y2K as a compelling reason to do certain things that you have wanted to or thought that you should, but that you had never gotten around to until now.

Let's take a simple example: paying off all your credit cards. You've probably thought about that many times and even made some half-serious attempts to get all the balances down. But something usually comes along that you have to handle— and the balances go back up. But now, based on your study and analysis of the Y2K situation, you decide that there's a real risk of a recession, with possible impact on your own employment. So you decide to really cinch in the belt this time and get those credit cards paid off. You do so—and find that your standard of living actually goes up, because you're not making all those payments each month.

That's a simple example, and one that won't necessarily apply to everyone, but you get the idea. It is commonly claimed that the Chinese ideograph for "crisis" comprises the symbols for "danger" and "opportunity." Y2K encompasses crisis and danger, so one hopes there is opportunity there as well.

ACTION. It is time to look at your financial portfolio. Making prudent investments and managing your money so that you avoid hardship are necessary steps to take now.

OUTCOME. Life is full of changes: mostly small, some medium, a few large. Y2K will likely fit somewhere between medium and humongous in your own life. One key to getting through it is to look for whatever opportunities open up for you.

Establishing Guiding Principles

Your next step in devising your strategy for each area is to come up with one or more guiding principles for that area. These principles are both for your Y2K preparations and for dealing with unexpected Y2K circumstances. Remember the words used earlier: emergent and dynamic. That means "unexpected" and "in real time." If milk prices tripled overnight, what would you do? What if key parts for your late model car weren't available? What if air travel were significantly curtailed and restricted to those who could prove need? What if curfews were suddenly declared in your area because of concerns over civil unrest or the threat of disruption by internal "militia" extremists or external terrorists? None, any, or all of these could happen; it's pretty tough to prepare for every eventuality, especially since there will be ones nobody thought of.

These principles, then, are your maxims, your guidelines, your rules of thumb to help you make quick decisions. For example, one principle might be, "Keep the family physically together and close to home." So if some situation comes up (such as the air travel restriction hypothesized above) that threatens to strand one or more family members hundreds of miles away from the others, then getting those members back home would be a high priority.

And priority again becomes the keyword. The guiding principles will be guided by the priorities and the commitments earlier established. To continue the case above, if the family member (one of the parents) is away from home to keep certain commitments (such as employment) that help meet other priorities (income for the family), the decision may be to have that parent continue where they are.

The real importance of the guiding principles is that they can act as a set of shared rules. If every family member understands and agrees upon the principles, then they'll have a good idea what to do—and what the other family members will do—even if they have to make choices on their own. The same may be true of religious or neighborhood groups. The individuals and families involved may have different priorities and commitments, but to the extent that they agree upon a basic set of principles, their responses to Y2K events will tend to be mutually supporting rather than interfering with, undermining, or conflicting with one another. It also forms the basis for social cohesion. The net effect: The consequences of Y2K events will tend to be dampened.

ACTION. Consider the following set of principles, which Thomas E. Ricks listed in an article unrelated to the Year 2000 issue:[4]

- Tell the truth.

- Do your best, no matter how trivial the task.

- Choose the difficult right over the easy wrong.

- Look out for the group before you look out for yourself.

- Don't whine or make excuses.

- Judge others by their actions not their race (or, I might add, by their profession, income level, political affiliation, or religion).

How would you adapt or modify this list for yourself? Your family? Your neighborhood? Your company? What would you add? What would you drop? Are there any principles here that you would expect of others and yet be unwilling to live up to yourself? (Hint: That's not a good sign.) Are the principles in your updated list consistent with each other? With your commitments and priorities? And what are the implied commitments (both ways) in your list?

Now do this exercise with others: your spouse or partner, your children, friends, colleagues, and so on. How do their modifications differ from yours? Can you reconcile them into an agreed-upon list for each circle of people?

OUTCOME. This is not some "touchy-feely" exercise. This is a hardheaded look while things are still calm at what principles will guide you and those around you if and when things get difficult. It's also an opportunity to see if your priorities, commitments, and principles are consistent with themselves and each other. If they aren't, they will fall apart at some point; the greater the inconsistencies, the more readily they will collapse. Likewise, if your principles are in serious conflict with those of people with whom you live or work, those conflicts will flare up and be intensified if and when trouble comes.

Step 3: Plotting Your Tactics

Each of the steps above was to help establish context and intent: what you're doing and why you're doing it. First you clarified your assumptions. You have a sense of your priorities; what your commitments are; and what Y2K events concern you. You have likewise laid out your strategy for each of the topics in Part II: what risks you face, and how to mitigate them; what opportunities exist and how you can approach them; and what your guiding principles are.

All this now gives you an intelligent, consistent framework for doing something. That something is simple: Figure out what you need, figure out what to do, figure out who is going to help you. With that, you should be ready.

Determining What You Need

When you've gone through this whole process for a given area—say, food and supplies—you should have a good idea of what you're going to need. So your first step is to see what you already have and how well it will meet your needs.

You'll need to distinguish between needs and wants; your priorities, commitments, and risk should help you to make those decisions. You may want a new car; you may need to pay the old one off and hold onto it until you see how things turn out.

ACTION. Imagine that you were suddenly cut off from your usual sources of food, water, a paycheck, a bank account and had to make do with what you had. What would happen? How would you handle it?

Now ask yourself what would you need to have on hand to get by for a week. For two weeks? For a whole month? If you're really adventurous, trying stocking up on groceries and then going for two full weeks without buying any.

The point here is not to presume that you'll be abruptly shut off from anything. It's to help you realize how much you count on having ready access to such things. The exercise of not buying groceries is great for emphasizing that.

It will also bring out an important psychological aspect in all of this: There is an intensity or desperation that can be out of proportion to the actual situation. For example, likely there have been days when you have gone for hours without getting a drink and even longer without eating anything, skipping both breakfast and lunch. Likely, you barely noticed it except for an occasional dry mouth or rumble from your stomach. But suppose someone had contacted you right after you brushed your teeth upon arising and said that you couldn't eat or drink anything until 7 P.M. that evening. Chances are that you would find yourself thinking constantly about eating or drinking, that your mouth would feel dry and cottony, and that you'd feel a bit weak and tired. Yet nothing has changed except this: You cannot have what you normally take for granted and thus get by fine without.

This aspect was dramatically illustrated back in the late 1970s during the gasoline shortages. Some states implemented even/odd rationing: You could only buy gas on even or odd days based on your license plate number. People were so concerned about running low on gas on an "off" day that they wouldn't let their cars get less than half or even three-quarters full. The results were frequent long lines of cars going down the block, waiting to get gas. The phenomenon was primarily psychological; if everyone had let their cars get close to empty before filling up, the lines would largely have vanished.

Creating the Plan

This is the capstone: writing down a sequence of steps to achieve what's implied or spelled out by your priorities, your commitments, the risks and opportunities, and what you need. The nature of that plan will vary based on the area (education, etc.). And it doesn't need to be detailed. Chances are, you can jot down a simple list of actions. In fact, you don't want to invest too much time into making it formal and intricate, because it's likely to change on a regular basis as the Y2K situation becomes clearer and as you actually start accomplishing tasks.

ACTION. Take a break. You've been doing enough so far in this chapter. Besides, you're going to do all the real work in the other chapters.

OUTCOME. A bit of relaxation, I hope. This won't be as hard as you thought. It won't be easy, but you can do it.

Enrolling others

Few of us can carry out a project like this alone; even fewer would want to. The actions detailed in your plan will likely require in some form the assistance, cooperation, or agreement of one or more other people. As you go through each of these areas and make your plans, you need to identify the key people to enroll in helping you accomplish those plans.

The challenge will be to keep them from thinking you've gone off the deep end. This may require several tactics. Avoid overexplaining what you're doing and why. Underplay it. Keep your sense of humor. Poke a bit of fun at yourself. Don't bury them in Y2K printouts and literature.

ACTION. Make a list of the most important people in your life. For each one, determine if they know more or less about

Y2K than you do, and if they are more or less worried than you are. Now judge what they're likely to do when you start making and following plans of action.

OUTCOME. This is an area to treat with caution and sensitivity. If you are obsessive, overbearing, or one-sided about how you approach this, you could alienate the very people you care the most about. I know of one couple where the husband is a bit more enthused/anxious about Y2K than the wife. For example, he went out one day and spent several thousand dollars for a year's supply of food for the entire family—without clearing with her ahead of time. Her response: "I can shoot you, you know." She's grateful for the food; she would just have liked to have been consulted in the decision and timing.

Conclusion

The pattern of the last two steps (strategy and tactics) will be followed in each of the following chapters. This may seem a bit repetitive at times, but that's part of learning this approach. By the time you've finished Part II, it will be second nature to you. The chances are you won't need to follow it formally after that point. You'll go through the steps of education, risks, opportunities, principles, needs, plan, and support without having to refer back here. You may not even do it sequentially, but you'll cover all the bases.

Each chapter will then end with two more sections: **Y2K JumpStart** and **Tips and Traps**. Y2K JumpStart will provide a default list of Y2K preparation activities to go through, in case the planning process seems a bit involved or daunting, while Tips and Traps provides practical observations on these activities.

In all this, be sure that you *not* go off the deep end. It's good to keep some perspective in this and realize that it is far better to be pleasantly surprised than to be right about how bad we think Y2K going to be. This may seem obvious, but it is an unfortunate human trait that we'd often rather be right than happy. Just keep in mind that the best outcome is that we all look a bit foolish as 1999 ends—but, boy, do we have our grocery shopping done for January.

6

Education: Things You Need to Know

A human being should be able to change a diaper, plan an invasion, butcher a hog, conn a ship, design a building, write a sonnet, balance accounts, build a wall, set a bone, comfort the dying, take orders, give orders, cooperate, act alone, solve equations, analyze a new problem, pitch manure, program a computer, cook a tasty meal, fight efficiently, die gallantly. Specialization is for insects.

— Robert A. Heinlein

This may seem a funny place to start, but education is the foundation of self-reliance. The more you know, and the more you know how to do, the better you can deal with unanticipated events, not to mention anticipated ones. It's also the best single investment you can make in yourself. This may sound a bit like a public service announcement, and in a way it is: We'll all get through this a lot better if we know what we're going through and how to do it.

The first subject for study is Y2K itself. I won't claim that knowing more about Y2K will ease your anxieties per se. When I was interviewing a candidate who wanted to work for the corporate Y2K contingency planning team that I was on, she asked me, "Is this work interesting?" I replied, "Yeah, it's interesting, all right. You may not sleep as well at night, but it

137

is interesting." But the more you know, the better you can judge how valid what you're hearing from various sources is.

Beyond that, if you're already involved in other educational pursuits, you need to realize that Y2K could impact those, and you should prepare.

How to Become a Y2K Expert in Your Spare Time

The more you know, the less you are at the mercy of others. This is nowhere so true as in the Year 2000 arena. The lack of visible national leadership to date has left a vacuum filled with conflicting claims, rumors, anecdotes, and assertions, largely transmitted by the national media. It is essential that you become informed—and stay informed—on Y2K issues and status. Here's how.

Dig Out Information

Buying this book was a good first step, but it's just that: a first step. Now that you're this concerned about Y2K, you'll notice when news reports appear in the newspaper, in magazines, or on TV. What you'll find is that the amount of new, accurate, relevant information through the mass media is relatively small. You may have to read two or three accounts of the same news item to figure out what happened and whether it's important.

There are plenty of other Y2K books out on the market, but like this one, they are snapshots, frozen in time. Seek out those that explain what you need or want to know. It's good not to rely too heavily on any one source of information, including this one. A list of Y2K books is given in the Resources section at the end of the book.

There are several Y2K-related magazines out on the market, though obviously few publishers want to make a major investment in a periodical with a time limit to its market. These journals are largely aimed at corporate and legal markets and so may hold little interest for the average person.

The best and most current information on Y2K is found on the Internet. Unfortunately, so is the worst or, at least, the most extreme (in both directions), irrelevant, and misleading. And there's a tremendous amount of information to sift through. Still, if you want to stay current on Y2K—and you should—you'll want to get access to the net somehow. The Resources section lists recommended Web sites and other net sources of Y2K information.

Consider the Source

In evaluating Y2K information for accuracy and relevance, you need to consider the source. First, you need to ask yourself what is the information's **provenance**, that is, its origin and history. Sensational Y2K information tends to show up most often in the news media and in e-mail chain postings. Some of these items may seem quite credible but, on examination, turn out to have no verifiable source. I was burned by one such e-mail back in 1997 that provided a documented case of Y2K problems in a specific set of car models. I passed it on to several of my Y2K contacts and got e-mail back from Ed Yourdon saying that this message had been traced and turned out to be a hoax. I quickly sent a disclaimer to all those to whom I had forwarded the original e-mail. After that, I was far more cautious about what I passed along.

Second, you need to ask yourself what are the source's **motives** or **agenda**, that is, what is the source's intent in providing this information. This doesn't necessarily invalidate the information per se, but it does mean that you might not be getting a balanced view or that some details or suppositions might be emphasized and others downplayed or omitted. This also doesn't necessarily impugn the sincerity or honesty of the individual involved; it just means that they are giving the information they feel is relevant, based on their priorities.

Third, you need to ask yourself what are the **potential repercussions** that the source has to consider. When I testified before the House Committee on Transportation and Infrastructure,[1] I received some pointed questioning and a bit of a tongue-lashing from Rep. Dennis Kucinich (D-OH), the ranking member of the House Subcommittee on Government Management, Information, and Technology, which had been invited into the hearings as well. He challenged me for mentioning "martial law" when describing possible Y2K repercussions, and he reminded me of the seriousness of going before Congress and giving official testimony.[2] Now, I'm relatively unknown; by contrast, consider the situation when, say, Alan Greenspan or another member of the Federal Reserve Board of Governors goes before Congress or speaks publicly. Markets rise and fall based on what key phrases are (or aren't) uttered; such individuals have to weigh very carefully what they say or even what they are perceived to believe.

Finally, you have to ask yourself the source's level of **understanding** and **information**. It has been an unfortunate truism for far too many corporations and government agencies that the higher you go in the organizations, the more optimistic— and less accurate—the information about that organization's Y2K status. Things are improving—reality has a way of asserting itself forcefully. But through much of the past few years, the blithe assertions coming from CEOs and even CIOs have been reminiscent of this old joke from the early days of personal computers: What is the difference between a used-car salesman and a personal computer salesman? The used-car salesman knows how to drive and knows when he's lying.

Track How Things are Going

Beyond informing yourself, the point of sifting through all this information is to get a sense of just what's going to happen. First, be aware that there's going to be a lot of good news. That's because a lot of organizations—government agencies, corporations, utilities, and so on—are working very hard on Y2K, and they are fixing many, and probably most, of their Y2K problems. As they do, they are going to publicize it.

Unfortunately, such reports—and they will predominate through 1999, I believe—do not address the Y2K problems not yet solved by those and other organizations. That information will be much harder to come by. Those organizations, particularly those in other countries, will have few incentives for revealing such details and many reasons not to do so.

In many cases, they won't realize until well into 1999 that things aren't going as well as they had hoped; remember the parable of the bungee jumper back in Chapter 1, not to mention the joke a few paragraphs back. One individual posted the following "Pollyanna Progression" to a Usenet user group about Y2K:[3]

1. We will fix all the systems.

2. We will fix most of the systems.

3. We will fix all the mission-critical systems.

4. We will fix most of the mission-critical systems.

5. All of the mission-critical systems cannot be fixed.

6. There will be some mission-critical systems failure.

7. We will use paper and pencils to work around what was formally called "mission-critical." It is now recognized that the formerly mission-critical system was never needed in the first place.

Not all organizations follow this sequence; I know of major corporations that have fixed, replaced, or retired all their systems, eliminating—to the best of their knowledge—their Y2K bugs. But here's the fundamental challenge with tracking Y2K progress. One can roughly divide all organizations into one of four classes:

1. Those that will fix all significant Y2K problems and know it.

2. Those that will fix all significant Y2K problems but don't know it.

3. Those that will not fix all significant Y2K problems and know it.

4. Those that will not fix all significant Y2K problems but don't know it.

We can set aside class 2 for now as a small, curious, and irrelevant class of organizations that tend to migrate quickly into one of the others. Looking then at classes 1, 3, and 4, we're faced with this challenge: To the general public, *all three are likely to appear identical.* Organizations in class 1 will honestly and knowingly assert their status. Organizations in class 4 will tend to think they are in class 1 and will make the same assertion, falsely but ignorantly. And those in class 3 will do their best to present themselves as being in class 1 or, failing that, in 4. Why? Because it is generally neither safe nor beneficial for the organization to reveal that it's in class 3. Businesses face loss of market share, loss of partners, drop in stock prices, and various liability issues. Government agencies face political pressures, panic among citizens, and investigations from other branches of government.

In short, it's not going to be easy.

Ask Questions

All Y2K remediation starts with awareness and assessment, as you learned in Part I. As you look at your needs, commitments, and dependencies, ask the people and institutions involved about Y2K. Chances are you'll get a puzzled look or a bland but optimistic answer. But the more you ask, the more seriously others will take the issue and will start thinking about it themselves.

The question you should not bother asking any organization, particularly a commercial one, until late in 1999 is, "Will you be Y2K compliant in time?" Again, if you consider the four classes above, you'll find that the chances are slim of getting any answer other than "Yes" or a more weasely worded, "We are confident that we'll have all important systems done in time" (see the Pollyanna Progression earlier). This is not to say that there aren't exceptions. For example, Suzanne Peck, Chief Technical Officer of the District of Columbia, should get an award for telling the House Government Oversight subcommittee, "What we don't know is which of the operations in our 75 agencies will fail. But what we do know is that some will fail."[4] That may seem like a simple, honest statement, but those are still uncommon in all this.

What information should you seek? Here are some suggestions.

- *How large is the organization?* A small business can go through Y2K remediation in a matter of weeks or even days, but it scales up rapidly. A mid-sized corporation (200+ employees) can count on months; a Fortune 500 corporation has its Y2K remediation time measured in years (1-3).

- *Where is the organization in its Y2K remediation efforts?* Look for an answer in one of the phases mentioned in Chapters 1 and 3: awareness; assessment; repairs; testing; integration; contingency planning. The "right" answer depends upon the size of the company and how late in 1999 you are asking this. A small business could be just fine starting assessment as late as September of 1999; a large corporation is facing problems if they're not well into testing by early 1999.

- *How much work has the organization done on end-to-end integration?* It's one thing to repair each individual system or piece of software. It's something quite different to make sure they all still work together correctly, especially if old systems have been retired and replaced with new commercial or custom programs.

- *How much work has been done on external interfaces?* This is the next step beyond internal integration: making sure you can still trade data, and so forth, with other organizations. The nature of complexity is such that as the number of systems you have modified grows large, the chances of them all still working together correctly drops.

- *How much work has the organization done on contingency planning?* Most organizations will be at three stages: no planning done yet (though some lip service); planning for internal failures, that is, systems not repaired in time or whose repairs don't work; and planning for external impacts as well. They should be at the third stage; if they're at the other two, they are behind, in denial, or both.

One other strong recommendation: If you want as honest an assessment as possible, ask people doing the actual Y2K work or those close to them. The farther you get from them, either up the organizational hierarchy or horizontally into other divisions such as Marketing, the less likely you are to get an informed accurate answer.

More Things You Should Know

Obviously, Y2K isn't all you need to know; it merely lets you know how much to worry about all these other matters. Based on what you think will happen, you may find yourself wanting to learn—or at least gather information—on the various areas of self-preparation. Each of the remaining chapters in Part II will talk about what you might study in those topics, but here's a brief survey:

- Education: Find out what educational resources exist for what you need and want to learn. Look for ways to improve some of your fundamental learning and study skills.

- Health and Fitness: There are few areas that have such divergent opinions and transient fads as health and fitness, but there are basics that have stood the test of time. Be sure you have an excellent first-aid manual, one of the popular home diagnosis guides, and a good book on alternative or home remedies.

- Home and Hearth: The obvious areas are home repair and alternatives for power, heat, light, water, and other basic household functions.

- Food and Supplies: Again, emergency preparedness and home storage would be your main focus.

- Work: If we go into a recession, unemployment will rise—which means that you may lose your job. Now is the time to improve yourself professionally so that you are either more attractive to keep around as an employee or better able to find a new job should your current one get cut.

- Money and Law: Learn how to budget your money and manage your resources, with an aim to getting out of debt; now is probably not a good time to start playing the stock market. Likewise, become familiar enough with law as it applies to the everyday person to avoid any liabilities.

- Family, Friends, Community, Nation: Study how to strengthen your family and how to improve your relationships with others. Study your community's history and how your local government works.

Impact of Y2K on Education

Now we need to shift gears a bit, moving from what you need to learn about Y2K to how Y2K might impact your education. You might be in high school or college, taking night classes, going to a professional institute, involved in distance learning, or otherwise bettering yourself through education. Y2K could disrupt those efforts in a variety of ways:

- Your education institution—school, college, university, or other—may suffer disruptions in operations, administration, records, and finance due to internal Y2K problems or external Y2K-related problems (power, water, heat, supplies, banking, etc.).

- More specifically, Y2K problems could impact functioning of computer systems and other equipment required for your classes; they could also interfere with production and delivery of textbooks and other classroom supplies.

- Disruptions in transportation may make it hard to get to and from class; on a larger scale, it may make it hard to get back from Christmas vacation.

- Y2K problems at home or work may take up your time or otherwise get in the way of attending class, doing assignments, and so on.

To be honest, we all tend to welcome a break in our studies; it's probably a legacy of our elementary school days. But disruptions on a high-school level can lengthen the school year, since most states mandate a certain number of school days per academic year. If the high schools are functioning, but the students and their families are experiencing Y2K issues, problems can arise for the students if tardies and absences begin to mount.

On a college or university level, Y2K problems could have more of an impact. Many students face delays in graduating due to difficulties in scheduling required upper-division classes. If such classes are interrupted or delayed to the point of being cancelled for the semester, those students could find themselves having to wait for months or even a full year to repeat the class.

This is a smaller issue compared to, say, power and food supply. But that does not mean that it is unimportant. It's just one more thing to think about. And since it is simple, it should make a good introduction to the Y2K planning template.

Education: Your Plan of Action

You're now ready to create a Y2K plan regarding education. The goal here is twofold: Figure out what you need to learn and adjust to ways in which Y2K might impact your current and planned education.

Identifying Risks and Corresponding Mitigations

Look at what risks you face because of the Y2K events that might impact you, the commitments you have with others or that they have with you, and your personal priorities.

ACTION. Review the current educational activities of yourself and your family members and note possible Y2K risks involved. For each risk you face, establish as best you can its likelihood (low, medium, high), its impact (low, medium, high), the possible mitigations, and the issues you face. Here are some general examples:

Risk/ Symptom	Prob.	Impact	Possible Mitigations	Issues
Disruption in normal operations of elementary and secondary schools.			Likely to be taken care of by school	
Disruptions in operations of post-secondary school (college, university, institute)			Take a light load; avoid critical classes, if possible	Possible disruption of required and hard-to-schedule classes
Y2K issues at home interfering with ability to prepare for and attend classes (all levels)			Getting assignments, materials in advance	Lack of concern or cooperation from the school or instructor.

You'll want to make these more specific to your circumstances, but you get the idea.

OUTCOME. When we have family members still in elementary or secondary school, we tend to take for granted that every will go well and the members will be able to graduate on schedule. Indeed, we expect it.[5] This exercise should help us to be aware of the potential interruptions and setbacks, though in most places they are likely to be small.

Looking for Opportunities

These will depend upon your profession and goals, but the dynamic and volatile conditions in the business market and the economy that Y2K are likely to introduce may translate to new or expanded opportunities within your firm or in the job market at large. For example, you may use the shortage of information technology workers as a way to get into the IT marketplace, and your employer (or another firm) may be willing to hire you with a minimum of training or even provide the training for you.

On a different level, and as noted above, you can use Y2K as a reason to educate yourself in a broad range of practical matters. The quote by Heinlein at the start of the chapter presents an interesting challenge. Working your way through that checklist would keep you busy for months, if not years.

ACTION. List three things that you would like to learn more about that will help your employment prospects, help you be more self-reliant, or will just make you feel better about yourself.

OUTCOME. You should see Y2K as a chance to develop your talents and improve your skills.

Establishing Guiding Principles

Based on your risks and opportunities, you need a small set of principles that will guide you through obstacles and discouragement and help you achieve your goals.

ACTION. Come up with one or two guiding principles relating to education. They should be short, pithy, and bold or funny. For example,

1. Those who know the most are seldom at the mercy of those who know the least.

2. Specialization is for insects.

OUTCOME. These should be punchy enough to keep you slogging through when your educational efforts don't seem nearly as interesting or relevant as when you started them.

Determining What You Need

Time now to figure out what you'll need to learn (or continue learning) or what you want to learn.

ACTION. List what you need to pursue your educational opportunities and reduce your risks. These should be general to education; education on specific topics (first aid, home storage, work) will show up in those chapters. For example, suppose you have two kids in school, one in elementary school, the other who will be a senior in the fall of 1999 and who plans to apply to several colleges and universities for the fall of 2000.

- Test schedules and materials for college entrance exams (SAT, AP exams, ACT)

- Application information for the colleges of interest

- Books, videos, and materials relating to educational needs for the other chapters in this book

That's about all you would need at this point until and unless you had some indication that either school (elementary or secondary) anticipated any type of Y2K impact.

OUTCOME. Depending upon the educational requirements of you and your family, this may be a minimal task. But you should have an idea of what you might need.

Creating the Plan

Here's where you put together the actual steps.

ACTION. Come up with a small list of steps. Don't bite off too much. A good first pass is to focus on acquiring and using the list of needed items. So you might come up with the following steps in your plan:

- Find out what the elementary school has done for its own Y2K.

- Find out the same for the high school; note in particular when the semester break is (before or after New Years). If finals are shortly after Christmas break, find out what the school's plans are.

- Verify the test schedules for the various college entrance exams. Note that SAT tests include ones offered in December and January—these are probably good ones to avoid.

- Verify application deadlines for the colleges themselves. If you're feeling really ambitious, you can find out what their Y2K status is.

- When you do send in applications, be sure to keep complete copies of all the forms and to send in the applications using certified mail or a courier service (e.g., FedEx or UPS), and that you apply well before the end of 1999.

And so on.

OUTCOME. You now have a simple list of steps to take. When done, you'll know more and be better prepared to ensure that your family's education continues without interruption. Note, however, that you'll want to revise later in 1999, as you (and these schools and companies) know more.

Enrolling Others

The more important people that may need to be enrolled will be teachers, counselors, and administrators at the educational institutions involved, to help out with any special issues, concerns, or problems that might arise.

ACTION. Based on your actual educational situation, look at contacting the appropriate people within those institutions, probably around the start of the fall 1999 school year. There's a good chance that by this point Y2K awareness will be such that the schools themselves will be proactive in dealing with this; however, if you have any special needs or concerns, this is a good time to bring them up.

OUTCOME. You want the support and cooperation of those responsible for the education of you and your family members.

Y2K JumpStart

If you're not sure where to start, here's a quick plan to follow. Adapt and expand to meet your own needs, but do *something*. Check off the boxes when you're done.

❏   After finishing this book, find and read at least one other book on Y2K. Compare and contrast with this one.

❏   If you can get onto the Web, go to www.wdcy2k.org/resources and bookmark it. Now start browsing the sites listed there.

❏   When you get tired of that, go to www.yahoo.com, enter "Y2K" (no quotes needed), and click on the Search button. When the list of categories comes up, click on "Computers and Internet: Year 2000 Problem." Browse through the various sites you find there.

❏   Make a list of schools and other educational institutions that family members attend. Call each one and ask about their Y2K remediation efforts. Keep on until you find someone who actually understands what you're asking and has an answer.

Tips and Traps

Here are a few suggestions in dealing with the suggestions and issues above.

•   As you browse through the Web, bookmark sites that appear of interest. Take time to keep your bookmarks/favorites organized, so that you can go back and find those interesting sites. If the site description is cryptic or misleading, change it to something you'll remember.

- Use your experience in trying to determine Y2K status of schools as a measure of general awareness of Y2K itself. Compare and contrast your understanding with that of the people with whom you deal.

Closing Thoughts

The Year 2000 problem in and of itself provides a tremendous learning opportunity for the public at large about the nature of information technology, global economics, national infrastructure, and what we depend upon in our everyday lives. For many of us, it may provide motivation to learn more of how to do for ourselves what we count on from others. One hopes that with all that additional knowledge comes a bit more wisdom as well.

7

Health and Fitness: Be Active and Proactive

You should pray for a sound mind in a sound body.
—Juvenal, *Satires*

The health industry faces multiple risks due to the Year 2000 problem. First, there are the regular Y2K remediation issues. Many hospitals and medical centers have a data processing center and information technology infrastructure that has grown by accretion year after year under the tight leash of a thin budget. The result is often a hodgepodge of various technologies, sharing data through ingenious but fragile means. Embedded systems have become widespread as microprocessors have made their way into a wide array of medical equipment. As you could expect, reports conflict.

Producers of medical equipment state that they're doing fine. For example, of the 1,782 manufacturers of medical devices responding to a U.S. Food and Drug Administration (FDA) Y2K survey, 1,649 reported that their products do not use date-related data or are compliant.[1] On the other hand, the U.S. Department of Veterans Affairs (VA) did a thorough survey of the medical devices used throughout the VA health system and found that 855 models of devices and equipment were not Y2K compliant, and that about 20 percent of these will not be

157

made compliant by the manufacturer.[2] They also noted that about 30 percent of the manufacturers did not respond to the VA's request for information even after repeated letters.

The real crisis, though, may be the U.S. Health Care Financing Administration (HCFA). This little-known agency is responsible for processing and paying Medicare claims: some $207 billion in 1997 and a (pre-Y2K) estimate of over 1 billion claims and $280 billion in payments in 2000.[3] Unfortunately, HCFA is in very poor shape with regard to Y2K—as of mid-1998, only a third of its 98 mission-critical systems had completed the repair phase, and none had completed testing or integration. Besides being late, HCFA's Y2K remediation effort is also complicated by one *million* different health care providers it must reimburse, the 73 contractors that provide information technology services to HCFA, the 25 different groups that maintain internal systems, and the other government and financial institutions it works with. If you correlate the numbers, you find that those million health care providers (hospitals, doctors, clinics, pharmacies, etc.) received an *average* of $207,000 in Medicare funds in 1997. Any significant disruptions in those reimbursements could seriously impact the planned-for cash flow of those providers.

In short, as Senator Robert Bennett has quipped on a few occasions, one of the three places you don't want to be on December 31, 1999 is in a hospital.[4]

So, what does all this mean for you? First, you may need to change your lifestyle to improve your health and fitness to help reduce the risk of illness or a medical crisis. Second, you may need to push ahead on those dental and medical checkups and procedures that you've been avoiding for months (or years or decades), to get them out of the way well before Y2K. Third, if you depend upon prescriptions, medical supplies, or special equipment, you may need to stock up so that you have what you need through any Y2K disruptions. Finally, if you have or are developing a serious medical problem, you need to ensure that you can continue to get safe, effective treatment through the Y2K transition. Let's take a look at each of these.

Getting Physical

There are those among us who live on bran, carrots, and that mythical "8 oz. of lean protein," have low blood pressure and body fat, and who could probably run a marathon while carrying on a conversation. Then there's us, the remaining 99 percent of the population. We feel virtuous when we have a diet soda or Wow™-brand chips with our cheeseburger and fries. Our daily exercise consists of taking the stairs to and from the third floor. And we keep switching dry cleaners to find one that doesn't shrink our clothes. Through it all, we make (and break) resolutions about how this time we're really going to do it, really going to swear off Ho-Ho's, really going to lose that 10 (20, 30, 50, 80) pounds, really going to get up an hour earlier and jog in the faint light of dawn—but tomorrow. This morning we just have to have that extra sleep.

Now would be a good time to get out of bed.

Look, being fit is no panacea. After all, James Fixx, who popularized running for fitness, died at age 43 of a heart attack while jogging. But for every untimely and inexplicable death like that, there are a thousand of us who die or get seriously ill precisely because of how we eat, live, and exercise. Here's a silent survey. How many of you have avoided getting that physical exam or applying for a different life insurance policy because you want to get into shape first?[5] In the meantime, entropy works against us; things fall apart; our belts cannot hold. Except for those of you blessed with the right genes and metabolism, each year it becomes easier to become less fit, harder to become more.

What we eat has a lot to do with this, too. The biggest accomplishment of the Food and Drug Administration in the 1990s was, in my opinion, mandating the uniform nutritional labeling of commercial food products. (I don't know about you, but I'll probably never again eat a large Marie Callender's Turkey Pot Pie.[6]) Yet for all the low-fat and nonfat foods we have available—and it's a pretty amazing assortment—we still don't necessarily eat *well*. The U.S. Department of Agriculture has their new-and-improved food pyramid[7] showing how much of what things we should be eating. For too many of us, the pyramid is inverted, or at least irregularly shaped.

As for tobacco—well, if you really believe it's harmless (or that you're immune), that's your right. But there is a very, very long sequence of medical studies linking tobacco use with increased incidents of everything from the obvious (lung cancer) to the unexpected (genital warts[8]). Even more suspension of disbelief is required for the various illegal substances.

All this isn't meant to scold, lecture, or preach. We all make choices and trade-offs, and we deal with the consequences sooner or later. But as noted above, Y2K is coming, and it might have a real impact on the health care system, the one that will have to bail you out if your lifestyle finally catches up with you or, at least, leaves you less able to cope with other health issues. So if you've wanted to clean up your act, to eat better, to become more fit, now is the time to do it. Because for a period starting toward the end of 1999 and continuing for some time into 2000, you do not want to have to visit a doctor, hospital, or other health care provider any more than you have to.

Besides, you'll feel better, probably a bit smug, and you'll deserve to.

Time to Stop Procrastinating

As mentioned above, we tend to avoid going to the doctor, dentist, or other health care provider. We do so for several reasons. One is money, especially if we don't have health insurance. But even if we do, we still have deductibles and co-pays, or we have only so much in our Medical Savings Account (MSA), or we don't want to run up the costs for our firm. We always have other things to spend our money on, and so we do.

The second is time. There are few prospects less inviting than to spend an hour or so in a doctor's or dentist's waiting room, spend another 10-30 minutes in an examination room (often largely undressed or with tubes in our mouths), through the procedure or exam itself, get things pulled back together, and then head back to home or work, the better part of a morning or afternoon shot. Actually, it is almost never as bad as described above,[9] but that's how we anticipate its being, and so we put it off and put it off.

The third is fear. We don't want to know how bad our teeth really are, or just what the doctor might discover if she biopsies that mole on our neck or examines our creaky knee. We would prefer to remain ignorant, thinking that will somehow make it all easier, hoping consciously or not for some form of spontaneous remission.

The last is pride. As noted above, we don't want to have a physical until everything's in top shape; we want to lose that weight, firm things up, not be embarrassed to be seen. The same is true for dental exams, though it's less clear just how we're going to clear things up on our own. When we've gone a long time without a visit, especially if there's some condition that we know needs to be looked at, we may also be embarrassed about going in and having the health care provider chew us out or even just silently disapprove of our procrastination—and so we procrastinate even more.

Come to think of it, these same four behaviors go a long way toward explaining how we got into the current Y2K mess in the first place.

Speaking of which—again, you face the possibility of a Y2K impact on the health care system. So if you're due (or overdue) for a physical, in need of a dental exam, or if you have some nagging problem that should be looked at, do it now. Get it done and out of the way. It will be one less thing for you to worry about, and if you do need some special attention, you can get it handled well in advance of Y2K.

Taking Care of Prescriptions and Medical Supplies

Back in the summer of 1998, I gave a presentation at a church one Friday evening on basic Year 2000 issues at the request of various members of the congregation. Afterwards, one family came up, an older couple with an adult daughter. The father asked me about any impact that Y2K might have on access to prescription drugs; his daughter, an epileptic, depended upon an uninterrupted supply of a key medication to prevent seizures.

I had already looked at this issue some months earlier in discussions with a human resources director in charge of employee benefits at a large corporation. My comments weren't exactly reassuring. Without knowing the Y2K status of any of the major or minor pharmaceutical companies, it was still very easy to list several points at which the prescription supply chain could break down:

- The first and most obvious involves any unresolved Y2K problems within the pharmaceutical company itself: operations, administration, communication, physical facilities, and especially the highly sophisticated and computerized equipment used for drug production and quality assurance, including the certificate of quality required for each batch of drugs.

- The pharmaceutical companies rely upon other firms for the extraction, refining, and delivery of various raw and processed chemicals and biologicals from which they create the drugs, as well as the components used to deliver the drugs (tablet manufacturing, bead manufacturing, packaging).

- Various aspects of drug production can be farmed out to other firms that specialize in contract manufacturing of pharmaceuticals. This introduces more issues of delivery and communication, as well as whether the contract firms are Y2K compliant and in a way that ensures that they are correctly exchanging critical data with the contracting firm(s).

- Once the drug is produced and packaged, it enters the pharmaceutical distribution system, going first to distributors and from there to hospitals, pharmacies, and other institutions, and from there to patients. This system makes significant use of computer technology to warehouse and monitor movement of drugs, track both prescriptions and patients' records, and authorize and transact insurance payments.

- All these institutions could experience disruptions if they face Y2K problems with power, water, telecommunications, and/or transportation. Note that an isolated or regional problem at just one point in the chain, if persistent, could impact drug production and delivery.

- The FDA, which regulates the pharmaceutical industry here in the United States, is part of the Department of Health and Human Services (HHS)—which received an "F" on Rep. Steve Horn's Y2K report card of September, 1998. It's unclear how the FDA proper is doing, but Y2K problems at HHS could in theory hinder the FDA's ability to regulate and certify drug production and thus slow it down.

All this works fine for the most part; the only clue we have of problems in the supply chain are when we find our prescription is back-ordered a few days or weeks, or that it's hard to get a particular brand or make of drug. Y2K, however, could have a more significant impact, causing greater scarcity and longer shortages of certain drugs, or impeding the ability of pharmacies to receive, dispense, and get insurance payment for prescription medications.

In other words, if you are dependent upon prescription medications, you may need to build up an extra supply to get you past any interruption or slowdown that could happen at the start of 2000. However, you may face some challenges here. First, your doctor obviously has to be willing to help you with this. Second, your insurance company may balk at the stockpiling; many will pay for only a month's prescription at a time and will do it only once a month. Third, some medications may have a limited shelf life and so not be amenable to stockpiling.

Similar, if less critical, issues may exist for key nonprescription supplies needed to treat or relieve medical conditions. These can include over-the-counter (OTC) medications, food supplements and vitamins, ointments, lotions, syringes, braces, and the like. Likewise, make sure your first aid kit is completely up-to-date. These are easier to stockpile, since they are less regulated, though certain restrictions may be in place based on the locale and item involved; for example, some states have limits on the quantities you can purchase of certain classes of OTC medications at one time. Again, you need to check shelf life and expiration dates as you build up whatever supply you need.

Dealing with Chronic or Critical Medical Problems

Now we come to the most serious cases. You already suffer from a serious condition—cancer, HIV, heart disease, emphysema, diabetes, and so on. You may be in a hospital full time. You may be an outpatient receiving treatment, such as dialysis, blood transfers, or chemo or radiation therapy. You may be receiving health care at home or in a hospice. You may be mobile with a truly "embedded" device such as a drug pump, a pacemaker, or some other device for dispensing, monitoring, or controlling. Whatever your condition, your health, well-being, and very life may depend upon continuing to receive medical treatment.

Because of that, you face potential risks on several levels. These include the following:

- Your health care provider (HCP)—hospital, HMO, doctor, hospice—may be impacted by Y2K problems in its own information systems (administration, operations, security, patient records, etc.).

- Your HCP's cash flow may be seriously disrupted by Y2K problems at HCFA, as noted at the start of the chapter.

- The biomedical devices you or your HCP uses may have Y2K problems, again as noted at the start of the chapter.[10] You may face delays in certain treatments because of devices being replaced or repaired. The HCP may have its budget significantly impacted by the cost of doing this replace/repair effort, impacting quality of care elsewhere.

- Any disruptions in vital utilities—water, power, heat, telecom, transportation—can impact your ability to receive treatment at home or in an HPC facility.

- Problems with telecommunication can also interfere with getting hold of a particular medical professional. (When the Galaxy IV satellite failed in mid-1998, many hospitals were scrambling to adjust to the fact that they could no longer page doctors and nurses.)

If you find yourself in this category, you will need to do some serious, careful research into the ways that Y2K could impact your medical care. It is important to create contragency plans to avoid disruptions in your care. This is especially true if you are receiving outpatient treatments. You must maintain access to your care and setting up alternative sources of care is an important task to accomplish.

Health and Fitness: Plan of Action

You're now ready to create a Y2K plan regarding health and fitness. Maintaining or improving your health is critical; without it, all your other activities will be constrained. Remember, though, that you cannot solve all your problems in a year; use wisdom and caution in all that you try to tackle.

Educating Yourself

To start with, become informed on general health and fitness issues. As noted in Chapter 6, there is a constant stream of health and diet ideas that come and go, but core basics exist that have withstood the test of time. Learn about them. Learn about first aid, home diagnosis of common (and uncommon) illnesses, and home remedies. If you depend upon prescription medications and/or biomedical devices, find out more about them, about alternatives, and about the consequences of any interruption. If you have a chronic or critical medical condition, you probably already know a fair amount about it, but it won't hurt to learn more; the Internet is often a good source of information. Above all, make sure you are an informed consumer of medical and dental services.

ACTION. Having gone through the paragraph above, make a list of three topics to study. For each topic, attempt to do the following: find and read (or, if reference, have on hand) a book on the subject; talk with a professional about it; find a web site about it.

OUTCOME. You will likely have neither time nor inclination to become an expert on these subjects, but you may be pleasantly surprised how much even just a modest amount of additional knowledge adds to your understand and leads you to study more.

Identifying Risks and Corresponding Mitigations

Look at what risks you face because of the Y2K events that might impact you, the commitments you have with others or that they have with you, and your personal priorities.

ACTION. Detail (on paper) the Y2K risks you or members of your family face through the spectrum of health and fitness issues. Analyze the areas above for risks: fitness and lifestyle; need for medical or dental procedures; dependence upon medications and biomedical devices; chronic and critical medical situations. For example, list the prescription medications that you take, as well as any OTC medications, food supplements, and medical supplies that you use regularly. What would happen if you had to go a few days without them? A few weeks? A few months?

For each risk you face, establish as best you can its likelihood (low, medium, high), its impact (low, medium, high), the possible mitigations, and the issues you face. Here are some general examples:

Risk/ Symptom	Prob.	Impact	Possible Mitigations	Issues
Requiring medical treatment due to health problems caused by poor physical fitness			Exercise, change of diet, weight loss, medication	Lifestyle patterns, demands of work and family, priorities, pre-existing physical or medical conditions
Requiring medical treatment due to health problems caused by lifestyle			Change of diet, cut back or abstain from tobacco, alcohol, other substances	Lifestyle patterns, addiction, social pressures
Requiring medical treatment due to a neglected or undetected condition (acute or chronic)			Schedule physical and/or dental exam ASAP; be consistent with medication, treatment, or therapy	Cost, time off
Pending need for a medical or dental procedure.			Make an appointment	Cost, time off
Interruption in supply of prescription medications			Stockpiling, alternative (OTC) remedies	Insurance, doctor, cost, effectiveness of alternatives
Problems or failures with necessary biomedical devices			Research compliance and alternatives	Lack of information from manufacturer

Risk/ Symptom	Prob.	Impact	Possible Mitigations	Issues
Disruption in treatment of chronic or critical medical condition			Work with HCP on compliance and service issues in Y2K time frame	Condition doesn't care about timing or convenience

Though it's not spelled out above, each risk above is specific to Y2K. For example, the first risk is not the general risk of having to seek medical treatment per se, but the specific risk of requiring medical treatment at a time—Y2K—when it might be harder to come by.

OUTCOME. You should now have an idea of your health and fitness risks. You may want to rank the ones you have in priority based on probability and impact. You can do this based on your own judgment, or you can do it by assigning a numeric value to probability and impact (high = 1, medium = 2, low = 3) and multiplying the two values together. The possible values will range from 1 (high * high) to 9 (low * low); the lower the value, the higher the priority.

Looking for Opportunities

This is a great area for opportunities. After all, you've probably wanted for some time to change your eating habits, start exercising, give up smoking, cut down on alcohol, or other improvements to your lifestyle. Many of these opportunities directly tie into your risk mitigation. Getting a clean bill of health from your doctors, making sure you are prepared for potential medical problems, and addressing them will, for some, eliminate long-standing fears of medical problems. Or in the worst case, you may find problems that will only get worse if undiscovered.

ACTION. Look at the highest priority risk you have. See if the mitigation presents an opportunity as well (e.g., exercising and changing diet in order to lose weight and increase physical fitness). If not, move down to the next highest risk, and so on. Continue until you have an opportunity identified. Since almost all of these involve lifestyle changes, you want to start with just one **and stick with it.** You can go back and add others later, but you shouldn't worry about them until the first one is established.

OUTCOME. You should now have something on which to base the principles you're going to create in the next section. You should also have an idea, based on the priorities of the risks, of the nature of the opportunities you have and the order in which you'll tackle them.

Establishing Guiding Principles

Based on your prioritized risks, corresponding mitigations, and potential opportunities, you need to come up with a small set of principles that will guide you as you deal with issues and unexpected problems, or that will hold you fast to your goals and commitments as distractions, pressures, and temptations arise.

ACTION. Come up with one to three guiding principles relating to health and fitness. They should be short, memorable, possibly a bit humorous, and written as a maxim or proverb. One should relate to your top opportunity; the others, if any, should deal with your top risk(s).

For example, suppose you have a chronic but controllable medical condition that requires regular medication or treatment of some kind, certain restrictions on diet or lifestyle, and a need for some form of exercise or physical therapy. You might come up with something like this:

1. A pill a day, come hell or high water.

2. Nothing tastes as good as being alive feels.[11]

3. When in doubt, walk; when sure, walk anyway.

OUTCOME. The principles you come up with are your real plan. There's more you will do to deal with risks and opportunities, and you still have more planning to do later on, but these form the heart of your effort. Feel free to add, throw away, or modify your principles depending upon what you achieve, what roadblocks you hit, and what new things you learn.

Determining What You Need

Time now to figure out what you're going to need to reduce your risks, exploit your opportunities, and live true to your guiding principles. It'll probably cost money and/or time.

ACTION. Come up with a prioritized list of goods, services, supplies, actions, and equipment that you need to accomplish the above. Tie these directly into risks, opportunities, and principles. If you face hard decisions, scarce resources, and/or trade-offs, fall back to your original set of priorities and commitments.

Continuing with the previous example, you might build the following list:

1. Seven-day pill dispenser to keep track of pills through week.

2. Two extra months of medication on hand; it is best to avoid refrigerated medications if possible.

3. Insulated lunch container to bring lunch to work.

4. Make sure you have alternative heat sources in your home and that you are well prepared for potential outages.

5. Both dress and exercise shoes geared for walking.

Distinguish carefully between true needs and mere wants, but make the list longer rather than shorter. Some items that are lower priority may get acquired sooner because they are cheaper, easier, or more available.

Creating the Plan

Take the time to put it all together. Think carefully about what you're doing.

ACTION. Come up with an initial list of steps—tasks to accomplish—based on all of the above. Again, start out modestly; you have several other areas (and chapters) to get through. Recognize that even a few steps are better than nothing and that several excellent steps are better than a long list of irrelevant or mediocre ones. Cut yourself some slack, too; if you're too tough on yourself or try too much, you may fall short on other priorities.

A good first pass is to focus on acquiring and using the list of needed items. So you might come up with the following steps in your plan:

- Buy seven-day pill dispenser, insulated lunch box at drugstore; fill dispenser with pills; put both in briefcase.

- Make appointment with your doctor for next month; talk about Y2K, stockpiling; get increased prescription, if possible.

- Clear inappropriate foods out of cupboard, and refrigerator; donate to local hunger project.

- If you need special care, check into alternative nursing programs in your area.

- Contact manufacturers of medical equipment you use to make sure it is compliant.

- Go to mall and sports shop; buy walking shoes for work, exercise.

- Take lunch to work every day for the next month, eating out just once a week.

- Walk to park (one mile each way) three times each week, listening to audio book in cassette player.

Note that the tasks are clear, matter of fact, and often have specific time frames, usually in the short term. Write them down on an index card or "To Do" note pads.

OUTCOME. You now have a plan for dealing with your health and fitness issues. When you have accomplished most or all of the tasks, go back through this whole process, starting again with identifying risks and mitigations. You'll find that it gets easier and faster each time.

Enrolling Others

You're not in this alone. Your tasks in your plan may explicitly or implicitly require the approval, cooperation, support, or tolerance of others. Get them involved.

ACTION. For each task in your plan, ask yourself: Who must help to make this succeed? Whose support and help would be most useful? Who is most likely to oppose or disapprove of this? And why did you select each person as you did?

OUTCOME. You should end up with a small group of people—perhaps just a friend, partner, or spouse—who understands what you're doing and supports you in that. Notice how much it helps.

Y2K JumpStart

If you're not sure where to start, here's a quick plan to follow. Adapt and expand to meet your own needs, but do *something*. Check off the boxes when you're done.

❏ Buy a good-sized first-aid kit, something in the $50 range. If you're tight on cash or prefer to customize your own, then buy an inexpensive waterproof box of some kind (such as a fishing tackle box) and start to put together a first-aid kit as time and finances allow. Pick up a practical book on first aid; Amazon.com lists 271 books under that subject, and your pharmacy or local bookstore should carry a good selection.

❏ Do you or any family members take prescription drugs? If not, skip this step. Otherwise, make a list of all active prescriptions. For each one, note who takes it, which doctor prescribes it, what it's used for, how much you have on hand, and—to the best of your knowledge—what will happen if you run out. If you're unclear, call your doctor's office and ask. If the consequence of not taking it are serious or unpleasant, then plan on seeing your doctor to see how to make arrangements.

❏ Do you smoke? Drink? Use drugs? If not, skip this step. Otherwise, consider eliminating or seriously cutting back on at least one of the three.

❏ Are you out of shape and/or overweight? If not, skip this step. Otherwise, introduce some form of exercise into your life. This may be no more than struggling through sit-ups and push-up (or something equivalent) each morning. Or it may be as much as joining a health club and hiring a personal trainer. But do *something*. Do it consistently. As you get better, push yourself more.

❏ Do you have a serious medical condition, either chronic (long-term) or acute (short-term)? If not, skip this step. If so, on your next appointment with your physician, raise the issue of potential Y2K impacts on your treatment.

❏ Buy a book on home treatment of illnesses and other medical conditions. Again, many such books exist; look for a comprehensive volume from a reputable publisher. Use it as a guide in building up a home supply of common over-the-counter (OTC) medications and treatments.

Tips and Traps

Here are a few suggestions in dealing with the suggestions and issues above.

• Before buying first aid supplies and OTC medications, inventory what you already have, checking carefully for expiration date, amount left, and general condition. Replace items older than their expiration dates.

- When you do go to shop for these items, check at warehouse stores (Costco, Sam's Club). You can find them in greater quantities at lower prices.

Closing Thoughts

The temptation may come to change many things at once. That isn't necessarily in and of itself a bad thing (though it can be), but it does often set you up for failure. If you really do want to change many things, still do it one or two at a time, but shorten the period until you start the next change.

8

Home and Hearth: Make a List, Check It Twice

It is good to moor your ship with two anchors.
—Publilius, *Maxim 119*

We most often think about home and hearth when thinking about Y2K and its impacts. We wonder about all the utilities, umbilical cords to the world, upon which we depend: power, gas, water, telephone, TV, and the Internet. We wonder about food in the cupboard, milk in the fridge, oil in the furnace, gas in the car, mail in the mailbox, and a newspaper on the front porch. And we wonder what exactly we need to prepare for and how to go about doing it.

External Feeds

We depend upon various services in our home. This century has seen a steady transformation in the standard family dwelling, with various services starting as luxuries only for the rich and powerful, then going on to be novelties, then options, and finally essentials. My move from Washington, DC to Texas in 1998 reflects that. I have a sheet of paper in my day-planner that I used to track all the services, obligations, and registrations that I had to terminate or wrap up on one end and then establish on the other. There are over 15 categories, and some have multiple entries.

Most of us have experienced some kind of interruption in those services, usually unexpected, at one time in our lives or another. The possible reasons are various: storms, accidents, earthquakes, billing or servicing errors, floods, fire, or even non-payment. When it happens, we realize what we've lost, what things we take for granted to be there when we count on them.

Y2K has the potential to be yet another reason for interruption or degradation of services. How likely that is remains an issue of significant debate at this time. The potential scenarios—mostly centered on failures in various control systems, embedded or otherwise—can be credibly spelled out. What we lack is hard information on the true scope of Y2K problems in these areas and how readily the various entities involved—corporations, utilities, and government agencies—can respond to get things fixed. So we have to decide how much preparation to do.

Electricity

Remote cabins and farms exist here and there in the United States that use no electricity, but they are a vanishing minority, a tiny fraction of a percent. Virtually every dwelling in the United States uses electricity; most require it to function, providing light, heat, air conditioning, and power to appliances of all types. Almost all of us have suffered a power outage at one time or another, ranging from momentary blackouts—just long enough to reset clocks and VCRs—to week-long interruptions in the wake of hurricanes, tornadoes, floods, and ice storms. Our experience has taught us that the novelty value of a power outage vanishes within minutes—sometimes seconds—and as it stretches out into hours or even days, it moves from annoyance to inconvenience to minor crisis to major problem. And that doesn't begin to address its impact on the rest of civilization.

It's no wonder, then, that the Y2K readiness of the mythic **power grid**—the collection of facilities and infrastructure to generate, transmit, distribute, and regulate power across North America—has been one of the predominant issues in the entire Year 2000 discussion.[1] It was the topic of the first public hearing of the Senate Special Committee on the Year 2000 Technology Problem on June 12, 1998. Various claims and counterclaims have appeared in media reports and spread across the Internet. The power industry itself has been late responding to Y2K, both internally and publicly, and so we lack both information about the scope of their Y2K problems and confidence in their progress resolving them.

The single most disquieting piece of news came from the Senate Y2K hearing mentioned above. In his opening remarks, Senator Robert Bennett, the chairman, said that the committee staff had surveyed ten of the largest power companies in the United States about where they stood in their Y2K remediation efforts. Eight of the ten were still in the inventory and assessment phases—that is, they were still trying to figure out how many programs and embedded control systems they had and which of those had Y2K problems.[2] For a large power firm to still be in assessment halfway through 1998 is not a good sign. For at least eight of them to still be in assessment is a very bad sign. Senator Christopher Dodd (D-Conn.), the ranking minority member of the committee, concluded, "Quite honestly, I think we're no longer at the point of asking whether or not there will be any power disruptions, but we are now forced to ask how severe the disruptions are going to be."[3]

The power companies are vulnerable from several different directions. Most obvious are their own Y2K failures, including various embedded and control systems. Nuclear power plants must prove themselves Y2K compliant by the fall of 1999 or face being taken off-line and shut down by the Nuclear Regulatory Commission. Beyond that, many power generation plants depend upon timely deliveries of oil, coal, or natural gas, and so are vulnerable to any interruption in those supply chains. Power generation and transmission relys heavily upon telecommunications, so any significant problems there could have an impact.

Having gotten late out of the gate, the U.S. power companies know that any Y2K failures on their part will bring very unhappy responses from government and business at all levels, not to mention the population at large. More significantly, any power firm that disrupts the power supply due to unrepaired Y2K failures on its part will likely face a slew of liability lawsuits. It's not as though they can blame this on weather, sabotage, or an unanticipated equipment failure. They have been served notice, and they don't have many excuses.

Because of all that, these companies will do whatever it takes to prevent or minimize any disruptions. They do still face the same problems and issues discussed at length in Chapter 3, along with the simple fact of the calendar. But they have well over a year (as of this writing) to find and fix as many Y2K problems as they can—and their first priority will be to keep the power going. So it's hard to give much credence to the more extreme predictions of the entire power grid or large portions thereof going down for weeks, months, or longer.

On the other hand, it's hard to believe that everything will work just fine everywhere. While most people are likely to experience little more than a flicker or brownout, some of you will probably face a power outage lasting somewhere from a few hours to a few days. And while it's likely to happen within the first few days of 2000, it might come days, weeks, or months later as unexpected problems crop up or temporary measures break down.

How do you prepare for such an outage? The first step is to make a list of what would be impacted. You can generate the list pretty easily.

- Anything directly wired into the house: built-in lights, doorbell, intercom system, some smoke detectors (though these usually have battery backup that will last for months), and security systems (usually with backup that will last for hours or days).

- Appliances: washer, dryer (even if it's a gas dryer), electric water heater, refrigerator, freezer, dishwasher, furnace/heater (even if oil or gas), air conditioner, garbage disposal, trash compactor, automatic sprinkler systems, and jet/filtration systems for bathtubs, hot tubs, and pools.

- Anything plugged into an electrical outlet: lamps, clocks, radios, TVs, VCRs, stereos, computers, kitchen appliances, and so on. Pay special attention to phones that plug into electrical outlets; most will not work in the absence of power, so you should be sure you have at least one phone that doesn't require external power.

The simple question: If you turned off all power to your house for eight hours, how well would you get by? How about for a day? For three days? For a week? Keep in mind that we're talking about the middle of winter, so both heat and light will be a serious concern, especially the further north you are. Loss of power and heat can also have an impact on your water supply in very cold climates.

Many people think first of a power generator for their home. That isn't a bad idea if you live somewhere where the combination of power outages and climate make that a reasonable idea independent of Y2K, such as in Canada or the northern part of the Midwest and Northeastern United States. But it raises some serious questions as a Y2K contingency plan. To justify buying and installing a generator, you would have to believe that there is a significant probability that you will undergo Y2K power outages lasting long enough to be more than an annoyance or discomfort. On the other hand, if you think the power outages really are going to be prolonged, then you have to deal with issues of fuel supply and storage; depending on the size and power output of the generator, it will typically run one to nine hours per gallon of fuel. You'll also have to determine what you actually want to have power for and what size generator you'll need accordingly.

Be aware that the nine hours/gallon is for a small portable 300-watt generator; most generators of a size to run a full household (2500-5000 watts) get one to two hours/gallon.[4] As a compromise, suppose you get a 1500-watt generator; for example, the Honda EM 1800XK1, which costs around $1000, gets three hours/gallon. If you want 12 hours of power each day (such as 6 A.M. to noon, 3 P.M. to 9 P.M.) and want to plan for up to two weeks of power outage, you would need to have a 55-gallon drum of fuel on hand to run it.

If you don't think that the risk is sufficient to justify the expense and effort of setting up a generator, or if you live in a dwelling where it just isn't feasible (such as an apartment or condominium), what else can you do to prepare for power outages? Simple. Analyze what you use the power for and come up with alternatives. The three main uses are to provide heat (including for cooking), to provide light, and to power up electric appliances. Consider your alternatives (camping equipment, wood-burning stove, battery-powered devices) and plan accordingly.

Water

You can argue whether power or water is more critical, but it's usually easier to prepare for and deal with an interruption or problem with the water supply than with power. Generally speaking, as long as you can get enough water (or equivalent) to drink, you can live for some time with not being able to bathe, wash clothes or dishes, water your lawn, and so on. It may be unpleasant, especially for those around you, but it can be done.[5] The most serious issue: human waste disposal. If you have untreated or unsafe water available, you can still flush toilets, but if you don't have water at all, you can develop sanitation and health problems very quickly.

How could Y2K affect the water supply? The primary answer is a familiar one: embedded control systems. Thousands of water processing, purification, and delivery facilities exist in the United States. These facilities depend upon control systems to monitor and control the flow of water. They depend upon such systems and laboratory equipment to carry out various treatment processes to reclaim waste water, purify water from rivers and lakes, and add chemicals to avoid problems with bacteria and algae within the water network itself.

You shouldn't underestimate the need for such utilities to also correct their various data processing systems. While these are of secondary concern to delivery of potable (drinkable) water, Y2K failures in such systems could end up disrupting the normal flow of business within the utility itself, causing problems with cash flow and ordering supplies. They could also lead to erroneous shutoff of service due to billing errors.

As with power utilities, water utilities are also vulnerable to secondary Y2K problems. They require power and telecommunications for sustained operations; they usually depend upon production and delivery of chemicals and other supplies; and the people who run the plants have to be willing and able to come to work. Concerns also exist where utilities are replacing noncompliant equipment as to whether new versions that are Y2K compliant will be available

In many cases, city or county governments run, or control, these water utilities. This is not a comforting thought, given how many such governments are tight on resources and behind on Y2K. Web sites dealing with water treatment and Y2K reflect a high level of concern among some key groups, but they do little to clarify how well the work is progressing among the broad base of water utilities.

Unlike the other external feeds, water can be stored. You can buy drinking water in bottles of varying sizes, sealed and safe. If water service is interrupted, you still have drinkable water in your hot water heater; on the other hand, if you water supply becomes compromised (under- or over-treated), you may not be able to us that water for drinking. If you have a hot tub or pool, you already have a significant source of emergency water, though it may require additional treatment, such as boiling and/or filtering, to drink. On the other hand, if you have a waterbed, the water inside may be unsafe to drink; check with the manufacturer.

Phone: Local, Long Distance, and Mobile

Telecommunications (telecom) is seen as the third leg of the so-called "iron triangle," along with water and power. Not only do these three utilities form the foundation of modern business, they are also heavily interdependent upon one another: A significant interruption in one can impact the other two.

We know that the breakup of the AT&T phone monopoly back in 1982 opened the door for a host of new telecom companies. We've watched the various commercials come and go for the major long-distance companies, not to mention the various local firms, the so-called "Baby Bell" regional bell operating companies (RBOCs) that at times seem intent on recombining into one large entity again. But most of us don't realize that there are over 1400 telecom companies in the United States alone, serving rural and isolated portions of the country.[6] Add to that the wide-open marketplace for telecommunications equipment, including the various companies that have come and gone over the past 16 years, and you have a profoundly complex system that we count on to work every time we pick up the phone.

The remarkable thing is that it does work so well, even though our demands and expectations have increased tremendously during the last four decades. I'm old enough to remember the phasing out of exchange names (e.g., HOpkins 5-5979) and the advent of direct-dial long distance and touch-tone phones. Now I carry a small portable phone that has a six-line alphanumeric display, caller ID, a 200-entry phone number directory, conferencing, voice mail, a clock (with alarm), and a calendar (with notes). It also receives e-mail, plays four different games, and can go for days without being recharged.[7] My service plan works across most of the United

States and has no long distance or roaming charges. People dial my number—which has the area code of a city over a thousand miles from where I live—and this vast, complex telecom network we've evolved tracks me down somewhere on the North American continent in the space of a few seconds and rings my phone, telling me who's calling.

Our economy, our government, and our society all run on that network. For most of us, the Y2K telecom risk is not that our phones at home or in our purses won't work. Most of us have experienced that at one time or another, and while it can be inconvenient, it brings some blessings of peace and quiet. The real risks is that the vast array of businesses, utilities, and service providers upon whom we depend will have their operations disrupted by telecom problems, and we'll suffer the second- and third-hand consequences.

When Y2K does come, it's likely that your phones at home will work just fine, that you'll get a dial tone when you pick up the handset. What is less clear is how many of the various organizations—business, government, educational—will have their telecom systems working just fine. Many of them depend upon **private branch exchanges** (**PBXs**), the office systems that support and manage a number of phone extensions off a single central phone number, providing voice mail, intercom capabilities, and the ability to answer, transfer, conference, and put on hold the calls that come in. There are tens of thousands of PBXs in use—the Internal Revenue Service has several thousand all by itself—and many of them have Y2K problems.[8]

Even less clear is the Y2K impact on the millions of cellular, digital, and PCS phones in use. These would be impacted by any disruptions to the regular telecom network, since they still depend upon it for various portions of a connected call. Beyond that, they have their own systems and networks, again built on heavy technology. And while it would be hard to conceive that any portable phone would have in and of itself a Y2K problem, more unbelievable problems have cropped up in all this.

Even household phones may be impacted by power outages. Portable household phones—with base units that plug into a power outlet as well as into a phone jack—typically won't work unless the base unit is getting power from the outlet. Some of the more sophisticated non-portable phones, such as those with data banks and text screens, also require power and won't function without it.

Natural Gas

A smaller—but still very substantial—percentage of homes use natural gas. Those that do vary in how they use it: heating systems, air conditioners, ovens and stoves, water heaters, clothes dryers, and gas fireplaces. Depending upon the mix in your home, the impact of any Y2K-related problems with the local gas utility could range from irrelevant to critical. It would be good to do a survey of your house to determine just where on that spectrum you lie.

That aside, problems in production and transport of natural gas could still impact you. Even if you don't use it directly or in a critical fashion in your home, many power generation plants burn natural gas. An inability to get the expected volume of gas could lead such plants to cut back their power output or even shut down.

Natural gas production, transport, storage, and delivery form a complex system that depends heavily on information technology and embedded systems. Various companies handle different sectors, exchanging gas, information, and money in appropriate measure. While electrical production and distribution are heavily coordinated and regulated by government and industry organizations, the natural gas industry is fragmented and lacks regional control.[9]

As with most other sectors, the problems lie not in any technical challenge or breakthrough required to deal with Y2K, but with the simple tedium of inventory, assessment, repair, and test. The fragmented nature of the industry adds complications, though a variety of industry organizations are focusing on Y2K awareness and coordination.

Television and Radio

TV transmissions—broadcast, cable, and satellite—could in theory be interrupted at any number of points, from origination to delivery at home, due to Y2K problems in various control systems, embedded or otherwise. Secondary impacts from infrastructure (power, water, telecom) and other problems could disrupt transmission also; those same factors, along with other Y2K events, could also hinder or shut down production of TV shows, live and taped. These same factors could also apply to radio, though radio is probably less vulnerable than TV, all things considered. And, of course, power outages at your house can hinder your reception of whatever is being transmitted.

One could argue, half in jest and half-seriously, that disruption of television service could be a good thing. A long-term disruption—which is extremely unlikely—might have some arguably positive side effects. But in the short term, such a disruption would just increase panic, concern, and misinformation. Our family lived in the Santa Cruz mountains just outside of Soquel in 1988 and 1989—which put us about three miles from the epicenter of the Loma Prieta earthquake that hit October 17, 1989. Our house made it through just fine, but we lost power and so lost TV (such as it was—we only got one or two channels, and those poorly). We went out to the car and turned on the radio. At first, we could pick up only two stations on the air. All that came from one station were sounds of the disk jockey trying to sort through the damage in the studio, coming to the mike every now and then to state the obvious: There had been a big earthquake. The other station didn't have much more to report. For the next half hour or so, as near-constant aftershocks rattled us physically and emotionally, we were left to wander if we had been on the fringes and the real disaster lay in the Bay Area. We had no way of knowing what the devastation was like over there.

Then the other radio stations slowly came back on the air, and we found out—bad, especially with the collapse of the Nimitz freeway and the fires in the Marina district, but still not the Big One.[10] We literally listened to a battery-powered radio all night long as the nature and scope of the damage unfolded. It was a psychological lifeline. Even if the news on the other end wasn't all that great, at least we were learning how things stood and what emergency measures were being taken.

There's little you can do if transmission and delivery of radio and TV are interrupted. But you can get portable radios—and even a small battery-powered TV set—to ensure reception should you have power problems at your house.

Internet

The Internet was designed originally to operate in the aftermath of a nuclear war. It assumes that any number of its supporting nodes may be knocked out and so will automatically reroute packets of information trying to get from one spot to another. It will likely survive Y2K with no more than an upsurge in traffic among users trying to find out what Y2K events, if any, have occurred. If significant problems develop with telecom and/or

TV, traffic will be even higher as people attempt to use it to contact one another via e-mail and read news from various sites.

The Internet came in handy in the aftermath of the Loma Prieta earthquake. Phone lines into the Bay Area were jammed for days by people trying to call to check on family members and friends. However, once power was restored (for us, about 24 hours after the quake), I could make local calls just fine and so get on-line. I became part of a group that received e-mail messages from people unable to get through to specific people on the phone. We would drive over to those people's houses and check on them or leave messages instructing them to call those concerned. I suspect the Internet may serve a similar role, particularly on a global basis.

Deliveries and Pickups

We don't just count on those automatic feeds, coming in through wires and pipes. We also expect live humans to show up in cars and trucks, or even on bikes or on foot, to bring things to us or to take other things away. Most are conveniences, but some can be every bit as critical as the automatic feeds listed above. And most could, in theory, be impacted by Y2K as well.

Oil, Coal, and Wood

Another personal story here. Late in 1996, while living in the countryside of northern Virginia, our family woke up one crisp winter morning to find we had no hot water. We called the oil company, with whom we had a service contract, to come look at the oil-burning hot water heater. A representative came out late in the day, serviced it, got it going again, and left. The next morning, we woke up to no hot water *and* no heat. We called the oil company again, the same service rep came out to check the furnace—and discovered our oil storage tank was empty. Due to a mix-up in its records, the oil company had never come out during the fall to check and refill the oil tank. The rep put in all the oil he had (about 20 gallons) and said the company would send out a truck later that day. It never came. We did have a chance to shower and to warm up the house a bit before the oil gave out again, but we had another frigid night. We had by this time gone out and purchased a few electric heaters, which we placed in key spots, but most of the house had become quite cold by this time. The oil truck finally showed up late in the afternoon—our third day, now, with little or no oil—filled up our tank and got everything going again.

Those of you living in cold climes—and northern Virginia is quite mild compared to the Midwest and the Northeast, not to mention Canada—probably have similar stories of your own. It doesn't take a large breakdown or a disaster for some number of houses to be missed or neglected in deliveries of heating oil, coal, or wood. But what's key to note here is how long it took the oil company to figure out what was wrong and to fix it, when all that was involved was a simple (if, for us, significant) mistake on their part for a single house. If that oil company had been dealing simultaneously with ten or a hundred houses that had not been serviced in time, the time required to straighten things out and catch up on oil deliveries might have taken days or even weeks.

The good news is that most such services are not high tech and not are likely to be impacted directly by embedded systems failures. But there is potentially bad news in several areas. First, such enterprises are likely to have lower-end computer systems to manage accounts, supplies, and deliveries but are less likely than large firms to have completed Y2K repairs in time. This means that you could be simply overlooked, and you might not notice until you start to run low on oil, and so on. It also means that if there's a problem with many customers, the time it takes to get what you need could be stretched out. Second, such firms depend upon oil or coal being delivered to them—and that supply chain is susceptible to interruption as well, particularly oil production. Third, these firms could be impacted by second- or third-order Y2K effects (infrastructure, economics, transportation, employees not choosing or able to show up for work), which in turn can have an impact on your getting what you need to stay warm.

The obvious contingency efforts—scheduling deliveries shortly before the Y2K deadline, stockpiling extra coal and wood, being prepared to use fireplaces, wood-burning stoves, kerosene and even electric heaters—should be made appropriately. Just be aware that a large number of your fellow-citizens will likely be doing the same, which itself could make for delivery problems and shortages.

Trash and Sewage

Many of us have experienced an interruption in trash removal service. It may have been due to some form of work stoppage, to equipment problems, to closures of landfills, through failure to pay a bill, or some other reason. We're also aware how quickly trash and garbage can pile up when it isn't being hauled away on a regular basis. Fortunately, the set of Y2K events that could impact trash removal is relatively small and fairly drastic: shortages of fuel or repair parts, inability or unwillingness of employees to come to work, or major disruptions in power, water, and telecom. If those Y2K events are happening that close to home, then trash removal is probably far down on your list of concerns. And those of you living in colder climates get this additional benefit: garbage left outside will be well preserved for some time.

On the other hand, this may be a good time to become more proactive on recycling and conservation than you have been before. Purchase bulk items stored in reusable containers. Use items that can be washed and reused rather than disposable equivalents. Learn to separate the trash and garbage you produce. If feasible, dig (before the ground freezes) a compost pit to hold garbage; keep a pile of soil to sprinkle on each layer. Likewise, if feasible and permitted by law, prepare a safe, screened location outside to burn paper-based items. Recycle cans, bottles, papers, and plastics where it makes sense (it often doesn't).

Sewage disposal requires less direct human intervention and for the most part shouldn't be impacted by Y2K. If you have a septic tank, you're unlikely to have it pumped in the middle of winter, so you have nothing to worry about. If you're hooked up to a sewer system, things should continue to work well at your end—as long as you have water. If water is in short supply, you may have to learn to ration flushing the toilet or collect wastewater from other uses (including showering) in a bucket to flush.[11]

Mail and Delivery Services

We'll take the United States Postal Service (USPS) at its word as far as making sure the mail goes through. For all we joke about them at times, they have an excellent track record in more difficult circumstances, such as various natural disasters. Recognizing what an important role they might play should Y2K events prove serious, the USPS has prepared a detailed contingency plan, not just to keep itself running, but to help pick up the slack should other communication and delivery networks be affected by Y2K.[12] They are taking this seriously: between their own Y2K remediation and their efforts to deal with possible Y2K impacts, they plan to spend well over half a billion dollars before they are done.

One can only assume that Federal Express, United Parcel Service (UPS), DHL, and other major carriers are likewise focusing both on their own Y2K repairs and their contingency plans. UPS, having gone through a 15-day strike back in 1997, knows just what an inability to provide its usual level of service means to its bottom line and that of its customers. Likewise, UPS's competitors know what it's like to have a sudden jump of shipping business because of that same strike.

Still, the Postal Service and the delivery firms could be significantly impacted should there by any Y2K disruptions in the transportation sector, especially in air traffic. And all of them may face a massive surge in shipping volume in December 1999 as businesses schedule shipments and deliveries ahead of Y2K. Your bottom line: Get those Christmas cards and presents sent before Thanksgiving. Just to be safe.

Household Y2K Remediation

Our homes themselves have become havens of technology. While only about 40 percent of U.S. homes have a personal computer, over 90 percent have refrigerators and televisions, and a majority has VCRs, washers, and dryers. The potentially bad news is that many of the more recent models of these appliances have embedded systems. The good news is that virtually none of them care about Y2K. The few that do will in all likelihood suffer the electronic equivalent of a hiccough, a bit embarrassing but quickly remedied.

Home Appliances and Electronics

Nevertheless, it is worth doing a survey of your house to find those items that may have time and date sensitivity. Again, personal computers are the most obvious, but others might include

- VCRs and cameras, included camcorders and digital cameras

- Phones, including cellular and digital phones

- Heating/cooling systems, including both the thermostats and the HVAC units

- Home security systems

- Automatic sprinkler systems

Most of these are likely to be unaffected by a year change, if indeed you can set the year at all. However, as mentioned back in Chapter 1, at least one friend found a serious problem with her camcorder: She did a Y2K rollover, and the camcorder ejected the tape inside and then froze in the "eject" position. She couldn't get it to unfreeze and eventually had to send it back to the factory for repairs. Lesson: You may need to do such testing (either that, or find out while filming your historic New Year's Eve 1999 celebration), but be sure you have your purchase receipts handy.

Personal Computers

You certainly do *not* want to do such a test on your home computer(s) for at least two reasons. First, you could cause problems for yourself, causing erroneous dates to be associated with some of your files or worse. (As Jim Lord says, "Running your system clock up to the Great Date Rollover to see what happens is like sticking your finger in a light socket to find out if the light is working."[13]) Second, you might not be able to tell if there are any problems and so mistakenly think that your system is fine.

Instead, run a PC Y2K assessment program on your system. Several commercial programs exist that will scan your PC to detect Y2K problems and, in many cases, fix them. Since they aren't terribly expensive (e.g., Check 2000 PC, a well-reviewed product from GMT, costs $29.95), it's worth spending the money. Various freeware, shareware, and demo programs can be downloaded from the Internet, but they come with their own warnings and limitations. If you're very computer savvy, they may be fine; otherwise, a commercially supported product is a better option.

Transportation

As you may remember from Chapter 4, one of the most common Y2K myths is that our cars are going to stop working. After hearing this for over a year and a half, I have yet to be presented with a single credible instance of Y2K failures in a car. That's not to say that there aren't any such problems; if there are, though, they've been kept under wraps, unlike Y2K problems in oil supertankers, critical medical systems, and power plants. The chances of your having a Y2K problem with your car appear to be very small.

A more likely (if still unlikely) Y2K risk would be in public transit systems, particularly those dependent upon computer systems: trolley, subway, and commuter trains. These systems do have various sensors, embedded control systems, safety systems, and centralized control systems that all must work for the trains to run. Some of these systems have computer problems independent of Y2K and there may not be the time, money, or foresight necessary to initiate and complete Y2K repairs in time.[14]

The most credible overall personal transportation risk could come as a rise in gasoline prices and/or gas shortages and rationing. Those of us old enough to have been driving in the 1970s remember the aftermath of the formation of the OPEC oil cartel. Not only did gasoline prices jump dramatically, but shortages also occurred, first in 1973–1974 (an OPEC embargo as a response to United States support of Israel in the Yom Kippur War.) Gas prices doubled again in 1978 due to oil shortages caused by the revolution in Iran and OPEC's subsequent hiking of prices. Efforts by President Carter to increase conservation led to restrictions on when you could fill your tank with gas (typically odd or even days, based on your license plate) and long lines.[15]

Oil companies have documented Y2K problems in just about every aspect of oil production, shipping, and refining. OPEC has been unable to raise oil prices or significantly cut production for several years due to global excess production of oil; in many parts of the country, we pay less (adjusting for inflation) for a gallon of gasoline now than we did in the 1960s, before OPEC. Y2K could change that. Actual Y2K problems could cause enough of a breakdown in the global oil production chain to cut production and cause prices to rise sharply. Just as significant, OPEC member states could use such problems as an opportunity to deliberately cut production and raise prices. Gasoline prices in the United States have a habit of responding sharply and immediately to oil price increases, but declining very slowly when oil prices drop. As happened in 1978, gasoline prices could easily rise 50 percent to 100 percent in a matter of weeks or even days, pushing into the $2 to $3 per gallon price range, particularly in urban regions that have higher gas prices (such as southern California). The corresponding jump in aviation fuel prices would dramatically increase the operating costs for commercial airlines as well, causing ticket prices to jump.

The realities of any or all of these problems will become more apparent as 1999 advances. Transportation alternatives—walking, a bike, a motorcycle—will depend upon your circumstances and needs, as well as what those realities are. If you use a car, the driving factor (so to speak) will be economic; looking for some way to buy and use less gasoline. If you use mass transit, you should have alternatives and contingencies should there be disruptions in service. As an example, for work you could car pool, telecommute, and/or work more flexible hours. Grocery shopping could be a bit more problematic, but then any disruption is likely to be temporary.

Home and Hearth: Plan of Action

This will be one of your more detailed efforts; the previous few chapters were a warm-up for this chapter and the next. The key here is not to go overboard—or, as we used to say at a place where I used to work, "Start out stupid and work up from there." Make a modest set of plans; carry them through; look around to see what else has developed; and then refine and expand your plans if necessary.

Educating Yourself

The first wave of Y2K education was focused on corporate and business issues; the second wave has been focused on personal and consumer issues. Many books and Web sites now focus on how to prepare yourself and your family for a range of Y2K possibilities; more will come, as will likely a CD-ROM or other software package to guide you in your Y2K planning.

ACTION. Find and read at least one or two other books on personal Y2K preparation. If you have Internet access, locate several web sites on the subject; a good one to start with is the Cassandra Project (http://millennia-bcs.com/).

OUTCOME. The more you read and surf, the more you'll realize that there are a variety of opinions on Y2K: What will happen, what the odds are, and what you should do to prepare. You should also understand why it's important to educate yourself, to make your own evaluations, and to follow your own judgment. Don't depend upon or trust any one source too heavily—not even this book.

Identifying Risks and Corresponding Mitigations

This exercise should be familiar to you now. Take your time on this; you have a lot more to deal with, and you'll have less solid information initially.

ACTION. For the major areas in this chapter that you are concerned about, list a risk. Leave the probability column blank; assign what you think the impact would be, and detail how you might mitigate the risk, while noting issues.

Risk/ Symptom	Prob.	Impact	Possible Mitigations	Issues
Rolling brown-outs or short-term blackouts			Propane lan-terns, heaters, stove; flash-lights; battery-powered radios	Need extra cau-tion with flames; be sure smoke detec-tors all work
Unsafe drinking water			Boiling and chemical puri-fication; melt-ing snow or ice from outside; bottled water	Cannot store enough water for a long-term problem
Inability to call to check on family members in other states			E-mail con-tacts; agreed-upon third-party contacts	Hard to guar-antee contacts
Cut-off of natural gas			Use propane stove top for cooking	Propane supply
Inability to receive TV, radio in case of power outage			Battery-pow-ered (or cranked) radio; battery-pow-ered TV	Supply of bat-teries
Oil supply for furnace			Schedule fill-ing in early December; rig fireplace for heating; buy wood	Heat in rest of house
Y2K problems in personal com-puter			Buy Y2K pack-age to check it out	What if I have to replace it and/or upgrade my software?
Cost of gasoline rising			Get a second, more efficient car	Money, repairs

OUTCOME. By making choices about the risks, you help to sort through your real concern. As a follow-up exercise, make a second list with an entirely new set of risks. Note the differences between the two lists; for each area, ask yourself which you think is more likely.

Looking for Opportunities

For years you've had various groups and speakers urge us to live simpler lives, to tread lightly upon the earth. Now is a chance to look at your lifestyle and see where you can do so. Not that simplicity is an inherent virtue; to paraphrase Leo Tolstoi, it is amazing how complete is the delusion that simplicity is goodness.[16] Still, our lives tend to weigh in on the side of undue and costly complexity springing from convenience, and some simplification may reduce costs and increase well-being.

ACTION. Select three or four opportunities that arise, even indirectly, from looking at these risks. For example, you might get out that bike sitting unused in your garage, have it tuned up at the bike shop, and start riding it. You might also finally get around to having your chimney professional cleaned and the fireplace set up to actually be used for fires. And you might even cut down on those utility bills.

OUTCOME. More silver linings and a certain self-satisfaction that comes from doing virtuous (or, at least, sensible) things long delayed.

Establishing Guiding Principles

As always, you need a small set of principles that will prepare you for and/or guide you through the unexpected.

ACTION. Come up with several guiding principles related to the risks and opportunities in this area. Humor and memorability always help. A few examples based on items above might be

1. Walk if you can; bike if you can; drive if you must.

2. Be prepared to camp at home.

3. Redundancy is the key to survival.[17]

OUTCOME. These principles act as reminders for your preparation efforts. They are what you quote to yourself, your spouse, and your kids when questions arise about what needs to be done and where money needs to be spent.

Determining What You Need

Given all that has been covered in this chapter, this again will not be a single act, done once and handled quickly. Revisit this list as you acquire information about how things are actually developing.

ACTION. Come up with a prioritized list of goods, services, supplies, actions, and equipment that you need to accomplish the above. Tie these directly into risks, opportunities, and principles. If you face hard decisions, scarce resources, and/or trade-offs, fall back to your original set of priorities and commitments. Where possible, make the purchases have value even if Y2K events don't materialize.

Continuing with the previous example, you might build the following list:

- High-quality sleeping bags for every family member.

- Propane lanterns, stove; kerosene heaters, and other camping paraphernalia.

- A bike for each family member.

- Each fireplace set up for use and firewood on hand.

- Flashlights, radios, batteries.

OUTCOME. If done right, most of these supplies will have benefits independent of Y2K, giving you alternatives for other circumstances or emergencies that might arise.

Creating the Plan

Once again, time to put it together.

ACTION. The risk mitigations and items to be acquired make a good start. Your first pass might include some of the following:

- Have the chimneys professionally cleaned and checked out. Install glass screens, possibly with blowers, in each fireplace. Get any necessary fireplace tools. Find a reputable source for good quality firewood; prepare a storage area and buy a few cords. Be sure to also get kindling, matches, and other necessary items. Make sure all smoke alarms are functioning properly.

- Make sure that each family member has a good sleeping bag.

- Put together a camping chest: lanterns, stove(s), propane and/or kerosene, other items.

- Repair and tune up usable bikes; buy new ones so that every family member who can ride a bike has one. Organize family bike rids just to get everyone used to using them.

- Make sure every room in the house has one or more flashlights in it, and that there are plenty of extra batteries.

- Make sure that you have one or more radios that can run on batteries.[18]

OUTCOME. Your household will be better prepared for any emergencies, not just Y2K. Avoid going overboard; it's easy to get into a sporting goods store and drop hundreds or even thousands of dollars. Spend wisely; be frugal. You'll want to use some of that money to pay off debts, as we'll discuss in Chapter 11.

Enrolling Others

Since this is focused on home and hearth, the most important people to enroll are family members. This is an important task; don't approach it casually or arrogantly. Other family members may be more or less concerned than you are, and spending money can raise tensions considerably.

Y2K JumpStart

If you're not sure where to start, here's a quick plan to follow. Adapt and expand to meet your own needs, but do something. Check off the boxes when you're done.

❏ Go through your entire house and determine what each of the following uses:

    ❏ Heat: electricity, gas, oil, coal, wood

    ❏ Water heater: electricity, gas, oil

    ❏ Clothes dryer: electricity, gas

    ❏ Stove: electricity, gas, wood

    ❏ Oven: electricity, gas, wood

    ❏ Air conditioning: electricity, gas

    ❏ Sewage: septic tank, sewer system

❏ Go through and around your house and locate the following items. If you're not sure what you're looking for, get a friend, neighbor, or family member to help.

    ❏ Electricity: meter

    ❏ Electricity: circuit breaker panel(s) and/or fuse box(es)

    ❏ Gas: meter and master shut-off valve (usually by the meter)

    ❏ Gas: shut-off valves for each appliance that uses gas (water heater, etc.)

    ❏ Water: master shut-off valve

    ❏ Oil: tank refill pipe

❏ Buy at least two battery-powered radios. At least one of these should also run off of regular wall current; no sense using up battery power unless you have to. Both should be good enough to pull in a wide variety of local stations; try before you buy.

❏ Buy at least one flashlight for every room in the house, plus one for each car. Spend a little more and get well-made flashlights. Put each flashlight in a well-known, agreed-upon location.

❏ Buy at least one propane camping lantern and several of the small propane cartridges. Don't forget plenty of waterproof matches stored in a location that you can remember and get to in the dark. Stick a few thick, sturdy candles in with the matches, so you have something to light immediately.

❏ Buy enough batteries to have at least two complete changes of batteries for all of the radios and flashlights above.

❏ For each member of your household, build up a two-week supply of drinking water (15 gallons per person, minimum). Have a few gallons of plain laundry bleach set aside as well. If you're really ambitious, you can purchase a water filtration system, but seek advice from someone who knows about them before taking this plunge.

❏ Buy a propane camping stove, even if it's a single burner.[19] You can get these at camping, sporting goods, and military surplus stores, as well as at some department stores. Buy several of the small propane canisters. On the other hand, if you have (or get) a gas BBQ grill, you can skip the propane camping stove. Be sure to have a few extra large propane canisters for the grill.

❏ Make sure you have at least one phone that doesn't require a power outlet. For example, all portable phones (that is, those that you can carry around the house and that have a base unit) require power.

❏ If you have a mobile (cellular, digital, PCS) phone, get a car power adapter for it so that you can recharge it even if your house doesn't have power. (Note: if you have a notebook computer, you may want to do the same thing for it.)

❏ Buy and put away a large box of extra-strength trash bags to be used in case of any interruption in trash service.

❏ Do a Y2K assessment of anything in your household that allows you to set the year except for your personal computer(s). This will likely be limited to watches, VCRs, cameras, camcorders, mobile phones, and more sophisticated desk phones. Be sure to have your purchase receipts handy in case of problems; or, if you don't want to risk your device and the model is current, go to a store that sells it and ask the salesperson to let you do a Y2K rollover. In either case, set the date to December 31, 1999, and the time to 11:59 PM, then let it roll over into 2000 while using it. If it works fine and you're really ambitious, repeat the test with February 28, 2000. It should roll over into February 29th; if it rolls to March 1st, you've got a bug.

❏ If you have a PC running Windows or DOS, buy a Y2K evaluation package, such as Check 2000 ($29.95 list). Before running it, back up all your important files: documents, spreadsheets, e-mail, and so on. If they will take up lots of floppies, now would be a good time to invest in a backup device, such as a Zip™ drive. Then install and run the software according to the directions.

❏ If you have a Macintosh, don't worry about Y2K. But you may want to get a backup device for your Mac anyway.

❏   If you don't already have at least one decent bike in good
    working condition, either fix up one you already have or
    buy a new or used one.

Tips and Traps

Here are a few suggestions.

*   In purchasing battery-powered devices (lights,
    radios, etc.), try to focus on those that use C-cell
    batteries. I discovered this in the aftermath of the
    Loma Prieta quake. Within 8 hours, there was
    scarcely a D- or AA-cell battery to be found in
    the Santa Cruz area, but the stores literally had
    piles of C-cell batteries. That's because most bat-
    tery-powered devices you see these days use D-
    or AA-cells.

*   Warehouse superstores (Sam's Club, Costco,
    etc.) sell larger packs of batteries that are usually
    much cheaper than anything you'll find at the
    grocery store.

*   If you think your water service is about to be in-
    terrupted or otherwise compromised, fill every-
    thing in the house that you can with tap water;
    tubs, sinks, pots, pans, vases, and so on. It may
    seem like a pain, but if your service is cut off for
    any significant period of time, you'll be grateful.

*   If you have a large freezer, fill washed-out soda
    pop and milk bottles about 80% full of water
    and store in the freezer along side your frozen

food. In case of a power outage, these will help keep the freezer cold as well as providing some extra drinking water should that be necessary. Or you can move some or all of them to the refrigerator to help keep *that* cold instead.

• Test everything you buy at least once, and preferably as soon as you buy it. Make sure all the flashlights and radios work to your satisfaction. Try out the propane lantern. Attempt to cook (i.e., warm up) something on the propane stove. If anything doesn't work to your satisfaction, return or exchange it immediately.

Closing Thoughts

Again, the theme here is not to run off in the hills somewhere, or to spend thousands of dollars to turn your house into a self-contained fortress. The goal is to be prepared for any number of events, whether they are cause by Y2K, the latest weather-related disaster, or some poor squirrel biting into the wrong line. Above all, focus on what's practical, affordable, and able to be used for something other than Y2K problems.

9

Food and Supplies: Your Daily Bread, and More

year's supply — *Enough containers of wheat, honey, pow-*
ered milk, and dried fruit to last a family for a year. Actually,
the average family will only need a four month's supply, since
it takes one month to get hungry enough to eat that stuff, and
after four months of eating nothing else, most family members
would rather die.

—Orson Scott Card,
Saintspeak: A Mormon Dictionary

Many of the preparations touched upon in Chapter 8 are
widely accepted and understood for a variety of reasons: alternative uses (camping), efforts to cut down on utility bills (fireplaces), and preparation for severe weather or regional natural
disasters (blizzards, ice storms, hurricanes, earthquakes, and so
on). But this topic—home storage of food and other supplies—
tends to be a bit more controversial. It carries strong overtones
of survivalism, bomb shelters, nuclear holocausts, hoarding, the
end of the world as we know it (or TEOTWAWKI, as it's abbre-
viated in Y2K discussions on the Internet). And because of that,
many people who would have no problem buying a generator or
stocking up on firewood will hesitate about having extra food
set aside.

They shouldn't. *You* shouldn't. Home storage makes tremendous sense from several points of view. First, it, too, can be critical preparation for severe weather and natural disasters. Grocery shelves often empty out in advance of a hurricane, tropical storm, and blizzard; likewise, they empty quickly after unexpected events, such as earthquakes, floods, and tornadoes. New supplies can be slow coming in, due to road damage or blockage. And since such events are often associated with loss of power, water, and other utilities, the food you normally have on hand—such as in your refrigerator or freezer—may not stay edible long. Having been through both a major tropical storm (Claudette, 1979, 45 inches of rain) and a major earthquake (the Loma Prieta quake, 1989, 7.1 on the Richter scale), I can personally attest to the advantages of having home storage and the problems of being without.

Beyond that, home storage provides an economic safety net. Most people know that the Church of Jesus Christ of Latter-day Saints recommends that its members have a full year's supply of food and other necessities stored up. What most people don't know is that this recommendation has its origins not in some millennial anticipation but in the Great Depression, which also spawned the Church's extensive welfare program.[1] The goal then and now was that Latter-day Saints be self-sufficient, or receive assistance from the Church in exchange for work, and not depend upon state or federal government welfare programs. Again, I can personally attest to those benefits of home storage. Our time in the Santa Cruz Mountains included over a year of chronic underemployment while I was attempting to shift my career back to software engineering. There were weeks and even months where we got by on very little cash, living on the home storage we had built up while money was coming in.

Finally, a well-thought-out home storage plan can actually lead to eating habits that are healthier, cost less, and have less of an environmental impact. By purchasing food items in bulk and storing them in reusable containers, you save money and you reduce the amount of trash you produce. At the same time, you can shift your diet away from high-fat, high-sodium, and/or high-sugar convenience foods toward one that more closely matches the "food pyramid" recommended by the U.S. Department of Agriculture.[2]

The irony is that the most widely accepted form of food storage—having an enormous freezer, well stocked with cuts of meats, ice cream, and frozen entrees—is the one most vulnerable to disruption and loss. If you have a power outage due to weather, disasters, or just not getting the bill paid in time, you may find yourself having a major barbecue party—but there goes most of your food storage. On the other hand, the advent of shopping warehouses (Sam's Club, Costco, etc.) has broken down some of the reluctance and hassle of buying everyday food and household items in mass quantities, and has reduced the cost as well. Home storage is just the next logical step: a private shopping warehouse tailored to your family's needs and wants.

How Y2K Might Show Up in Your Pantry

While giving a presentation on Y2K contingency planning at a Fortune 100 corporation, I briefly covered the results of the WDCY2K membership survey on Y2K impact within the United States (see Appendix B). I explained the 0 to 10 scale used in the survey, describing each level. When I got to level 10, which included collapse of the U.S. government and possible famine, one of the listeners snorted—not at the idea of the government collapsing, but at the idea of having famine here in the United States, much less it somehow being caused by Y2K. After pointing out that level 10 was *intended* to be extreme, I then briefly summarized some of the ways in which Y2K could impact food production and delivery in this country and the world:

- Production and delivery of agricultural chemicals, including fertilizers and pesticides

- Production and delivery of hybrid seeds

- Production, delivery, and operation of farm equipment, including spare parts, fuel, and lubricants

- Computer and embedded systems' control of irrigation systems and storage facilities

- Interruption of power, water, natural gas, phone, or other services to farms, food processing companies, warehousing firms, and grocery stores

- Difficulty of farmers getting loans due to banks' own Y2K problems as well as a general recession

- Interruptions and delays in transportation systems, especially trains

- The whole spectrum of Y2K problems within food processing firms, especially embedded systems within the food processing equipment

- Y2K problems in transportation, communication, and storage in the food warehousing and grocery store network

This list alone should be enough to underscore that the possibility of Y2K-induced shortages and/or price hikes at the local supermarket isn't far-fetched. We see such shortages and price jumps now when bad weather or natural disasters impact crops, when food producers renegotiate prices, or when labor disputes disrupt the normal grocery supply chain. Why is it so hard to believe that Y2K events could have a similar impact?

A parallel set of factors applies to the household items and consumer goods we take for granted every day. Instead of food production, that chain depends upon production of fibers and skins, metals and plastics, rubber, wood, and pulp. But all the same weak spots exist in one form or another. We have become so accustomed to low inflation, inexpensive imports, and constant competition that we presume that things must, of course, always continue to work that way. In so doing, we ignore both our own past as well as the present circumstances of much of the world. We have no guarantee that things will go on as well as they have except for our own blithe assumption and desire. It's a classic logical fallacy—I want it this way, therefore it must be so—that keeps us blindly moving ahead until reality intervenes, sometimes harshly.

One last major factor is public reaction to and/or anticipation of these factors and their consequences. That factor predominates when a hurricane or blizzard threatens; it's not the weather that makes milk (in the north), water (in the south), and bread (both places) vanish from store shelves in a few hours. It's a dramatic surge in demand, anticipating shortages caused by the weather and the demand itself. The most dramatic example, though, occurred in December 1973. This was right in the middle of the OPEC oil embargo and subsequent gas shortages, which had started back in October. One evening, during his monologue on the "Tonight Show," Johnny Carson cracked a joke about how the United States was facing an even more critical shortage: toilet paper. Of course, there was no such shortage, but the next day, people panicked about running out of toilet paper and quickly emptied store shelves of it. That, of course, merely confirmed the shortage and fueled the panic even more. This continued for nearly three weeks, despite an apology and retraction by Carson and ads by the paper companies.[3]

This may seem a bit far-fetched, but the psychology isn't all that different from what drives the various financial markets. And the effect is already setting in with regards to Y2K. Manufacturers of home storage food products—vacuum-sealed, freeze-dried, and the like—were already reporting backlogs measured in months as of October 1998. Part is just the demand rising above the relatively low level that has existed up until now. But people aware of the backlog are hurrying to put their orders in, driving demand even more past supply.

Again, the response is: Don't panic. You may not need or want home storage. If you do, you may not need or want these specialized products. Read through the points in this chapter and think carefully about what your needs and concerns are. And then decide.

If you do decide on home storage, what should you store? The basic answer: what you need and what you can. This seems obvious, but it's important to consider this carefully. Many books and Web sites on home storage, as well as many home storage vendors, prescribe a standard set of items that sometimes have little bearing on your particular circumstances. It's important that you think carefully about what you'll need and what you'll use; otherwise, you may pay too much for supplies that do you no good. Let's talk about the biggest set of challenges—those involving food storage—and then touch upon other items that you may want to store.

Storing Food: Issues and Challenges

Having dealt with water back in Chapter 8, we turn to the next essential: food. The goal is to be able to go for some period of time buying few if any groceries because you don't have the money, you cannot get to the store, or the store doesn't have what you need. In a food storage program's simplest form, you would just buy more than usual of what you normally would. Based on your circumstances, concerns, and habits, that might work just fine. But most of us would run into one or more problems with that approach.

I've know families who have lived in the same house for over 30 years, who have a large basement with built-in shelves dedicated to home storage. On the other hand, I've known retirees and single moms living in small apartments on fixed incomes who have a hard time keeping food in the refrigerator. Conditions, circumstances, needs, and resources vary. We may not be able to prepare in the manner we'd like, so we have to be willing to prepare in the way we can. Let's look at some of the issues and challenges involved with food storage.

Planning

The very first question you must ask yourself is how much of a food supply you want, and what events (Y2K or otherwise) do you want it to serve? Suppose you live by yourself and just want to be able to get by for a month or so with minimal grocery shopping should you find yourself between jobs. Your food storage plan will be quite different from that of someone setting up a year's supply of food for a family of six with a presumption of on-going power interruptions and no real access to the grocery store.

Questions you must answer to help plan your food storage include

- How many people is this for?

- How much do they eat?

- How long do I want this to last?

- How much money do I assume will be available for grocery shopping during that period?

- What foods and other goods do I assume will be available (or not) during that period?

- What external events do I think might impact food production and availability?

- What events do I think might impact in-house food preparation?

- What do I really want to eat? How about the rest of the family?

- Are there any dietary/health restrictions or requirements?

Your fundamental plan rests upon the first three bulleted items: the number of people, how much they eat, and how long this is to last. For example, a teenage boy can eat as much as several younger children. The Y2K JumpStart section later in this chapter has you monitor what is currently being consumed so that you have some real idea of the scope of what you're tackling. But it's more than just the volume. As noted above, if you're just taking care of yourself for a month or so, a single trip to a shopping warehouse can probably load you up with enough canned and packaged foods to get by.

The next three questions have a key impact on what you choose to store. For example, if you presume that you'll be able to buy and keep fresh milk, eggs, cheese, and other refrigerated items, then you don't have to worry about stocking up on their equivalents; ditto for fresh fruits and vegetables, meat, poultry, and so on. If, on the other hand, you feel these items might not be available or affordable, then you'll likely want to get powered milk, freeze-dried fruits and vegetables, and TVP (Textured Vegetable Protein) products for your storage.

Your food storage needs to match your expectations of external events that might impact food preparation. If you choose to store wheat to make bread, what will you do if power interruptions make it hard to grind the wheat into flour and then bake it in your oven? If you have dehydrated foods, have you ensured enough of a water supply to prepare them? Do you have a few spare can openers?

The last two questions should not be ignored or dismissed. The quote at the start of the chapter touches lightly on a serious fact: Eating food you cannot stand for weeks or months at a time can have a profound negative impact on the psychological and, ultimately, physical well-being of family members. At the same time, you need to ensure that what you store and plan on eating won't cause or aggravate existing health problems. If someone in the family is diabetic, you need to ensure that they have a sufficient store of the right foods. If someone else is allergic to, say, wheat, then you need to provide alternatives.

Finances

Money is usually the first constraint or, at least, concern. If you're having a hard time making ends meet—and especially if you're trying to reduce your debts (as recommended in Chapter 11[4])—then how are you going to find the money to buy more groceries than you're using?

The problem is real. But I also know first-hand that most of us could get by spending less on groceries—and many other items—than we do. There were times, living in the Santa Cruz mountains that Sandra and I would go to the grocery store with $20 to $40 and have to do a week's worth of shopping for a family of nine. It was a major indulgence to buy an extra half-pound of ground beef and fix the two of us grilled hamburgers for a "lunch in" together. Nowadays, I find myself dropping $20-$40 on a single "junk run" to the grocery store to pick up various treats for a much smaller family. For that matter, Sandra and I spend more going out to dinner and a movie than we spent at times back then in a whole month's worth of grocery shopping.

In short, chances are if you're honest with yourself, you can probably find similar places to economize. On the other hand, it is almost certainly a bad idea to go into debt for home storage. That added financial burden is a more likely Y2K risk than not having all the food storage that you think you should have. Your best bet is to scale your plans to fit what you can afford. If nothing else, you should be able to put together a 72-hour plan, which we'll discuss later in the chapter.

Storage Space

The next question you have to wrestle with is where to put this. Storage space available within a detached house, townhouse, condominium, or apartment can vary widely depending upon region, zoning, and architect. Some places have attics, some have basements, some have lots of closets, and some—including larger homes—have surprisingly little storage space at all. Most have garages. The amount you need will depend upon the (number of people) x (how much they eat) x (period of time) calculation you did above and so could vary from the existing cupboards in the kitchen to a storage locker or tool shed. Some enterprising souls have built furniture on top of or around food storage containers.

Climate and Preservation

Given the investment you are making in this food storage, you need to be sure that it stores well. Several factors are at work here. First are the quality and nature of the food itself. Food that is dry or dried tends to store better and longer than food that is moist and/or fresh. A simple, if obvious, example is that low-moisture whole wheat stores better than flour, which stores better than baked goods.

Second is the manner in which the food is stored. Low-moisture whole wheat stored in an airtight container or metal can, possibly vacuum-sealed or filled with nitrogen, will store better than whole wheat sitting in a burlap sack.

Third is the climate where the food is stored. Food products kept in a cool, dry basement or pantry will last better and longer than those kept somewhere where there are greater temperature and humidity extremes. This is a challenge we face. Our house doesn't have much storage space except in the garage. But the temperature in there was easily 120 degrees most days during the extended heat wave last summer, and I suspect it will get quite cold in there come winter.

Independent of these factors, you should avoid buying food storage and then let it sit unused for months or years. All food will lose quality and nutritional value with time. Ideally, you should rotate your food storage; that is, you should be living on it, at least in part, consuming the oldest items while replacing them with new. (Dating your stored food is a very good idea.) Rotation not only ensures that your stored food remains fresh, it also ensures that you know how to use what you've stored and that you're used to eating it—which brings us to the next point.

Food Preparation

You have to be able to prepare and serve the food that you've stored. This may seem a bit obvious or simple, and it is. But some people store wheat with no real idea of how they would actually fix and eat it should they need to. I think they had some vague notion of boiling it into cereal or sprouting it. While it is true that people will eat just about anything if they get hungry enough, that's probably not the standard of living you're hoping for, even in an emergency.

Shortages

As noted above, backlogs and shortages already exist for a lot of the prepackaged food storage items. Assuming that you're interested in these products, don't be overly concerned about the backlogs. Unless you're reading this fairly late in 1999, you still have plenty of time to order and receive those products.

On the other hand, if you do choose to build up your food storage, don't wait until November or December 1999. At that point, there may be enough spot shortages of things you'd like but you may not get them until after Y2K.

Other Things to Store

Man and woman do not live by bread alone. There are other consumables that we go through on a regular basis that you would probably not want to be without. Virtually all of these have the advantage over food of not requiring special storage or preparation. And, as with food, your decision of how much to store (if at all) depends upon your circumstances and what you anticipate might happen.

Let's take a quick look at what you should consider storing if you do decide to do so.

Bathroom Supplies, Personal Hygiene, and Grooming

Again, the advent of warehouse stores has made this already a way of life for many people. We go and find ourselves buying essentials such as soap, toothbrushes, toothpaste, mouthwash, toilet paper, tissue paper, cotton balls and swabs, deodorant, shampoo, and various feminine hygiene products in larger containers or multiples of the regular sizes. All home storage entails is buying more of these jumbo sizes/ assortments than you do currently. As mentioned in Chapter 7, you'll want to make similar preparations for basic over-the-counter medical supplies—not just first aid, but pain relievers, cold remedies, antacids, rubbing alcohol, hydrogen peroxide, and so on. And you may want to stock up on basic grooming supplies, including hair sprays, cosmetics, and other items that you'd just as soon not be without.

Laundry and Kitchen Supplies

Those of you who have been through natural disasters know how tedious and difficult the cleanup afterward can be, and how quickly you run out of cleaning supplies. Laundry detergent is important, but bleach—the all-purpose disinfectant—is even more so. All-purpose cleaners, soap both for washing dishes and for electric dishwashers, paper towels, dishtowels and dishrags, cleansing powders, glass and surface cleaners, and the rest will help to keep things clean.

Clothing

Most of us have more clothing and shoes than we ever wear anyway; we could probably go for months or even a year or two without buying more if we had to. But if there are serious gaps in your wardrobe—maybe you're overdue for a new suit or dress shoes—it might not be a bad idea to fill them in sooner rather than later. What you do want to consider storing are the items that you "consume": briefs, boxers, T-shirts, bras, lingerie, socks, nylons, and so on.

The 90% Solution:
Putting Together a 72-Hour Plan

A simple lesson has come out of various natural and man-made disasters: Life usually stabilizes and gets back to a semblance of normalcy within 72 hours. That doesn't mean that your house, flattened by a hurricane or earthquake, magically springs back up. But it does mean that by then the network of personal, community, and government resources has responded enough to help those in need. The trick, then, is getting through those first 72 hours.

Because of this, various organizations from the American Red Cross on down recommend putting together a disaster supplies kit to get through those first three days.[5] Several approaches exist; one of the most popular is to assemble "72-hour kits" for the family. This is usually a backpack or shoulder bag that contains food, water, and other essentials to support one person for that period of time. In case of disaster or emergency, each family member grabs his or her kit and can leave via car, bike, skateboard, or on foot. Another variant is a larger container that can be thrown into the back of a car and that can support four or five people for three days.

Our family had a real-life alert with our 72-hour kits, a few years ago. A large brush fire broke out in the San Diego suburb where we were living. Two ridges of dry, highly flammable brush and one row of houses were all that lay between us and the fire, and the fire was moving our way. Tanker planes dumping water on the fire were flying directly over our house, just a hundred or so feet up. I had two of the kids up on the roof, hosing it down in case sparks blew our way, while Sandra and I loaded up the car with our 72-hour kits, critical papers, and a large suitcase in which we keep all our irreplaceable family photos and negatives. The fire had crested one ridge; if it crested the second and headed down towards us, we would have hopped in the car and evacuated.[6] The firefighters, however, stopped its progress, and we didn't have to leave.

These kits provide an approach that just about anyone reading this book can afford and carry out and that has use outside of the scope of Y2K. Given the degree of mobilization that is likely to be in place to deal with Y2K events, most situations that arise are likely to stabilize within three days. So creating a 72-hour plan, with 72-hour kits for your family, will help increase your family's general emergency preparedness as well as ensuring that you can handle the majority of Y2K impacts, if any, that you are likely to experience.

Any number of companies will sell you prepackaged 72-hour kits at prices ranging from $40 to a few hundred dollars each. Beyond that, many Web sites discuss what a 72-hour kit should and could contain. The idea is pretty simple: Get a sturdy school-size backpack for each person and fill it with the following items:

- Nine meals. You can decide how to put these together, but your best bet is probably to use camping food or MREs (meals ready to eat) purchased at sporting or surplus stores. They have a better shelf life.

- Nine (at least) sealed water pouches. These usually hold about a half-cup each. Again, you can buy these from a number of sources. Alternately, you can wash out a two-liter pop bottle and fill it with water.

- Some high-energy snacks, as well as hard candies.[7]

- A lightweight folded thermal "space blanket" and a lightweight poncho.

- A change of underwear and socks; if space permits, also a warm shirt and a pair of long pants.

- A small first-aid kit, lighter, candle, flashlight, whistle, Sierra cup, and pocketknife.

- Paper or note cards, pencil, pen, and a paperback book to read.

- Travel-size toothbrush, toothpaste, liquid soap, packaged hand wipes, comb.

- A half-roll of toilet paper (i.e., when a roll in the house starts getting low, replace it and put it in someone's 72-hour kit).

You can adjust and adapt based on your needs, preferences, and budget, but you get the idea.

Food and Supplies: Plan of Action

This is likely to be your single greatest challenge. To build up your home storage of food and other items will require more time, money, thought, planning, and storage space than any of your other Y2K efforts. The good news is that you and your family should be able to eat or otherwise use everything you get.

Educating Yourself

Most of us have a very set manner in which we buy, store, and prepare food. For many of us, that manner is based on frequent trips to the grocery store, heavy use of prepared foods, and the assumption that we can store perishables in the refrigerator and replace them as they get too old. Home storage requires a different mindset and approach to eating. If you don't recognize and reconcile these differences, you and your family may run into serious problems should you have to rely upon what you have stored.

ACTION. Do research into home storage. Again, the Web is a good starting point. Sites on home storage have been out there for some time, but Y2K has brought a new emphasis. Some books on the subject also exist; check out the Resources section at the end of this book.

OUTCOME. You should have a better idea of just what home storage of food and other supplies could entail.

Identifying Risks and Corresponding Mitigations

We're now into the usual drill.

ACTION. Fill at the risks chart based on your own concerns.

Risk/Symptom	Prob.	Impact	Possible Mitigations	Issues
Shortages of food			Home storage of food	Space, money, diet, preservation, preparation
Shortages of key household items (hygiene, cleaning, other)			Home storage of key items	Space, money
Power disruptions causing food in refrigerator, freezer to spoil			Home storage of non-refrigerated food; generator	Fuel for generator; what to do with food

OUTCOME. These risks and the mitigations are fairly well known; see if you can come up with some new ones.

Looking for Opportunities

As in Chapter 8, your opportunity here may be to make a shift in your consumption habits to lower costs, eat better, and create less trash.

ACTION. Take note of the trash currently generated by your family in its food consumption. Look for ways in which it can be reduced, either by purchasing food in bulk or by changing what you eat.

OUTCOME. As you cut down on the trash you are generating, you are likely to find yourself saving money and eating better as well.

Establishing Guiding Principles

These principles will help as gentle reminders when you question just why you're doing all this.

ACTION. Here are just a few guiding principles related to the risks and opportunities in this area. For example,

1. Grocery money should go toward food, not paper and plastic.

2. Use it up, wear it out, make it do, or do without.

3. It may not be much, but at least it's not SPAM®.

OUTCOME. Humor may be even more critical here. We tend to get cranky when we don't get the food we want and expect.

Determining What You Need

In this case, it literally is what you need: what you are going to eat or otherwise consume.

ACTION. Figure out what your anticipated duration is, how many people need to be fed, and what special considerations you might have. For each person, figure out the basics for one month, including

- Meals and snacks

- Beverages

- Bathroom supplies

- Other needs

Now, for the entire group as a whole, figure out the group basics for one month, including

- Cooking and baking basics (oils, yeast, herbs and spices, etc.)

- Laundry and cleaning supplies

Now multiply this by the number of months that you want your storage to last.

OUTCOME. You should have a rough idea of the scope of what you are proposing to store.

Creating the Plan

Take your time in doing this. Start out simple and work up from there. The virtue of home storage is that it's easy for you to scale up as money, space, and time permit.

ACTION. Put together a first-draft plan for home storage.

- Evaluate your current consumption of food and other supplies.

- Determine what your (initial) level of concern is: 72 hours, a week, a month, three months, and so on.

- Examine your life and figure out what the impact would be in terms of money and storage conditions.

OUTCOME. From your plan, create a shopping list of what you intend to buy. Each time you do grocery shopping, buy and set aside some of the items on the list.

Enrolling Others

Eating habits and preferences are highly personal. Every parent knows the challenges of getting kids at any age to eat what you have prepared, even (or especially) if it's what you prepared and they loved the night before. This effort may involve some definite changes in eating patterns and habits. If so, you will be far better off getting the other family members enrolled ahead of time.

ACTION. Sit down as a family (even if that's just two of you) and discuss the factor behind starting up a home storage program. Note in particular disagreements in priorities, approach, or food preferences.

OUTCOME. With patience and understanding, you will all be largely in agreement on both the need and approach for home storage.

Y2K JumpStart

If you're feeling a bit overwhelmed by all this, here's a simple start.

❏   Put together (or buy) a 72-hour kit for each family member.

If you want to move beyond that, here's the next set of steps.

❏   Monitor your family's eating and grocery shopping habits for two to four weeks. Don't worry if your log isn't 100% (or even 80%) complete or accurate; the goal is to just get a sense of what the family is eating. Track especially the following categories:

   ❏   Bread, cereal, rice, and pasta

   ❏   Vegetables; where possible, note canned versus fresh versus frozen

   ❏   Fruits; again, note canned, fresh, or frozen

   ❏   Dairy products: milk, cheese, yogurt, butter

   ❏   Other proteins: meat, poultry, fish, beans, eggs, and nuts

   ❏   Fats, oils, sweets

❏   During the same period or a similar one, note consumption rate for the following:

   ❏   Toilet paper

   ❏   Tampons, pads, and other feminine hygiene products

   ❏   Soap, shampoo, and other cleansing products

   ❏   Cosmetics and grooming products

❏   Based on this information, create a "template" for each
      family member, showing how much they consume during
      a typical month. This gives you a baseline of what you
      have to maintain or replace.

❏   Build up a one-month supply for each person. For items
      that normally have to be refrigerated or frozen, buy room-
      temperature equivalents or replacements (e.g., powered or
      sterilized milk).

❏   Start rotating the stock, that is, using what you've stored
      and then replacing it.

Tips and Traps

Vicky Tate, author of the book *Cooking with Home Storage*,[8]
published an article entitled "Seven Major Mistakes in Food
Storage," which has been posted in several places on the Web;
here's a synopsis.[9]

- Not having enough variety in your storage.
  Don't load up on wheat, sugar or honey, and
  powdered milk without thinking about what it
  would be like to eat that for months on end. Be
  sure to include spices and flavorings.

- Only focusing on one type of food storage (e.g.,
  bulk items). Use freeze-dried and canned foods
  as well, and be sure to include baking necessities
  (oil, yeast, baking power and soda, shortening).

- Not including vitamins, especially for kids.

- Not having quick and easy "psychological" foods. These include snacks, desserts, fun meals, and other indulgences.

- Not keeping the food storage balanced. If you're trying to build a three-month supply, don't buy three months of one item, then three months of another, and so on. Build a one-month's supply of everything, and then move on to a two-months' supply, and so on.

- Not properly storing foods. If you buy a 25- or 50-lb. sack of flour or sugar at the local shopping warehouse and throw it in a corner of your garage, you're likely to be very disappointed when you go to use it some months later. Invest in quality storage containers.

- Not using the food you store. As you build up your food storage, you should actually start using it to some extent, replacing what you use as well as continuing to add to it. This will not only provide very real feedback about how feasible your storage is, it will also soften the "culinary shock" if you do have to switch abruptly from your current eating habits to living on food storage.

To these I would add a few tips of my own:

- Replace what you use as soon as possible. This is especially important for nonfood items (toilet paper, etc.), which are usually far easier to get into than food items.

- As you rotate through the food you're storing, look for the items you avoid or never use. Make a deliberate effort to use them. If you just cannot or don't want to, then they probably shouldn't be in your storage. Find something that you are willing to use that will replace them.

- For food that isn't in presealed containers (cans, cartons, etc.), check it monthly for spoilage or infestation. It can be very disheartening to go to get some flour and find bugs crawling through it.

Closing Thoughts

It is very convenient (provided one has the money) to plunk down several hundred to several thousand dollars and buy a configuration of foods packaged for long-term storage. However, that's a solution that many of us cannot afford; even if we could, we might be hard pressed to make the transition to eating it. Instead, maintain the idea of a private warehouse supermarket that you keep stocked and which you can live on should circumstances—employment, the economy, bad weather, natural disasters, or Y2K—dictate.

Work: Nine to Five in 2000

I don't like work—no man does—but I like what is in work—the chance to find yourself.
—Joseph Conrad, *Heart of Darkness*

With all the focus on power, water, transportation, and food, it's easy to overlook where Y2K will likely have its largest impact: on working people. The global economy has been faltering for well over a year, the stock market indices have become volatile, and Fed Chairman Alan Greenspan has cut interest rates multiple times in an attempt to forestall a U.S. recession. Into this weakened setting comes Y2K, like a new strain of flu introduced into a weakened and exhausted population. It remains to be seen whether the "flu shots" of Y2K remediation around the world have been sufficient and in time, but Y2K can only make things worse.

The bottom line: If you work, then your job may be affected directly or indirectly by Y2K. This is true whether you work for the U.S. government, a Fortune 500 corporation, state and local governments, a nonprofit organization, a small- to medium enterprise (SME), or even yourself. Because of that, you need to be aware of how well prepared your employer is for Y2K. You also need to look carefully at what influence Y2K might or should have on your career choices, job hunting, and training.

Potential Y2K Impacts on Employment

Many books and a vast number of articles have been written on Y2K's impact on organizations and the efforts required to carry out Y2K remediation. In the space of just a few years, Y2K has gone from being a nuisance for CEOs, agency directors, and cabinet members to being their top priority. The Internal Revenue Service expects to spend close to $1 billion; U.S. Postal Service and AT&T, around $500 million each; Merrill Lynch, $375 million. That's not nuisance money.

This raises the first possible impact of Y2K. Those vast sums of money aren't coming out of thin air, not even (or especially) within the federal government. Each dollar spent on Y2K is a dollar less spent elsewhere or else a dollar less in profits. And that can affect positions elsewhere in an organization.

For example, Merrill Lynch announced significant layoffs in mid-October 1998, in the wake of the declining stock market: 3400 full-time employees and 900 consultants. However, Merrill Lynch noted that the consultants released worked primarily on non-Y2K technology projects, and that it was slowing work on such projects while maintaining focus on Y2K and Euro conversion.[1] It is not unreasonable to conclude that were it not for Y2K many of those consultants would still be working at Merrill Lynch on projects that would be getting more resources and attention than they are now.

This brings us to the second possible impact. The need to do Y2K remediation has caused many organizations to slow down or put on hold non-Y2K projects. Several reasons lead to this. The company may have to divert funds to its Y2K effort.

It may have to divert development resources as well. It may want to stop those projects until after Y2K remediation is done so that the existing source code base isn't being changed in the middle of repair and testing. Or it may be all three reasons. In any case, it does mean that employees and managers associated with those projects may find themselves treading water, drafted into Y2K work, or shown the door.

Third, as we approach the Y2K crossover, internal Y2K problems may arise from systems that weren't repaired in time or tested sufficiently. This could have an operational impact on the company, causing processing plants, assembly lines, or company divisions to go into a crisis mode, slow down, or even shut down for a while. That, it turn, could impact employees at all levels.

But fourth, as has been cited repeatedly, even if your firm is 100 percent ready for Y2K, it may still be at the mercy of all its suppliers, customers, partners, and all the other organizations that impact its business operations and profitability. Consider the General Motors shutdown of June-July 1998, caused by strikes at just two supply plants. By the time the strikes were settled, GM had shut down 27 of its 29 North American assembly plants, idled nearly 200,000 workers, and lost over $2.5 billion.[2] If there were alternative sources for the metal stamping done at one plant and the parts at the other, GM would have used them. Dependencies such as these exist at all levels; few are perhaps as drastic, but the impact on the business can be very real nevertheless. Remember: 200,000 people don't have to be laid off for you to be affected. It can be just one person: you.

Fifth, the overall economy could slow down as a consequence of Y2K problems, here and abroad. Frankly, the global economy is quite shaky right now (October 1998) as it is, with

Asia threatening to slide from recession into depression, Russia's economy in free fall, and economic tremors coming from South America. If your employer depends upon firms from those countries, you may already be feeling the pain, and Y2 could only make things worse.

At this point, you may be looking back at Chapter 9 and rereading the part that talks about home storage as a hedge against unemployment. But here's something to remember: Even at the height of the Great Depression, two-thirds of non-farm workers had jobs.[3] It's highly unlikely that we're looking at anything like that. Even with what would be considered a severe recession here in the United States, employment would be at 90 percent or better. The key here is to be informed about the Y2K status of your employer (or, if you run or own a business, your own business) and to understand how Y2K can impact it. That's what the next section is about.

While some firms, such as Merrill Lynch, are capable of swallowing the cost of the Y2K investment, other less stable companies or those companies that are simply unprepared or unaware of their exposure, may lose business and find themselves in financial jeopardy. This chapter is devoted to making you aware of this possibility so that you may evaluate your course of action.

Determining Your Employer's Y2K Status

This section isn't intended to explain how to do a Y2K assessment of your firm; we all hope that has been done by now. Instead, it's meant to help you nose around and get a sense of what progress is actually being made.

(Note: Through all this I'll refer to "your firm" as if you were working for a business. However, most of this applies just as well if you work for a government agency, a branch of the military, an educational institution, or some other organization.)

General Approach to Snooping Around

You're going to have to do the legwork, but here are some suggestions:

- Your firm should have someone in charge of Y2K. Find out who it is and find out what people generally think of them. Get to know that person. Find out the organizations they run. Get to know people on it, particularly one or two levels down.

- Your firm's Y2K group should be producing a report on internal Y2K progress on a regular basis. Get your hands on a copy. For a specific department/division/whatever in the report, find some folks doing the actual work in the trenches and see how their assessment measures what's being reported.

- Your firm may have an internal Y2K Web site and/or newsletter. Read both.

- Your firm may be compelled to make disclosures on its Y2K progress. For example, the Securities Exchange Commission (SEC) requires public corporations to disclose the financial impact of Y2K remediation in 10Q and 10E statements; a searchable database of these Y2K disclosures is available on-line.[4] Likewise, federal departments and agencies have to report to the OMB their estimates on Y2K progress and schedule.[5]

Internal Applications and Infrastructure

Information technology within your company is where most honest-to-goodness Y2K problems lie. The list of technologies to be assessed is long, perhaps depressingly so. It includes (but isn't limited to)

- All computers, from hand-helds to mainframes

- The operating systems and system utilities

- The networking hardware and supporting software, including network operating systems and protocols

- Specialized third-party hardware systems, within accompanying software

- Databases, supporting server utilities and applications

- All the various forms of middleware

- Third-party productivity applications, including office automation

- Software development tools and libraries

- Software utilities and applications developed for your firm by outside parties

- Software utilities and applications developed within your firm

- Control systems (embedded or not) in key manufacturing, processing, monitoring, and transportation equipment

And so on, and so forth. This is where your organization is probably spending the vast majority of its Y2K budget, not to mention most of its time. However, the remaining items shouldn't be neglected.

GOOD SIGNS: Repairs are complete and testing is well underway, preferably on dedicated hardware. Status reports are made weekly. The CEO heads up the Y2K steering committee. The engineers doing the testing are bored because almost everything passes. A significant percentage of applications have passed testing and are back in production. Application development and revision have been slowed down or halted until Y2K is done.

BAD SIGNS: Inventory and assessment are still going on. People are talking about replacing noncompliant systems. Testing only makes up 30 percent or less of the entire Y2K schedule. There is no one person in charge of Y2K. Department heads are using Y2K resources to add functionality to existing applications or, worse yet, write new ones. Y2K testing is being done on production systems nights and weekends. Your company plans to spend more money in 1999 on Y2K than it could possibly spend in that period.[6]

Internal Operations, Staffing, and Business Processes

Independent of the IT infrastructure, your firm operates within a physical setting: buildings, offices, lights, heating, cooling, phones, security systems, and so on. There are potential Y2K problems within that setting; most are at best annoying, though problems with the heating system in mid-winter would be less than amusing in many parts of the country.

Concerns about Y2K could lead many people to stay home or vacation with friends and relatives in warmer and/or more isolated climes. Others may simply choose to stay home to see what all is happening. This could cause problems with staffing at the end of 1999, at a time when having the right staff on hand may be critical. Many organizations have already established policies prohibiting vacation time during the Y2K crossover for staff members deemed "critical."

Key business processes within your firm depend upon a coordinated sequence of actions, events, and responses to work toward its core business goals. As a rule, these require that all of the above be in place and working reasonably well.

GOOD SIGNS: An active Y2K contingency planning effort exists and is focused on more than just whether the IT stuff above will work. Human Resources is already doing Y2K planning.

BAD SIGNS: The rest of the firm sees Y2K as being just an IT problem. No contingency planning is being done, except to have SWAT teams to hurry and fixed missed Y2K defects (or new ones introduced in the repair process).

External Interfaces, Partners, Customers

Many of your computer systems will communicate with systems outside of your firm. They will do this via direct wire or fiber-optic connections, phone lines, microwave signals, and other media. They will also do it via punched cards, magnetic tape, diskettes, portable hard drives, and various other forms of storage. As your systems become Y2K compliant, they have to continue to work with programs via interfaces and data format standards that may or may not be in agreement.

Likewise, your company usually conducts business in cooperation with some number of other organizations, coordinating efforts, exchanging information on a variety of levels, and working toward shared goals. Y2K disruptions among those partners impact the function of your company.

Continued existence usually depends upon enough customers giving your organization money in exchange for services. If those customers are unwilling (because of economic conditions) or unable (because of their own Y2K problems) to buy your goods and services, then you face your own cash flow and credibility problems.

GOOD SIGNS: A complete list of external interfaces exists, showing the type of data interchange (file in, file out, direct connection), the external parties involved, and any Y2K issues. Your firm has contacted and is working with each of the external parties. Y2K contingency planning is dealing with "what if?" scenarios centered on Y2K problems with partners and customers.

BAD SIGNS: No one person knows and has documented all the external interfaces. Form letters have been sent out with no follow-up. Each division is on its own for Y2K contingency planning. People in your firm accept at face value the assurances of partners and customers that they will be Y2K compliant.

External Supply Chain

Your company depends on many other firms for goods and services that it cannot or chooses not to produce for itself. Some are more critical than others; as noted in the General Motors strike, even just a plant or two can bring the entire company to a halt. So even if all your Y2K repair efforts are done, you are still vulnerable to how your suppliers are doing. And even if they are all done, they are vulnerable to their suppliers, and so on.

You cannot force your suppliers to be compliant on schedule, especially when your firm may be struggling with that also. But your firm—and you—can attempt to find out as much as you can about how suppliers are doing. Your firm should then make contingency plans should key suppliers be unable to deliver.

GOOD SIGNS: Someone has analyzed the firm's financial records, built a list of everyone to whom the firm pays money, analyzed that list to see who is critical and who isn't, and started contacting or visiting the critical ones.

BAD SIGNS: Someone has made a dozen or so phone calls (or sent out several dozen letters) to suppliers, but there has been no follow-up. No one can definitively say who your suppliers are, much less which are critical. No one is very worried.

External Infrastructure

We've talked enough in other chapters about the Iron Triangle of infrastructure: power, water, and telecom. Any problems or disruptions for more than a few hours could become serious enough to shut down commercial operations in affected parts of the company. Likewise, other infrastructure disruptions, such as in transportation, could have a serious impact on the organization.

GOOD SIGNS: The firm already has business continuity plans and is extending or adapting them.

BAD SIGNS: The firm doesn't have business continuity plans. Or the firm has business continuity plans and considers them to be the entire Y2K contingency plans.

Legal, Liability, and Market Issues

This remains the true wild card for each organization facing Y2K issues. For a publicly traded corporation whose stock suffers because of its own Y2K problems, there remains the specter of class action shareholder lawsuits on the quite accurate grounds that this problem has been known for years without repairs being started.

GOOD SIGNS: The firm's legal department is an integral part of the Y2K contingency planning team. It is providing guidance to the Y2K team's public announcements and interactions with outside firms, but does not get in the way. Your firm is looking long and hard at how its assets and sources of income might be impacted by Y2K and is taking steps to reduce that risk or cushion the blow.

BAD SIGNS: Legal has not a clue about Y2K and/or legal is absolutely refusing to let anyone else in the firm say anything concrete, pro or con, to the firm's various partners and customers or to the public at large. The firm seems clueless or unconcerned about possible Y2K impact on its income and assets.

Making the Evaluation

The scope and breadth of the set of possible firms, as well as the variety of complex factors involved, suggests that there's no easy, mathematical way to combine these results into a score. But that won't stop us. Here's a quick and dirty scoring method:

- Assuming you're reading this in 1999, start with a negative score equal to two times the value of the month (Jan = –2, Feb =–4, Mar = –6, and so on).

- Add one for each major good sign that you find.

- Subtract three for each major bad sign that you
  find.

If your score is negative, your firm is in trouble. The more
negative it is, the bigger the trouble.

Job Moves and Career Plans

So now that you have an idea about how your firm is doing
with Y2K, two questions arise: How will that impact you, and
what are you going to do about it? Let's take a look at those
questions and how you might answer them.

Y2K and You

You face a spectrum of outcomes with your job based on
how Y2K affects your firm. Here's a rundown on the possibilities where you have no real involvement in your firm's Y2K
remediation effort:

- New opportunities open up for you. Because of
  other people being drawn into the firm's Y2K effort, you have the chance to work on new
  projects and technologies, and you may be given
  even more responsibility.

- Your future becomes brighter. Your firm has
  done a good job on Y2K and is reaping the rewards of better competition, public confidence,
  and freed-up resources. Or your firm is suffering
  from Y2K impacts, but sees you as a critical asset
  to help recover and wants to be sure you stay.

- Nothing happens. Whatever impact Y2K has on your firm (if any), it doesn't impact you.

- Your future becomes darker. Your firm is behind on Y2K, and it doesn't look good. Or your firm is cutting back on raises, promotions, and benefits because of costs and other issues connected to Y2K. Or it becomes increasingly apparent that Y2K events outside the firm may have a major impact on your firm's profits, growth, or even existence.

- You find yourself cut back to part time, laid off, or otherwise asked to leave. Your firm's Y2K expenditures and/or external economic or operational factors connected to Y2K have forced the firm to reduce costs, either temporarily or permanently.

Here are some possibilities if you are actually involved in the Y2K effort:

- You are a Y2K hero. You end up working part or full time on Y2K, and your firm is so grateful for the job that's done (by you personally or by the Y2K team as a whole) that they give you monetary and/or career rewards, such as a promotion, your choice of projects, and/or training in some new fields.

- You use Y2K as a bridge to a new career path. Working on Y2K in your firm allows you to move into a new field of interest to you (project management, configuration management, test automation), and you continue in that field when the Y2K work is done. Or you find yourself hired as a consultant by other firms for your expertise, either with key legacy technologies or with Y2K itself.

- You have a Y2K detour. You end up working part or full time on Y2K efforts within your firm for some duration, then go back to what you were doing before, coming back up to speed with what you left behind.

- You hit a Y2K slow zone or dead end. You end up working full-time on Y2K efforts, but when you're done, your old position/project/career track/technology initiative doesn't exist or has been taken over by someone else. Your firm isn't quite sure what to do with you or, worse yet, it is, and that involves your departure.

- You have a Y2K crash landing. You are part of the Y2K team, and your project doesn't finish in time. You get caught in the bloodbath afterwards and have to leave the company (or are fired).

What to Do

Both lists of possibilities above are listed from best to worse outcome. As such, both lists are only loosely tied to how well your firm does on its Y2K efforts; there are potentially negative outcomes even if the Y2K effort does well and positive ones if it doesn't.

There's an important point in this: As with so much else dealing with Y2K, what matters most is how people choose to act and react. Y2K events—or the expectation of them—act as an intensifier of thoughts and trends that are already there. Besides Y2K impacts on your firm, you need to focus on the likely choices and responses of those people within the firm who, directly or indirectly, will affect your career path. Of course, that may range from the CEO, COO, or CFO deciding to cut costs by cutting staff to your immediate supervisor looking for a chance to help you advance.

The purpose of this book isn't to plan your career for you or tell you how to win friends and influence people. But the next few sections should give you some ideas.

Work: Plan of Action

The question here is: How might Y2K affect your employment situation and what you should do about it? You can see it as a chance for some new opportunities, or you may focus on the need to maintain job stability through any economic uncertainties.

Educating Yourself

You've been learning about Y2K; now you need to learn about your own firm.

ACTION. Find out where your company stands with regards to Y2K, both its internal effort and its external Y2K contingency planning. Use the "good signs/bad signs" criteria as starters, but dig deeper. Find out how its industry may be impacted by Y2K. Look at what competing and cooperating firms are doing. Above all, focus on the people who will make decisions that affect your job, for good or ill.

OUTCOME: After all this, you should have a better idea of how your employer is going to deal with and come through Y2K—which leads to the next step.

Identifying Risks and Corresponding Mitigations

Having been through the education part, now you need to see what risks you've found and figure out what to do with them.

ACTION. List what risks you think you might face in your work because of Y2K.

Risk/Symptom	Prob.	Impact	Possible Mitigations	Issues
Diversion of resources to Y2K may slow or block current career path			Find internal mentor to look after you	Not a good time to find a mentor
Y2K costs may force layoffs			Impress superiors sufficiently to be kept on	Have to decide whether to attempt to stay or attempt to go
Firm will suffer significant loss of business due to Y2K directly or to national or global economy			Find another job. Soon.	Accuracy of prediction; whether new job will be any more secure

These are quite general; be sure to make these specific to your circumstances and to sort them according to what you think the probability is.

OUTCOME. The key is whether your position is at risk, and if not, whether your advancement is. Once you understand that, you can see better what you need to do.

Looking for Opportunities

If you are a typical employee in a firm, the chances are that your situation will be dictated by the overall health of the firm. However, if you are working on the Y2K problem in your firm, you may be given a chance to have impact; it may also give you a chance to move into a more hands-on role in information technology. On the other hand, it may just be a dead end, and you may want to look for opportunities outside your firm's Y2K effort.

You now have risks to consider and opportunities to pursue. You should be ready to figure out how to use the opportunities to guard yourself against the risks. If you believe the firm may be in trouble, you may want to make a move to a new career now. The key word here is "now." Waiting until later could mean unemployment at the worst possible time. Now is the time to make sure you are secure in your position and that you are comfortably employed as the Y2K arrives. If not, take action immediately to remedy the situation.

It is possible that the Year 2000 issue may offer a business opportunity for you—for instance, consulting on the Year 2000 issue can be a lucrative business. However, if you have been considering leaving your company to start your own venture, this may not be the best time. Major change of life plans like buying a new house, having a baby, starting a new business, elective surgery, and the like probably can wait till after January 1, 2000.

Establishing Guiding Principles

You need something punchy to tell yourself on a daily basis so as to keep yourself focused on your opportunities while mitigating the risks.

ACTION. Come up with a few catchy principles specific to your situation. Write them on a 3x5 card and post them in your cubicle or office.

1. Reliability, proficiency, courtesy.

2. It's amazing what you can get done if you don't worry about who gets credit for it.

3. No guts, no glory.

OUTCOME. Use these to help keep you focused on what's important and what isn't.

Determining What You Need

Most of what you need here is information about your firm.

ACTION. Get the information you need to figure out where your company stands and how you might be impacted. Here are some of the things you might get:

- Get all internal materials you can get about your firm's Y2K remediation and contingency planning efforts: reports, newsletters, internal Web sites, budget documents, and so on.

- Where relevant and possible, get your firm's annual report or financial report for the last year or two. Look at what the firm's trends are. Find out how much the firm is spending on Y2K.

- Track down articles and other reports about the market or sector your firm is in, particularly those that discuss Y2K's impact in that sector.

- Find someone more senior, higher in management, whom you respect, and ask them to serve as your mentor. They will probably be flattered by your request and will likely help or recommend someone who can.

OUTCOME: You should have a better idea at this point as to what risks (and opportunities) your firm faces as a result of Y2K.

Creating the Plan

Here's where you put together the actual steps.

ACTION. The plan will vary, based on your goals. Suppose you're working for a small to medium-sized business that's still floundering about with Y2K, and you want to become a Y2K hero. Here's what you might do:

- Do the research to determine just where your company truly stands in its Y2K remediation.

- Likewise find out what all the external factors and issues are.

- Find someone higher up to act as a mentor or, at least, as a sounding board.

- *Without impacting your work on current assign-ments*, put together a succinct approach to Y2K that you feel will help get the company on track. Have your mentor review and critique it.

- Put the plan in whatever form is best received by the key decision makers (report, memo, presentation); again, get it reviewed by your mentor.

- If your mentor is willing to act as a champion for you or for the project, let them take the plan from there; otherwise, get on the calendar for the appropriate person or committee and pitch your plan.

And so on.

OUTCOME. You now have a plan; start working it.

Enrolling Others

Success within organizations depends heavily on relationships with others. It helps to be outstanding, or at least good, at what you do, but we've all seen too many situations where people who are less than competent still move up through the ranks. This is a situation where it's good to seek out relationships and let others help you.

ACTION. Start by lining up the mentor/champion described above. But beyond that, to effect change within an organization, you need to put out a simple message and put it out consistently for a long time. Come up with two or three one-sentence descriptions of what you want to get across. Bring them up in conversations with people at all levels in the firm. Don't preach, dispute, or argue; just make the simple assertion and leave it at that. Keep it up until other people start saying it to *you*. Then move on to the next set of items.

OUTCOME. Through techniques such as these, you can have a significant influence within your organization regardless of your actual position. By using them, you may be able to blunt the Y2K impact on your firm.

Y2K JumpStart

Here's the quick-and-dirty plan if you work for someone else.

❑   Find out who is responsible for all of Y2K at your company. Then find out what they have to say (internal and confidential) about how your company's Y2K effort is progressing. See if you can get a copy of whatever report is being produced on a weekly or monthly basis to track Y2K remediation status.

❑   Go back to Chapter 6, the section entitled "Ask questions." Find out the answers to those questions. Pay particular attention to your project/department/division/business unit/whatever.

❑   If there is a Y2K contingency planning team associated with your department, find out who's on it and befriend them. Ask them lots of questions.

❑   Figure out what needs to be done that isn't getting done now. Come up with a plan to fix it.

Here's a plan if you own or run a business.

❑   If you don't have someone in charge of Y2K for your firm, put someone in charge. They should be bright, an excellent organizer, honest, and fearless; if there's no one like that in your firm, pick the nearest match. Tell them that their top priority is Y2K remediation of the company. Make sure they understand all that it entails. (If you're self-employed, then you're probably elected.)

❏ Get a good book on Y2K and business. Read it.

❏ Make sure your direct reports (in any) understand that Y2K is a top priority and that they are to cooperate with the person in charge of Y2K.

❏ Get weekly reports until it's done. Ask questions. Hold feet to the fire, if necessary.

Tips and Traps

Here are a few suggestions in dealing with the suggestions and issues above.

- Be careful not to step on any toes (at least, not unnecessarily) in gathering information and putting your plan together. Realize that it takes a lot less effort on someone else's part to trip you up than it does for you to succeed.

- Recognize that change in individuals almost never comes as the aftermath of a single, well-done, logical and valid presentation; people almost never slap their foreheads and say, "Oh, I understand *now*! I'll change right away." Effecting change is more like steering a supertanker: You start miles ahead of time and you keep the wheel held over for a long time.

- Remember that no good deed goes unpunished.

Closing Thoughts

As with most of the other topics covered in Part II, the chances of Y2K events actually impacting your job in a significant way are not high. But as with these other topics, there is a need for education, for preparation, and for preemptive action to reduce risk and pursue opportunity. And somewhere in it all, looking at the other issues at stake, remember: It's just a job. Your goal is to make sure you are happy, content, and that the Y2K effect on your employment is minimized. It may be a time to hold off on major change of life plans or it may be time, now, to make a move so that you are prepared when January 1, 2000 comes.

11

Money and Law: Keeping Yourself Whole and Well Documented

Gives me some kind of content to remember how painful it is sometimes to keep money, as well as to get it.
                    —Samuel Pepys, *Diary,*
                        October 11, 1667

In November 1997, I attended a Y2K breakfast meeting in Northern Virginia sponsored by ITAA. During a break at one point, I was speaking with another attendee about Y2K issues and what impacts we might see. He told me that just a week or so earlier he had gotten his monthly mortgage statement from whatever company currently owned his mortgage—and it was wrong. It didn't have the right balance for his mortgage, nor the right monthly payment. So he called up the mortgage company. He spent time on the phone with a customer representative, trying to get things straightened out. Finally, the representative asked if he had the statement from the previous month. He did. So she asked him to make a copy of it, write out a check for the same amount he paid the month before, and mail them both in.

Here's what's important about this story: The problem wasn't caused by Y2K, at least not as far as he knew. And that's the point. So much of the software that runs business, government, and other institutions is less than perfect. Software tends towards imperfection. It's written to handle whatever situations the developer considered at the time and doesn't always do that perfectly. If a new situation is introduced, if something the developer never thought of shows up, if changes are made without careful testing of existing functions, or if the developer just plain made a mistake in actually creating the software and associated data, then an error pops up. "The computer made a mistake" became a cultural catchphrase a few decades ago; it's what we expect, though the blame usually lies with managers, marketers, developers, testers, and all the other human beings involved in determining the quality (or lack thereof) of the software.

Y2K is just a spike in the usual scattered stream of software defects, and we're even fixing most of the Y2K problems. The question is, will we fix enough, and if we don't, what happens when defects surface and systems shut down? But before we address that, let's look again at an issue that's been touched on a few times already: the potential impact of Y2K on the U.S. economy.

Y2K and the Economy

A growing debate has been going on since 1997 when Dr. Ed Yardeni, chief economist of Deutsche Bank Securities and a Wall Street analyst with a very good track record over much of the 1990s, estimated that there was a 30 percent chance of a global recession caused by Y2K. Other Y2K analysts had already said as much, but the financial world couldn't dismiss Yardeni—a Wall Street economist with a solid reputation—as readily. As the U.S. government continued to show lack of progress over the winter of 1997-98, Yardeni upped the estimate until it stood at 70 percent in mid-1998.[1] In the meantime, the currency crisis in Indonesia started knocking over financial dominoes in Japan and the rest of Asia, the legs went out from under the Russian economy, and the U.S. stock markets took a big dive.

Some of the those who dispute that Y2K could have any consequences on the national economy focus largely just on the actual repair costs for government and industry, which—while not insubstantial—probably aren't enough to trigger a U.S. recession. But that's not what Y2K analysts are focused on. They see the following factors contributing to a possible recession here in the United States:

- Disruptions and inefficiencies in mining, extraction, and refining of minerals and petroleum.

- Disruptions and inefficiencies in manufacturing and production, due both to internal problems and problems with suppliers.

- Disruptions and inefficiencies in transportation, logistics, customs, distribution, and warehousing.

- Buildup of stockpiles (manufacturing, business, consumer) during 1999, resulting in a drop-off of new orders in early 2000.

- Disruptions and inefficiencies in business processes, including administration, accounting, and operations.

- Disruptions in information and financial transactions.

- Reduced earnings among firms due to all the factors above, actual Y2K repair costs, and increased fiscal caution among consumers and investors.

Here's something important to remember: We don't have to suppose a total breakdown to end up with a recession. If there were a total breakdown, we'd have a depression or worse. All we need is the introduction of enough disruptions and inefficiencies to cause an economic contraction.

For that matter, all we need is enough worry and concern on the part of investors, big and small. In December 1996 while testifying before Congress, Federal Reserve Chairman Alan Greenspan expressed caution about what he saw as "irrational exuberance" of investors in the market.[2] The flip side—irrational panic—could cause a tremendous transfer of funds from stocks and similar investments into notes and bonds or even cash.

On top of all this, as noted, the global economy is in bad shape. When the WDCY2K group survey was conducted in March 1998 (see Appendix B), 85 percent of those responding felt we'd have at least a 20 percent drop in the stock markets, and 56 percent felt that we'd have a mild recession. That was considered sufficient news for the survey to get significant press coverage, including a full-page write-up in *Newsweek*.[3] The irony is that as of this writing (October 1998), the various stock market indices have been down close to 20 percent below their record highs in mid-year, and the threat of a recession here in the United States in 1999 has led the Federal Reserve Board to cut interest rates twice so far.

This is all *before* any apparent Y2K impacts have set in. The late start that many countries have gotten on Y2K—in many cases, the very countries that are the most troubled economically, in Asia, South America, and Africa—suggests that they will be worst hit by Y2K problems and least able to cope with the economic consequences. And that will have an impact on the U.S. economy just as the current troubles have, just as we're dealing with whatever Y2K problems of our own we have.

The Complexities of Life

What does all this mean to you? It means that you could find your income and investments threatened at the same time when a higher-than-normal number of errors could occur in the various organizations with whom you have financial and legal relationships. One or the other could be unpleasant; the two combined could result in significant financial and legal risks.

Even if we apply the 90 percent rule of thumb—that 90 percent of everything is going to work just fine—you face the probability of problems with one or more of those organizations, since there are so many of them. Here's a sample list of such organizations; ask yourself how many you have dealings with.

- Your employer, clients, business partners, employees, investors, shareholders

- Your family: living expenses, school expenses, personal loans, child support, alimony, wills, trusts

- Tax agencies: IRS, state, city, property

- The U.S. Government: Social Security, passport, military service, Selective Service

- Your insurance companies: life, medical, dental, automobile, homeowners/renters, disability

- Your mortgage company, rental agency, or landlord

- Savings and checking: banks, credit unions

- Credit: credit cards, secured loans, credit records

- Investments: brokers, mutual funds, stocks, bonds, royalties, retirement accounts

- Transportation: car loans and leases, car registration and taxes, driver's license

- Utility companies: electricity, gas, oil, coal, water, sewer, trash, cable/satellite, Internet

- Telephone companies: local, long-distance, mobile

- Education: tuition, student loans, school records

- Professional services: legal, accounting, counseling

- Real estate: titles, deeds, inspection documents, blueprints, surveys, reports

- Subscriptions: magazines, newspapers, book clubs, collectibles

- Donations: churches, charities, nonprofit organizations, candidates

- Health care: hospitals, doctors, dentists, other
  professionals, pharmacies, Medicare, Medicaid

- Dues: health clubs, other clubs, professional organizations

You probably didn't expect the list to be that long or for so
many of the items to apply to you. But there it is. All of these
pretty much boil down to one or more of these:

1. A financial commitment on your part toward someone
   else, possibly in exchange for services or goods

2. A financial commitment on someone else's part toward
   you, possibly in exchange for services or goods

3. Documentation of assets, ownership, obligations,
   rights, agreements, and achievements

As noted before, we deal with minor (or occasionally not-so-
minor) problems in these different areas on a regular basis. As
such, just about any book on the subject of personal finances or
law recommends keeping good records in these areas.

Most of us, however, tend to be a bit haphazard in doing so.
We are often "interrupt-driven" (to use a technogeek phrase[4]).
That is, we ignore a lot of these until something sufficiently
urgent arises that requires we deal with it. We handle it, then go
back to whatever we were doing. Most of the time, we can get
away with handling things that way, so we continue to do so.

However, sometimes the lack of advance planning and pre-emptive action can get us into trouble. Something sufficiently serious arises that would have been easier (and cheaper or more lucrative) to handle earlier. Or we find ourselves facing several issues simultaneously and lacking the time and attention ("bandwidth," to use another technogeek term[5]) to deal with them well. We may especially lack the money and other resources to deal with problems, meet obligations, or exploit opportunities.

Well, guess what? Between the potential economic impact of Y2K and the higher probability of problems and mistakes cropping up due to Y2K defects, we all may well face such a time in the 1999–2000 time period. So consider this your interrupt: Now would be a good time to take preemptive actions to protect your assets, reduce your obligations, and document your life. As with most of the activities in Part II, these steps would probably help out your life even if Y2K weren't coming. It's just that now you have incentive...and a bit of a deadline.

Risks to Your Income and Assets

We count on our income to meet the necessities of life and to enjoy some of its niceties. More than that, we carry an expectation, conscious or not, that our income and assets should increase over time, that our standard of living five or ten years from now should be higher than it is now. We also expect that somehow we'll be able to retire when the time comes to do so and that somehow we'll have the assets and income to do so.

However, as many of us have discovered, there is nothing in life that guarantees such constancy and security. Circumstances change; events intervene; reality all too often bites, and bites hard. In some cases, there was little we could have done to prevent things, and we just have to roll with the punches. However, quite often we could have done a lot. We could have seen what was coming, we could have prepared, we could have sidestepped the large heavy cannonball that life fired our way. Y2K has the potential to be such a cannonball; we need to understand where to look for it and how to duck.

There are three fundamental risks that Y2K can pose to your income and assets. The first is a threat directly to the organizations upon which you depend for income. We spent Chapter 10 looking at the ways that Y2K could impact you if you are an employee of a typical organization. But there are many other forms of employment: commission-based income, multilevel marketing, consulting, self-employment, and others. All these have the potential to be impacted by a recession (Y2K-related or not) by the simple fact that organizations and individuals spend less during a recession. Beyond that, the Y2K preparedness (or lack thereof) of your employers, partners, and/or customers can impact their ability to do business with you.

In a similar fashion, if you receive pension payments, survivor's benefits, Social Security payments, or other regular payments from a given organization, then Y2K problems within that organization—or within organizations that administer those plans or deliver the payments to you—could disrupt or delay those payments. The Social Security Administration itself is in good shape. But it is the Financial Manager Service, a department within the U.S. Treasury Department, that actually issues the Social Security checks—and Treasury got an "F" in the August 1998 grading by Rep. Steve Horn.[6]

The second risk is that of a devaluation of assets because of Y2K's impact on the economy. The 1990s have been the decade of personal investment. Americans have become investors to an extent unprecedented in history, pouring literally several trillion dollars into various financial markets. As the Dow, NASDAQ, and other indices continued to climb all through the decade, the money continued to pour into the stock market. Should Y2K cause an economic downturn or even a recession, those assets will lose value. In the long run, this probably won't matter as much—the stock markets are likely to recover and start another bull market after the Y2K downturn—but if you have short-term (0–5 years) needs for that investment money, you could find yourself hurting.

The last risk is an administrative one: having records of assets impacted by Y2K. We assume that the records we receive of our assets—bank statements, investment statements, deeds, titles, and so on—are accurate and correctly executed, and the vast majority of the time they are. However, Y2K bumps up the probability of errors creeping in, either from unrepaired Y2K defects or from **iatrogenic** defects, that is, new defects inadvertently introduced while trying to fix the old ones.[7]

Risks Due to Outflow and Debts

We live in an era of easy credit, and we use it to the hilt. Per capita credit card debt has increased constantly for years; it now stands at about $7000, with 7.5 credit cards per person, for a national total of $523 billion. Total consumer debt on car loans and revolving credit is $1.24 *trillion*, which represents a doubling since 1991.[8] And the growth in debt continues.

Y2K poses risks to us because of our debts and commitments. The first, and most obvious, comes from the risks to our income detailed above. When you think of it, most of us serve as mere conduits, with most or all of the cash coming in each month going out that same month and only a little bit staying around at the end of the month. But should the income shrink, we may not be able to shrink the outgo the corresponding amount due to monthly debt payments and fundamental living costs (housing, utilities, food).

The second risk is less likely, but still possible: an increase in common living expenses due to Y2K-related shortages. The most likely of these is a rise in prices of petroleum products due to Y2K problems in pumping, shipping, and refining oil. However, other disruptions could cause other price increases. For example, we depend upon South America for many of our fruits and vegetables during the winter months; Y2K problems could impact harvesting, processing, and delivery to the United States of those products.

The last risk is the same administrative risk as above: having records of debts and obligations impacted by Y2K. The true story about the mortgage statement at the start of this chapter, while not Y2K-related, shows what indeed could happen. As with assets and income, errors in the systems that track and process our debts could come directly from Y2K defects or from iatrogenic defects.

Losing Your Identity

As technology has advanced the ability to track who we are, we are placed under increasing demands to document who we are. One may see this as either ironic or a direct consequence, but those key pieces of paper that establish our lives and those of our children have become more and more important. When we recently moved from Washington, D.C. to the Dallas-Ft. Worth area, my wife and I carefully collected (or thought we did) into a single file box all the key documents we would

need to register our children at the local high school. But
between the cross-country car trip, the various hotel stays, and
the whirlwind of unpacking at our new home, some of them
vanished—and we went through quite a scramble to reassem-
ble the complete set required by the school.

At the same time, the rapidly growing *fin de siecle* crime of
"identity theft" has given a new importance to the ability to
establish who you are and who someone else isn't.[9] The documented cases are unnerving, not just because of the theft itself,
but because of the lack of effort by credit card companies,
employers, and law enforcement to prosecute such cases. Here's
one of many such cases reported by the Privacy Rights Clearinghouse at the Utility Action Consumer's Network (UCAN), a
nonprofit consumer rights organization based in San Diego:

> *Robin's wallet was stolen with all her ID and checks in it.*
> *The thieves opened up several credit accounts in her name,*
> *using her SSN and name and address. Even after she had*
> *fraud alerts put on her credit reports, the thieves were still*
> *able to get new credit cards. They even paid a small amount*
> *of the balance to continue to use the cards. The total fraud is*
> *more than $30,000. Robin recently got married and*
> *changed her name. Somehow, the thieves obtained her cur-*
> *rent address, home and work phone numbers. She is worried*
> *they might commit crimes in her name. Robin has tried to*
> *get the banks and credit card companies to press charges*
> *against the thieves but they are not interested. It frustrates*
> *Robin that the credit grantors won't take action.*[10]

Again, neither of these is tied to Y2K; they just reflect the
challenges and risks that now exist in the world. However,
Y2K increases the risks associated with establishing your identity in two ways. First, Y2K defects may cause errors in systems
holding information about you, either introducing errors into
your information or making it harder to call up the information. If you then have to prove who you are to that organization or get records from it to establish your identity with

others, you could run into problems. Second, Y2K defects cause errors and inefficiencies in systems that need to track identity—credit approval, credit billing, licenses, utility accounts, and so on—then those firms may either err in confirming identity or lower their standards for accepting identity as a workaround to an ailing system.

In either case, the consequences could range from annoying to profound, with tremendous financial and legal liabilities as a result.

Defending Your Life

If there's an underlying theme here, it's that we tend to live our lives on the presumption that many things will go on turning out just as well as, if not better than, they have been up until now. We consider everything working well to be norm—that we'll keep our job and get that promotion, that we'll be able to pay off all our debts even as we incur new ones, that whatever inadvertent errors or deliberate acts may occur in the vast complex systems in which our identity, our assets, and our obligations reside, they won't affect us, at least not for the worse.

Time to wake up.

The fundamental risks detailed in the chapter aren't unique to or caused by Y2K. They can and do happen for a variety of reasons. But Y2K shows all signs of increasing these risks across the board. That means that the measures you could take to reduce these risks become even more important. The basic steps are simple, though, as usual, the devil is in the details.

Documenting Your Universe

This is where you start, though you shouldn't wait to finish this to begin the other tasks. You start here, because you need to collect and organize the documents associated with your debts and assets as part of your efforts to deal with both. And you need to assemble the critical documents for your identity and that of your family members just in case Y2K makes that more difficult or more necessary.

Above all, you are establishing a **baseline** for your life, that is, a set of documents that can be used to prove who you are, what you've done, what you own, what you owe, and what you are owed. Chances are you'll find one or more errors just in the process of gathering and reviewing; again, it's better to correct such now rather than later.

What should you collect and organize? The essentials about the essentials. There are three lists given in this chapter, one above, two below; I won't repeat them here. Use them to figure out what you need and what you can use. Here's a rule of thumb: If a given organization (county recorder, credit card company, IRS, stock broker) came back and needed you to document exactly where you stood with relation to them, what would you need?

Reducing Your Outflow and Debts

The most sure protection against an economic downturn, however severe, is to reduce how much money you need to have coming in each month to stay current on your financial obligations. Several steps can be taken here. The first is to stop incurring debt. Put away your credit cards, avoid consumer loans, pay by check or cash.

The second is to pay off existing debts. Interest rates on credit cards are so much higher than virtually any return on savings or investments that you are almost always better off taking cash out of those accounts to pay down credit cards. Each credit card you pay off is one less monthly payment to make and that much less interest charged and one less potential error to have to check.

The third is to look for other ways to economize, to spend less than you bring in. Moderately wealthy people are often known for being frugal; this is how they become and stay wealthy. This was well documented in the best-seller *The Millionaire Next Door* by Thomas Stanley and William Danko (Longstreet, 1996). Stanley and Danko found, among other things, that 50 percent of the millionaires in one survey had never spent more than $29,000 for a car; 50 percent in another survey had never spent more than $399 for a suit.[11] In other words, $20 saved is still $20 saved, whether you're a millionaire or not.

The last is to build up a hedge against having your income drop dramatically. This means putting some portion of your cash resources into safe and liquid investments that can be drawn upon in case of financial reversal. It can also mean building up home storage as described in Chapter 9, so that you can live on the food and household supplies if needed.

Protecting Your Income and Assets

Even as you are reducing your outflow and debts, you should take steps to ensure so far as possible that your income continues uninterrupted and at the same level, if not higher. Chapter 10 talks at length about issues concerning Y2K problems at work and mitigation strategies. If you have income from other sources—Social Security, pensions, and so on— then you very much want to establish a record of what you are

owed and find out as best you can what potential Y2K problems might exist that could cause problems.

You also want to document your ownership and the value of
investments, accounts, real estate, and other items of worth, such
as vehicles. These should be current values, balances due on real
estate and other items, a record of payments made to date, and
the appropriate documentation of ownership (title, deed, etc.).

Finally, you need to look at how to manage your investments
in the face of Y2K. This remains an area of some dispute and
controversy, since there are varying and strong opinions as to
what exactly Y2K will bring, even among analysts and economists who are agreed upon the seriousness of Y2K. For example,
in Ed Yardeni's Y2K Action Day conference held over the Internet on August 17, 1998, he and three other investment special-
ists stated their opinions.[12] Three of the four saw deflation; one
saw inflation. They varied in their estimates for drop in growth.
And even where they did agree upon impact, they didn't necessarily agree on investment strategies.

In the end, all the chapters in Part II, up to and including
this one, tie together. They all build upon the themes of preparation, self-reliance, and taking responsibility for and control
of your life. This is an immense challenge, not one to be taken
lightly. But we all face the daily chances of error and misfor-
tune, and Y2K threatens to increase those odds significantly.
Some preparation is better than none.

Money and Law: Plan of Action

While the home storage effort outlines in Chapter 9 may be
your single greatest challenge, this one may be intellectually
more demanding, not to mention more tedious. But, in the
end, it may also be the most rewarding, not just fiscally but also

emotionally. Most of us know that we should do a better job of managing our financial and legal affairs. If you go through this plan, you'll likely feel very self-satisfied, and with good reason.

Educating Yourself

Most of us could be better served by knowing more about money and law. You would be well advised to find at least one book on personal finances, investments, and/or legal matters that covers topics you don't already know. Read it, making notes about things you should do or find out.

Identifying Risks and Corresponding Mitigations

ACTION. Review your assets, liabilities, and obligations, and note the risks you personally face from Y2K events. For each risk you face, establish as best you can its likelihood (low, medium, high), its impact (low, medium, high), the possible mitigations, and the issues you face. Here are some general examples:

Risk/ Symptom	Prob.	Impact	Possible Mitigations	Issues
Loss of job.			See Chapter 10	
Decline in value of investments			Seek qualified financial advice; shift investments	Short term vs. long term
Error or disruptions in other sources of income or reimbursement: Social Security, pensions, dividends, loans, Medicare			Get updated copies of all records; use for post-Y2K comparison	A lot of other people doing the same (in other words, don't procrastinate); getting by until problems are solved

Risk/ Symptom	Prob.	Impact	Possible Mitigations	Issues
Errors in records of assets			Get updated copies of all records; use for post-Y2K comparison	
Errors in records of obligations				
Error in vital documentation			Gather copies together; replace those you don't have; put in a safe place	

Make these more specific to your circumstances and concerns.

OUTCOME. It may be hard to come up with probabilities, but you can certainly come up with the impact should these happen.

Looking for Opportunities

As always, there are opportunities. And, as before, the best may be doing the things that would benefit you regardless.

ACTION. Identify opportunities that you see in this area. Some may be financial opportunities related to Y2K; just try to avoid any get-rich-quick schemes. The most important: to reduce debts.

OUTCOME. With opportunities, your efforts become more proactive instead of being simply defensive. That can help give you the motive and encouragement to push through discouragement and weariness.

Establishing Guiding Principles

Based on your risks and opportunities, you need a small set of principles that will guide you through obstacles and discouragement and help you achieve your goals.

ACTION. Come up with your own guiding principles relating to money and legal obligations. For example,

1. Simplify, simplify, simplify.

2. Interest never sleeps, even if my creditors do.

3. Get it in writing—or, at least, in hardcopy.

OUTCOME. Again, shape these to your own goals and opportunities.

Determining What You Need

This will largely have to do with documents and the like.

ACTION. Make a list of the specific relevant documents and other items you need to collect. Here's a general list to work from. You probably have a lot of these around; if you don't, determine whether it's worth the time, effort, and expense of getting them. In many cases, the original needs to be in a specific place (e.g., your driver's license, in your wallet); make a copy to keep filed.

- Vital documents: birth certificates, baptismal and christening records, immunization records, passports, Social Security cards, marriage certificates, divorce decrees, adoption papers, military service records, selective service, wills, trust and estate documents, living wills, powers of attorney

- Bank and credit union records: statements, cancelled checks

- Investment records: stock certificate, investments and 401(k) statements

- Loan documents: loan statements and agreements, including credit cards

- Tax documents: local, state, and federal, organized by year

- Donations: whatever records you need for tax purposes

- Medical: copies of medical, dental records; statements for medical services; copies of prescription information; record of Medicare/Medicaid payments

- Real estate documents: mortgages, titles, deeds, liens, leases, inspection documents, blueprints

- Educational documents: report cards, transcripts, tuition receipts, student loan documents

- Insurance: policies, statements

- Car: registration, title, driver's licenses, proof of insurance, service records, car loan/lease agreements

- Utilities and phones: account numbers, records of payment and usage (e.g., a year's worth of statements)

- Subscriptions: account numbers and obligations for book club, collectable subscriptions; records of payments

OUTCOME. At this point, you may feel exhausted. You probably feel a bit overwhelmed. And you probably have a greater appreciation for the Ralph Waldo Emerson maxim above ("Simplify, simplify, simplify.") But consider this: Between now and the end of 1999, you can either have some portion of the records above gathered and organized—or you can be right where you are now, plus a year more behind.

Creating the Plan

ACTION. Your plan will be based on your circumstances, needs, and priorities.

- Document your life

  — Set up a filing system that you can live with

  — Organize your existing documents (see list above)

  — Get those documents you are missing

- Protect your income and assets

  — Pay attention to your job (see Chapter 10)

— Check into your other sources of income (pension, Social Security, dividends)

— Document title to your assets (real estate, cars, boats, other valuables)

— Seek professional advice on your investments

• Decrease your debts and outflow

— Stop using credit cards; start paying them off

— Don't start other new debt unless it's absolutely necessary

— Consolidate debts to lower monthly payments, interest where possible

— Examine spending patterns; separate wants and needs; look for cheaper alternatives

And so on.

OUTCOME. If you can put together a plan and stick to it, you will not only substantially lower your risks due to Y2K, you will put yourself in an excellent financial position generally.

Enrolling Others

ACTION. Sit down as a family and make out a plan of how you want your assets and debts, income and outflow to look by the end of 1999. Then figure out what that will mean for your family's monthly budget, especially if you're trying to build up home storage as well.

OUTCOME. You need to agree on this as a family, because it probably means a deliberate lowering of your "standard of living"—that is, the disposable income you have available each month—for a sustained period of time.

Y2K JumpStart

Here's a way to get started immediately. This plan isn't comprehensive, but it'll get you moving in the right direction.

❑ Stop incurring debt. Put all your credit cards away; use checks, cash, or check cards to pay for everything. Consider seriously before you purchase a car, home, or similar big-ticket item.

❑ Get a file box and file folders of some kind. (But see Tips and Traps below.)

❑ Make a list of all your income, assets, debts, and obligations: employment, bank accounts, credit cards, mortgages, investments, real estate, cars, and so on. For each one, do the following:

  ❑ Create and label a folder and put all papers related to that income source or asset in there.

  ❑ Take a note card or blank sheet of paper and make a list of the tasks to do for that item in preparation for Y2K: documents to request, things that you need to have done, changes to make. Put that in the folder.

❑ Sort the folders in order of priority based on your needs and concerns.

❏   Start working through the folders in that order. For each
    folder:

    ❏   Take out the list of tasks. Do as many as you can,
        checking them off as you complete them, but *do at
        least one*. Your inclination will be to do the easy ones
        first and to avoid the hard or awkward ones. That's
        understandable, but when you get to the hard ones,
        you need to bite the bullet and do them. When you
        feel that desire to put them off again, remember this:
        That is exactly what got us in the Y2K mess in the
        first place.

    ❏   If you write or receive any letters, keep copies in the
        file.

    ❏   As you get updated documents, put them in the file.

    ❏   As you think of or discover new tasks to do, add
        them to the list.

❏   Get a separate, portable file box; one that you can grab
    and take out of the house in case of fire or flood. Use this
    as your identity box. For you and each family member,
    build a file with key identity documents: birth certificate,
    Social Security card, immunization record, Selective Ser-
    vice card, passport, voter registration card, photocopy of
    driver's license, appropriate legal documents (will, trust,
    power of attorney, living will), credit bureau reports, and
    so on. Get copies of the documents that you don't have
    on hand.

❏   Get a book on personal financial management, particular-
    ly one with a focus on getting out of debt. Read it, apply
    it, and start reducing and consolidating debts. Strongly
    consider selling assets where possible to reduce or elimi-
    nate debts.

❏   Seek professional financial and tax advice on any investments and assets you might have. Either look for ways to
reduce risk or decide that you're taking a long-term view
(if you can).

It's a simple plan, but by and large it's what you need to do.

Tips and Traps

Here are a few suggestions in dealing with the suggestions
and issues above.

- If you're setting up a filing system, don't spend a
  lot of money on a big file cabinet until you see
  how much storage you really need. On the other
  hand, be prepared to create and label a file folder
  on the spot each time you need one. However,
  make the labeling easy to change; you'll figure out
  better ways to organize things as you go along.

- Some books and articles suggest sending certified letters to the various entities you deal with
  (banks, etc.) asking what their Y2K remediation
  status is. My recommendation: Don't bother, at
  least, not until late in 1999. Experience to date
  has taught that it's unlikely you'll get any answer
  other than one that boils down to "We're fine
  (unless something unexpected happens)."

- Nowadays, it is very convenient—and sometimes
  a necessity—to have a credit card of some kind,
  particularly if you have to travel. Your bank may
  offer a check card, which acts like a Visa or Mas-

terCard but deducts directly from your checking account. However, there are some firms that won't take check cards in certain settings; for example, most major rental car companies won't accept one to rent a car (though they'll let you use it to pay for it at the end). Consider getting an American Express card, which will force you to pay off the balance in full each month.

Closing Thoughts

It is curious to think upon money, possessions, and debts and how much they are founded upon intellectual and philosophical concepts rather than reality. Value and expectations come from a complex set of agreed-upon expectations; few of the many attempts over the centuries to break free of that net have worked. And yet I keep coming back to Douglas Adams' observation in *The Hitchhiker's Guide to the Galaxy*:

> This planet has—or rather had—a problem, which was this: most of the people living on it were unhappy for pretty much of the time. Many solutions were suggested for this problem, but most of these were largely concerned with the movements of small green pieces of paper, which is odd because on the whole it wasn't the small green pieces of paper that were unhappy. (p.1)

We often carry an expectation that contentment, if not outright peace and joy, would come if only we had more of those small green pieces of paper. Yet my own experience is that attempting to smother the desire for things by pouring money on it is too often like attempting to smother a fire by pouring fuel on it—it merely increases the flame.

What is the solution? To use one last quote, this time from Herodatus, "The secret of success is that it is not the absence of failure, but the absence of envy." We can manage our money and investments all we like, but the ultimate clue to financial security is to lower the thermostat, to set our level of wants to some point below our means.

12

Family, Community, Nation: What Really Matters

We must all hang together, or assuredly we shall all hang separately.
　　　—Benjamin Franklin
　　　　(at the signing of the Declaration of Independence)

It's true, you know. In the end, for the vast majority of us, what really matters is our relationships with others. There are a few people who are emotionally, socially, and intellectually self-sufficient, but they are few. Most of us wish we had more relationships, more friendships, more acceptance and support from those around us.

And in the end, what really matters is how those relationships hold up in the face of facts and fears about Y2K. It may be that Y2K turns out to truly be a false alarm, a hurricane that degrades into nothing more than a squall line before it comes ashore. But if the alarm is true, then it will be our individual choices, shaped and acted out within the dynamic, emergent, complex system of relationships and social contracts, that ultimately determine what the consequences of Y2K are.

Nation: Cohesion Rather than Separation

Douglass Carmichael, who heads up Shakespeare and Tao Consulting, has been giving some long, hard thought to Y2K in the context of society. In a presentation on Y2K contingency planning at the January 1998 meeting of the WDCY2K group, he put up a diagram similar to Figure 12-1.[1]

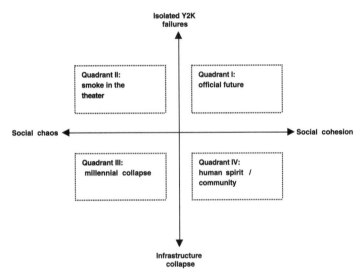

Figure 12.1   Y2K scenarios. Adapted from a diagram
© 1998 by David S. Isarberg

The vertical axis represents the range of possible Y2K impact—from isolated problems here and there to a profound collapse of our infrastructure. The horizontal axis represents the range of possible social reactions to Y2K events: From a complete collapse of social order to an orderly pulling-together in the face of whatever happens. The axes divide the area up into four quadrants, I through IV, each representing a general type of outcome:

I.   Official future: Few problems, either technically or social-ly. The best of all outcomes, and the one most often asserted by official sources.

II. Smoke in the theater: Social overreaction to relatively minor Y2K consequences. Fear and lack of leadership make Y2K worse than it had to be, for example, like people stampeding out of a crowded theater when an orderly evacuation would have worked just fine.

III. Millennial collapse: Profound infrastructure and social dysfunction. The further down and to the left you got, the more you move toward TEOTWAWKI.[2]

IV. Human spirit/community: pulling together in spite of (or because of) significant Y2K problems. Our equivalent of Great Britain rallying in the face of the sustained German air assault in WWII.

One can argue about probabilities and complexities, but this diagram illustrates clearly the point that has been underscored by virtually every thoughtful and informed Y2K analyst:

The single most important factor in how we come through Y2K, regardless of the actual technical failures, is social cohesion.

In this context, social cohesion refers to the willingness of the vast majority to support legal and social standards and to seek to pull the community together even in the face of significant breakdowns in infrastructure, local government, and law enforcement.

It is hard to overemphasize this point. With social cohesion, we can best get through whatever Y2K events occur. Without social cohesion, we could end up with far worse consequences than actual Y2K events warrant. And what we need is social cohesion on a national level.

Social Cohesion and National Leadership

Unfortunately, a key ingredient for social cohesion is credible national leadership on Year 2000 issues, which to date (October 1998) has been profoundly lacking. As mentioned back in Chapter 4, President Clinton and Vice-President Gore jointly gave their only public addresses on the Y2K in a non-televised morning appearance at the National Academy of Sciences back in May of 1998. That came only after nearly two years of growing pressure by Democrats (starting with Sen. Daniel Moynihan in 1996), Republicans (Sen. Bennett, Rep. Morella, and Rep. Horn, among others), and Y2K analysts and other IT leaders (Dr. Howard Rubin, Harris Miller, and others). While the talks were actually quite good, they received very little media coverage, and likely less than 1 percent of the American public ever saw or read of the talks. Since then, the profound silence has returned.

Similar issues arose over the appointment of John Koskinen as the chairman of the President's Council on Year 2000 Conversion, which made him the President's "Y2K czar." Again, the appointment of a Y2K czar had been urged for nearly two years by many of the same people above, including Senators Moynihan and Bennett. But the expectation was that it would be a nationally known figure with public influence and credibility—perhaps the vice-president himself. Koskinen, while a very gifted, intelligent, and capable public servant, has no such visibility and cache—again, as of this writing, I doubt that even 1 percent of Americans know him by name. Not only that, but his appointment in February 1998 by the Clinton Administration was very low key and drew little attention.[3]

Any number of speculations exist for why the administration has maintained such a low profile on Y2K, in spite of efforts by leaders in both parties to have it given more visibility.[4] But no matter the reason, the results have been clear. There is only limited public awareness on Y2K, and most of what the public believes—and, frankly, the media reports—about Y2K is irrelevant, distorted, or flat wrong. But the absence of leadership creates an information vacuum that is rapidly filled by a wide variety of sources.

Beyond that, the fraction of the public that's aware of Y2K often reasons—and understandably—that if Y2K were really important, the president would be addressing it publicly at least as much as he does such issues as Social Security and education, not to mention terrorism and the global economy. But, with that one barely reported exception, he hasn't addressed it at all—therefore, it must not be a real problem.

The president will almost certainly address Y2K publicly in an increasing manner in the first half of 1999. One key date is the March 31, 1999, deadline set by the office of Management and Budget (OMB) for all federal computer systems to be Y2K compliant and tested. That will be an opportunity for him to show leadership in this area, help establish social cohesion on a national level, and so minimize whatever level of Y2K impact we experience.

But if the information and progress by then indicate that we are indeed in for something more serious than a bump or two, the president (and the vice-president) will face a significant and classic credibility issue. By then there will exist a well-documented three-year history of Congressional and technology leaders trying to get the administration to pay attention to Y2K and to show public leadership sooner. The painful, but legitimate, question that arises in such situations is: Were they dishonest, deliberately burying the seriousness of the situation, or merely incompetent, not taking seriously what so many solid, credible people were asking them to for so long?[5]

Social Cohesion vs. Survivalism

Another factor working against social cohesion is the **survivalism** faction within the Y2K community.[6] These are people who have reached the conclusion that the combined levels of infrastructure collapse and social chaos will put us somewhere well into Quadrant III (millennial collapse), and that the best solution is to set up a completely self-sufficient homestead somewhere far from urban areas. A very common theme is having plenty of guns and ammunition for self-protection.

The United States actually has a strong foundation of survivalism dating from the early days of the Cold War, when building a bomb shelter in your backyard wasn't that out of the ordinary and elementary schools had air raid drills and other emergency drills dealing with nuclear war. It's easy to look back and mock it now, but the threat was quite real. I can still remember coming to school in October 1962, during the Cuban missile crisis, and discussing with other fourth graders that nuclear war might actually happen that day—and it might have.[7] Nuclear war and its aftermath was a theme for serious literature—*On The Beach* (Nevil Shute), *Triumph* (Philip Wylie), *Fail-Safe* (Eugene Burdick and Harvey Wheeler), and *Alas, Babylon* (Pat Frank), among others—and, of course, it became a staple of science fiction writings and movies, from the thoughtful to the schlock.[8]

But survivalism as a national trend has faded with time, perhaps out of the realization that a backyard bomb shelter wouldn't do a lot of good in the case of a real nuclear exchange. It has, however, started to reemerge within the Y2K community, as noted above.

The single most visible proponent in this area is Gary North, who also happens to have one of the better-known and more extensive Y2K Web sites around.[9] However, unlike many

Y2K "bookmark" sites, North doesn't just provide the links; he has commentary associated with virtually every link presented—and the commentary is definitely Quadrant III (millennial collapse). Other sources on the Web cite writings allegedly by North that indicate his expectations (indeed, hopes) of social collapse and interests in survivalism predate his involvement in the Y2K issue and that his alarmist position is intended to help push things toward the "social chaos" end of the scale.[10]

North appears sincere in his beliefs that the technological failure will be at the "infrastructure collapse" level of severity. On the other hand, he appears to have little hands-on information technology or systems background and certainly has never spent any time working on an actual Y2K remediation effort. That is relevant to the extent that he makes repeated statements about how things must work and the extent to which systems must be 100 percent compliant to work at all. He seems unaware of the fact that the vast majority of software systems have plenty of defects and still manage to run. For example, it is not uncommon for commercial shrink-wrap software to be released with hundreds, if not thousands, of defects. That's why you get those alert boxes in the middle of using some application on your PC. This happens all the time in corporate and government settings. A lot of software and hardware systems are held together by the binary equivalent of chewing gum and bailing wire; Y2K-repaired applications will be no different. North's "all or nothing" assertion is a logical and technological fallacy.

Let's suppose for a moment, however, that there were the probability of a very serious technological collapse. The question then becomes, which is the more rational response: survivalism or social cohesion? As with any profound and apparently intractable issue, it comes down to fundamental assumptions. The survivalist reasoning boils down to this:

- There is no higher priority or cause than the physical safety of myself and my family.

- The social/technological situation is beyond repair and/or not worth preserving.

- When the collapse happens, I will be on my own for all the necessities of life: food, water, heat, and so on.

- When the collapse happens, roving mobs (or government troops) will come looking for whatever I have stored at home.

- Therefore, I need to set up an isolated, self-sufficient homestead with sufficient supplies and equipment to live independent of modern society and to protect myself and my family.

- Most people are too uninformed/shortsighted/ stupid/foolish/wicked/lazy to do what I am going to do or to track me down and find me where I go.

That last one may seem presumptively harsh, but it is an essential component of survivalism, perhaps more so than the first two. Why? *Because survivalism can only work if a relatively small percentage of people attempt it.*

Suppose just 10 percent of the U.S. population—around 28 million people, or roughly the entire population of California—were to attempt to follow a survivalist course of action.

Where would they go? They would immediately exhaust the market for survivalist-type supplies and equipment; they would quickly fill up and overflow what isolated, habitable areas exist; and they would rapidly consume the resources (e.g., wild game, firewood, edible plants, potable water) available for such regions.[11] This isn't like 1880, when the United States only had 50 million people total and half the continent was nearly empty.

Let me put it in its starkest terms:

The fundamental survivalist assumption is that the vast majority of the population of the United States will suffer significantly or die.

This is a necessary condition from the reasoning above. The only way you can avoid it is to start toning down those assumptions—and as soon as you do that, you also begin to undermine the survivalist argument.

Here we get to the subtle but significant different between the old Cold War survivalism and the current Y2K survivalism. The former assumed that nuclear weapons would devastate metropolitans areas, wiping out large portions of the population in a matter of minutes and killing another large portion within days through radiation exposure and fallout; infrastructure would collapse only catch up with the survivors.[12] The latter assumes that everyone is still going to be around and doing fine (relatively speaking) until the infrastructure starts to collapse, at which point some 280 million people in the United States alone will be living in a system that can no longer support that kind of population. The former was fleeing foreign nuclear weapons; the latter seeks to flee fellow citizens and/or the U.S. government.

This is why Peter de Jager has called such an attitude "cowardice"—and why I fully agree. The irony, of course, is that this book will likely be considered "survivalist" by those unconvinced of any possibility of Y2K failures.

The Argument for Social Cohesion

What are the fundamental assumptions of the social cohesion viewpoint, at least as I see it? They can probably be summarized as follows:

- The technical impact of Y2K can and will be reduced by on-going remediation efforts.

- The social impact of Y2K can and should be reduced by social cohesion.

- This is an opportunity to strengthen community—reducing the probabilities (whatever they might be) of the anti-social behavior survivalists fear.

- The risks to myself and my family are lessened by working with others rather than by separating from society.

Let's talk about each of these.

Chapters 1–3 discussed the state of Y2K efforts, how we got into this mess, and why it's not easy to fix. It is critical to understand that we won't get everything fixed in time. But it is also critical to understand that the vast majority of systems, particularly in the United States, aren't affected, will be fixed by the end of 1999, or will be readily fixed when problems actually occur in 2000. The Y2K breakdowns will not be massive, complete, and irreparable, as some Y2K survivalists contend. They may be painful, but with each week that passes between now and Y2K, their potential to be so is less.

We've already talked above about the benefits of social cohesion. A diagram and an assertion do not an argument make. But we have enough examples within the twentieth century alone of where social cohesion has brought endurance and survival out of a difficult situation (such as the Battle of Britain) and where social chaos or factionalism has made a difficult situation truly hellish (such as Bosnia).

While recognizing the potential for the behavior that the survivalists fear, social cohesion proponents seek to reduce that probability by building the sense of community. Efforts in the United States to solve other urban problems have shown the impact that even a modest level of community mobilization can have on reducing crime, drug dealing, and other antisocial activities. It is precisely because no one can step in and solve this problem for us that communities need to be prepared to deal with it themselves.

Finally, we get to one of the most profound and personal issues, one that would almost seem to be too serious to be addressed here—except that the highly visible survivalist faction in the Y2K community requires that the problem be addressed. That has to do with the needs of the community versus the needs of the individual or the family. The survivalist assertion is that no community needs are worth any risks to a family; the social cohesion assertion is that there are indeed needs worth that risk. The survivalist wants to hide out in the wilderness with food and with guns for protection; the social cohesion advocate is willing to stay in the community and, if necessary, share resources—and believes that her or his family will gain by doing so.

For all the allure of the pseudofrontier, rugged individualist way of life, the truth is that the life-style we desire for ourselves and our families requires the active cooperation of thousands or possibly millions of other people, plus the vast, complex systems that support us all. We forget that without basics we take for granted such as antibiotics and tetanus vaccine, a simple puncture wound can cripple or kill. And that doesn't begin to list the benefits of society itself. Well did Thomas Hobbes famously describe the "back to nature" lifestyle:

> No arts; no letters; no society; and which is worst of all, continual fear and danger of violent death; and the life of man, solitary, poor, nasty, brutish, and short. (*Leviathan*, pt. I, chapter 13)

Civilization is built upon mutual loyalty and shared risk. Put simply, the social cohesion advocate opts for civilization; the survivalist opts out.

Community: Familiarity Rather than Isolation

OK, we've been talking about social cohesion and communities; what does that mean, exactly? Do we go around with Velcro on our upper arms so that we stick together when we brush past one another or enter a building together? Super glue on our hands? Shared ankle bracelets?

The simple key, I think, is familiarity. I'm embarrassed to say that I have lived in places in which I never spoke to the neighbors on either side more than a few times in a few years, and where I could almost never remember their names. Part of it may be just a bit of self-containment on my own part.[13] But I think it's so easy and comfortable to remain disconnected from our neighbors that we fall into that rut without thinking.

But I've been struck by the efforts that our neighbors have made to get to know us since we moved to the Dallas area. We've been invited to housewarmings; had people bring over loaves of bread; and even had the teenage girl next door—a high school senior—come over just a few days after we moved here and invite our sophomore daughter to go hit the mall with her.[14] In short, we've discovered what it's like to have neighbors who are, well, neighborly.

We plan to build on those relationships. We want to get to know these neighbors better, know their names, know their kids, even their dogs. We want to keep an eye on each other's houses (and kids). We want them to know that if they need something or just someone to talk to, they can call or come by and ask. Should Y2K look as though it's going to be more serious than less, we want to start coordinating to whatever extent we can our preparation efforts with others in the neighborhood. And if actual Y2K events turn out to cause problems in our area, we'll know and trust each other enough to pool resources, share skills, and pull through it together.

Family: Unity Rather than Division

Let's go from the national and community perspective to the family one. As you've gone through the last several chapters, you've repeatedly encountered the planning section "Enrolling others," and it has almost always focused on your family members. This is important. It is enough of a challenge just to get all the members of a regular family together at the same time to go see a movie, much less to agree on which movie to see. If you're suddenly talking about cutting back on spending, stockpiling food, and going to the local city council to ask them about Y2K, your kids may think you're nuts, or at least being silly. And if you start changing what you fix for dinner, you may have a real rebellion on your hands.

First, you need to invest the time in educating your family about Y2K. You don't have to drown them with information, especially if they're younger children. But don't be condescending or protective, either. This is their lives as well. Above all, give them chances to ask questions and voice fears and concerns.

Second, the principle of social cohesion works on a family basis every bit as much as on a community basis, if not more. How do you build family cohesion? That is perhaps the greatest challenge of marriage and parenthood, and not one that you solve for once and for all. But I'm reminded of a story that I once heard a philosophy professor tell. He was riding in a cab in New York City during a period when he was researching a set of essays on the nature of love. He struck up a conversation with the cabby and asked him what he thought love was. The cabby thought for a minute and said, "Love is what you've been through together." The professor said that he considered that one of the more thoughtful and profound answers he encountered on the subject.

What does your family go through together? How often do you actually do things with your partner, spouse, and/or children, in home or out? We're not talking about sitting in front of the TV together; we're talking actual interactions, either serious or amusing. How often does the entire family sit down to dinner together? Turned off the TV and dragged out a board game? Went to church? Sat around and debated politics or current events? Went jogging or biking? Went out to a movie? Threw a Frisbee around? Made plans and set goals together as a family?

When was the last time you talked to one of your children for more than five minutes? Without arguing or lecturing.

As with the possible preparations described in previous chapters, activities such as these make sense and have benefits quite independent of any Y2K issues, But, as with those other preparations, these activities could be essential should you face significant Y2K impacts. As noted, the quadrants diagram at the start of the chapter applies to families, too: A family with strong unity can get through just about anything; one without it can be torn apart by relatively small problems.

Family, Community, Nation: Plan of Action

The title notwithstanding, this book isn't about just surviving. It's about getting through as well as possible and finding ways to come out ahead. The greatest risks and greatest opportunities may, in the end, be here. We face a chance to do things that we probably have thought of doing a hundred times but just never have made the effort. As with the other chapters in the book, now would be a good time to start.

Educating Yourself

Education here deals with people and relationships more than anything.

ACTION. Find out what each of your family members knows and thinks about Y2K. Find out who your neighbors are. Know where and when your city council meets. Find out who your Congressional representative and two Senators are and what they think about Y2K.

OUTCOME. Just by these acts you'll develop a greater sense of community and will be laying the foundation for a complex network of your own acquaintances.

Identifying Risks and Corresponding Mitigations

There are probably less active risks here than in previous chapters, but you may still come up with some.

Risk/Symptom	Prob.	Impact	Possible Mitigations	Issues
Kids have heard about Y2K but aren't clear what it is			Have a family evening devoted to discussing it	Getting everyone together
Unsure who neighbors are or what they are doing about Y2K (probably nothing)			Get to know neighbors; raise issues of Y2K	They might laugh at me or think I'm strange
Lack of national leadership making Y2K problems worse			Public speaking; letter writing to officials	So, who'll pay attention

You'll want to make these more specific to your circumstances, but you get the idea.

OUTCOME. It will be interesting to see the risks you identify and the mitigations you envision

Looking for Opportunities

This is full of opportunities. We talk about being more civic minded, more neighborly, more involved with our families. Well, here's the chance.

ACTION. Make a list of opportunities that you see from this effort. For example, you might decide to turn off the TV for an hour or so one evening a week and use that as a family activity/planning time. You might use up those aging bananas to make banana bread for the neighbors. And you might discover how seriously your Congressional representatives take calls or letters from you.

OUTCOME. Now you have some motivation to pursue this. Think how virtuous you'll feel.

Establishing Guiding Principles

Time for the standard exercise.

ACTION. Here are a couple of principles worth considering, one each representing family, community, and national efforts on your part.

1. Home is where they have to take you in.

2. Good fences make good neighbors, but fresh bread makes better ones.

Determining What You Need

This list will likely be shorter than other chapters; you're not stockpiling goods, you're stockpiling goodwill.

ACTION. Come up with a list of things that you need.

- The names of your neighbors around you.

- Get to know your police chief, fire chief, mayor, and other emergency services personnel.

- Know whom you can talk to or get help from in an emergency.

- Get to know your plumber, electrician, oil service provider, grocery and hardware store managers, gas station manager, oil service provider, grocery store managers, druggist, and so on.

- The type of city/country government you have and the appropriate people there.

- Your own Congressional representative (name, address, phone); ditto for your two Senators.

You get the idea.

OUTCOME. You'll be using this information to contact and coordinate.

Creating the Plan

As always, this is the plan itself. And, as always, start off modest and work up from there.[15]

ACTION. Create a plan with steps such as these:

- Spend part of an evening (order in pizza) with the rest of the family, explaining Y2K and the sorts of things you think the family should be doing to prepare.

- Write letters to President Clinton, both Senators, and your local Congressional representative.

- Attend a city/government council meeting; find out who is in charge of Y2K (if anyone) and emergency services.

- Get to know your neighbors

And so on.

OUTCOME. You should have a good sense of progress and a better sense of where things stand.

Enrolling Others

This is the ultimate act of enrolling others, from family members up through the administration.

ACTION. Be informed, be rational, listen carefully, speak clearly. Understate and overprove.

OUTCOME. With patience, you'll have a whole bunch of people all working to the same end.

Y2K JumpStart

Here is a series of escalating steps you can take, depending upon how far you want to get involved.

❏ Set aside one night a week for family discussion and activities, both serious and fun.

❏ Get to know ten of your neighbors whom you don't already know.[16]

❏ Find out when the city (country) council meets. Attend. Raise an issue about Y2K.

❏ Contact your Senators and your Congressional representative and ask them about Year 2000 issues and any committees that they are on that might be holding hearings about Y2K. Let them know about your concerns and your desire for more national leadership and exposure on the subject. You can track down contact information via the Senate and House Web sites.

❏   Write the President a letter expressing those same concerns. His address is

The President of the United States
1600 Pennsylvania Ave. NW
Washington, DC 20500

You can also use his e-mail address (president@whitehouse.gov), call (202.456.1414), or fax (202.456.2461).

Tips and Traps

Here are a few suggestions in dealing with the suggestions and issues above.

- As noted above, always start out with understatement. It's easier to document and prove an understated assertion.

- Change, whether in families, companies, or government agencies, is usually slow in coming. Be patient, but persistent.

Closing Thoughts

We view reality from the context of our own experiences; consciously or not, we see in it reflections of our own hopes, fears, strengths, and weaknesses. The fact that you're holding this book—entitled *The Y2K Survival Guide*—and are reading it says something about your thoughts, curiosities, and concerns about Y2K; contrast them with those of all the people who have no interest or desire to read this book.

Ultimately, the point of this book is personal empowerment, not panic or fear. You now have the tools to prepare for Y2K. In Part III, we're going to look at what it is that you might face.

PART III

THE WINTER OF OUR DISCONNECT: GETTING THROUGH

Setting the Stage: November 1999 through January 2000

> *It was a monstrous big river down there.*
> —Mark Twain, *Adventures of Huckleberry Finn*

Y2K has been compared to various dramatic disasters—an earthquake, a forest fire, a ship striking an iceberg. However, the unfolding of Y2K will be more like a quiet, inexorable flood, a river rising ever higher over a period of time, breaking through with some fanfare here and there, then finally subsiding and leaving behind its damage.

We are now working hard and long at filling sandbags, building dikes, evacuating valuables, and dredging channels.

What remains to be seen, what we still don't know, is how high the river will rise before it crests. If the crest is low enough, and our preparations thorough enough, then the flood tide will come and go with little effect. If the crest is high and the preparations few, then the water will spread far and wide, the damage will be extensive, and the cleanup long and tedious.

Whatever happens, we will likely no longer look at technology or at ourselves the same again.

13

Bracing for Impact

*And it came to pass at the seventh time, that [the servant] said,
Behold, there ariseth a little cloud out of the sea, like a man's
hand. And [Elijah] said, Go up, say unto Ahab, Prepare thy
chariot, and get thee down, that the rain stop thee not.*
                                                    —2 Kings 18:44

So, you've been through all the chapters in Part II. You've
developed your customized plans for each of the different
areas, even if they're just the various Y2K JumpStart checklists.
You've started working through them, collecting the items you
need, tracking down information, updating records, meeting
neighbors—in short, getting ready for Y2K.

Now what do you do?

Tracking the Storm

For the most part, you go back to living life. The fundamental principle here is to take your life back, to be empow-
ered, to not be obsessed with or controlled by Y2K. The more
you get through your plans, the less your exposure, and the
less you have to worry about.

At the same time, you need to track what's going on with Y2K, both in general and in regard to your different planning areas (education, health and fitness, home and hearth, food and supplies, work, money and law, family, community, nation). You may need or choose to adjust those plans based on new information and on your efforts to date. Or you may have held off pushing ahead in a particular area until you had more data on how certain things were going.

Besides, at some point, issues and events surrounding Y2K are likely to start to pick up. We're going to have a much better idea of just where things stand around mid-1999. By then, the organizations that believed—or tried to believe—that they would be done in time are going to know one way or the other. Those organizations that knew they probably wouldn't make it but that had been trying to hide or ignore that fact aren't going to be able to do so any longer, at least, not without leaving themselves increasingly open to various liabilities, legal, political, and/or economic.

Back in Chapter 6, you learned how to educate yourself about Y2K, how to dig out information and what sources to trust. Now is the time to put them to use. Read and cross-check the Y2K press clippings. Send e-mail to the folks whose opinions you trust. Compare what the Office of Management and Budget says on the Government's Y2K remediation with what the General Accounting Office says. Look at the 10Q filings for the companies whose stock you own and see which ones appear to be making progress and which ones are stalling for time.

Your goal is to decide which of the 11 scenarios in Chapter 14 you believe we're headed for at any given point. So you want to compare the information you are getting with the descriptions of the scenarios and figure out which scenario is most likely. This may—and probably will–change from month to month. You might start out thinking that we're headed for Level 5 and by late 1999 decide that it's actually going to be Level 3—or Level 7.

In all this, keep in mind this important disclaimer: **The scenarios in Chapter 14 may be inaccurate**. They represent a best effort to devise a spectrum of Y2K consequences, from no consequences at all to a complete collapse. But the details may end up being quite different for the reasons outlined at the end of this chapter: complexity, humanity, and simultaneity. The more specific the details of a given scenario, the more likely that they are wrong.

Why the Future Remains Hard to Predict: A Reminder

Back in Chapter 5, we discussed the challenges of contingency planning. As you may recall, there were three: complexity, humanity, and simultaneity. These three reasons are why the future is generally hard to predict and why Y2K in particular is tough.

First is that we are enmeshed in a vast network of complex systems—technology, communications, politics, economics, business, sociology—that adapt and change themselves in ways that we cannot necessarily predict or control. Behavior of such systems tends to be dynamic and emergent. In other words, new attributes and trends appear in real time, apparently on their own. A simple, yet dramatic example is the World Wide Web. Who back in 1994 would have predicted that by the end of the decade hundreds of millions of people worldwide would be using the Web? Or its impact on advertising and business, initial public offerings, schoolwork, book selling, and laws on privacy, copyright, and pornography?

Second, we as human beings—and our choices and reactions—are a critical, yet unpredictable component of those complex systems. Why does a given toy—Tickle Me Elmo, Cabbage Patch Dolls, Beanie Babies—become hot for a time while others just as nice or fascinating sit on shelves? Why do elections swing one way or the other, often against all analyses? Who (besides James Carville) would have predicted that President Clinton's poll numbers would have remained so high through all the various allegations, revelations, and confessions? Key here is that human behavior can skew an unremarkable situation and cause problems (Tickle Me Elmo) or it can take a highly volatile situation and dampen its impact (President Clinton).

Finally, with Y2K we may find ourselves dealing with increasing numbers of overlapping or simultaneous events, with the undermining and multiplying impact that can have. We grasp this readily on a personal level. If I injure my left Achilles' tendon and have to go around on crutches for a while, it's a pain, but I can cope. If my car has to go in the shop for a week or so, it's a pain, but I can cope. But if I'm on crutches *and* my car has to go in the shop for a week—and, oh by the way, we're having ice storms, and I have a project at work to finish up—then I may find myself utterly overwhelmed, especially if the ice storm is delaying further the delivery of the parts my car needs. Any one of those I could handle, but to handle two at once is a major challenge and more than that is not only difficult but also leaves me out of control of my own situation.

Keep all this in mind when tracking what's going on with Y2K and attempting to map it to one or more of the scenarios in Chapter 14. Expect at least one major Y2K event not anticipated in any of those scenarios, nor in the public press at large.

Revising Your Approach

As your tracking efforts yield more and better information on Y2K, or as other events in your life cause you to reconsider, you need to go back and review your approach in each of the seven areas of preparedness (education, health, home, food, work, money, family/community). For a given area, here's some of what might change:

Risks/mitigations: New risks might appear; existing ones might go away; mitigation approaches might turn out to be impossible or not effective.

Opportunities: You might accomplish the opportunity; it might go away; or new (and more attractive) ones might appear.

Principles: The ones you have may need adjusting, or they may have become so ingrained (or irrelevant) that you can move on to new ones.

Needs: As you obtain the items on your list, or as you determine that you don't really need them, you can cross them off; in the meantime, there may be new items to add.

Plan: As you achieve tasks in your plan, or as they become unnecessary, check them off; modify them as needed; add new ones.

Enrolling others: Review to see whose help, support, and/or understanding you need and revise accordingly.

This shouldn't take a lot of time; maybe a few hours a month, if that. But it is worth the investment. It not only keeps you thinking about Y2K and your preparations, it also helps make the planning process a natural part of your thinking about Y2K, as opposed to something you have to sit and learn over and over again.

Acting Preemptively

A simpler approach is to take any preemptive actions that are appropriate, particularly in the seven areas of preparedness. The intent is to forestall or defuse potential problems ahead of time when possible, thus reducing cost, effort, and impact.

Suppose, for example, that you think based on evidence coming in spring of 1999 that Level 5 appears to be likely, though you had previously estimated the impact to be Level 3. For each of the seven areas, determine what actions you can take to increase your level of preparation. They might look like this:

Education: Curtail night law school plans for now; push to finish Java certification by July.

Health/fitness: Get those dental crowns put on now.

Home/hearth: Increase water storage supply to one month. Expand list of light, heat alternatives.

Food/supplies: Bump up home storage from two weeks to two months.

Work: After finishing Java certification, angle for position on development project.

Money/law: Put off getting new car; pay off old one by end of year. Shift 401(k) completely out of stocks and into bonds and cash. Finish next level of document organization.

Family/community: Talk activist neighbor into organizing a community Y2K group.

These can be worked back into your plans, if you are so inclined. However, remember that the entire reason for the priorities and principles is so that you can act and react without having to go back and dig out a plan. You'll know what's important and what you're trying to do, and that will help you make the decisions. However, don't underestimate the usefulness of a plan in helping you to stay on track and not forget or overlook details previously noted.

Responding to Y2K Events

A common assumption is that all of Y2K's consequences will occur in the weekend of January 1-2, 2000 in one grand burst of failures, leaving us to pick ourselves up afterwards. Unfortunately, this is almost certainly wrong.

Far more likely is that Y2K events will follow what you might call the "microwave popcorn" pattern. You stick a package of popcorn in the microwave and turn it (the microwave) on. Nothing happens for a while. Then there's an isolated pop. And another one. And another. Then several. The frequency of popping builds until there's a near-constant roar. Then the popping slows down to an intermittent rate and continues at that level for quite some time, then drops to a much slower level. If you left the popcorn bag in there long enough, you'd reach a point where all the kernels that were going to pop had done so, and no amount of microwaves would cause any more popping.[1]

That's how Y2K will likely happen, though on a scale of months or years. We've had individual "kernels"—Y2K events—popping for years. They have started to pick up some—the Information Technology Association of America reports that 44 percent of the firms they surveyed have experienced at least one Y2K failure in actual operating conditions[2]— but they're still isolated and well contained. However, as we get closer to Y2K, we'll see the rate of Y2K events increase, possibly dramatically, as they overlap in ever-higher numbers: *simultaneity*. The rate of Y2K events and consequences should reach a peak sometime around the Y2K crossover, and then start to taper off and drop back down to largely invisible levels.

What we don't know yet is exactly how many kernels are in the bag, where they, and how they'll interact, impact, or trigger one another: *complexity*. Various organizations seek to remove or disarm them as fast as possible. But most are late in starting. The hope is that the numbers drop enough to minimize the interactions and the impact.

The real wild card is how the populace at large, or even relatively small slices, will be reacting: *humanity*. As noted above, this can have an intensifying effect or a dampening one. Effects are already starting to be felt. For example, producers of food storage products, used to a small, steady sales rate, now find themselves with backlogs that may take months to fill— but they are leery to ramp up too much, less the demand for their products evaporate after Y2K.[3] And yet the peak demand for food storage products probably hasn't even hit yet. If significant numbers of people wanting to order those products in March 1999 find that they have a 12-month wait wherever they try to buy them, where will they turn next, and what backlog or shortage might be created there?

It is in that context that you will face Y2K events and have to choose how to respond to them. You can predict general classes of events—examples are given in the scenarios in Chapter 14—and you can make plans for how to respond to such. But there's a good chance you will be facing at some point an ever-increasing series of Y2K events, many of which were not thought of ahead of time.

This is where spending the time in determining priorities, establishing principles, and taking care of as much as you can ahead of time pay off. Look again at the "Acting Preemptively" section above and the proposed changes to the various areas of preparation. When you read through the list of changes of each area, you probably understood very quickly what was behind each change and what the intended outcome was. For example, the item to get certain dental work done now likely reflects a set of concern about there being money and/or dental insurance later, about not wanting to worry about it in the thick of Y2K events, and about whether the dentist's operations might be impacted by Y2K.

Minimizing the Impact

Should the frequency and/or impact of Y2K events rise in your own life beyond a certain point, you may find yourself in a fire-fighting situation, trying to control the damage and hold things together until things die down a bit. If the priorities/ principles/preparations approach was important above, it will be absolutely critical here.

Suppose that your post-Y2K area—far north and very cold—is suffering massive, weeks-long power outages over a wide area, causing water-supply interruptions as well due to bursting pipes and nonfunctional water pumps; in addition, oil deliveries have been delayed. Temperatures are plummeting; the house is getting unlivable; and your refrigerated/frozen food is either spoiling (inside) or frozen (outside). You are going to have to relocate the family farther south, at least temporarily. But your employer has relocated offices temporarily to a branch office in town that has sufficient power and heat. They badly want you at work. Your supervisor makes it clear that you are critical and expected to be there. Gas supplies are limited, and the city and county governments are struggling to keep the streets clear of snow and ice. And your mortgage payment is due.

What do you do?

Lest you think this example is an extreme case, it reflects exactly what a lot of Canadians went through in the first few months of 1998. A series of ice storms hit Ontario and Quebec and knocked out power to over a million homes for an extended period—in some cases, for days or even weeks—and was then followed by a sharp drop in temperatures. There are several accounts on the Web of the storm and its aftermath. One of the best is by Dave Brown of Rideau Canal, Ontario, who describes all that he, his family members, and his neighbors went through.[4] It gives you a sense of all the things that can go wrong (including a tree coming through the roof and a chain saw injury to the leg) and the various ways that you can scramble to cope with them. Another account that is both humorous and a bit sobering is Lorie Truemner's "Ice Storm Diet," in which she describes how to "lose at least 10 pounds in 2 weeks."[5] If you question the usefulness of food and water storage, this account should make you reconsider ("Breakfast: Choice of:…any fruit that hasn't started to smell funny…but all you really want is: WATER! any drinking water, anywhere you can scavenge it—all you can drink…").

This is why you have gone (will go) through the process of creating your plans for each of the seven areas of preparation, and why you should continue to adjust and update them as circumstances change. It is also why these preparations need to be specific to your needs, circumstances, and priorities—so that they can be of value in any serious or emergency situation, not just something related to Y2K. The difference can be minor as convenience vs. inconvenience, or it can be as serious as life and death. To quote Dave Brown:

> In summary, 23 people have died as a result of the storm to date. There are heart attacks related to clearing trees, to hypothermia, to carbon monoxide poisonings caused by people running their generators in their houses or garages to keep them from getting stolen. A number of deaths are related to fires caused by candles and unattended wood stoves. One man died while trying to heat his house with his car. Farmers have lost millions in livestock as cows die of cold related illness and lack of drinking water. Dairy cattle are drying up as farmers milking machines are inoperable without power. One farmer lost 13 cattle to electrocution when a felled power line charged the steel grating in the barn. He narrowly escaped himself. Rural areas will be without power for weeks to come as Hydro must work harder to service these remote areas. [6]

This is serious business, and it's worth your serious attention. Your next step: To review the scenarios in Chapter 14 and see which ones you think you need to prepare for.

14

Forecasting the Storm

Prediction is extremely difficult. Especially about the future.
—Niels Bohr

Now we come to the heart of things, the real questions that are on everyone's mind, including most likely yours: What's going to happen? How is Y2K really going to affect you? What exactly do you need to prepare for?

Good question.

We already discussed in the last chapter a few of the reasons why it's hard to predict what impact Y2K will have. Besides all those, extrapolations based on current trends and assumptions are almost always wrong,[1] because complex systems adapt—that's why they're called complex *adaptive* systems. The essential factor in Y2K consequences will be whether the number, timing, and types of Y2K events—and in particular, Y2K failures—will be such as to overwhelm the systems' ability to adapt or to perturb them into a new direction.

Because of that uncertainty, this chapter won't present a single speculation about the future. but rather a set of eleven scenarios. These represent a sample range of consequences, from a complete nonevent to the proverbial TEOTWAWKI.[2] Your responsibility is to track developments in the real world and use them to determine which scenario or set of scenarios seems most likely.

The triggering factors for these scenarios are several: Y2K problems in software and embedded systems in all sectors (corporate, infrastructure, government); self-protective measures in the financial and corporate sectors, including shifting of investments, avoidance of liability, and stockpiling; caution, self-protection, fear, and anger in the social sector; efforts, legislation, and leadership (or lack thereof) in the government sector; availability, accuracy, and tone of information available, including media coverage; and Y2K failures and consequences in the rest of the world. None of these can or should be considered independent of one another; they depend upon one another and interact in complex, dynamic, and nonlinear ways.

These scenarios track five major levels of Y2K impact within the United States: the economy; business; infrastructure and supply chain; society; and government.[3] As noted there, the groupings are a bit arbitrary; you could well get a Level 3 impact on the economy and infrastructure, a Level 4 on government, and a Level 5 on society. It's also important to note that each scenario level assumes the consequences of the lower levels. For example, the consequences in Level 5 include, build upon, or replace the consequences described in Levels 0 through 4 as appropriate.

Here's a description of what each of the fields in a given scenario means or is used for:

In a nutshell: A one-line description.

How it looks: A longer description of the scenario.

Time to recovery: How long it will take to get back to where we were pre-Y2K or the equivalent. This *doesn't* necessarily include a full economic recovery.

Economy: Possible impact on the economy, including financial markets, GDP and unemployment.[4]

Business: Possible impacts on businesses of all sizes.

Infrastructure: Possible impacts on power, water, transportation, telecom, and the supply chain.

Society: Possible social reactions and incidents.

Government: Possible impacts on federal, state, and local governments.

Education, and so forth: possible impacts and concerns.

Tracking clues: Evidence that might point toward this scenario, organized by six-month periods.

Commentary: Personal observations on this scenario.

Probability: A *highly subjective and tentative* estimate on the likelihood of this specific scenario or something close to it. The value is drawn from the survey results, with some (conservative) adjustments reflecting my own opinion. It reflects both the uncertainty about the real state of things and the uncertainty of what choices, events, and responses will occur through the entire Y2K period. (The value in parentheses indicates the cumulative probability that things won't get this bad.)

Wild cards:[5] Events and choices not directly caused by Y2K failures, though possibly coming in response to them, that could help this scenario come to pass.

Scenario Level 0: Just Kidding

In a nutshell: It's all a false alarm.

How it looks: Everything gets fixed in time. Y2K error rates in embedded systems turn out to be fewer and farther between. Business, government, and everyone else gets their various information systems repaired. The party goes on as planned.

Time to recovery: None required.

Economy: Irrational exuberance lifts Dow to 12,000, helps buoy up global economy.

Business: A lot of money spent, but improved quality and efficiency due to Y2K efforts.

Infrastructure: Everything works just fine.

Society: New era of good feelings and optimism.

Government: Democratic sweep in 2000, led by President-elect Gore.

Education: No impact.

Health/fitness: No impact.

Home/hearth: No impact.

Food/supplies: No impact.

Work: No impact.

Money/law: No impact.

Family/community: No impact.

Tracking clues:

> 1H99:[6] The U.S. Government declares itself Y2K compliant (with minor issues), and the GAO agrees; 50 percent of the Fortune 500 say they're done with Y2K work; a massive small-business mobilization starts.

> 2H99: The balance of the Fortune 500 are compliant; Europe, Asia, South Africa mobilize and get things under control more quickly than expected. Y2K becomes the "swine flu" of the century.[7]

Commentary: This is in here for completeness and intellectual honesty. Given the few public acknowledgments that have already been given by organizations that will not make the Y2K deadline, this is nearly as improbable as Level 10, though more pleasant to contemplate.

Probability: Less than 1 percent.

Wild card: A national and global mobilization unprecedented in history helps to get assessment and repair done ahead of time.

Scenario Level 1:
A Bump in the Road Ahead

In a nutshell: Local impact for some enterprises.

How it looks: Not quite a nonevent, but the Y2K equivalent of Comet Kohoutek.[8]

Time to recovery: A weekend.

Economy: Y2K's impact on the economy and markets is lost in the noise.

Business: Some small to medium businesses have Y2K problems.

Infrastructure: Some failures, but all caught in time and handled well.

Society: No impact.

Government: Both parties praised in handling of Y2K; "antipartisanship" movement in 107th Congress elected in November, 2000.

Education: No impact.

Health/fitness: A few hospitals, medical centers have Y2K problems.

Home/hearth: No impact.

Food/supplies: No impact.

Work: Possible problems at work.

Money/law: No impact.

Family/community: No impact.

Tracking clues:

1H99: Full-blown national mobilization underway by start of year. Congress takes over Yardeni's Y2K compliance database for publicly traded firms. Similar databases started up in regions and cities for local businesses, government agencies.

2H99: Businesses compete to establish Y2K compliance. Volunteers mobilize to help remediation for state and local government agencies.

Commentary: It's still hard to believe we could get off this lightly.

Probability: 5 percent (better outcome than this: <1 percent)

Wild card: Colin Powell appointed new Y2K czar before end 1998, gets full mobilization on fixing problems.

Scenario Level 2:
Well, Maybe a Large Pothole

In a nutshell: Significant impact for many enterprises.

How it looks: About 10 percent of all organizations find themselves either running out of time or dealing with uncaught Y2K problems. Some systemic problems show up.

Time to recovery: A week or two.

Economy: Some market adjustment (down 10 percent), but recovered within 6 months.

Business: Businesses are jolted a bit and scramble to fix things. Several instances of supply chain failure shut down businesses that would otherwise be ready.

Infrastructure: A few short-lived (1–3 days) water quality warnings and equivalent problems. Air traffic slowdown for Y2K weekend due to consumer caution.

Society: Y2K jokes in late night monologues for a few weeks before and several weeks after. At least one late night host triggers an inadvertent shortage or panic with a joke.[9]

Government: At least one state government runs into serious Y2K problems.

Education: Some public schools close for a few "Y2K days" (instead of "snow days") to get things going.

Health/fitness: Most hospitals face temporary loss of a few critical pieces of equipment due to inability to test and replace all of them in time. At least one highly-publicized death due to a Y2K failure is reported.

Home/hearth: Use of bottled water in many areas due to concerns about water purification systems.

Food/supplies: Stores have a hard time keeping certain items in stock during last few weeks of 1999. Some entrepreneurs set up special "Y2K warehouses" selling case lots of canned and packaged goods, water in 5- and 55-gal. containers, other items.

Work: Some Y2K ripple effects through workplace, but short lived.

Money/law: A few billing errors show up.

Family/community: Communities organize Y2K parties.

Tracking clues:

1H99: The Administration doesn't really address Y2K until sometime in the first part of 1999. Media coverage continues to follow hype/anti-hype cycle.

2H99: First public acknowledgment of one or more major corporations, and at least one state government, facing serious Y2K problems.

Commentary: This is probably the best result we can hope for.

Probability: 15 percent (better outcome than this: 5 percent)

Wild card: The President makes Y2K the top—and sole—issue in his January 1999 State of the Union address and appoints himself as national Y2K coordinator, delegating all other responsibilities to his Cabinet.

Scenario Level 3:
The Dow Drops Some More

In a nutshell: Markets drop 20 percent; some business bankruptcies occur.

How it looks: The serious struggles of several Fortune 100 corporations due to Y2K problems whacks the Dow.

Time to recovery: A month.

Economy: Dow drops 20 percent within a week or two and doesn't recover before the end of 2000. Economic growth is flat for 2000.

Business: Businesses have "Y2K holidays" in which all hands report to help solve remaining Y2K problems.

Infrastructure: At least one regional brownout/blackout (2–3 days) with other scattered problems; most airlines scale back flights some for Y2K weekend.

Society: Surge in stockpiling at end of 1999; drop in consumer confidence, spending.

Government: Y2K dominates 2000 elections; Gore fails to get Democratic presidential nod.

Education: Colleges (incl. universities) face some disruptions of internal information systems.

Health/fitness: Shortages of some prescription and OTC medications.

Home/hearth: Use of some flashlights, candles, fireplaces; at least one death attributed to blackouts.

Food/supplies: Shortages of a few key items at end of 1999; spot shortages of random items in first part of 2000.

Work: Some hiring freezes, layoffs due to flat economy, market decline.

Money/law: At least one mid-sized bank discovers pervasive errors in its accounts and records.

Family/community: Increased anxiety in families and communities, especially in lower-income areas.

Tracking clues:

1H99: The Federal government resets its Y2K deadline from March 31 to June 30 with a vow for a "crash priority effort."

2H99: Media reports start to explore Y2K impacts between the two extremes (Level 0 and Level 10). More and more businesses go public with their contingency plans.

Commentary: This reflects the most commonly held opinion of what Y2K will bring and represents the most probable optimistic outcome.

Probability: 20 percent (better outcome than this: 20 percent)

Wild card: National Y2K movement starts independent of U.S. government and provides leadership and information.

Scenario Level 4:
It's The Economy, Stupid

In a nutshell: The Fed versus Y2K.

How it looks: The Federal Reserve Board makes a few more interest rate cuts. However, Y2K failures begin showing up outside of the United States well in advance of Y2K itself and have both an operational and a psychological impact.

Time to recovery: Two months

Economy: Economic slowdown (–1 percent over a three-month period); unemployment rises.

Business: Bankruptcy/acquisition of at least one Fortune 100 company due to internal Y2K problems, supplier problems, foreign Y2K issues, and/or Y2K litigation.

Infrastructure: Transient (3–7 days) interruptions in utilities; cutbacks in various transportation systems.

Society: A few isolated social incidents, including discovery (and prevention) of a militia-type terrorist plot timed to coincide with Y2K.

Government: At least one major government agency (HCFA, FMA, FAA) requires that some contingency plans go into effect.

Education: Problems with college admissions, testing, financial aid.

Health/fitness: Some problems with health insurance companies.

Home/hearth: Common use of heaters, cook stoves.

Food/supplies: Manufacturers temporarily suspend production of some product offerings to focus on production of best-sellers.

Work: Increase in layoffs, time off without pay.

Money/law: Errors in billing, records not uncommon. At least one arrest of a consumer trying to claim more money in bank accounts than was actually there.

Family/community: Some neighborhoods form purchasing associations.

Tracking clues:

1H99: The OMB and the GAO have a series of increasingly sharp and public disagreements as to how ready the various federal agencies and departments are.

2H99: The news that a major government agency will need to use its contingency plans causes a ripple effect through private industry and actually leads many corporations to make the same admission.

Commentary: The cumulative probability up to and including this level is 65 percent. That range of scenarios (0 through 4) presume no real surprises about Y2K defects themselves; the major distinction is the timing and level of mobilization to deal with Y2K.

Probability: 25 percent (better outcome than this: 40 percent)

Wild card: The global economic crisis rolls over Latin America; Brazil, Argentina, and finally Mexico face major currency and economic issues.

Scenario Level 5:
The 1982 Recession, Revisited

In a nutshell: A sharp, short recession, combined with isolated infrastructure problems

How it looks: Y2K turns out to have some real teeth, both here and abroad. Foreign Y2K consequences drag the global economy down even more, and we are unable to escape the consequences.

Time to recovery: Three to four months

Economy: Mild recession (–2.5 percent over six months); unemployment up to 8 percent.

Business: Major disruptions in production and processing of raw materials, as well as the manufacturing and supply chain.

Infrastructure: Scattered infrastructure/supply chain problems lasting up to two weeks.

Society: Some population shifts to states and regions that appear to be better prepared and have milder climates.

Government: HCFA not ready for Y2K. Administration blamed for Y2K problems, economy; Republican sweep in 2000.

Education: Many colleges delay start of classes for a few weeks, as do most public schools.

Health/fitness: HCFA problems cause cutbacks, closures, bankruptcies in health care industry; media keeps track of "HCFA death count."

Home/hearth: Ten percent of population experiences some form of outage, however short.

Food/supplies: Shortages, especially in urban areas, of some food and household items through January 2000. Many grocery stores implement per-person limits.

Work: Turmoil in job market; worst for new graduates since early 90s.

Money/law: Voluntary arbitration centers set up to handle disputes over records, accounts.

Family/community: Short-term "housesharing" common to deal with outages.

Tracking clues:

1H99: Many corporations and government agencies shift completion dates to November 1999.

2H99: Government files suit against several HCFA contractors for failure to complete work; most simply declare bankruptcy and walk away.

Commentary: This is the first (and mildest) of the "nasty" scenarios. While the probabilities decline from here on out, once we get into this level of Y2K impacts, we risk a "vicious circle" effect that could drag us into higher (worse) scenarios.

Probability: 15 percent (better outcome than this: 65 percent)

Wild card: Senate Special Committee on Year 2000 holds a special set of hearings with whistleblowers (identities hidden) from the public and private sectors, establishing how far behind many of these organizations really are. This is followed by a wave of resignations and firings in both sectors.

Scenario Level 6:
Make That the 1973 Recession

In a nutshell: A longer, broader recession

How it looks: We discover how tied in we are to the rest of the world, and how far behind the rest of the world is on Y2K. The economic decline is more and longer than expected.

Time to recovery: Six months (not including recession)

Economy: Strong recession (–3.5 percent over 18 months); unemployment up to 10 percent.

Business: Most businesses suffer some form of Y2K impact. Significant die-off in small to medium high-tech firms as funding, markets dry up.

Infrastructure: Urban infrastructure/supply problems lasting two to four weeks, with lesser outages elsewhere in the country. Significant transportation disruptions, especially overseas.

Society: Stockpiling starts earlier in 1999. Protests and isolated incidents of looting in some cities, both before and after Y2K.

Government: IRS not ready in time. Congress votes in flat tax, but the deficit explodes due to reduced collections, recession, increased social services.

Education: Significant financial problems at colleges due to declining enrollment, tax revenues, federal grants, alumni donations.

Health/fitness: Significant increase in hospital deaths due to shortages of supplies and medications, interruptions in utilities, unrepaired equipment.

Home/hearth: Most urban/suburban dwellings suffer some period of utility disruption.

Food/supplies: Shortage/surplus cycle runs through 1999 as manufacturers deal with consumer stockpiling. Some shortages persist into February 2000.

Work: Sudden (if short-lived) glut of high-tech workers on market, making job market even worse. Sudden shift in tax laws causes headaches, costs for businesses.

Money/law: Shift in tax laws causes significant problems, errors in financial systems, records.

Family/community: Some communities set up food banks.

Tracking clues:

1H99: Panic begins to set in over in Europe as real scope of Y2K becomes apparent.

2H99: IRS acknowledges that it won't be ready until close to the end of 2000. Facing a total collapse of revenue and continuing public antipathy toward the IRS, the President reverses field and takes the lead on abolishing the personal income tax, leading to record approval ratings—until the recession sets in.

Commentary: At this point, the various complex systems—economic, social, political, technological, informational—have been perturbed enough to cause them to settle into new forms irrevocably.

Probability: 10 percent (outcome better than this: 80 percent)

Wild card: China devalues its currency, plunging Asia into a deep depression and intensifying the recession in Europe and the Americas.

Scenario Level 7: Things Get Worse

In a nutshell: The U.S. escapes a depression—barely.

How it looks: The global infrastructure is seriously impacted by Y2K, intensifying and prolonging the global economic crisis, and triggering political crises in many countries, including the United States.

Time to recovery: Six to twelve months.

Economy: Very strong recession (–5 percent over two years); unemployment up to 15 percent.

Business: Widescale layoffs, cutbacks. One of the Big 3 auto manufacturers collapses and/or is acquired.

Infrastructure: Regional infrastructure/supply problems for one to two months. Significant problems with internal transportation. At least one major environmental disaster due to Y2K.

Society: "Peoples Needs" movement organizes groups to distribute food, other necessities.

Government: Significant problems in government delivery of social services. Both parties blamed; centrist third party arises and wins enough seats in Congress to deny either party a clear majority.

Education: Rise of neo-Luddite movement on campuses. Public schools take "summer vacation" during Jan.-March 2000 period.

Health/fitness: Health care centers implement informal triage in admittance policy. Medical research centers close or are set back years in research due to power, equipment malfunctions.

Home/hearth: Dwellings in affected areas adapt to intermittent feeds and deliveries.

Food/supplies: Fresh fruits, vegetables, meats scarce and expensive until spring due to problems in foreign countries, transportation. State- or city-mandated rationing on key items, causing long lines at stores.

Work: Vandalism of technology firms in Y2K protests.

Money/law: Debt/account negotiation becomes a way of life.

Family/community: Federal government asks states to help implement key social programs.

Tracking clues:

1H99: U.S. supply chain becomes clogged with stockpiling requests by businesses, consumers, leading to backorders and shortages throughout 1999.

2H99: Attempts for national and global Y2K mobilization fall apart in acrimony.

Commentary: This scenario presumes that Y2K problems are much worse than currently believed and that we will do a much poorer job of fixing them in time, here and abroad.

Probability: 5 percent (outcome better than this: 90 percent)

Wild Card: Christian millennialists trigger a new Arab-Israeli war—as well as a Muslim *jihad* against Christians—by destroying the Al-Aqsa Mosque (including the Dome of the Rock) in Jeruleaum so that the new Jewish temple can be built.

Scenario Level 8:
Brother, Can You Spare a Dime?

In a nutshell: The Great Depression: The Sequel.

How it looks: We get sucked into a systemic collapse by a greater-than-expected rate of Y2K failures in the United States and a host of developing countries going through economic crises similar to Indonesia's but all at the same time. The GDP drops an average of 7–9 percent per year for two to three years, in spite of near zero interest rates from the Fed.

Time to recovery: Two years.

Economy: Depression (–21 percent over three years); unemployment hits 25 percent by 2001.

Business: Major meltdown, with massive consolidation or failure in manufacturing, production industries.

Infrastructure: Infrastructure/supply chain crippled for three to six months.

Society: Protests and riots in many large metropolitan areas; at least one foreign terrorist attack on U.S. soil.

Government: Curfews and/or martial law imposed in many large metropolitan areas.

Education: Large cutbacks at colleges; some state campuses consolidate, close for year. Public schools implement part-time home schooling programs.

Health/fitness: Presidential order (via Dept. of HHS) mandates triage for health center admittance, treatment, prescriptions.

Home/hearth: Measurable relocation of populace from urban to rural areas causes problems, conflict.

Food/supplies: Federal food rationing and distribution implemented.

Work: Congress (106th session, 2nd term) passes emergency legislation to suspend federal regulation of businesses.

Money/law: Congress passes legislation to halt all Y2K-related lawsuits.

Family/community: Congress turns all social services over to states.

Tracking clues:

1H99: A major news source breaks a well-documented story of how bad Y2K is throughout the world. Panic and millennial fever begin to set in across the globe.

2H99: Country after country sinks into economic and political problems.

Commentary: I consider this the worst of the foreseeable Y2K outcomes, absent some separate and very profound shock to the system (e.g., nuclear or biological terrorism).

Probability: 3 percent (outcome better than this: 95 percent)

Wild card: Nuclear civil war within Russia. China becomes involved in an effort to seize disputed territory; the conflict spreads to include India and Pakistan. The United States is not involved, though the Pacific Northwest suffers from fallout blowing across from Asia.

Scenario Level 9:
Welcome to The Third World

In a nutshell: America discovers how the rest of the world lives.

How it looks: The complex systems that have supported America so well for half a century are unable to adapt and collapse to a lower level of functionality. Immigration— legal and illegal—plummets to its lowest recorded levels.

Time to recovery: Three to five years.

Economy: Profound depression (–40+ percent over five years); unemployment hits 30 percent before government stops keeping track.

Business: Radical cutbacks, mergers, or failures of 50 percent of the Fortune 500; 80 percent of small to medium business fail.

Infrastructure: Collapse of infrastructure, supply chain (6–12 months).

Society: Widespread social disruptions, including internal terrorism from militia groups.

Government: Widespread but ineffective martial law. Elections in 2000 disrupted or cancelled. *De facto* (if not *de jure*) secession of at least one state.

Education: Closing of many colleges. Many public schools help administer home schooling program.

Health/fitness: Massive closures of hospitals, research facilities. Most health care shifts to small centers. Severe shortages of medical supplies, equipment.

Home/hearth: Suburban homes converted to operate without external power, water, and so on.

Food/supplies: Food production and distribution chain breaks down.

Work: "Microtech" businesses spring up locally to provide products, services to remaining businesses.

Money/law: Congress (107th, 1st term) passes "Jubilee" legislation to cancel all debts (including a complete tax amnesty), dismiss all civil lawsuits, and halt new ones for a year.

Family/community: States turn over most of social services to cities, counties.

Tracking clues:

1H99: Communist resurgence in Russia increases global tensions, diverts attention and resources away from Y2K worldwide.

2H99: Assertions of Y2K progress in public and private sectors continue up until November, at which point mass panic begins to set in.

Commentary: Highly improbable based on current information and estimates.

Probability: 1 percent (outcome better than this: 98 percent)

Wild card: Rise of "strong man" leader within Europe leads to collapse of NATO, threat of European "warm war," reformation of (smaller) Soviet Union.

Scenario Level 10:
It Can't Happen Here

In a nutshell: The End Of The World As We Know It.

How it looks: Quadrant III: Millennial collapse. Complete infrastructure breakdown combined with pervasive social chaos.

Time to recovery: Five to ten years.

Economy: Collapse of economic systems, including currency, banking system, financial markets.

Business: Collapse or radical transformation of most mid- to large-sized businesses.

Infrastructure: Long-term (> one year) shutdown of infrastructure, supply chain, with scattered operating centers.

Society: Social chaos.

Government: Radical downsizing, transformation, splintering, or collapse of U.S. government; global political chaos.

Education: Colleges become communes.

Health/fitness: Health care set back 50 years or more; collapse of medical system.

Home/hearth: Flights from dense urban areas.

Food/supplies: Possible famine, especially in winter of 2000-2001.

Work: Post-service economy: Mix of preindustrial, industrial, and technology.

Money/law: Collapse of monetary system, replaced by barter variants and local currencies. Personal records largely irrelevant.

Family/community: Social services provided (if at all) by communities.

Tracking clues:

> 1H99: Significant Y2K failures show up in more systems than expected, causing problems and leading to panic. Global economy drops into full-blown depression, lead by Chinese devaluation of currency. United States drops into recession; unemployment starts a steady climb.

> 2H99: The vast majority of businesses (including utilities and government agencies) find themselves unable to complete Y2K work because of economy, resources.

Commentary: Again, this is here for completeness. Given the current state of Y2K repair efforts in all sectors, it's hard to see a credible Y2K-only chain of events that could result in this level of disruption.

Probability: Less that 1 percent (outcome better than this: 99 percent)

Wild card: Nuclear or biological attack on Washington D.C. and New York City, either by rogue Russian military units or by terrorists. That, combined with a feasible worst-case Y2K scenario, leads to the collapse of the U.S. government.

Building Your Own Scenarios

As stated back in Chapter 13, these scenarios represent a best effort to put together a reasonable and complete spectrum of possible Y2K consequences. However, they may be wrong. New political, social, or economic developments might arise. Or you may decide that the "spectrum" approach is wrong, that there should be a set of scenarios with some that can lead to others, but not vice versa.[10]

As such, a blank scenario follows. Feel free to copy it for noncommercial purposes and fill it out.

Scenario Level

In a nutshell: .

How it looks:

Time to recovery:

_____

Economy:

Business:

Infrastructure:

Society:

Government:

_____

Education:

Health/fitness:

Home/hearth:

Food/supplies:

Work:

Money/law:

Family/community:

_____

Tracking clues: 1H99:

2H99:

_____

Commentary:

Probability:

Wild card:

Concluding Thoughts

It is a bit presumptuous to attempt to shoehorn the range of Y2K possibilities within a single chapter and with a simple format. But this represents a far broader spread of Y2K outcomes than are typically presented in the media or in many books on Y2K.

In all this, remember that these are guesses and estimates based on information and speculations available as of the fall of 1998. Your responsibility is to learn as much as you can about Y2K, track these scenarios, and prepare accordingly. Above all, don't panic—that serves no one, least of all yourself.

Part IV

HOPE SPRINGS ETERNAL: GETTING UP OFF THE GROUND

Setting the Stage: January through June 2000

Life is change; how it differs from the rocks.
—John Wyndham, *Rebirth* and Jefferson Airplane,
  "Crown of Creation"

If our occasional blindness stems from an unwillingness to acknowledge that history will bring unpleasant changes despite our assertions that life (when good) can and should remain the same, our occasional greatness rises from a willingness to take the worst that history has to give us and to build a future upon it. A hospital and an apartment building sit at what was ground zero for the atomic bomb dropped on Hiroshima, with the Hiroshima Peace Memorial Park nearby.

Whatever the Y2K consequences, our task is much less daunting, and we have so much more to work with. Let's see what we can build.

15

Taking Stock, Setting Direction, Moving On

The art of life is a constant reqadjustment to our surrounding
—Kakuzo Okakauro

Let's say that it's sometime in January 2000.

There you sit, having made it through whatever it was that the *fin de siecle* brought, somewhere in that range of scenarios in the previous chapter. There is a vast array of outcomes to cover—not just the scenarios as given, but your particular preparations (or lack thereof), geographic location, local events, reaction to events, and so on. All may be well, or you may find yourself in a setting you never imagined. How are you going to deal with whatever it is that comes up, and how will you know what to do?

Once again, don't panic. If you've been following the advice in this book, you have established your personal and family priorities, as well as your commitments to others, be those financial, legal, or personal. You considered the set of possible Y2K events and decided which ones might affect you. You went through seven major areas of your life—education, health and fitness, living quarters, food and supplies, work, debts and assets, and social relations—and for each one determined what you needed to learn, what risks and opportunities

357

you faced, what your guiding principles were, what you were in need of, what your plan for Y2K preparation was, and whose help and cooperation (or, at least, understanding) you wanted. Then, you monitored developing events and fine-tuned (or radically rethought) your plan based on what was happening and what seemed to be just over the horizon.

Bingo.

If you did indeed do all that, then you don't need much advice. You just need to go through this process again, only this time you're applying it after Y2K, not before. You have learned how to plan your life according to what you consider important, how to shape those plans to what's feasible, and how to redirect those plans when things change.

Of course, if the Y2K transition was relatively uneventful, you can just skip all this and go on with your life however you choose. On the other hand, consider this. The process that's been described here isn't just a way of getting through Y2K or even any potentially difficult event or period. It can also be used to get control of your life in general—to know where you stand, where you want to go, how to get there, and how to deal with surprises, especially the unpleasant ones, along the way.

Because of your post-Y2K condition or just because of your personal inclination, you may feel a bit overwhelmed at the thought of going through any kind of planning process. As with Part II, this chapter has a "JumpStart" section at the end. Feel free to skip to that and come back here later, if at all.

Important Note: The ACTION sections below are for doing *after* (or in the midst of) Y2K, not before. That should be clear, lest you be confused about just what this book is asking you to do.

Taking Stock

So, Y2K has come and possibly gone. Before you decide which way to go, you need to know where you are. That means evaluating where you currently stand in each of the areas of personal and family preparation.

Consider this chart:

Preparation area	Current status	Pressing needs	Risks	Opportunities	Issues
Education					
Health and fitness					
Home and hearth					
Food and supplies					
Work					
Money and law					
Family, community, nation					

ACTION. Create this chart or an equivalent. Note that you don't have to actually do this as a table or grid. You might not have that big a sheet of paper to fit all you need to in each box. But it helps to see it and think of it this way.

OUTCOME. You're ready to start filling in the boxes. You also have a way of making sure nothing is ignored or falls between the cracks.

Current Status

The first question is: Where do you stand in each area? Here are some more specific questions.

- **Education.** What is the status of anyone currently enrolled in any kind of educational institution? Is the institution itself functioning well? Are you trying to complete a particular course? If you or your children are applying to a college or university, what is the status of that process and of the institution itself?

- **Health and fitness.** Is everyone well? What is the status of any medical conditions or issues that predate Y2K? Do you have any prescriptions or other medical supplies that need to be replenished? Are there any new medical needs requiring immediate attention?

- **Home and hearth.** What are your water supplies and how long can they last? What is the status of all the various external feeds (electricity, phone, etc.)? Is the house safe? Livable? Comfortable?

- **Food and supplies.** What food is on hand? Is any in danger of going bad? Are there any problems with grocery shopping? What other supplies might you need?

- **Work.** Can you get there? Do they want/need you? Are they able to pay you? What impact has

Y2K had on them? How long does it look as
though it will last?

- **Money and law**. What bills are due? Do you
  have any problem in paying them? Are the statements you're getting accurate?

- **Family, community, nation**. How is everyone
  in the family holding up? Have you gotten hold
  of everyone? How are your neighbors doing? Do
  they have all that they need? Are they able to
  help you with some of your needs?

These, by the way, are pretty much the same questions that
you go through after something like an ice storm, hurricane,
or earthquake: How is everything and everyone?

ACTION. Fill in the first column of the chart with the status of each area. Useful information should come to mind by
answering these or other relevant questions. You should be
able to come up with plenty of questions for each area in just a
few minutes.

OUTCOME. You should have a well-rounded idea of how
things stand. It's good to go through the entire list, even
though your priorities (original or revised) might lead you to
focus on just a few. You might end up with some high-priority
items in areas you didn't expect.

Pressing Needs

The next question is, what are the most pressing needs you
have in each of these areas?   Here are some examples; yours
will vary depending upon your status and circumstances.

- **Education**. Transcripts, grades, or certificates; response on applications; homework or other instructions for disrupted classes.

- **Health and fitness**. Prescription refills and other medication and devices; treatment for new or existing conditions.

- **Home and hearth**. Water; heat; light; power; gasoline.

- **Food and supplies**. Basic foods; dairy products; fresh fruits and vegetables; household supplies.

- **Work**. Callback to work (if furloughed); supplies and utilities required for company to function; ability to sell to customers; paycheck.

- **Money and law**. Payment of creditors; access to financial resources; correction or updating of accounts; information required to file taxes in April.

- **Family, community, nation**. Get in touch with family members in other cities/states/countries. Check on status of neighbors and friends.

Again, the actual list will depend on what has actually happened. If the scenario level is 4 or less, the focus is likely to be on work, education, and money; if it's 5 or higher, then the other areas become more involved. On the other hand, if you've been furloughed and it's unclear when you'll get back to work, then food and supplies may suddenly be of significant interest.

ACTION. Go down the second column of the chart, putting the three or four most pressing needs for each; if there are fewer than that, don't worry; if there are more, pick the most important.

OUTCOME. This column is your emergency response plan. Your ideal is to take care of your needs. If time and resources don't permit that, then you'll use your priorities to select the most important.

Risks, Opportunities, and Issues

Beyond the current status and pressing needs, you need to look down the road and ask yourself what risks you face (aside from your pressing needs), what opportunities you might pursue, and what issues remain unresolved. These will, of course, depend on a host of factors, but here are some hypothetical examples; be sure to come up with your own.

- **Education**. Risks: Delays in graduation, admission; loss of credit. Opportunities: Educational institutions willing to be less restrictive due to losses elsewhere. Issues: What are the best jobs for 2000? For 2001? For 2005? 2010?

- **Health and fitness**. Risks: Impacts on medical facilities and solutions; greater scarcity of drugs and treatments; interruptions in Medicare/Medicaid payments (HCFA). Opportunities: More chance for physical activities, alternative remedies. Issues: What to do for critical medical situations.

- **Home and hearth**. Risks: Persistent or intermittent interruptions of feeds, deliveries, pickups;

services cut off because of computer errors, difficulties in payment. Opportunities: Adjust lifestyle to use less utilities, save money. Issues: What is that minimum set and level of services?

- **Food and supplies**. Risks: Persistent or intermittent shortages of food and supplies; jumps in price. Opportunities: Reexamination of eating habits; switch to lower-cost, healthier foods. Issues: Can you get everything that you need?

- **Work**. Risks: Layoffs; scaled-back hours; reduced profits. Opportunities: Potential upsurge in your profession (information technology, accounting, construction); chance to change jobs. Issues: Figuring out what you'd like to do and how to make yourself qualified.

- **Money and law**. Risks: Damage to credit rating; accounts referred to collection; loss of value of investments. Opportunities: Potential upsurge in investments. Issues: Knowing what will go up, what will go down.

- **Family, community, nation**. Risks: Uncertainty of condition due to communication, transportation problems. Opportunities: Get everyone together in one place. Issues: Do you really want to?

Again, these are general examples, and they're all over the map.

ACTION. Put at least one risk, one opportunity, and one issue in the chart for each area of preparation. Don't get too tied up in the examples given above; you need to tailor them to your circumstances and the conditions where you find yourself.

OUTCOME. You now have a decent assessment of just where you stand. If you compare this with the planning you did in Part II, you can get a sense of just what impact, direct and indirect, Y2K has had on you. You're also now ready to get on with your life.

Setting Direction

Now that you have assessed where you are, what you need, and what might get in the way, it's time to review—and possibly modify—the priorities that drive you and the commitments that bind you.

Reviewing Priorities

Once you have gone through—or are in the midst of—the various events surrounding Y2K, you may find that your priorities have changed. New ones, not on your original list, can be added; old ones dropped; and the order changed. Here's the list in Chapter 5; if you're reading this post-Y2K, see if they look different than they did then:

- Current living quarters, neighborhood, geographic area

- Career or profession

- Your personal well-being

- Various assets (savings, investments, posses-sions)

- The well-being of your spouse/partner

- The well-being of your children or other depen-dents

- Adherence to certain religious or philosophical beliefs or standards

- Standard of living, including diet, clothing, transportation

- The well-being of relatives, friends, neighbors, co-workers

- Level of income, or some sizable fraction thereof

ACTION: Take the list of priorities you made in Chapter 5 (if you have a copy sitting around) and review it. See how well they've held up. Then make a new list of priorities and stack rank it as you did (or were supposed to) in Chapter 5, that is, put them in an absolute 1-2-3 ... order. As you do so, see if you look at things differently.

OUTCOME: As before, these priorities will guide you when you have to make difficult decisions, such as deciding which needs in your table get handled first and which are deferred.

Reviewing Commitments

Your post-Y2K list of commitments may have changed signif-icantly from what you came up with in Chapter 5. For starters, if you made a serious effort to reduce or eliminate debts, then you may have fewer and/or less demanding financial commit-ments. On the other hand, you may have made more serious social commitments with your neighbors and others.

ACTION. Take out your old list to modify, or start a fresh one. Again, list all your commitments, noting the nature of the commitment, whom it's with, what it entails, and where you want to go with it. Do the same for commitments made to you. Note their relative importance and how the commit-ments relate to one another.

OUTCOME: While your priorities guide you, your com-mitments constrain you. Between the two, you should be able to determine where to spend your resources.

Looking Ahead

Now comes the really challenging part: predicting the future. Y2K as an event has come and gone, but you still live in a world full of complexity, humanity, and—though perhaps not as dramatic as Y2K may have been—simultaneity. And whether or not Y2K has changed the landscape, there are many other forces and factors that will continue to make the world a dynamic and challenging place to live.

Welcome to the future. You're now living in it.

Moving On

If you really have worked through to this spot, congratula-tions. You have a level of awareness, control, and power in your personal life that few ever achieve. You have also probably been of great service to your family, your neighbors, and your community; by so doing, you have also served your country and your species.

At this point, you can use your decisions concerning priorities, commitments, and future events to refine and prioritize your needs and tasks in the seven areas of personal and family preparedness.

Post-Y2K JumpStart

For those of you who need something quick to work from, here's a checklist. Adjust it to your circumstances.

❏ Write down the four or five top priorities you have.

❏ Write down the commitments you have and what each implies or requires.

❏ Make a survey of what you have on hand or can get readily, based on the seven areas.

❏ Determine your most pressing needs, organized by the seven areas, based on your priorities, commitments, and family needs.

❏ Set up a plan to take care of those pressing needs while meeting your commitments.

❏ When things have settled down a bit more, come back to this chapter and work through it to make plans for the rest of the year.

Tips and Traps

A few last suggestions

• Don't make this harder than it needs to be. It's easy to become obsessed with forms and checklists and plans. The goal isn't the paper you produce; it's the choices you make, consciously and with a good understanding of the risks and trade-offs.

• At the same time, try to exercise the discipline to go through the entire process. Otherwise, you may find yourself blindsided by unquestioned assumptions, unexamined conflicts, and unanticipated risks.

Closing Thoughts

The Year 2000 issue was just a special case of the context of life that we created for ourselves. As noted above, the factors of complexity, humanity, and simultaneity will continue to dominate our lives. We must choose how we act or react as we move on.

16

Lessons Learned

Experience keeps a dear school, but fools will learn in no other.
—Benjamin Franklin,
Poor Richard's Almanac

What, then, should we learn from all this? That will depend, of course, upon one's point of view, as well as what happens; the lessons of Level 0 are not the same as those of Level 10. But there are several lessons worth getting out of this. And since several groups have estimated worldwide Y2K costs to be on the order of hundreds of millions of dollars, we might as well profit from what we have paid for.

This chapter presents some of those lessons and suggests how they can be applied from here on out. Some of them may seem a bit focused on technology, but that's where Y2K shows up. If you're not familiar with software development, you might learn a few interesting facts about the profession. Each lesson also gives my personal assessment as to the chance of this happening on any significant basis, rated on a scale of 1 to 5 snowballs.[1]

So, let's see what we learned.

Lesson 1: Quality Counts; It Also Pays Off

For literally decades there has been an ongoing argument in software engineering. It is between those who advocate a strong emphasis on Quality Assurance (QA) at all points through the process and those who see QA as at best an after-thought, something to be done as briefly as possible before releasing the program or system into production. The latter point of view tends to dominate in organizational settings; even where QA exists, it is often underfunded and lacks clout within the organization. For every mid- to high-level manager who supports the time and money that QA requires, there are at least a dozen who could not care less and have only two questions about the project: Have you started coding[2] and when will it be done?

Y2K was decades of poor quality come home to roost. Let's just posit for a minute that all the software for the past 50 years had been developed in a professional, quality-oriented manner. That means it has adequate documentation, good source-code control, professional design and code reviews, well-written test scripts, decent testing at all levels, and so on. Now suppose that it still had used two-digit years with the same level of frequency, that is, there was just as pervasive a Y2K problem. The expense, effort, and time required to repair all those systems would have been a small fraction of what the effort will end up costing. But it gets even better, because had those quality practices been followed, the Y2K issue would have been raised and dealt with many years ago. Better yet, the massive maintenance costs that eat up such a large portion of typical information systems (IS) division budgets would be much smaller as well.

How to apply: Y2K projects themselves have required many organizations to implement a level of quality previously not attempted. If those organizations will continue to follow those practices—and pay professional quality engineers to ask a lot of good "what if?" questions—then the organizations will benefit greatly.

Chance of this happening: Three out of five snowballs. The forces and tendencies that drew organizations away from quality in the first place are still there, so the question for a given organization will be how well it learned the lesson from Y2K.

Lesson 2: You Can Pay Now, or You Can Pay Later with Interest and Penalty

This could be the official motto of the Internal Revenue Service. But it's actually something a good friend used to chide me with when I'd grumble about the hard tasks life presents: It's almost always easier and cheaper to deal with problems now than to postpone them until later.

Outside of, say, failing to stop Hitler before he plunged us all into World War II, it's hard to come up with a more dramatic global example of this lesson than Y2K. This problem has been known for decades. The resource constraints that caused it in the first place went away 10 to 15 years ago. The information technology (IT) industry started focusing on it in 1993. Yet the vast majority of organizations using or relying upon information technology—business, government, educational—did nothing until 1996 or later and an amazing percentage didn't start their initial inventory and assessment phase until 1998, with less than two years left. Those delays dramatically drove up the cost of Y2K remediation; they also increased the chances of organizations not being done in time and suffering further financial losses thereby.

How to apply: Upper management needs to support IS management in their efforts to find problems in advance and resolve them. Just as important, upper management needs to quiz IS management regularly on what they (IS) should be dealing with now so that greater and more expensive problems don't arise later on.

Odds of this happening: I give this one just one snowball. As Capers Jones notes in his book on Y2K, "…for sociological reasons the human species is not very effective in disaster prevention."[3] Frankly, when a news item came out in March 1998 that a newly detected near-Earth asteroid might come close enough to impact Earth in 2028,[4] my first thought was, "And I'll bet we wait until 2025 to do anything about it." Luckily for us, the orbit calculations turned out to be in error.

Lesson 3: Details Matter

The question that comes up time and again when people first encounter the Y2K problem is: "How could two digits cause such problems?" One answer: Well, if you drop the first two digits off your paycheck, would it matter? We're talking about a different type of error, but it still gets the point across: 1900 and 2000 are not the same number, and any system that is doing calculations on 2000 but thinks it's actually dealing with 1900 is going to get confused very quickly.

Frankly, vast numbers of Y2K-like defects and limitations exist in software worldwide. What makes Y2K different from most is the largely synchronized—literally—nature of the defects, tying them to an external, constantly incrementing calendar.

How to apply: This lesson can be applied by having those who specify, design, and implement information technology in its various forms to focus more on the consequences of the details of their decisions.

Odds of this happening: Four snowballs. Y2K is going to cause a lot of software engineers and technical managers to think more carefully about the consequences of their design and implementation choices. The catchphrase "We don't want another Y2K on our hands" will probably become common.

Lesson 4: Small Causes Can Yield Large Effects

This isn't the "details matter" lesson, which applies to how you build software. This lesson states that in a functioning complex system, a small event may have a major impact on the system. We were already learning this lesson before Y2K became a public issue. It is an essential aspect of complex systems. The classic example from complexity theory is that of dumping a large pile of sand on a table, letting it settle down, then allowing a tiny stream of sand (or, if you're amazingly patient, one grain at a time) trickle down onto the top of the pile. Most grains hit, slide, and settle. From time to time, you'll get a tiny "sandslide." Less often, you'll get a larger sandslide. But keep it up long enough, and you'll eventually get a major sandslide, sufficient to carry sand off the table.

In the same way, most failures or unintended behaviors in complex information systems are dampened and have little effect. Occasionally such an event will have some kind of

noticeable, though not major, impact. But every now and
then, you'll get a doozy. Real-life examples of this phenomenon abound; a great source is the ACM Risks Forum.[5] We've
just never had anything with the scale and visibility of Y2K.

How to apply: Awareness and caution are the first steps; as
we help build complex systems, we need to be constantly asking "what will happen if" questions and put defensive safe-
guards into place. The truth is that the systems we work with
are too complex for us to understand, predict, and debug completely; the best we can do is to protect ourselves.

Odds of this happening: Three to five snowballs, depending upon the actual severity of Y2K consequences; the more
severe, the greater the chances that it will happen.

Lesson 5: Community Counts More Than Technology

This isn't some touchy-feely, neo-Luddite statement. This is
a hard-nosed assertion of what is more important in maintaining civil order, standard of living, and civilization itself in the
face of significant breakdowns in infrastructure and government. Put another way, social cohesion can hold things
together even in the face of significant technological failures,
but even small failures can have very bad effects if social chaos
predominates. This was the point of David Isenberg's diagram
at the start of Chapter 12.

How to apply: We talk about family and community values, about getting to know the people around us. Now we
need to actually do something about it, do it well, and do it
for a long time.

Odds of this happening: Either one or four snowballs, depending upon Y2K's impact. If the impact is at the lower end of the scale (Level 0-5), I'll pick one snowball—because I think people will just go along the way they are now. If the impact is 6 or higher, I think that the probability jumps up to four snowballs.

Lesson 6: Most Technical Failures Are Rooted in Human Failings

For close to 50 years, we have lived with the myth that problems and failures with information systems projects are rooted in technology and therefore have technical solutions: **silver bullets**, to use Fred Brooks' classic designation.[6] Upper management, technical managers, and even developers kept looking for that next great breakthrough in tools, languages, algorithms, or methodologies that would help us to get projects growing ever complex completed on time and under budget. The expectation of a silver bullet for Y2K has permeated the discussions of those uninformed or uninvolved, most often in the form of an expectation that Bill Gates was going to come up with some magic solution (see Chapter 4, Myth 7).

Instead, Y2K is teaching these folks in a very painful fashion what many people within the software engineering community have known for years: The development and deployment of information technology are largely issues of human factors and communication, and that most project failures stem from human issues. Numerous books have addressed this over the last 30 years;[7] Y2K has merely reconfirmed it. Indeed, as I've said elsewhere on the subject,

Humanity has been developing information technology for half a century. That experience has taught us this unpleasant truth: virtually every information technology (IT) project above a certain size or complexity is significantly late and over budget or fails altogether; those that don't fail are often riddled with defects and difficult to enhance. Fred Brooks explored many of the root causes over twenty years ago in *The Mythical Man-Month*, a classic book that could be regarded as the Bible of information technology because it is universally known, often quoted, occasionally read, and rarely heeded. Most publications and books on IT since then have debated, discussed, and deplored these same problems. And they are with us still. Their causes stem not from technology but from human frailties. Indeed, when asked why so many IT projects go wrong in spite of all we know, one could simply cite the seven deadly sins: avarice, sloth, envy, gluttony, wrath, lust, and pride. It is as good an answer as any and more accurate than most.[8]

It's been a painful lesson, but all the more necessary for that.

How to apply: Our entire approach to the development and deployment of information technology needs to be rethought and refocused on these realities.

Odds of this happening: Only 2 snowballs. I believe that certain organizations will learn from Y2K and will make significant changes in how they develop and deploy information technology. I think most will go back to (or continue with) the usual way of doing things.

Lesson 7: We're Not Done Yet

If you think the Y2K problem will vanish sometime after January 1, 2000, think again. One of the two major solutions to Y2K is windowing, which—if you recall—uses a pivot year and merely shifts the interpretation of the two digits. For example, with a pivot year of "40," the values "00" through

"39" are used to represent 2000...2039, while "40" through "99" represent 1940...1999.

Programs that use windowing aren't really fixed; the problem has just been postponed some number of decades. For example, a program that uses "40" as a pivot year has a "Year 2040" problem. Yet of the millions of programs that have been or are being repaired, the majority it would appear use windowing, since it is a faster and (for now) less expensive solution. But these programs will have to go through the entire Y2K process again in the future: inventory, assessment, repair or replacement, testing, and integration.

Beyond that, there are other **bounding issues** that are very prevalent in computer software. One that received some attention in 1998 (before stocks dropped) and may yet again if stocks continue to recover and climb is the "D10K" problem: What happens if the Dow Jones Industrial Average hits the 10,000 market? Obviously, this is only of concern for a relatively small number of firms, but those firms account for a massive amount of financial transactions. Capers Jones has pointed out two other bounding issues that actually exist outside of computers but will impact them are phone numbers and Social Security numbers. The former could be exhausted by 2010, the latter by 2075; the effort required to update existing software for changes in either will be massive.[9]

How to apply: The D10K issue affects only a small number of companies and will likely be solved before it becomes a problem; indeed, the drop in stocks in mid-1998 helped buy the companies several more months at least. Work needs to start on the phone number problem now; the level of effort won't rival Y2K nor have the risks (most programs don't do calculations based on phone numbers, nor are they used in most embedded systems), but it will be massive nevertheless.

And the Social Security Agency should make the creation of a 10-digit SSN one of its first major initiatives of the twenty-first century, establishing it immediately as an acceptable alternative. That way, new software code from here on out can be written to use it. Beyond that, all the corporations and government agencies now doing Y2K repairs using windowing are going to have to upgrade to date expansion at some point; a sustained, if low-level, effort to repair or replace these applications

Odds of this happening: 0.5 snowballs. The half-snowball is for the phone companies, which I suspect are already looking long and hard at the phone number problem; ten years is a blink of the eye, given the scale of changes that will need to be made. I think far too many of the other groups involved will procrastinate until they have to go into crunch mode to fix the pending pivot year problems or replace the applications.

Closing Thoughts

At some point not too many months from now, we'll stand on the threshold of the year 2000 and see which set of Y2K events actually unfold and which lessons are indeed relevant. Still, I persist in wondering if we must always learn by pain and experience, when we learn at all. From here on out, let's see how many lessons we can learn the easy way. Experience may keep a dear school, but wisdom's school is priceless.

EPILOGUE

THE ENDLESS MILLENNIAL SUMMER?

July 2000 and beyond

Keep cool: it will be all one a hundred years hence.
— Ralph Waldo Emerson,
Representative Men

About ten years ago, a massive wildfire raged in Yellowstone National Park. A debate ensued about whether to fight it actively or merely contain it and let it burn. The "let it burn" faction won the debate, though not without criticism and controversy, especially when the devastation to the park was surveyed once the fire was out. Ten years later, the explosion of new growth and return of long-missing species to the park testifies to the validity of their approach. The fire, a natural part of the ecosystem, did what it was supposed to do: clear out deadwood and underbrush, opening the way for rejuvenation.

The Year 2000 problem will have—is having—something of the same effect in information technology (IT). Systems and software that should have been retired years ago are being replaced. More importantly, old mindsets and approaches to developing and deploying IT are likewise being retired and replaced in many organizations. Those organizations that develop good software and develop it well are thriving; those that don't are facing the consequences of their choices. Think of it as evolution in action.

On a grander scale, Y2K is helping to illuminate hitherto-unknown aspects about our economy, our society, and our civilization, with all its technological underpinnings. We are learning about the connectedness of all things, and the long-tired phrase "global village" may yet make a comeback—not out of a sense of community, but more from the interdependencies, welcome or not. No country is an island, not even Indonesia.

Consider all this a warm-up for the next hundred years. The world we live in now is as different from the 1950s—or more so—than 1950 was from the end of the 19th century. The year 2050—well within the lifespan of most readers of this book—will widen that gap further. The complex systems that ensnare, enmesh, and sustain us aren't going to vanish because of the wishful fantasies of a few backwoods survivalists who would rather blast their VCR with an Uzi than spend the few minutes and IQ points required to make it stop blinking "12:00." We will adapt; our children will thrive; our grandchildren will think us quaint with our digital phones and laptop computers.

There is a very simple secret to complex systems, one that has emerged from research into complexity theory. Complex adaptive systems are very difficult to control from above or outside; they adapt in response to such efforts. What governs complex systems and determines their responses are the individual rules, priorities, and behaviors of the elements in those systems—namely us. The irony is that the various conspiracy theories about how some small or secret group is running everything really are paranoid delusions, escapes from reality and responsibility. What we live with is the consequences of billions of daily choices and acts, including—especially—our own.

This, then, is the core lesson of Y2K that we should carry with us through the year 2000 and on into the twenty-first century: what we do matters. Y2K was not some sinister plot or grand error by a few people. It has emerged from thousands and thousands of individual decisions over a 50-year period, some defensible, many not, especially those made during the last 15 to 20 years. Those decisions were not independent of one another, either. Organizations with individuals who showed forethought and leadership solved their Y2K problems a long time ago, or are wrapping up even now; those with individuals who didn't are facing vast expenses and critical problems.

The only question remains: how often do we have to learn the same lesson? How often do we have to prove yet again that the virtues of honesty, dependability, sacrifice, service, accountability, and tolerance benefit us and all around us? Conversely, what will it take for us to learn once and for all that greed, anger, sloth, envy, lust, gluttony, and pride—the famous seven deadly sins—are not mere conventions of arbitrary morality or outdated religious hang-ups but the foundation of virtually every ill our society faces, be it in business, government, cities, communities, or families?

Experience keeps a dear school, but fools will learn in no other. The twentieth century has been a bloody, painful, costly education; Y2K has just been a last simple and, we hope, relatively inexpensive class. Let's see if we can individually and collectively pass the final exam, graduate, and leave the school behind. We have better things to go on to, and we could all use a vacation right about now.

The choice, as always, is up to you.

Testimony Before Congress

I had the privilege of testifying before several different Congressional committees about the Year 2000 issue. This appendix contains the official statement submitted for each occasion. For the first testimony (June 22, 1998, House Subcommittee on Government Management, Information, and Technology), my submitted statement is longer and more detailed than my oral testimony, which must be limited to five minutes. For the other occasions, my written statement was identical to my oral testimony. I came to prefer that, figuring that whatever I could say in five minutes was probably as much detail as was relevant at the moment. It also forced me to focus on what was important and not just talk for the sake of hearing myself talk. This is undoubtedly why Congressional rules about speechmaking and debate are very focused on minutes and seconds.

Submitted to the Subcommittee on Government Management, Information, and Technology Hearing on "Year 2000: Biggest Problems, Proposed Solutions," U.S. House of Representatives, June 22, 1998

Mr. Chairman and distinguished members of the Subcommittee, I am honored to appear before you today. I do so representing not just myself but also the 1300 members of the Washington D.C. Year 2000 Group, most of whom work on or deal with this problem full time in the government, the military, corporations, educational institutions, and other organizations.

I didn't come to Washington to do Year 2000 work—it's not what my company does—but like many others, I was drafted into it. Once involved, I became profoundly concerned, both because of the scope of the problem and my own professional experience with information technology projects, large and small. A quote from Shakespeare has repeatedly come to mind during the past 18 months while observing those who arbitrarily set schedules and deadlines, or who make blithe statements about how simple the problem is and how readily they will solve it. It's from *Henry IV*, act 3, scene 1. In it, the character Glendower boasts of his supposed command over the leading technologies of his day, declaring, "I can call spirits from the vasty deep." Another character, Hotspur, with a firmer grip on reality, replies, "Why, so can I, or so can any man; but will they come when you do call for them?"

Humanity has been developing information technology for half a century. That experience has taught us this unpleasant truth: Virtually every information technology (IT) project above a certain size or complexity is significantly late and over budget or fails altogether; those that don't fail are often riddled with defects and difficult to enhance. Fred Brooks explored many of the root causes over 20 years ago in *The Mythical Man-Month*, a classic book that could be regarded as the Bible of information technology because it is universally known, often quoted, occasionally read, and rarely heeded. Most publications and books on IT since then have debated, discussed, and deplored these same problems. And they are with us still. Their causes stem not from technology but from human frailties. Indeed, when asked why so many IT projects go wrong in spite of all we know, one could simply cite the seven deadly sins: avarice, sloth, envy, gluttony, wrath, lust, and pride. It is as good an answer as any and more accurate than most.

In the midst of these human challenges, we place ever-growing demands on information technology. Like ratcheted gears on a torture rack, the tension only increases; there is no relief; things never simplify. Part of that is beyond our control, a natural consequence of the complex systems—social, economic, informational, technological, logistical, and even political— that we have nourished and which now enmesh us. Those complex relationships have made our miracle economy possible, giving us low inflation, low unemployment, low interest rates, and steady growth. But they also create the situation where a currency crisis in a small Southeast Asian country roils financial markets around the world and impacts the monetary policy of the richest nation on earth, or where a single strike at a single supplier can cause the world's largest company to shut down most of its North American manufacturing operations, furloughing tens of thousands of workers.

The other part of the problem comes from our fundamental ability to conceive and demand systems more complex than we can safely build, and our unwillingness to acknowledge and deal with those limitations. While only optimists successfully build complex systems, many complex failures come from those who are both optimistic and ignorant, or perhaps just arrogant. In the field of information technology, we have begun and abandoned the tower of Babel repeatedly in the past half century, ranging from innumerable small project failures to the incomprehensible 11-year, $4 billion IT modernization fiasco at the IRS. New foundations start each day.

In the midst of all this, we face the chasm on the road ahead known as the Year 2000 crisis, which has its roots in all the sins related. True familiarity in this case breeds deep concern; it is ignorance of the problem's actual scope and ramifications that yields popular contempt. Indeed, the Y2K controversy differs from most popular scientific disputes—such as global warming—in that there are few ideological overtures, the reality of the problem is trivial to prove, the consequences are sure and soon, and it is the most technical, informed, and involved practitioners who are most worried. Two surveys were done of the membership of the Washington D.C. Year 2000 group, one in March and a repeat survey in May, to ask their projections of the Year 2000 impact in the United States. Both surveys yielded the same results. Two-thirds of the members responding felt there will be at best an economic slowdown; one-third felt there will be at least a strong recession and regional infrastructure failures; a tenth foresaw a second Great Depression or worse. Even when the votes from those who might stand to profit from such concerns—vendors, consultants, and lawyers—were factored out, the results remained largely the same.

Likewise, anxiety has begun to set in through the public and private sectors as the true scope and difficulty of the Y2K problem—with its foundation in all the regrettable IT and business practices of the past half-century—become apparent. For the first time in those 50 years, these organizations face a problem that is inexorable with a deadline that is unmovable. The difficulties cannot be finessed, buried, rescoped, bought off, reorganized away, or dragged out until they're finally fixed. There is too much complexity to handle, too much damage to undo, too little time to allocate, and too few people to deploy.

What, then, can and should we do? I believe the best course lies in four principles: recognize; resolve; repair; and refrain.

Recognize. We need a broad, public acknowledgment of the nature, scope, difficulty, and potential impact of the Year 2000 problem, starting with President Clinton and followed by other leaders in the administration, in Congress, in the military, in industry, and elsewhere. (A good friend of mine told me that many years ago he went through a substance abuse program; because of that experience, he is fascinated by all the classic and well-documented forms of denial and self-deception he's observed among people at various levels confronting the Year 2000 problem.) Each organization needs to discover and be honest with itself about the status of Y2K challenges inside and outside. Industry and society must realize that the Federal government isn't going to solve their problems—indeed, the government will be hard-pressed to solve its own—and that no other organization, vendor, or individual, least of all Bill Gates, will come riding up with a miracle solution.

Resolve. We need to resolve that whatever the nature and level of Y2K consequences, we will pull together as communities, as industries, as a society, and as a nation. With that cohesion, even major Y2K events can be weathered; without it, even minor Y2K events could be disastrous.

Repair. We need to do the work. It will be long, difficult, expensive, and tedious, and it will probably last well into the next decade. We cannot get it all done in time; simple mathematical exercises demonstrate that for the embedded systems alone, we can only hope to get a small percentage tested, repaired, and replaced by the end of next year. This means we will also have to repair whatever economic, infrastructure, and even ecological damage is caused when Y2K problems hit. But what we can repair or replace, we should, and as quickly as possible.

Refrain. We must refrain from our long-established and self-defeating patterns in information technology, business, law, and government. Without that, we have little hope of making things better; as another friend is fond of saying, if you keep doing what you've always done, you'll keep getting what you've always gotten. The most critical restraint: As far as humanly possible, and perhaps a bit beyond that, we must voluntarily refrain from Y2K litigation

One of the best-run Year 2000 repair projects in America—and therefore in the world—is right here in Washington at Fannie Mae. The head of that effort, Carol Teasley, distributed to her staff some months back a clipping from an article in *Parade Magazine* (November 9, 1997) written by Thomas E. Ricks based on his book, *Making the Corps*. The clipping details what Ricks felt the fundamental lessons were at the USMC boot camp at Parris Island. Carol told her staff that these were their operating principles for the duration:

- Tell the truth.

- Do your best, no matter how trivial the task.

- Choose the difficult right over the easy wrong.

- Look out for the group before you look out for yourself.

- Don't whine or make excuses.

- Judge others by their actions not their race (or, I might add, by their position, political party, or profession).

I would suggest that a top-to-bottom application of these principles—in government, the military, industry, and society at large—is our best hope for determining the true scope of the problem, repairing as much as we can, and minimizing the impacts that do occur. I would also suggest that virtually any major Year 2000 repair or contingency effort not following these principles will fail.

Exactly 58 years ago last Thursday, Winston Churchill gave what is perhaps his most famous address. He sought to rally the British nation in the wake of Dunkirk and the fall of France, asking them to brace themselves for the task ahead. What, then, will those of the mid-twenty first century say of us? Will they say that January 1, 2000, was—to paraphrase our own great WWII leader, Franklin Delano Roosevelt—a virtual day of infamy, a sad and tragic symbol of short-sightedness, incompetence, denial, blame, and political maneuvering? Or will they look back at midnight of December 31 of next year and say of our generation, as Churchill felt the future would say of his, "This was their finest hour." The choice, I submit, is still ours—but won't be for much longer.

I would be happy to answer any questions that you or any of the other committee members might have.

Submitted to the Subcommittee on Oversight and Investigations, Committee on Education and the Workforce, U.S. House of Representatives, September 17, 1998

Mr. Chairman and distinguished members of the Subcommittee, I am honored to appear before you today, representing not just myself but also the 1500 members of the Washington D.C. Year 2000 group.

Let me start today with a parable of sorts. A man spotted something valuable over the side of a bridge in a deep ravine below. So he carefully estimated the depth of the ravine at that point, subtracted his own height, and purchased bungee cords of that length. He carefully tied them to the side of the bridge and to his ankles, then leapt off. He smashed, fatally, into the floor of the ravine, his descent barely checked by the long, elastic cords.

This story may appear silly, since only a fool would bungee jump with cords that reached almost to the ground. Bungee cords stretch well beyond their measured length, and a bungee jumper would plan accordingly. Indeed, one would wish to err on the side of safety, given the possible consequences.

The history of information technology projects is a history of missed deadlines and overrun budgets. It's not that we don't know how to make decent estimates or to track progress reliably. The concepts, books, techniques, and tools exist to help us. But far too often, those responsible lack the training, skill, intent, or will to employ them. They are often overly optimistic on how quickly work will get done or how well things will go. And they often face unrealistic deadlines mandated from above.

All these factors affect efforts to deal with the Year 2000 problem, which has additional complications of its own. First, the deadline in this case really is fixed. It cannot be slipped or postponed or cancelled. It just won't budge.

Second, a Y2K repair effort aims to keep existing systems functioning. In other words, if we don't get it done, things that now work, won't. This dramatically raises the cost of failure. To use a recent government example, the Internal Revenue Service's 11-year IT modernization effort failed, but the IRS kept right on functioning. However, if the IRS's Year 2000 repair effort were to fall significantly short, the IRS would have great trouble doing its job.

Third, the attempt to distinguish between "mission-critical" and "noncritical" systems is often arbitrary and sometimes misleading. The criticality of a given system is a function of time. I can go longer without food than I can without water, and longer without water than I can without air. But if all I worry about is air and water, I will eventually starve to death. In much the same way, systems designated "noncritical" can still impact an organization adversely if left unrepaired. The only truly noncritical system is the one you can live without.

Fourth, Y2K remediation involves simultaneous changes to a large number of interacting systems, which, having been through Y2K repairs, must then be reintegrated so that they all function together again. It's as if for some reason we were compelled within a short period of time to change all our electrical wiring, extension cords, and appliances to use four-prong electrical outlets and then to get everything working again.

Finally, it requires that these modified systems be tested to see if they will work correctly under Y2K circumstances. This testing is not as easy or straightforward as it might seem. It can be difficult to set up a proper environment for time-shifted testing, that is, testing as if it were in the year 2000 and beyond. You don't just go into a major production mainframe and play around with the internal clock. You need to ensure that current systems continue to function properly and are not impacted by Y2K testing. Put another way, you don't play around with the hydraulics of a Boeing 747 while it's in flight with a load of passengers. Some organizations have solved this problem by setting up test labs with separate computer systems, up to and including mainframes. But many are relying on using existing hardware during off-hours and weekends, a dubious proposition. Add to that the task of producing time-shifted test data and results, and you have a serious challenge.

Let me stress that Y2K testing is essential. Some organizations, because of these challenges and shortage of time and resources, plan little or no real verification. They feel that the Y2K date change itself will provide all the testing required, and that any uncaught defects that show up will be corrected then. To use the earlier analogy, this is a bit like turning the power off, changing all the wiring, outlets, cords, and appliances, plugging everything in, and then turning the power back on—at which point sparks fly, wires fuse, motors burn out, and fires start.

Virtually every Y2K effort to date has taken longer and cost more than estimated. In particular, the latter phases of a Y2K remediation project—testing, integration, and redeployment—usually account for as much or more time and effort as the earlier phases—inventory, assessment, and actual repair work. In most cases testing alone has taken from 40 percent to 70 percent of total time required.

Because of these factors, any Y2K remediation effort should carefully reexamine its plan for inaccurate or overly optimistic assumptions and deadlines. Special attention should be placed on time and resources allocated to testing and integration. Above all, absolute honesty must be the rule. Like the ravine floor, the reality of Y2K is certain, solid, and unforgiving.

I would be happy to answer any questions that you or the other members of the Subcommittee might have.

Submitted to the Committee on Transportation and Infrastructure, U.S. House of Representatives, September 29, 1998

Mr. Chairman, as well as Mr. Chairman and Madam Chairman of the House Joint Task Force on Year 2000, and distinguished members of your respective committees, it's an honor to appear before you today, representing not just myself but also the 1500+ members of the Washington D.C. Year 2000 group.

There are many countries today where gasoline costs $2 to $5 a gallon, where great factories run half-shifts and unemployment has crept into double digits, where intermittent shortages of various consumer goods cause inflation, long lines, and even government-imposed rationing, where the power system suffers rolling brownouts, and the water in some cities is not safe to drink without treatment, where martial law is imposed from time to time in certain areas to help calm domestic unrest.

Now imagine that this is the United States some 16 months from now.

The Year 2000 crisis is distinct from any challenge that humanity has faced to date. We have spent the past 50 years constructing a complex, planetwide network—technical, informational, economic, logistical, social, even political—that none of us can completely comprehend or control. It has served us well, especially here in the United States, where its benefits have given us a strong economy. But we have planted and left unchecked in it the seeds of disruption. These flaws may cause a million unpredictable, overlapping errors, big and small, disturbing the flow of information and affecting that which information creates and moves: energy, water, food, freight, raw and processed materials, people, money, and more information.

Let us be clear: The Y2K problem will not bring destruction and death as a hurricane or a war. Nor will it, in my opinion, bring our civilization to a halt, ushering in the post-apocalyptic world found in science fiction and survivalist literature. But that doesn't mean it won't be painful or serious. It will be more than a mere bump in the road ahead or a brief hiccup in a long economic boom. We must not reject all serious consequences because we reject the most severe and improbable. Wishful disbelief and blind optimism won't shield us from the very real and likely consequences of Y2K. In fact, it could well make them worse.

The Cutter Consortium was asked by the International Finance Corporation to assess a specific list of global economic sectors for potential impact by Y2K. They determined the following to be vulnerable: financial services, utility and power industries, telecommunications, manufacturing, industrial and consumer services, social services (including health care and education), food and agribusiness, chemicals and petrochemicals, and hotels and tourism. Cutter also singled out transportation as being vulnerable, even though they had not been asked specifically to evaluate it. In addition, they identified several smaller sectors tied to those above and so also at risk, including mining, cement and construction materials, textiles, timber, pulp, paper, motor vehicles and parts, oil refining, fertilizers and agricultural chemicals.[1]

Such sectors face Y2K disruptions in multiple ways and on different levels. First are Y2K problems in corporate information systems that support accounting, administration, operations, business processes, workflow, and external communications. Next are potential Y2K problems in the physical facilities: buildings, equipment, plants, vehicles, sensors, and so on. Legal issues impact not just sharing of information but actual operations; some firms may scale back or shut down operations for a short period around the Y2K crossover to reduce liability. Beyond that are Y2K problems in the infrastructure upon which these firms depend—telecom, utilities, external facilities, and services, not to mention timely deliveries of raw materials, processed goods, equipment, and supplies. Finally, even if a given firm or sector is itself in good shape, it may still be impacted by Y2K problems among suppliers, partners, customers, and government agencies.

When you consider the range of sectors vulnerable to Y2K, the various ways and levels in which they can be affected, and the complex, global, and interrelated nature of many of the sectors, you begin to grasp why there are such concerns about the Year 2000 problem. And while it is good to remember that the duration of most such disruptions will be measured in days or possibly weeks, we need to also remember that it only took a few weeks of work stoppage at one supplier of one key part to cause General Motors to shut down its entire North American manufacturing system, lay off 200,000 workers, lose $1 to $2 billion, and—all by itself—impact the U.S. economy. With Y2K, we may face dozen of simultaneous scenarios like that,

---

1. "Y2K Impact Report: Economic Sectors," The Cutter Consortium, May 1998.

all interacting with and intensifying one another. Add in possible disruptions to transportation, infrastructure, and social services, and place it all on top of the weakened global economy, and we may face profound economic and social consequences. Because of that, the Year 2000 problem must be for the next 16 months the most pressing issue for Congress and the administration.

I would be happy to answer any questions you or the Committee might have.

Two Surveys of the Membership of the Washington D.C. Year 2000 Group on the Impact of Y2K in the United States

Two surveys were conducted via e-mail of the membership of the Washington D.C. Year 2000 group. The first was done in March 1998 (over 700 members at the time); the second was done in May (over 1000 members). The survey asked the recipients to estimate the impact of the Year 2000 problem within the United States on an escalating scale of 0 to 10, with definitions given for each value, and to identify their type of organization (government, corporate, military, etc.) from a given list. The respondents could add optional comments. Both surveys were anonymous.

The first survey resulted in 229 usable responses, and a white paper was issued on April 21, 1998. The results showed two-thirds of the respondents believe that there will be at least an economic slowdown; over one-half think there will be a mild recession; over one-third think there will be a strong recession and local social disruptions; and a tenth believe there will be an economic depression and widespread failures in infrastructure, supply chain, and social cohesion.

The second survey, conducted in May 1998 after the white paper had been distributed electronically to the membership and posted to the WDCY2K Web site, resulted in 283 usable responses. The overall results were largely unchanged, though there were some shifts among responses in specific groups. Most notable was a shift in pessimism among those working in the U.S. Department of Defense and Armed Forces.

These results were tabulated and press releases were issued at a Year 2000 conference hosted by the Center for Strategic and International Studies on June 8, 1998. However, no white paper was issued, and the press releases contained only a sampling of the comments included in some of the responses. This appendix represents the first time that the full set of responses have been published.

The Surveys

On March 3, 1998, an e-mail message[1] went out to the notification list of the Washington D.C. Year 2000 group (WDCY2K). This list contained at that time well over 700 e-mail addresses of individuals who are notified about the meetings and other activities of the WDCY2K. The overwhelming majority of these individuals deal with Year 2000 issues in their respective organizations at some level: workers, technical managers, high-level managers, consultants, vendors, lawmakers, and so on. The stated intent of the e-mail was to conduct a survey of the notification list membership as to what they thought the impact of the Year 2000 problem would be within the United States.

The survey asked the recipients to identify themselves as belonging to a particular category: corporate/business; government; military; educational; organization; consultant/analyst;

Y2K vendor of products or services; legal; press; recruiter; other. (Due to sparse and ambiguous responses, "press" and "recruiter" were later merged into "other.")

The survey then asked the recipients to estimate what they felt the impact of the Year 2000 problems would be within the United States, using an explicit scale of 0 to 10^2 (see Table B-1):

Table B-1   Levels of impact in the WDCY2K surveys.

Scale	Impact of Year 2000 Problems within the United States
0	No real impact
1	Local impact for some enterprises
2	Significant impact for many enterprises
3	Significant market adjustment (20%+ drop); some bankruptcies
4	Economic slowdown; rise in unemployment; isolated social incidents[3]
5	Mild recession; isolated supply/infrastructure problems;[4] runs on banks
6	Strong recession; local social disruptions; many bankruptcies
7	Political crises; regional supply/infrastructure problems and social disruptions
8	Depression; infrastructure crippled; markets collapse; local martial law
9	Supply/infrastructure collapse; widespread social disruptions and martial law
10	Collapse of U.S. government; possible famine

Each of these levels of impact comprises all the previous ones, so that impact level 5 includes the consequences of levels 1–4 as well.

The recipients had the option of appending any comments they wished to clarify or elaborate on their choice. They were told that their responses would be kept confidential, which they have.

The survey was sent out on March 4th to the e-mail addresses that then constituted the WDCY2K notification list. One week later, a follow-up message was sent, encouraging the recipients to respond to the survey. The survey was closed at the end of March. During that time, over 230 responses were received, 229 of which contained the requested information. In some cases, the category of a given response (government, etc.) was changed to more closely reflect the intent of the survey.

The results of this survey were presented at the April 21, 1998, meeting of the Washington D.C. Year 2000 group. They were also written up in a white paper that was then published on the WDCY2K Web site and mailed out in electronic form to the WDCY2K membership. These results have been cited in several national publications, most notably in a *Newsweek* article that focused entirely upon them.[5]

At the start of May 1998, the survey was repeated for three reasons: to see if there was any significant variation in the results; to see if the results of the first survey had an impact on the members; and to extend the survey to the 300 new members who had been added to the WDCY2K notification list since March 4. A few minor changes and clarifications were made to the request.

The second survey was closed at the end of May. During that time, over 280 responses were received, of which 283 contained valid responses.

The Results

Table B-2 contains the responses to the March survey. Each entry in the body of the table indicates how many individuals within that category (row) predicted a given level of impact (column). The right side shows the total number of respondents in that category and the average impact voted. The bottom rows show the number of respondents for each level of impact, what percentage of the total response that represents, and the percentage of the total who voted for that level of impact or higher. Where an individual gave a range of values, the lowest value was the only one tabulated.

Table B-2   Results of the March 1998 survey

Last update 4/1/98 12:00 PM	Level of Impact (see scale)												
Respondents	0	1	2	3	4	5	6	7	8	9	10	TOTAL	AVG
Other				1						1	2	4	8.0
Legal		1		1		2	1			1		6	5.3
Educational				1		3	1		1	1		7	5.9
Organization			2	5	1	2	1	1		1		13	4.2
Military		1	4	2	4	7		2				20	4.0
Y2K Vendor			4	6	2	3	3	11	1	1		31	5.2
Government		1	6	7	4	9	4	3	3	4	1	42	5.0
Corporate	1	3	8	11	3	12	3	7	1	2		51	4.3
Consulting	1	1	3	8	8	14	6	10	2	2		55	5.0
TOTAL	2	7	27	42	22	50	20	35	8	13	3	229	4.8
Percent of response	1%	3%	12%	18%	10%	22%	9%	15%	3%	6%	1%		
Cumulative % (up)	100%	99%	96%	84%	66%	56%	34%	26%	10%	7%	1%		

For example, Table B-2 shows that 11 people identified as belonging to corporations responded with a prediction that the level of impact would be 3; that there were a total of 51 corporate respondents, and that their average vote was 4.3; that 42 people voted for an impact of 3, which represents 18 percent of the total responses; and that 84 percent of the total response was for level 3 or higher.

Table B-3 shows the results of the May 1998, survey.

Table B-3   Results of the May 1998 survey.

Last update 5/29/1998 14:00PM				Level of Impact (see scale)										
Respondents	0	1	2	3	4	5	6	7	8	9	10	TOTAL	AVG
Other							1		2	2		5	8.0
Legal		1		2	1	4	1					9	4.1
Educational				2	1	2	1	1	1			8	5.1
Organization			3	4	2	3	3	4				19	4.6
Military			4	2	2	8	5	6				27	5.0
Y2K Vendor		3	6	4	4	6	5	4	1	2		35	4.5
Government		1	5	7	2	8	3	3	6	2		37	5.0
Corporate		1	8	12	8	18	3	3	2	1		56	4.3
Consulting	1	2	6	12	9	21	12	15	4	5		87	5.1
TOTAL	1	8	32	45	29	70	34	36	16	12	0	283	4.8
Percent of response	0%	3%	11%	16%	10%	25%	12%	13%	6%	4%	0%		
Cumulative %(up)	100%	100%	97%	86%	70%	59%	35%	23%	10%	4%	0%		

The results do not show any dramatic shifts, though there is a tendency to move toward impact levels 3 through 7; the May survey has no votes for level 10, though the March had three such votes, and it has only one vote at level 0 (March had two).

Analysis and Observations

The most obvious conclusion from both surveys is that the overwhelming majority of the respondents believe that the United States will experience a significant economic impact from the Year 2000 issue. Correlating the definitions in Table B-1 with the results in Tables B-2 and B-3, we find the following:

- An average of 85 % believe that it will trigger *at least* a 20%+ drop in stock markets—over 1800 points in the Dow Jones Industrial Average—and some business bankruptcies. The irony, of course, is that the DJIA has already dropped nearly 20 percent since the survey was done due to reasons unrelated to Y2K.

- Over two-thirds (66% to 70%) believe that Y2K will cause *at least* an economic slowdown, a rise in unemployment, and some isolated social incidents.

- Well over half (56% to 59%) believe that it will *at the least* result in a mild recession, isolated infrastructure and supply problems, and some runs on banks.

- One-third (34% to 35%) believe that Y2K will *at the least* result in a strong recession, local social disruptions, and many business bankruptcies.

- One-fourth (23% to 26%) believe that in addition to all the above, the Y2K problem *will at least* result in political crises within the United States, regional supply and infrastructure disruptions, and regional social disruptions.

- One-tenth (10%) believe *at the least* that the United States will suffer another depression (or worse), that financial markets will collapse, that the national infrastructure will be crippled, and that martial law will be declared in some local areas.

A graphical representation of the May 1998 survey results can been seen in Figure B-1.

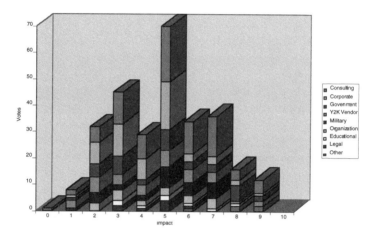

Figure B–2   Year 2000 Impact Survey Results

The overall shape of the graph shows a spike at impact level 5, with smaller peaks at levels 3 and 7.

Figure B-2 shows the May results broken down by category of respondent. This projection has been done to help show the

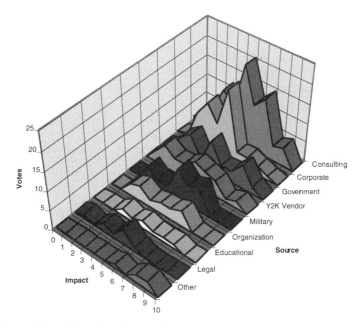

Figure B–3 Year 2000 Impact Survey

distribution of votes for each category versus the overall distribution of votes.

Due to the smaller sample size for each category, we must be careful in putting too much weight on a specific distribution of results. That said, we can make a few interesting observations:

- The military (including defense organizations) were the most "conservative" group in the March survey, that is, the group predicting the least impact (average score was 4.0). That shifted by a full level (average score was 5.0) for the May survey, even as the sample size increased by over 30%.

- Vendors of Y2K products and services, as well as lawyers, actually declined in their overall estimates, though the sample size of lawyers is too small to make the shift that significant. Still, the distribution of responses in both groups in both surveys undercuts the contention that those who stand to profit from Y2K are those who are most pessimistic.

- The single most pessimistic group was found among those involved in government work of some kind. In the March survey, of the 24 respondents voting for an impact in the range 8–10, one-third (8 out of 24) were in government. The same number of votes showed up in the May survey, but the overall number increased, reducing the government level to one-fourth (8 out of 28).

- The responses from both corporate and consulting sectors followed a distribution very similar to that of the overall group, with the consultants being a bit more worried about the Y2K impact.

Conclusions

Those observations having been detailed, a caveat is now in order. Polls and surveys do not establish facts, predict the future, or fix probabilities. They merely report how the surveyed group of people happened to respond to the question(s) put to them. As such, the results above are not actual probabilities of the associated consequences. They are just the collective guesses of a particular group of people at two particular points in time.

What makes these results of interest, however, is that these people for the most part work on or deal with the Year 2000 issue day in and day out in a wide range of organizations, settings, and levels. Collectively, the respondents probably know as much or more about the realities of the Year 2000 situation than any other group of people one could assemble. In that light, these results—and the supporting comments volunteered by some of those surveyed, found later on in this appendix—reflect as informed and broad-based an opinion on the subject as one is likely to get at this point in time. In that light, it is clear that the United States faces potentially significant economic and social consequences from the Year 2000 problem.

It is our intent to conduct follow-up surveys of the WDCY2K group in the future, both to track changes in opinion as experience increases and to capture the impact that this initial survey might have had upon the membership. Results will be posted on the group's Web site (www.wdcy2k.org).

Text of Year 2000 Impact Survey

Below is the complete text of the e-mail sent out to the WDCY2K notification list on March 4, 1998. Note that although the text estimates that there are some 400-500 addresses on the notification list, an actual count made in early April found almost 1000 addresses on the list—which means that there were probably well over 700 addresses at the time of the survey.

```
From: Bruce Webster <g8ubew@fanniemae.com>
Date: Wed, 4 Mar 98 12:59:44 -0500
To: WDCY2K@fanniemae.com
Subject: WDCY2K SURVEY: Estimation of Year 2000 conse-
quences
```

To the WDCY2K Group:

For some time, I've wanted to repeat formally a survey
that I did informally back in the October meeting, a
poll to see what you think the impact of the Y2K issue
is likely to be here in the United States. In light of
Sen. Bennett's visit and some of our subsequent planned
meetings, I'd like to get as complete a feedback from
all of you as I can, so please take a minute to respond
to this message.

Recognizing that this is a multi-dimensional and global issue, I'm nevertheless going to limit it to the
United States and squeeze it down to a 0…10 scale, this
time with the definition of each level spelled out a
bit more and escalating a bit more quickly. I'm adapting these consequences from the table of Year 2000
consequences given in Capers Jones's white paper, "How
Serious Is the Year 2000 Software Problem?" (Nov 29,
1997; contact www.spr.com for more details). I've set
up the scale to produce what I think will be a normal
(bell curve) distribution, so it'll be interesting to
see the actual results.

NOTE: I know these levels are arbitrary and that you
may foresee a different mix of events, but do your best
to pick what you think is the best representation of
what you think the impact will be. Recognize that each
level assumes the relevant consequences of all lower
levels. Based on response and interest, we may do a later survey that lets you choose the level of impact for
each of a series of areas (political, economic, infrastructure, etc.) and that addresses global issues.

What I ask from each of you is just two pieces of information: a categorization of your background from the
list provided (the survey will be anonymous; I will delete each e-mail response after logging the information) and the level from 0 to 10 representing your best
guess as to the overall impact. You may add optional
comments to expand or clarify, but keep them clear and
concise, please.

INSTRUCTIONS: reply to this message, but please delete
all extraneous text that's copied in (everything up to
the line below); likewise, delete all the categories
and consequences except the relevant one for each. Add
any comments or clarifications. Send it back.

When this is done, I will compile and distribute the
results. We have between 400 and 500 people on our
WDCY2K notification list, the vast majority of whom
deal with this problem daily, so I think the results of
this survey carries some weight. Thanks!…bruce..

Bruce F. Webster, CTO, Object Systems Group
Member, Fannie Mae Year 2000 Team
Chair, Washington D.C. Year 2000 Group
[address information removed]

================= DELETE UP TO THIS LINE
==================
CATEGORY (pick one; delete the rest):
Corporate/Business (non-Y2K)
Government
Military
Educational
Organization (e.g., a .org domain)
Y2K Product/Tool/Services Vendor
Consultant/Analyst/Consulting Firm
Legal
Press
Recruiter
Other

IMPACT IN UNITED STATES (pick one; delete the rest; see
notes below):
0 No real impact
1 Local impact for some enterprises
2 Significant impact for many enterprises
3 Significant market adjustment (20%+ drop); some bankruptcies
4 Economic slowdown; rise in unemployment; isolated social incidents
5 Mild recession; isolated supply/infrastructure problems; runs on banks
6 Strong recession; local social disruptions; many
bankruptcies

```
7 Political crises; regional supply/infrastructure
problems, disruptions
8 Depression; infrastructure crippled; markets col-
lapse; local martial law
9 Supply/infrastructure collapse; widespread disrup-
tions, martial law
10 Collapse of US government; possible famine

COMMENTS (be concise and clear):

===========-======== END OF SURVEY
======================
NOTES:
— "supply/infrastructure problems" have to do with food
shortages, fuel/heating oil shortages, disruptions in
public utilities (power, gas, telecom), disruptions in
transportation (airlines, trucking), and so on

— "social incidents" and "disruptions" have to do with
demonstrations, work stoppages, strikes, organized
vandalism, looting, and riots
```

A week later, a second e-mail was sent out, making a "last call" for survey results and asking specifically for responses from those were not inclined to do so. The message indicated the number of responses to date by category but gave no indication as to what the nature of the responses had been. While we did not keep specific track of the responses before and after this second request, we observed that the subsequent responses were more "conservative," that is, they tended toward the low end of the impact scale. A total of 148 responses had been received before the second call; another 85 were received afterwards. A few of the responses didn't give usable answers and so were not counted in the table above, resulting in a total of 229 tallied responses.

A similar mailing was done for the May 1998 survey. It made reference to the earlier survey and asked the respondents to take the time to review the results, available on the WDCY2K Web site and e-mailed to the membership list in late April.

Comments from Survey Respondents

In both surveys, the respondents were given the option of including anonymous comments to explain their answer or otherwise make observations on the Year 2000 issue. These comments are given below, sorted according to the estimated level of impact (0…10) and the survey in which the comments were made. Some reformatting has been done for purposes of minimizing document length, and spelling has been corrected.

Level 0: No Impact

MARCH 1998 SURVEY

Consultant/0: This issue has become the focus for free-floating anxieties relating to software (and perhaps to the millennium). However I am glad you are taking the survey and look forward to your results.

Business/0: Our business acts in a tenant/landlord relationship in most of the airports both nationally and internationally. We do not present a threat economically, except to our employees, we have 197 sites and over 22,000 employees. We have taken the necessary steps in preventing business disruption, but find ourselves very dependent on the airlines, FAA, airport authorities, utility companies etc. Our business has a marginal profit margin to begin with, and we seem to be completely dependent on the government agencies (airport authorities, FAA etc.) that are not Y2K compliant and will not be until after the year 2000. The government negligence could cause a rippling effect to our company's profit margin, and not to mention, unemployment factor. If the airport authorities have not yet addressed the seriousness of the year 2000, and airports close due to safety failures, it impacts our business directly. We are "sitting ducks" at the bottom of the priority and mission critical list for many airport authorities, not to mention dependencies on suppliers of produce, FAA etc. Would our company be in a position to sue the government agencies for Y2K negligence? Would this also apply toward the airline industry and the FAA?

MAY 1998 SURVEY

Consultant/0: This issue has become the focus for free-floating anxieties relating to software (and perhaps to the millennium). There are still VERY few facts chasing MUCH speculation.

Level 1: Local Impact for Some Enterprises

MARCH 1998 SURVEY

[No comments]

MAY 1998 SURVEY

Corporate/1: If the public and government officials are continued to be made aware of the problem the issues will be mitigated and defective systems taken out of the national economy.

Vendor/1: I think that your 10 levels do not provide enough options at the low end, where there is not significant damage/impact. I would recommend offering some lower-level states of despair (0.5: isolated nuisances, no regional/global impacts; 1.3: isolated problems, some portion of contingency/disaster recovery plans activated; 1.7: local/regional govts impacted, businesses experience multisite impacts; 1.9: enterprises continue to function but major portions of contingency/disaster recovery plans activated; etc.). Beyond Level 2 sounds like major economic disasters and/or social unrest in various flavors. I would reduce the many levels that address various disastrous combinations.

Vendor/1: Y2K is one of many possible impacts due to the increasing dependence on information technology and the assumption that technology is so cheap and reliable that contingency planning and management is not necessary. Two recent examples demonstrate the vulnerability of our information technology web; the ATM outage delaying credit card transaction response for major corporations and the satellite drift cutting off pager communication nationwide.

However, Y2K can be a catalyst for maturing information technology support, moving from an undisciplined art form to a responsible citizen, caring more about the people impact than the demand for righteous self expression. The industry can take advantage of the current popular and funding support to address serious infrastructure weaknesses.

Level 2: Significant Impact for Many Enterprises

MARCH 1998 SURVEY

Government/2: I do not speak for my organization, simply for myself based on my observations. The strong, prepared enterprises will do well and profit from the mistakes of others. Some businesses will fail, but businesses fail every day for various reasons. Some government organizations will be unprepared, but critical functions will go on. We will not be cowering in the dark and cold. We may find some unexpected inconveniences, but nothing that our social structure cannot cope with. Business as usual in that there will be lots of scrambling to take credit for success and assign blame for problems.

Government/2: I believe that we will experience significant impact on all information technology related aspects come year 2000. Systems that were developed 5 years ago might be OK. Systems that were developed 10, 20 years ago will probably undergo extensive re-engineering works to be compliant.

Corporate/2: Impact will be substitution of automated processes by manual processes which will cause a slowdown in some industries.

Vendor/2: If the U.S.A. is one of the leading countries in meeting the year 2000, yet we must operate in a global economy, what role can/should the government of the U.S. play to mitigate the impacts as well as drive the other countries to take more action to reach compliance in time?

Military/2: Recently retired from DoD. My opinion may not be consistent with present consulting company position. Does not imply doing nothing. Y2K characteristic of future information technological environment adjustments and management challenges. The biggest threat is intemperate, capricious litigation.

Corporate/2: I believe that inside the US, there will be enough financial motivation/forces to ensure that widespread, major disasters do not occur. I believe there will be isolated problems, ranging from inconveniences to near-disasters. I do not believe that any lives will be lost but I do believe that some companies will experience greater negative impacts than others, due to their own doings and/or the doings of those with whom they deal/interface. I also believe that some "systems" will experience undesirable behavior, in some cases to the detriment of the owner of those "systems."

Government/2: I think it's pretty difficult to predict the impact accurately. This is a unique problem, past experience doesn't help much. While I think if the Y2K problem "surprised" the US economy we'd have very serious problems, in fact, this is a clearly foreseeable problem. I'd assume that most organizations have strong incentives to "fix the problem" and that most will. As always, there will be some organizations that fail and that may lead to bankruptcies, but they occur all the time so the impact of a few more is hard to predict. I'd expect a reduction in economic growth and a probable recession between now and 2001 due to all the resources that will be spent on Y2K and draw away from other productive IS work. Still, I think serious social problems are unlikely. Recessions are common (although) less so than in the past but don't lead to social disintegration. Long term Depressions sometimes do.

NOTE: I think your list of choices is confusing. While I do think a recession is likely, I don't feel like that must be linked with a 20 percent market reduction. You should make them separate choices!

Similarly, I do see a moderate recession but not "runs on banks" or "local social disruptions." Again, I see those as separate choices. I'd choose a "recession" but not the other outcomes you assume they will predict. The last run on banks came during a VERY severe Depression.

Consultant/2: Modified 2. I'd give it a 4. I expect some infrastructure problems—power and telecomm distribution grid, transportation—air and rail in particular. Some security and emergency services problems—911, police, fire, hospital embedded systems, etc. I consider embedded systems the greatest risk in both the public and private sectors. A lot has to do with what is done to "set the mood." It also depends on what else is happening in the world—i.e., are we at war with Iraq etc. It would be easy to exacerbate the problem. I expect the problems to be more significant outside the US because they are not addressing it yet.

Organization/2: Predictions of impending doom are made from the present perspective and using linear projections of current trends, assuming constant progress and a constant level of remediation. In real life, everything goes in cycles, and the predicted catastrophic course turns out to be a tangent emerging from the true curve of happenings. Also in real life, when things get bad enough, they get more attention, common sense kicks in, and something is done about the matter. When the public's "threshold of pain" is exceeded, priorities change. We'll have disruptions, but life will go on. Most of the hype comes from those who are making a living from disseminating it.

MAY 1998 SURVEY

Consultant/2: Affects small to medium sized businesses. Will be a one to two month period of adjustment with many inconveniences and workarounds until things straightened out.

Consultant/2: I believe there will be numerous scattered outages and service interruptions. There will be severe problems in some hospitals, parts of the various grids—power, telephone, various pipelines, traffic management, etc.—embedded systems are most of the problem. Hackers and weather have the potential to make things worse. Transition from the current administration to whatever follows presents the problem of discontinuities in federal agency management. Outside the US the potential for chaos is much higher—problems caused by Y2K, Euro, winter, political change and instability, Asian and Russian economics,...

Consultant/2: Public Inattention reflects our credibility as a profession. The chickens have come home to roost. The largest casualty will be the computer.

Consultant/2: Had not attention been drawn to this matter, I think the results would have been much more severe. However, in the U.S., the awareness among those that need to know is quite high and even the owners of systems not renovated/replaced will be warned in advance of the possible problems and thus will be able to respond more effectively. I do think that there will be significant litigation facing those that knew in advance and did nothing to respond effectively. I don't think that there will be widespread interruptions in utilities and public services. Fortunately, the first work day is two days after the change, so many of the unsuspected problems and embedded chip problems will have surfaced and workarounds will be in progress.

This fairly optimistic view is not to say that Y2K efforts are meaningless—on the contrary, it is only because of the efforts of groups such as yours to publicize the problem and discuss solutions that lead me to believe that the transition will not be as painful as many have predicted.

Corporate/2: Computer software/hardware vendors have to put forth considerable time and effort to show that their programs are Y2K compliant. I predict that there will be Y2K problems in computer software/hardware, or in the input/output data formats, which will be identified only when it is the year 2000.

Corporate/2: The main worry over the past two years has been that people/business/government simply didn't know what the Y2K issue was and what was at stake. That has changed drastically over the last six months. Now, the key issue becomes timeliness. Did the awareness come too late for your particular organization? How much of a sense of urgency exists? Can the inevitable failures be limited to noncritical systems?

Corporate/2: Though it appears that more interest is being taken in the Year 2000 problem, the urgency for companies still does not seem to be there. Testing and Contingency planning are two areas that need to be addressed between now and post Year 2000.

Government/2: Most institutions will address the most serious problems in a timely fashion. There will be a significant number of delays and inconveniences.

Military/2: I think that in 2000 enterprises will delete many systems that do not work and are not really needed. But I expect some major impacts for unanticipated ramifications for some systems, such as air traffic control stopping for a few days.

Military/2: If asked again in two hours, my answer might be totally different, and I don't think I am alone in this vacillation...the ONLY predictable occurrence is the date.

Organization/2: The possibility that the IRS may not be able to collect taxes is such sensational news that Y2K awareness will now spread far and wide. Those whose business is critically dependent on computers will draw the appropriate conclusions. Others will make do. As always, money will solve what seems unsolvable when no awareness is the obstacle.

Organization/2: Predictions of impending doom are always made from the present perspective and using linear projections of current trends, assuming constant progress and a constant level of remediation. In real life, everything goes in cycles, and the predicted catastrophic course turns out to be a tangent emerging from the true curve of happenings. Also in real life, when things get bad enough, they get more attention, common sense kicks in, and something is done about the matter. When the public's "threshold of pain" is exceeded, priorities change. We'll have disruptions, but life will go on. Most of the hype comes from those who make a living from disseminating it.

Vendor/2: Many organizations are going to wait and see what happens. Several industries are in a full charge in attempting to identify the problems. I feel they will be too late to avoid any failures.

Vendor/2: In spite of the Y2K shouting, there are large pockets of individuals, businesses, and government agencies that are technologically deaf. They cannot fathom their problem large or small, hence little or inadequate actions. Example, the Nations Airports (non-FAA systems) upon which airlines and passengers rely for travel and commerce.

Consultant/3: I'm making my pick without a lot of firsthand knowledge. I've found it almost impossible to separate the facts from the speculation and I don't believe that anyone (short of those involved with the power grids) know what is going to happen. I'm preparing for a 7 or 8, but hoping that the rise in awareness will mean a 3 or a 4. I will add one note though, I believe that the Y2K exercise will force many organizations to replace many older outdated systems, leading to increased productivity in the long run. I also think that in 1999, those organizations that are Y2K ready are going to have one heck of a marketing advantage. :-)

Level 3: Significant Market Adjustment (20%+ drop); Some Bankruptcies

MARCH 1998 SURVEY

Legal/3: Although the problem will be rather severe at the outset, it will likely be resolved for most of the critical resources and functions rather quickly. However, it is likely that some companies will not recover from their failure to adequately plan for this contingency.

Consultant/3: Remember the Titanic!

Consultant/3: I believe there will be some adjustment to the marketplace, but that adjustment may be somewhere between 10 and 15 percent.

Military/3: I think there may be some runs on banks due to the fear of money "disappearing" on 1 Jan 2000. I think this can be avoided with some public education or by banks printing statements on 31 Dec for concerned customers, etc. If the current frantic media coverage continues, large numbers of banking customers are going to want to withdraw their funds prior to Dec. 31 to avoid losing their savings. I hear comments of this nature regularly.

Corporate/3: The outcome might be a bit like the great flood—it will wash away a lot of our dependencies upon systems that we don't fully understand and allow us to start afresh.

Educational/3: I think there will be many bankruptcies and unemployment, but few if any social incidents.

Corporate/3: There is a reasonable possibility of the others 2 or 3 on either side of my answer. The big question, I think, is whether the utilities (electricity, water, telephone) and food distribution systems will work, and we should know that within 6 months according to last month's speakers.

Consultant/3: I think people are starting to get the major issues tackled enough that the world will keep turning.

Consulting/3: Would call this a 3+ rating—difficult to discern between the two rankings. Believe that most companies are underestimating the impact. Also believe that the panic mongers are exacerbating the problem.

Consultant/3: The "impact" categories are too drastic. I think the scale should include only the items you have up to the seventh one, which is probably the "doomsday" scenario. Scenarios 8, 9 and 10 will not occur—the establishment cannot afford to let it occur.

Corporate/3: I see a drop in the market coming as soon as this spring due to the falling value of unprepared companies. I see lots of complete outsourcing of DP by large companies. I see lots of mergers and consolidations among business competitors. By 2001 I see a strong increase in efficiency and an upturn due to (1) economies of scale gained by larger merged companies, and (2) the increased use of packaged software which will replace expensive to maintain custom software. But, I see major backlogs in government services until about 2002. I see no increased unemployment at all.

Corporate/3: Businesses which don't effectively address the Y2K problem with the products they sell will be subject to lawsuits, loss of sales, and loss of jobs. I don't believe individual, group and corporate investors are tuned into the risks that their investments have due Y2K problems.

Corporate/3: The impact of Y2K may be even stronger in the rest of the world, particularly Europe and the more advanced developing countries of the world. This in turn may have a negative effect on world trade and world financial markets.

Corporate/3: I believe that this issue will have a significant impact, but that it will be short-lived. Most of the impact will be felt and corrected in the first month, but firms that are poorly prepared are at risk for going out of business. This will also cause an adjustment to the stock market.

Corporate/3: Prediction: The last month of 1999 will represent the most volatile period of financial turmoil the world has ever seen as people scramble to ensure their assets are safe by selling or withdrawing them from institutions. The first week of 2000 will represent the most dynamic market the world has ever seen as those assets flood back into the institutions able to withstand that massive short term cash flow problem. Although some suffering will occur in selected areas, history will record it as an amusing moment, unfortunately discounting the yeoman efforts of the countless professionals worldwide who toiled under adverse and stressful conditions to save the world as we have come to know it. In 2000, I suspect many of the unknowledgeable will speculate whether there really was a problem anyway.

Organization/3: Lots of workarounds; people will have to be resilient.

Consultant/3: The significant business slowdown will be problems in exchanging electronic data, even among compliant systems. These problems will be solved on a case-by-case basis, as they fail. It should take about a year to correct these problems. As a Y2K professional, I am personally staying away, as best as I can, from any devices with embedded chips from December 28, 1999 to January 2, 2000.

Government/3: Foresee significant failures/bankruptcies in small business, especially banks, that have failed to timely implement Y2K remediation strategies. Given our global economy, have major concerns with overseas financial markets that do not seem to have aggressive strategies (especially the diverse communications networks that traverse the globe) for dealing with the Y2K matter. Should be an item of concern that perhaps should be raised at the United Nations.

Government/3: There will be a significant impact on the US economy—people are still in "denial" mode with respect to this problem and its effects. So there will be chunks of the public and private sector which will cease to function in a normal manner.

Other/3: Local disruptions due to power outages and some telecom outages, but not a massive blackout. Some imports could be disrupted that depend upon shipping.

Vendor/3: Not much real data yet on actual tests of problem programs and applications. Seems like a lot of speculation.

Military/3: Am not sure how to respond as far as format is concerned, but here is my response: I feel the impact will be 3 and 7, but not necessarily everything in between. The recovery can be very quick or very long depending on the emotional state of the country. Although these are extreme examples, this is due to the following reasons:

There is a significant amount of hysteria being generated by various speakers, the media and other groups regarding the impacts of Y2K. It makes for sellable newsprint. I recently received a call by an individual who could not sleep at 2AM because of another friend explained there would be a total collapse on a worldwide basis of all electricity, computers, business and banking systems. This individual wanted to know if they should take all their savings and move out to the country. Whether it is real or perceived, this will influence what the public will do before Y2K.

There can be potential for significant political impact if these problems become excessive. There is a very high potential for vulnerability to terrorist/information warfare impacts if they timed problems in conjunction with the Y2K changeover. The terrorists could be long gone before the source of the problem was discovered. Some concerns have been raised regarding missile systems or nuclear systems accidentally firing based on an internal clock going to 000000. Assumption is these issues have been evaluated and this will not have an impact.

MAY 1998 SURVEY

Consultant/3: Here it is. Hope I'm wrong!

Consultant/3: There will be a major breakdown of the "food chain."

Consultant/3: It is encouraging to see serious attention on the part of major segments of government.

Consultant/3: I don't feel that famine or extreme unemployment will set it. I believe the United States is taking a good bit of precaution early enough to make a significant difference. The organizations that worry me the most are the small businesses because the news/media isn't making this potential problem clear enough to society! More needs to be done to get the word out on the potential problems (i.e. hospitals, elevators, airlines, nuclear power plants, etc.).

Another aspect is the international arena. I am concerned about the problems that could occur from external financial organizations that connect into our NYSE, etc. Reuters and Bloomberg are making good head-way, but they're just a drop in the bucket when you include all the other financial/international systems out there.

Corporate/3: I'm willing to select "2" next time if we see more action by small business and service companies.

Corporate/3: Y2K problem is already impacting productivity at our business as projects that would normally be funded/staffed are put on hold in order to deal with Y2K issue. I believe there will be an impact, but I'm optimistic that it will be minor.

Corporate/3: Initially, employment may increase as companies scuffle to correct latent problems that may surface, and to implement manually intensive workarounds.

Consultant/3: Several small vendors of Y2K related solutions will be unable to meet obligations of product warranty. Majority of corporations, governments, and public businesses will be operational with little or no effect. Overall, immediate panic will strike the stock market but will recover within 45–60 days.

Government/3: I see more than a few businesses being totally unprepared for Y2K—both in-house and with their suppliers/trading partners. They may wake up, but much too late to do anything other than wring their hands and bitch about "no one told me!"

The Federal Government should be in pretty good shape, but I doubt if state governments will be more than 60 percent ready. Local governments could easily be under 50 percent compliant since they have so few resources to throw at the problem. Plus, they are still in denial.

Very few small businesses will be ready for the millennium change. So, the market will be ripe for new businesses to come in and take the business from those who refused to be prepared for the changeover.

Legal/3: Corporate America is worse off than current disclosures suggest. Look for SEC disclosures to get more negative and dire as 2000 approaches. Corporate Earth is worse off than corporate America. As an attorney, I can offer no worthwhile insight into the technical reality or scope of the problem, and for that I defer to technologists and economists. However, I am competent to testify as to the general ability of corporations to handle complex technology projects (poor), and most year 2000 projects are going to be handled no better (and probably worse) than the typical technology project.

I think that the most dire consequences from the Year 2000 problem are the reactions in anticipation of the problem. My biggest concern for 1999 is how we can control the adverse and nonproductive public reactions stemming from the perceived consequences of Year 2000 failures; specifically, stock market problems, bank withdrawals, panic. If a company's business prospects sour because it has failed to address this problem, then that company's stock price should legitimately reflect the change in value. However, a great deal of market value may be lost simply as a result of anticipatory fear (panic), or the fear of anticipatory fear (fear of panic by others). How can we control this situation? Should we control this situation? As difficult as it has been proving the legitimacy of the Year 2000 problem, it is going to be even harder to prove that it is under control.

Military/3: I believe that awareness is heightening exponentially as we move closer to AD 2000 and that in the United States, we will see "yankee ingenuity" and a spirit resembling that which won WWII emerge minimizing the adverse impact of any overlooked Y2K glitches. I am personally backing out of any investments in foreign concerns because I envision a graver Y2K impact in most of the other countries in the world.

Organization/3: If all organizations pay serious attention and address their issues, I believe the situation can be handled with minor disruptions. However, are all organizations going to be ready? No.

Vendor/3: The drop in the market will be gradual beginning late next spring as more and more businesses adjust to a new fiscal year.

Vendor/3: Some large companies still seem to be ignoring the problem. Others seem unable to mount an effective renovation program: lots of velocity with no direction (Brownian Movement). What I suspect is that some companies will avert disaster by good luck, while others will have a major MIS or business application failure because of bad luck (whether or not either group performed Y2K remediation). What is likely to happen in LOTS of industries is that small and/or weak companies will be consolidated (merged, bought), as is presaged in the defense, telecommunications, banking, and insurance sectors. Y2K failures will be used for the reason, although underlying weak or mismanagement is the actual cause.

Vendor/3: Noncompliant businesses with critical automated interfaces (e.g., financial institutions) will be consumed by compliant businesses. Most of the remaining problems will be in data exchange between external organizations. These will be corrected over a five year period, on a case by case basis between the organizations.

Level 4: Economic Slowdown; Rise in Unemployment; Isolated Social Incidents

MARCH 1998 SURVEY

Corporate/4: Due to our current global economy (consider the "Asia crisis" going on now), I am especially concerned with the effects of other countries ignoring this problem.

Consultant/4: Y2K doesn't yet seem to be taken as the most important issue facing industry, or even facing data processing. The choice seems to be risking over-reacting, or risking under-reacting. Most votes seem to be for the latter — otherwise known as denial. Results will be delivered in about 21 months. Stay tuned...

Organization/4: I think that most big companies will have coped; most government agencies are incapable of coping. There will be bankruptcies, primarily in small businesses; there will be major problems in hospitals and universities. Many small businesses will be badly hurt, even the ones that manage to survive. The nonprofit community, for the most part, does not seem to be taking the problem seriously enough. Embedded systems (cash registers, elevators, pacemakers, heart-lung machines) will create havoc.

Vendor/4: Panic in the first half of 2000: among the public who depend on Government support (Social Security Benefits, Unemployment Benefits, etc.); among the retired veterans/public who have invested their life savings in stocks, bonds and other avenues. High anxiety due to imaginary and in some cases reported ill-consequences in travel, medical treatment and other vital areas. Severe Unemployment in general labor categories due to mild recession, business closures, and temporary lay-offs. Temporary shortages of fuels, utilities and the like, resulting in sharp price increases. Chaos in the service industry. Weakening of US dollar against currencies of nations who have vital natural raw-materials, strong service base and high-end skills. Very sharp increase in market price of skilled technical labor—both domestic and immigrant—until some of the major relevant Y2K problems are solved. Shortages of commodities, consumables and essential goods required for day to day living. Pattern of hoarding and price escalations by a series of business houses. To some degree, upsurge in anti-social elements, crime, arson and very difficult law-enforcement situation. And many more....

Military/4: I hope 4 is the worst.

Military/4: In light of the barely perceived ripple-effects of the Canadian/Northeastern US ice storms, and similar disasters in California's mud-slides and Florida's tornadoes, I think there will be impacts that won't generally be perceptible until the economists analyze the situation and tell us about he overall slow-down and shifts in hot and cold markets. I don't foresee many if any social incidents due the diluted aspect of the events.

Consultant/4: I expect major failures starting in the second half of 1999. I expect most major problems to be solved or worked around by second half of 2000. I expect annoying problems until 2002 or so. The widespread, basic error is a programming statement that includes a logic or arithmetic operation between two dates with unexplicit, different centuries.

Government/4: Economic slowdown for Y2K firms after 01 Jan 00. Rise in unemployment of COBOL programmers. Isolated social incidents of Yuppies/Baby Boomers whining that their cell phones don't work

Government/4: Comment on impact—a conservative choice.

May 1998 Survey

Consultant/4: The "Millennium Bug" will prove to be a wakeup call for politicians. For the first time since the dawn of the nuclear age they were faced with making a long term decision (i.e., fixing the problem in the 80s and 90s) based on a technological assessment. They failed. The electorate will recognize this failure and begin to hold current politicians accountable for the failure of past politicians to address the problem.

Consultant/4: I am in the process of changing banks because my old bank is too much a stick in the mud for changes that help the customer. One criteria that I plan to use is checking if the bank is year 2000 compliant and getting it in writing. It still seems that many organizations are behind in the year 2000 changes or just don't get it. I think that maybe there should be a change from the government to help these changes along (tax break, etc.). I plan on checking very carefully on this when I invest.

Consultant/4: There will be failures and they won't come as a surprise. What may be surprising is the elapsed time until the failures are corrected.

Corporate/4: I really think this subject is too complicated to summarize in a single impact statement from which many conclusions will be drawn.

Corporate/4: I find this business issue fascinating, very hard to predict due to the plethora of opinions on both sides of the spectrum. The prudent plan of attack may well be plan for the worse, but hope for the best! WHERE'S WALDO (Gore)?

Corporate/4: Because we are a global economy, the failure of other areas of the world to recognize and deal with the Year 2000 problem will be enough to cause economic problems in the US. In addition, social anxiety about the Millennium could transform even the most minor computer problems and snafus into social incidents.

Government/4: There are still too many who feel that the Year 2000 problem affects only governments, the banking industry, and large business. For these small businesses, small offices and home offices, the year 2000 will present a very rude awakening.

Military/4: I would respond with a 4. This is one level higher than the last item submitted. I mentioned in the previous survey that the hype created by the media may cause impacts to banks and other industries. During recent discussions with people not associated with Y2K, they mentioned they will take all their money out of the bank. If this attitude is much greater than expected, then banks will be impacted. Unfortunately this is mostly caused by the media playing up the millennium bug.

Organization/4: Slow pace of Awareness/Assessment due to denial and blissful ignorance, combined with reluctance to act cooperatively due to legal concerns has caused me to go up one notch in my impact selection.

Vendor/4: There will be significant disruptions in all areas, most important will be communications and commerce. I don't believe that there will be mass social unrest, but there could be localized incidents if people cannot have access to their money.

Vendor/4: The economical slowdown will be more psychological than a real concern. There are still a lot of people that do not understand what Y2K really means. I think they will visualize the worst things can get and will believe they will happen. Today most business travelers state up front that they will not travel the first few days of 2000. The public utilities and transportation lines will cause the most disruptions. These will be with the interfaces and the non-IT systems not the company internal functions.

Vendor/4: Like others from your first survey, I personally do not agree that all of the things in the number 4 option will occur. However, out of the choices I believe it contains the most realistic scenario.

Level 5: Mild Recession; Isolated Supply/ Infrastructure Problems; Runs on Banks

MARCH 1998 SURVEY

Consultant/5: When there is thoughtful preparations for 10 and all events listed below then reactions to the event will be dampened as people will know that the plans have been made and widespread panic will not occur.

Government/5: Major political impact on all incumbents and citizen opinion of effectiveness of Federal and State governments—a Libertarians dream come true.

Consult/5: Could easily be a 6 or 7 instead, depending on market psychology more than "reality."

Consult/5: This is a tough call. I'm somewhere between 5 and 8; went with the lower in an attempt to be conservative and not categorize myself as a "doomsayer." Also gives me more wiggle room for later. Certainly, there will be some level of disruption, and we just won't know until weeks (or even months) after "the day" hits.

Consultant/5: I believe Euro conversion will cause major financial problems to Europe and U.S. Y2K will cripple them.

Corporate/5: The government and regulators have an obligation to strongly address the issues in public and quasi public entities. For example: (1) We know today that utilities have an inherent problem in their distribution systems, but no one is doing anything to fix the problem; (2) We know that government agencies are behind in their Y2K projects, additional resources should be applied.

Military/5: I believe that the military will experience isolated problems depending on its defense posture at the time (engaged or not engaged). If, the military is engaged in action, the impacts could be severe and numerous. Lives could be jeopardized by Y2K issues. The military is doing well in looking at unit and system level items, however the weakness is in its testing of the whole enterprise. Supplier/vendor issues will place a significant burden on its ability to supply and sustain itself. Contingency planning is weak due to the nature of the imposed deadline Dec 1998 placed upon themselves. There is much activity toward putting fixes in place and disregarding contingency planning. However, it is very likely that this will be the focus in 1999.

The level of commitment in the leadership is high and the organization is clear on the mission. The area of greatest focus has been in the weapons system arena. The embedded chips in ammunition, tanks, aircraft, ships, are numerous and there are additional outside influences impacting them. If they are not fully tested (at unit, system and enterprise levels), a critical device may be impacted and lead to a safety concern or a failed mission.

Consultant/5: Like any catastrophe, those that are prepared will get through with minimal damage, those that are unprepared will suffer greatly. We (USA) are a resilient people; and as there are incidents of catastrophes, as earthquakes, floods, widespread power outages, etc.

we as a nation cope very well I believe. This situation, due to the widespread nature and the level of global integration of economies, will bring about a level of cooperation amongst partners and competitors alike that is unprecedented. At least, this is what I hope.

Consultant/5: An urgent need for Y2K labor and materials will be discovered by remiss organizations — nearly all at the same time, when skilled resources are already committed/exhausted.

Military/5: I believe there will be many supply/infrastructure problems.

Government/5: The recession will be industry specific; some industries will actually benefit from Year 2000. No run on banks. There will be a major backlash against the programming industry which ignored and then profited from the problem. Fortunately, it won't effect their paychecks.

Educational/5: I think there will also be a number of major bankruptcies.

Corporate/5: The media attention being given to the impending Year 2000 impact on daily life will create a self-fulfilling prophecy. This includes runs on financial institutions as citizens follow the advice of the experts to have cash on hand for several months survival. During the months to come there will be an increasing burden placed on all institutions to deal with requests for information about how the organizations are preparing to stay in business for the year 2000. This is being promoted by more than one television program on a regular basis, for example, The 700 Club. We must do all we can to proactively educate the people and continue to work on the fixes and the contingency plans to prevent REAL catastrophes that might be possible.

Military/5: I expect most (many) of the embedded systems to be found and corrected (or at least work arounds in place) but some will be missed and some will be corrected wrong. The closer the date comes, the more concerned management will be that most will err on the side of caution for the first days. They will realize, some too late, that failure to adequately address the problem in one part of a larger system can have serious repercussions elsewhere. I think that failure at the interface (point of interconnectivity between systems) will be most significant.

Military/5: I'm not sure if I am hoping it is no worse, or simply believe it will be no worse. I believe the government will take strong steps to assure the basic services are available, or at least unavailable for a short period of time. I think there will be pockets in most cities that do not have basic services for an extended time. I believe that there are still people who don't think this is a problem. I don't necessarily believe that doing patches on old programs (windows, bridges, etc.) is a good way to fix the problem. I think we may be increasing our problems in which case the impact "status" of 5 would rise quickly to 7 or 8. Some articles I have seen recently are saying people are not allowing enough time for testing. This is a concern.

Government/5: Six months ago, I would have chosen about an 8, but I am very impressed with the level of awareness now and the efforts being made across many industries, particularly in the large corporations. The key is to accelerate the rate of repair across all size companies. I still remember the time when the country ran itself without automation. I hope that the people running the organizations today can recall what it was like and what they may have to go back to in the event of a shutdown of their systems. That alone should jolt the remaining naysayers to action.

Government/5: I would have gone higher but I expect more impact on economy than on society.

Corporate/5: I believe that there will be a supply/infrastructure problem due to the fact that we cannot fully integration test our products through our third parties prior to 1/1/2000. I do not think that we are alone in this problem and thus, it will be a wide spread clean up effort. If we keep finger pointing to a minimum then we can work together and get things cleaned up quicker for the good of the whole.

Consultant/5: I believe there is a significant lack of awareness of the scope of the Y2K problem in small and mid-sized businesses that are not located in major markets. As an example, I recently spoke to the IS staff of a mid-sized manufacturing company in Roanoke, Va. They had decided, without doing a thorough assessment, they had no Y2K problem and therefore had no remediation plans. They had overlooked some of the most basic things such as the PC BIOS issue, and COTS compliance. They had done some testing by changing system clocks, but had done no data aging or regression testing. They had no idea if their suppliers were going to be able to continue to fill their orders and had no contingency plan. Awareness is slowly spreading but for some businesses it will be too little too late.

Corporate/5: Based on personal forecast as well as recent *Business Week* cover story on the impact of Year 2000 on the nation's economy.

MAY 1998 SURVEY

Corporate/5: Influx of capital from other parts of the world may off-set the recession somewhat but may cause other problems in the short term.

Corporate/5: I think that there will be problems and interruptions in services that may prevent people from being able to work. I will have frozen, canned and dried food, a generator and firewood. If my office is not open (phones don't work) I will stay home. And yes, we have a well.

Corporate/5: If there's a problem with financial institutions—whether internal systems or external due to lack of confidence (i.e.: run on the bank) there will be a ripple effect.

Consultant/5: Could be worse than 5.

Consultant/5: Just my personal opinion …the more I learn about how poorly prepared for Y2K that the world infrastructure is, the more I am concerned about the impacts that it will have globally. There is a very real possibility of runs on banks. I've already heard rumor that a well-known financial company is advising its employees to have 3 months salary CASH on hand at the turn of the millennium. Power companies are assessing their readiness and are being found lacking. All in all, very scary prospects. Enjoy the current economic boom while it lasts.

Consultant/5: My biggest concerns are the embedded chip problems in our nation's (and the world's) infrastructures. These apparently are being the last to be addressed, often because the IT Department "has the responsibility for fixing our problem," but usually has no control over manufacturing/plant/building infrastructure. Thus I believe that a significant number of these "supply/infrastructure problems" (as you described—food shortages, fuel/heating oil shortages, disruptions in public utilities (power, gas, water, telecom), disruptions in transportation (airlines, trucking), etc.) will occur. In many cases, these will take longer than just a few hours or days to fix.

Consultant/5: I've been trying to get my broker and his firm to focus on Y2K issues as an investment issue. I've finally gotten past his assurances that his firm will be fine, and his firm's investment research reports are starting to show Y2K assessment. Now I'm going to drill in and see what they're basing their happy talk comments on. And I'll be interested in what companies start to say in quarterly/annual reports, though that too may be happy talk, approved by lawyers, meaningless.

Consultant/5: The Federal Government is not going to get this done in time; although this will result in some good, i.e. a flat income tax, most will be bad. We rely more than we think on Washington and even a small fallout in Federal outgoing payments will have a large ripple effect on the rest of the country.

Consultant/5: Anticipate supply/infrastructure problems due to lack of adequate preplanning and contingency planning preparedness. Longer term problems will involve hackers manipulating or corrupting sensitive data and implanting time-bomb viruses during especially vulnerable time for industry when getting the job done fast means a lowering of quality control and security standards. Expect some fatalities due to cold, inadequate food, unclean water. Runs on canned foods. Stock market run due to late public awareness, exacerbating financial uncertainties. Substantial small business failures with ripple effects on business chains. Demand for qualified programmers, for chips that are Y2K compliant, and for information re how to fix embedded chip problems will outstrip supply, creating bottlenecks and escalating costs. Companies with adequate capital reserves will be able to hold on, others fail. Substantial redistribution of capital in market toward larger companies. Shortage of paper for making hard copies of critical information. Substantial lawsuits against CEOs and calls for holding accountable gov't officials who had responsibility for addressing these issues and who chose not to.

Consultant/5: I picked my best case scenario; there's a real possibility it could be much worse.

Consultant/5: Having been in the trenches repairing code for the past 8 months, I've seen how easy it is to miss a date that doesn't look like a date (i.e. two-digit fiscal year embedded in the accession number for archival of government records and tested as valid only if greater than 60). There are bound to be oversights which would be more catastrophic than old government records.

Consultant/5: As with the last survey, this continues to be my "best case" scenario. The human (and corporate) capacity for denial of the breadth of the issue continues to amaze me. I'm convinced that there will have to be a major Y2K related failure of some sort before there is a collective acknowledgment of Y2K impact at government, industry, and personal levels.

Consultant/5: It appears that there are a number of CEOs\CFOs\CIOs that are still in denial about the problem and their firms will not be able to respond in time to implement effective solutions in time. Subsequently, these businesses will most likely be out of business very early in 2000. What then will be the ability of surviving companies to meet the increased demand while coping with the Y2K problems that will still have slipped through the cracks of even the best prepared? Its the age old problem (and opportunity) of supply verses demand.

Another critical issue that I see as having the potential to be a huge problem is the dependence that a lot of large firms have as a result of having multitudes of business partners. A chain is only as strong as its weakest link. This still seems to be an area that only little attention is paid. The assumption is that the business partner (phone company, electric company, banks, service providers, etc.) will meet Y2K compliance because they have so much to loose. To further complicate matters, this assumption is often made without any contingency planning. In some cases, contingency planning is not an option. One only needs to look at all the mergers within the financial institutions. How many of these are being made because they recognize the fact that they cannot achieve Y2K compliance? Partnering with all business service providers is critical—complacency spells disaster.

Acceptance of the problem, allocating resources, mobilizing the workforce, and partnering together is of paramount importance and requires the immediate attention of all corporate management. My hope is that it is not too late.

Consultant/5: Even though actual Y2K problems may be marginal and not too threatening, I believe many individuals will react in a panic emotional state that will cause poor decision making. As a result, the Y2K problems will become more severe. My hope is that we all plan our contingencies now when we are of sound mind, before panic or anxiety sets in. For those of us who have faith in a personal God, we can rest in knowing that He will take care of us!

Educational/5: I do not believe public schools have adequately addressed this issue. Problems with student records, payroll, benefits, leave records, staff records, will be problem areas. School boards need to get more involved and demand that school administration have a plan to identify and correct problem areas.

Educational/5: Recently, I received the following assurance from my own organization's internal MIS staff:

"Thank you for your interest in the Y2K preparedness of [our] business, administrative and management systems. We are fortunate that ALL of the systems supporting such functions have been replaced within the last five years. As a consequence, we don't have the scale of challenge that many organizations have. However, we still have some major systems, those based on COTS software that need to be upgraded with new compliant versions (and we have had to wait until those became available from the vendors). Those upgrades are in process. When this is completed, we will still have a substantial amount of broad, systemwide testing to do. But we expect to be in good shape with our central systems well before the excitement begins."

Among the projects I manage is a small (approx. 2 programmer-year) software development which simulates a piece of communications equipment. When we tested it for Y2K compliance, we discovered that a single C++ library routine was noncompliant. The library routine took a compliant, 4-digit year date supplied by the system and subtracted 1900 to obtain a 2-digit year date. My programmer corrected our software by adding 1900 to the result of the noncompliant routine. While we plan to conduct more extensive Y2K testing prior to delivery of the software to the customer (in about 45 days), I do not anticipate that we will discover any more Y2K problems.

However, we are fortunate in that our particular application is relatively nonsensitive to dates, and that the documented "minor issues" with NT 4.0 compliance apparently will not affect it.

I am aware of at least one major U.S. military organization (a unified command) which claims to have reduced their systems from over one hundred to less than thirty in their process of Y2K remediation (which was largely complete last year). While I once worked for the Air Force general responsible for those MIS systems (during one of his previous assignments), I have no personal knowledge which would verify his claims. However, I do consider him to be credible.

The reports which I have read about the financial sector as a whole, and about the Federal Reserve and Master Card International (STLTM reports) specifically have convinced me there is a medium-to-high probability of this sector being generally remediated by Y2K. I am concerned about the ability of banks and other institutions to deal with Y2K-induced panic and runs on banks, but recent statements by Fed officials are somewhat reassuring in this regard.

Based upon what I have read about the corporate community, it seems likely that at least 10 to 30 percent of corporations will have significant business disruptions up to and including bankruptcy as a result. Probably all (90 to 100 percent) of corporations will have at least some disruptions, hopefully minor and of short duration.

Based mostly upon Rick Cowles's reports, I am cautiously optimistic about the power industry. There will almost certainly be some glitches, but it appears at least possible the industry may be able to handle these with little or no disruption to the national grid.

I am more skeptical about the capability of DoD as a whole and the remainder of government agencies to complete their remediation efforts in time. It appears almost certain that some DoD administrative systems will fail or have serious problems come January 2000, and may be inoperational or impaired for substantial periods. While there may be isolated failures of weapons systems, I expect the majority of those weapons to be normally operational (including our attack warning systems and nuclear control systems). Therefore, I expect U.S. military forces to be mostly combat operational; however, the failures in administrative and logistical systems will likely impair our capability to deploy forces and to sustain them.

Even if the worst projections of Y2K systemic collapses materialize, I believe that U.S. military forces—active components, reserve components, and National Guard—will be able to maintain order and organize the distribution of critical food and other supplies. I do not believe that we will be able to project combat power very effectively into southwest Asia or other OCONUS theaters; consequently there is a medium-to-high probability of significant disruption of petroleum supplies in the short-to-medium timeframe. (two months to five years) (I may not have adequately allowed for the impact of petroleum shortages in my estimates of domestic disruptions.)

Virtually all of the above are my personal conclusions, with all the biases and myopia of any such individual opinions. However, combined with the assessments of other experienced professionals, these may help to construct a realistic evaluation of the country's Y2K posture. (On the other hand, the general lack of previous experience with such an event makes it difficult to assign high confidence to such evaluations.)

Background: I am a project manager in a university affiliated research center which performs applied research and development, principally for DoD customers. I am a retired Army Signal Corps officer with an electrical engineering degree and twenty years of experience in tactical and strategic military communications and computer systems, with recent specialization in satellite communications and information security. Aside from the software application development mentioned above, I am primarily a user of MIS with no direct responsibility for Y2K compliance.

Apologies if the preceding is neither concise nor clear.

Government/5: Selection considered to be the least impact.

Government/5: (Government/FAA/electrical engineer installing new computers in 22 enroute facilities across the nation.) It is impossible to meet the schedule of complete installation and check out and debug this many facilities in 16 months. We are short of money, the new computers have not been fully tested in our Atlantic City test facility, there is a serious space problem in the facilities and the first computer installation MIGHT start in Sept. 1998. Any major upgrade of this nature normally takes three to four years so I see it as an impossible physical task to complete just one part of the FAA.s Y2K problem.

Legal/5: Have any of your speakers addressed the potential for social disruptions? Frankly, I haven't thought about it before.

Legal/5: My position has changed little since the March survey—while I HOPE [I used to say "pray" but then I get numbered with the religious millennialists, which ain't so] for a containment in the 4–5 range, I believe the reality may well prove to be 7 or worse, not because technology failures drive that result, but because the financial infrastructure and distribution chains [both of which have many unregulated/laissez-faire elements] will experience "5-like" isolated disruptions in Q3-Q4 1999, which, once the media gets hold of them, will become the basis of hysterical, prophecy-fulfilling responses, such as runs on banks, liquidity problems in markets, etc. Thus, I fear, handled "improperly" ["typically"?] anecdotal "5" events could crash the entire system to a 9 or 10—a media-brewed hysteria.

Governmental emergency management readiness, well publicized and supported by visible acknowledgment of its need might blunt some of the shock—but this scenario is unprecedented and probably hits FEMA like plans for an alien invasion. Along with the lateness of real useful institutional responses [John Koskinen?] the intellectual horsepower being applied to figure out how folks can sue each other, rather than prevent significant harm to the economy and our welfare still astounds me ['tho when in our history have we ever been free from carpetbaggers and snake oil salesmen?].

We need to use the time and resources remaining to do crisis management, real useful triage ["goodbye!" school lunch program, tobacco subsidies, end-of-model-year-rebates, global warming, "hello" to "this is an 80-column punch card"] and risk avoidance among all institutions. The big IT companies need assurance that they will not be driven out of existence by bs litigation, and then their resources need to be drafted by coordinated efforts between business and the government to maintain the core infrastructure institutions that our painfully short sighted Administration just announced on Friday we need a plan to protect. We know what we need; now we just have to get the idiots who post drivel on the Y2K websites out of the way and go and do it.

Or are we not going to do the extraordinary as a way of admitting the problem seems insoluble so we will all JUST GIVE UP? If so, shame on us—our children deserve then to condemn our memories.

Military/5: Almost all of the real problems caused by failure to fix the bugs will result in identifiable glitches that can be corrected by human intervention. Some corrections may take up to five years to effect, but the problems will be worked around in the meantime. The more serious problem will result from panic: people who do not understand the nature of the problem but have heard dire predictions will take defensive actions (e.g., withdrawing large sums from banks, hoarding food, and liquidating stock and bond holdings) that can be extremely disruptive.

Military/5: I still think there will noticeable interruptions in both commercial utility services to consumers and within home/business devices, at least initially. Some will be significant while most will be bothersome. I see the run on banks occurring during November and December as the naysayers and predictors of gloom become more vocal in declaring the impending catastrophe. Any recession we have should be extremely mild, relative the other parts of the world.

Military/5: It would be easier to pick and choose what degree each category will be affected. I believe there will be a mild recession, numerous (more than 50 percent, less than 75 percent) supply/infrastructure problems, runs on banks, power grids out (in small numbers), transportation gridlocked, medical devices (who knows), yadda, yadda, yadda.

Military/5: Stock market begins to drop in 4th quarter as people read the impact on MIS budgets. Runs on banks in 2d quarter 1999.

Organization/5: For me this is the range (5…7) which I believe likely. I am manic/depressive alternating between happiness at signs of progress and depressed at evidence of continued denial. I think the issue is not so much US as it is international.

Vendor/5: At this point in time, with many gov't agencies still unclear as to which applications they need to convert and test, knowing that we are nearing the point where companies and gov't will have to choose which applications to target (as we get nearer to 1999) for conversion and testing in a triage environment, it is difficult to believe the ramifications of Y2K will not have a major, negative impact within the US. Certainly globally the negative impact will be more significant.

Vendor/5: The major banks will operate intact and even benefit from a major inflow from foreign cash. Same for US brokerage firms, although the stock markets will be hit and certain (many) stocks will get hammered as real and imagined facts and impressions surface. The real deciding factor will have to do with basic infrastructure services. I believe the telcos will be ready. If the power companies/ grids aren't ready, it will be a longer, much longer recovery period. The same for the railroads, but to a much less extent. Overseas will be one crisis spot exploding after another.

Level 6: Strong Recession; Local Social Disruptions; Many Bankruptcies

MARCH 1998 SURVEY

Vendor/6: I'm an optimist. My pessimistic side pushed for me to select 7 or even 8.

Government/6: The unknown interrelationships between business areas and market sectors will cause dire consequences. In my role as a government agency Y2K testing coordinator I see a new and different way to "solve" the problem almost every day, yet no one is sponsoring or supporting true interface testing. The side effects of changes will be more harmful than the original problem. Once the media blows the Y2K problem out of proportion, like only the media can, there will be panic that will cause any small problem to be magnified so as to cause total mistrust of technology. This will not be a happy time.

Consultant/6: I am a pessimist. I am also seldom disappointed. I believe the Y2K problem, which could be addressed rationally and solved in the time remaining, will instead be politicized and that the efforts of business and government will be less than effective. Many brave speeches...little impact.

When this is combined with current trends of "It's not my fault...It's their fault...Punish them!" and the higher emotional charge (historically called Millennial Fever) I believe there will be substantial breakdowns in certain areas and that some people will try to take advantage of the confusion for their own gain or sport. For example, many of the people involved in the violence and destruction of the Los Angeles riots would not have recognized Rodney King if they tripped over him.

Consultant/6: I do feel that it is time for programmers to be paid what they are worth. Also some job security after the year 2000. For many of the past few years we have not had many rights in the workforce and have been under appreciated. How long do you think it would take for the teamsters to strike if they were not getting time and a half for overtime. Yet for many years no programmer that I know has gotten this and they are expected to put in extra hours. Without us right now working on this problem then most of the worlds computers and programs will have problems. This would most likely mean the collapse of major stock markets and many banks. This would lead to a collapse in the economies of many countries.

Corporate/6: I'm not sure that there will be many bankruptcies, but there will be failures and several distressed companies where layoffs will be required because of distribution, manufacturing or cash flow problems

Consultant/6: The strongest impact will be on those mid-sized companies which do not (did not) have the budget or forethought to resolve their Y2K issues. We rely so heavily on those organizations and I do not feel companies are making enough contingencies to protect them from this potential issue. Additionally companies who interface with or rely on international organizations will have a tremendous challenge. Government is not placing enough emphasis or budget on this issue and this will impact the nation as a whole.

Consultant/6: FYI, Usenet newsgroup comp.software.year-2000 has been running a quarterly survey, the results average about 7-8 on your scale. I'd guess that WDCY2K comes in with the same range.

Government/6: Too many uninformed key people not taking any action. The stock market reacts to what it perceives as the future in 6 months not the actual events. Embedded systems are everywhere including 20 percent of US power plants and are extremely difficult to fix. Communication between Y2K COMPLIANT and non-COMPLIANT computers on a worldwide basis is going to fail in many critical areas. ONE POSITIVE factor the Internet will be up and running carrying commerce and communications and will be Y2K compliant.

Educational/6: Slow down with Social Security, all retirement funds, and IRS will negatively impact all.

Vendor/6: The infrastructure will be affected by supply shortages of fuels, lack of power (Spotty/localized), inability of local governments to prioritize most needs because of the largeness of the emergency. The durations of services that may be out and the ability of law enforcement to keep a handle on the chaos that results. An inability of most to visualize Y2K as a global problem that will affect everyone in the industrialized world.

MAY 1998 SURVEY

Consultant/6: It still amazes me how many companies and governments have NOT started any remediation whatsoever!

Consultant/6: 6 instead of 5 because of PSYCHOLOGICAL factors in the financial markets.

Consultant/6: In the months since the first survey, I have seen no decisive action or even enhanced awareness by government at the local, state or federal level. Senators Bennett and Dodd and a very few of their colleagues are the exception that proves the rule.

The social impacts of the Year 2000 problem (financial, logistical, emotional/societal) will be completely out of proportion to the actual damage done by failures to fix programs/devices by 1/1/2000. In short, people will be emotional, overreact and follow the herd...all when it is too late for effective corrective action.

In the aftermath, do not be surprised at a new wave of Luddism, a reaction to the technology and technologists who will be blamed for these disasters. This feeling is stronger and runs deeper today than many of us who work in technology want to believe. A few days of working the phones at a help desk would vividly demonstrate this.

Consultant/6: The scale overlooks some truly worst case scenarios, especially the possibility that a nuclear nation loses significant command and control capabilities or Chernobyl class nuclear power facilities somewhere lose their ability to monitor activity and shut down gracefully in the face of failure.

Consultant/6: As a software engineer for the last 15 years, I have learned that most large software projects will be finished late and over budget. To think that the world can take on the global project of simultaneously ridding all critical systems of the Y2K bug by an immovable deadline is fantasy. US Fortune 500 companies will probably fix most of their systems in time because they have a huge financial incentive to do so, they have the resources and they respond vigorously to financial incentives. Without the same level of resources, smaller private sector organizations will probably not fare as well. With neither the financial incentives, the leadership of politicians nor the ability to compete with the private sector for scarce human resources, the public sector may fare worst of all.

Consultant/6: The economic effects will begin when the press gets serious on the subject and stops trying to make a joke about it. Clinton and Democrats will bear the blame for the government not being ready. The IRS will hopefully fold and a VAT-type sales tax will be instituted. A lot hinges on the seriousness of the problems with imbedded chips in manufacturing. A lot hinges on internal audit reporting to catch erroneous data, transmissions, etc. Basically, a lot hinges on how fast IT professionals can put out fires and band-aid everything back together.

Consultant/6: As noted in previous survey results, items at different levels will not necessarily only occur with those at the same level. I'd expect: Significant impact for many enterprises (especially government), including many bankruptcies; significant market adjustment given the companies which fail, but some companies will do extremely well in newly opened up arenas; temporary rise in unemployment; riots in some areas; possibly run on banks, although the financial sector seems to be one of the best prepared; political crises (given government's inability to overcome this problem) with possible martial law for a while—extent unpredictable at this time; enough food for the US, with shortages of certain foods in different areas of the country due to transportation coordination problems—very possible our food shipments out of the country will be halted for a while.

Consultant/6: Although the US will be well prepared, the economic impact of worldwide effects will directly affect the US economy and trade balance resulting in a large impact on the sale and transfer of goods and services both domestically and internationally.

Public utilities will be affected, more noticeably in smaller communities. Erratic fluctuations in the demand for electricity will overwhelm power control systems causing immediate shutdown of power grids. Systems will be brought online in small increments with major cities regaining power in a week to two weeks. Small communities resort to manual operation of water pumping stations; large communities are affected more.

Consultant/6: I am a self-employed consultant but not on Y2K. I am a project manager 29 years in the business; most recent projects have been website development. Although I've read Ed and Jennifer Yourdon's book and Capers Jones' book on the subject, subscribe to your list, read much of comp.software.year-2000 Usenet news group, and read the original general, business, and computer press articles linked to by c.s.Y2K posters. I've never worked in an IT shop or developed a major process control system, and have no first hand knowledge.

Consultant/6: As our clients (mostly small businesses) become more aware of the problem, many seem overwhelmed by the potential for the ripple effect on the economy as well as society. Even with more awareness, many are waiting to take remedial steps. If this attitude persists and is national in scope, Category 6 impact is inevitable.

Corporate/6: In the time since the last survey I have become slightly more pessimistic. Our Year 2000 Compliance project is continuing to run in our "spare time" as new business development takes the bulk of our resources. Senior management thinks we are exaggerating the impact of Y2K and that we'll figure out how to get past any problems that arise.

Corporate/6: Although many companies are taking steps to inventory and correct the Y2K internal systems, there are countless interfaces the companies can do nothing about. If those interfaces have a Y2K operation, they may fail. If the company responsible for the interface is a primary supplier then there is going to be a problem getting to market with the product.

For example, an airline or automobile company relies on hundreds of suppliers to provide a product—if any of those suppliers have to provide a critical component for the final product, then the airline or automobile company cannot market their product. If that happens, then the company must lay off workers, etc.

Because the United States has a global economy we are dependent on thousands of suppliers worldwide. If those suppliers cannot produce the parts or final products, then the business community will be forced to lay off workers, and the cycle will start all over again.

Government/6: It's clear that not everyone will be prepared—either because of (a) late start to fix, (b) no money for this or (c) they don't care. Since everyone depends on everyone else, it will cause bankruptcies and other major business disruptions. I can be sure [our] programs all run correctly but I cannot be sure our suppliers will survive or be able to produce. Imagine [our organization] unable to get a delivery of toilet paper! or copy paper! I think some suppliers of software will not fix their product and will simply go out of business on 12/31/1999; then open up 1/1/2000 as a different company. "Sure we'll fix the old company's software program. It will only cost you xxx." Well, some small companies may not be able to afford it.

I'm also concerned that Europe is more concerned with the Euro then Y2K—which might cause big problems. They took on two large scale projects at the same time—perhaps not a wise move.

Military/6: It is still incredible to talk to non-Y2K folks about Y2K. They still think it is not a problem. Or, an easy fix is available, but those Y2K contractors are just jacking up their rates, etc. NO ONE IS LOOKING AT THE END TO END FIXES. Everyone is focused on their "piece." Doing AWARENESS briefings to government personnel, sometimes I encounter the "1000 yard" stare. I can tell some are calculating if they will be in the same job, or retired and don't have to worry about Y2K. Some are thinking about how they can move and not be responsible. Those two groups, if they come up with an out, sit back and listen, and at the end, the only questions they have are how to fix their OWN HOME PCs, not the thousands they are currently responsible for! The US Government will not get the important systems fixed.

Military/6: The inherent danger of predicting the future is that it's a moving target. At any given point in time there is a new set of possible outcomes. It is still not too late to change course. However, based on the current trend of downplaying the seriousness of the Y2K problem and a general lack of decisive action, I would say that this country is headed for a rude awakening as to the extent that it depends on information technology.

Military/6: I guess you'd have to put me in the 5.5–6.5 range. My problem is that I would rate the issues into categories: Economic, Infrastructure, Social Impact, and Political. In these categories I would anticipate the following:

Economic: Mild recession, unemployment may dip at least temporarily as companies "go manual" in an attempt to survive, some local runs on banks. Bigger impact as the "velocity of money" drops from 75 mph. to 25mph for 6–24 months. Short term 90–120 day heavily cash economy.

Infrastructure: Regional supply and infrastructure problems—some localized blackouts, regionalized brownouts—6–24 month recovery—again by "going manual."

Social Impact: There will always be opportunists that will take advantage of social disruption—in some hotspots this may lead to rioting—nothing heavy duty unless someone fans the flames "the rich folks got (lights, water, heat, food,—you pick) some localized martial law.

Politics: This IS a political crisis! The only way to win is to "declare war" on the problem. To "declare war" and have less than an overwhelming victory, is political suicide—NO ONE is going to grab this bull by the tail! Calm words and assurances from the top will be essential to minimize the social impact. Will we have a capable messenger? Unknown!

Organization/6: I believe this problem to be entirely misunderstood by the American public at large, and a large portion of our nation's small businesses. Should small business in the U.S. be affected in even the smallest way it would have a profound effect on the economy (small business makes up over 50 percent of both our nation's workforce as well as our GDP).

Organization/6: While I'm not certain about the strong recession, I do agree with the rest of the statement. I think that the public sector, particularly local and federal govt. will be severely impacted. I think many of the states have a better handle on this issue, although some of the rural or western states do not, but they also have fewer IT systems. I am afraid that some of the worst disruptions will come from embedded systems that have been neglected. There will be more than one situation where the IT systems work, but the infrastructure will not, thus preventing employees from getting to work or being able to work due to heat, electricity, etc. The international implications are terrible with 70 percent of the world's countries barely addressing this problem. I am an optimist at heart so I still hope that we can minimize the worst of the problems in the areas of health and safety, but I fear that my optimism will be misplaced.

Other/6: It is very difficult to gauge where the US is in terms of fixing "mission critical" systems (infrastructure, banking, military etc.) but my feeling is that your major corporations will "fix" about 75 percent of their systems. The real problem lies in the interrelated economies of the world and how the inaction of Asia (Japan) and some European countries affect the US. The other problem I see is how the US public will react to the potential problems when it finally wakes up. By mid-99 we should begin to get nightly news stories about the associated problems and potential disasters. As the public begins to react by moving life savings out of mutual funds and stocks...the dominoes begin to fall.

Vendor/6: I fear that the economic fallout from this problem will start with a downward lurch and then gradually spiral further downward for a couple of years before the world economy turns back up. Barring extended infrastructure disruption, I believe the U.S. (if not the world) will work its way through this challenge without major societal upheaval. If the energy and telecommunications infrastructure fails in any substantial way, all bets are off.

Vendor/6: There was an impact on the market with the Asian crisis recently, even though the market was strong. American industry is addressing the Y2K issue, however, the International community is not reacting fast enough to mitigate the Y2K risk.

Level 7: Political Crises; Regional Supply/ Infrastructure Problems and Social Disruptions

March 1998 Survey

Government/7: I believe that the expected power grid collapse on the East coast will have a domino effect that will have the stated impact. Americans have experienced no electricity before, however only locally and for short periods of time. This expected blackout will result in a negative effect on each person in America. How long will it be before food spoils in the fridge resulting in food shortages, how long before the car runs out of gas resulting in transportation problems, how long can you work without computers, telephones, lights and heat resulting in no money if you could find what you need. Just stop and think how electricity touches our everyday lives. Without the power grid, life as we know and expect it will not continue after 1/1/2000. However, this is America. We will pull together and attack and fix this problem. We will get back on our feet and many people will be promptly fired and sued for ignoring the problem to a point that allowed the expected temporary grief to happen in the first place. Smile if you wish, I am preparing for self sufficiency!

Corporate/7: Depends on what the FAA is able to do in the next six months and if research agencies (Metagroup, Gartner, Forrester) are wrong about utility and health industries. Disruptions, even if only for a few weeks or months, in these infrastructure areas will cause chaos and panic.

Vendor/7: Our clients range from being very much in control and in time to fix the problem to people who have yet to tackle the bulk of the situation. It is unclear how the situation will play out at the last minute, but if things keep going at the rate they are going now, the U.S. will be severely impacted. The sense of urgency is still not there.

Vendor/7: On the one hand, the US currently runs quite well on computers with an infinite number of existing bugs. On the other hand, these bugs aren't the same one and they didn't occur at the same time, requiring the same limited skill set to resolve. Year 2K is a PEOPLE MANAGEMENT PROBLEM. And it will end causing more problems than it should, mostly because both Government and Industry are dealing with it as though it's normal project—to be evaluated slowly, carefully, taking into consideration all the vendors, making them go through all the normal motions, etc. IT'S TOO LATE FOR THAT! IT'S AN EMERGENCY!

The government should consider immediately forming an agency that immediately hires the thousands of needed skilled resources and vendors, at COMPETITIVE RATES and APPROPRIATE IN-CENTIVES, to have them available to any government organization who needs them.

Government/7: Where was "all of the above"? Political crises will come in the shape of some of the Defense infrastructure problems. Also, it will "overshadow" the inaugural events of 00, but a plus because this person will be "exhibiting" the leadership skill to pull things together nationally after "pockets" of social unrest are isolated. Regional supply chain problems will occur because "smaller" links will be scrambling to repair/exist/exit infrastructure.

Consultant/7: The government has not yet reached awareness!

Consultant/7: Nothing I can say that can't be sung...

Conslutant/7: Lots of creativity and effort, but too little too late and the utilities and government are in the worst shape.

Corporate/7: What is the government doing to ensure financial market systems will be compliant? (exchanges, broker-dealers, banks, etc.).

Consultant/7: We estimate that no more than 50 percent of the US companies have a sufficient Y2K activity to make it through the year 2000. From our observations, there are still 20 to 35 percent who have not addressed the problem and more than 60 percent have yet to begin remediation activity. In addition to the software/hardware problems which get the most press, embedded systems will have the most impact. There are too many unknowns in their use and application to everyday things to be effectively corrected in time. Even if the US was able to be 100 percent compliant, the rest of the world, which we have to interface with, will not be able to provide or receive reformatted data on January 1, 2000.

Consultant/7: Although I do not yet believe that the Y2K software crisis will mean the "end of the world as we now know it," I foresee regional impacts of a severe nature. Those regions most vulnerable are the most densely populated areas, where the supply chain/infrastructure will be absolutely stretched over a relatively short span of time. I'm reminded of a physics problem where a Heaviside function (abrupt, huge stimulus occurs) and the effects attenuate over a significant period of time (but not immediately). I am becoming more convinced that the unknowable side of the Y2K problem—embedded systems—will be the litmus test of how well or how badly our country fares in the first half of 2000 A.D.

Military/7: The problem is we don't KNOW the magnitude of the problem! Americans are very good problem solvers—once the problem is identified concretely. This problem is an example of chaos theory in practice. We do not have a command economy—the last 30 years of infrastructure—technical, social, financial, etc. were not designed and planned, they grew—organically in response to market opportunities. The market as it stands—dominated by "quick buck" experts—rewards "first" more generously than "best." "Best" will survive the shakeout better, but the "first" management will learn nothing from it! Sigh......

Consult/7: Historically, due to the emphasis on dialogue, our political system does little to prepare for impending problems unless the crisis is imminent. The imminence of this crisis will not be fully appreciated until a major infrastructure disruption occurs which affects life or fiscal stability; thereupon political interference will add to the magnitude of the problems and introduce its own dimension. If it were not for this, I would have chosen choice 6 instead of choice 7.

Consultant/7: The harder I work, and the more people I talk to in this industry, the more pessimistic the response... I waffled between 7 and 8.

Consultant/7: Opinion surveys are interesting, but models of failure scenarios would be more compelling. Particularly in the government, where progress appears to be slow and truth elusive.

Legal/7: As part of the industry team working feverishly to thwart a real crisis, by generating responsible vendor behavior, modifying customer (especially Fed Gov, large institutional [e.g.-bank, investment, telecom, aviation]) expectations and response, and generally avoiding the Bruce Hall/ Lou Marcocio chicken little outcomes, my HOPE is that we are successful and that the real result is somewhere in the 3-4-5 range.

But, as I look at US Gov posture, the naivete of many large corporate IT users, the European readiness posture, and other tea leaves, I really fear that the outcome will be "worse than 5." Given the cascading nature of phenomena like runs on banks—the herd mentality/feeding frenzy nature of our culture, until the media infrastructure collapses, hysteria will come, "isolated" runs on a few small banks will breed wholesale panic, and with the collapse of confidence in the financial infrastructure will come distribution/transportation failure, which, as the President's Commission blithely points out, will paralyze the rest of essential services of government, health care, etc. and

THWACK, you've got a "millennium"—or, put another way, anything 5 or worse won't stop till 9 or 10.

So, we need drastic measures NOW, (emergency supplemental Appropriation for essential government systems [beyond national security, otherwise only the soldiers and cops will have functioning systems], furlough of thousands of government employees who cannot be put to work writing Social Security checks, a PLAN for air traffic, rail traffic, bridges, highways, food supply, pharmaceuticals, electrical power, telecom, etc.) because by the time things get bad enough that the featherbedders in Congress do something about it, they'll be "tits up in the Potomac." I love Sen. Bennett for his foresight, but he's working inside a system that is part of the problem. Where do ya think two digit date fields came from—look at War Department ledgers for supplies during Custer's Campaign!

Consultant/7: Still too soon to evaluate because the awareness level is so low and so few assessments are underway for embedded systems. I expect significant regional power interruptions/reductions in grid supply due to loss of nuclear plant supplies. Impacts in military-industrial complex could be significant. Federal agencies are feeling no sense of urgency for Y2K embedded systems in my opinion.

Vendor/7: (a) Expect regional telecommunications outages on the order of days (1–5), regional electrical power distribution outages on the order of weeks (1–5), and air transportation impacts on the order of months (1–5, maybe years). (b) Expect items in (a) above will interact with one another and drive high demand for repair resources. (c) Pray we have a mild winter.

MAY 1998 SURVEY

Consultant/7: We work mainly in the medical systems area. Unless there is substantial improvement in their readiness, Y2K is going to kill people. Don't get sick, don't get hurt, don't go near healthcare facilities for the first six months of 2000.

Consultant/7: In examining the President's Y2K efforts and reading the list of government agencies that are in trouble, there is no way to avoid the element of "chaos" throughout this country, not to mention those outside our borders.

Consultant/7: We are facing the greatest crisis to worldwide public safety since the Cuban missile crisis and no one seems concerned. The Y2K bug will not wait, it will arrive on time if not early. This is a bullet that cannot be dodged. The minimum problems will be on the 7th level and could go right off of your chart if not prepared for and fixed promptly. Two weeks without power worldwide would throw our society into collapse and our technology back to the bronze age.

Consultant/7: A large amount of business is communicated and conducted with worldwide neighbors. I believe their inability to comprehend and accomplish the task will affect the U.S. much greater than is perceived. Therefore we will see enormous infrastructure problems in addition to the great impact of business beyond our borders.

Consultant/7: My comments and vote for # 7 remain the same; people are not realizing the seriousness of the situation and things are moving at a snail's pace compared to the monumental effort required globally. The interdependency factor will, in the end, drag much of the world into the vortexes of collapse that will be located at various places and in various industries throughout the world.

Consultant/7: The above is what I am planning for with hopes it is much less serious. All governmental agencies and corporate businesses need to cleanup the IT and non-IT portfolios, get control of inventory and configurations, apply standards within their organizations and promote standards across like business centers within major industries.

The critical systems will not be fixed in time, the band-aids will begin peeling off before we finish the critical systems, and because there was no standard fix applied to all linked and interfaced systems, enterprises and industries, the Y2K problem will likely be a cold war we fight for the next 10 years.

Consultant/7: I think there will be widespread impact resulting from a failure to deal with this issue in a timely manner. However, I also believe in the ability of the American people to find ways around problems. The lag between these two events is what will cause most of the problems. If we wait for government to fix the problem, the effect will be protracted severely.

Consultant/7: Since the last survey, I haven't seen any indications that the impacts of Y2K will be less severe than I originally thought. The general tone of Y2K activities is moving quickly towards risk/damage avoidance and minimization (as opposed to productive mitigation efforts).

In my opinion, the greatest threat to successful mitigation of Year 2000 problems in the U.S. is the rapidly evolving legal "feeding frenzy" now being born. Public companies are unwilling to freely share poor product Y2K compliance status for fear of corporate devaluation in the equity markets and of litigation. Otherwise capable vendors and service providers are unwilling to pursue Y2K work because of liability risks. States are now immunizing themselves against lawsuits for projected failures to provide public services. Legal practices are now "training" for Y2K class action efforts. Witness Peter de Jager's reasons for ending Project Damocles.

The American propensity for legal remedies, as opposed to developing and implementing real fixes, will not serve the country well for this issue. In fact, it may cause more economic pain and suffering than the original problem.

Consultant/7: I'm a software programmer/consultant with 14 years experience. I find myself vacillating between denial (it cannot happen/it's just a bad dream) and panic (I need to protect my family and head for the hills). When it comes to Y2K, it seems that otherwise intelligent, educated and rational people suffer from cognitive dissonance (i.e., the facts render a conclusion that is so unbelievable, the mind dismisses it and comes to a conclusion it can deal with).

On your scale of 0 thru 10 and based on a static snapshot on 5/13/98, I am in the 6 to 9 range—probably a 7.5—although if we don't get our act together, it is not too hard to envision a 10. With that in mind, I'll put down a 7 for the time being, with room for future adjustments up or down based on how events unfold.

I just finished a relatively small scale Y2K conversion that was originally estimated/budgeted to take two people six months. It took ten people two years. The hardest, most labor intensive part was identifying dates that were embedded in nondate key fields and other strings of data, as well as tracing dates through fields that have names that are not readily identifiable as dates. No automated tools can handle those tasks.

That lapse in schedule was for a small system. Extrapolate the numbers to a larger system such as Bank of America which currently has 1000 programmers working on it full time and only estimates its work to be one-third done (per Ed Yourdon 5/6/98).

The work cited above has nothing to do with embedded systems, the wild card in the Y2K deck. Astonishingly enough, the business community is only now realizing the scope and magnitude of this "potential" problem and it seems they have been stunned into a state of denial.

I subscribe to *Federal Computer Week* and have been anxiously tracking the Federal Government Agencies' progress on the Y2K problem for several years. The May 5th *Federal Computer Week* has no less than ten pieces dealing with Y2K, four dealing with failing Y2K remediation efforts in the federal government:

1. GAO Slams DOD's Y2K Effort—pg. 3,

2. GAO Says Interior Faces Y2K Meltdown—pg. 10,

3. Agencies Doubt They Can Make Y2K Deadlines—pg. 15,

4. Year 2000 Computing Crisis, Federal Regulatory Efforts to Ensure Financial Institution Systems Are Y2K Compliant—pg. 15.

Some of the most troubling insights are:

- The GAO reports "that it could be difficult to monitor or conduct military engagements" and "aircraft and other military equipment could be grounded" due to mission critical system's failure—pg. 3.

- "vendors are stonewalling requests for compliance info" fearing legal action—pg. 8.

- "systems that regulate… our nations dams could fail"—pg. 10.

- federal regulators were "late to recognize Y2K problem, are far behind schedule in fixing the problem and do not have sufficient technical knowledge" to ensure financial institution systems (i.e., banks, S and L's, Credit Unions) are Y2K compliant—pg. 15.

- the departments of Labor, Health and Human Services and Education face failures in many mission critical systems—pg. 15.

Given the facts that:

1. Most IT projects ARE underestimated and NOT completed on time,

2. That there is a worldwide labor shortage of Y2K skills,

3. That Y2K projects are the most costly, labor intensive projects that most business entities will ever undertake,

4. That 01/01/2000 is an immovable deadline,

5. And that many private companies and that most federal agencies, state agencies and local governments, have not moved past the assessment stage of Y2K work,

I am not optimistic that ALL the critical systems of ALL these entities will be completed and synchronized on time.

What% percent of the global/U.S. economy must shut down for the whole thing to shut down? I don't know, but we may find out. This will be an interesting case study in chaos theory and complex systems.

There is a lot of data out there and a lot of varied opinions on the post-Y2K future. Time will tell who is right and who is wrong. The important thing is for adequate contingency planning and disaster recovery planning by the Federal, State and local governments starting NOW. Emergency food and medical distribution hubs must be established and stocked prior to 01/01/2000. This means mobilizing FEMA, the national guard, the military establishment, and other appropriate federal, state and local emergency agencies and working out the logistics of such a disaster preparedness plan. The public must be educated about the risks and contingency plans in a way that prevents panic.

Each individual and family must determine a course of action based on their own individual assessments of the magnitude and potential impact of this problem and they must assess their own personal priorities and loyalties (e.g., if confronted with the level 9/10 doomsday scenario does the soldier, reservist, policeman, etc., answer the call to duty by his/her country or does he/she protect his/her own family)?

One last caveat—the inherent security risks associated with Y2K and its ensuing chaos present the optimal opportunity for terrorists and/or other "kooks" to wreak havoc (e.g., unleashing nuclear devices, or deadly chemical and/or biological agents). Keep an eye on Saddam.

Corporate/7: Although I think the Y2K effects will be severe, I think they will last a year or shorter in duration. That is the time I think it will take to regroup and restructure our way of life to survive/solve the Y2K problems.

Corporate/7: This survey is more like a consumer confidence survey because the people answering these questions are not trained to do so. But, even so, the survey definitely gives an indication of "knowledgeable Y2K" sentiment.

Corporate/7: Still not enough attention and urgency and explanation of problem breadth to average citizen. A recent *Washington Post* article even dismissed the problem as hype—much ado about nothing. Clinton is worried about his legacy and how history will view him, and his lack of leadership to this problem may well become his long-term legacy.

I also worry that many corporate leaders believe all is well in their companies, based on assurances from their managers, when the truth is otherwise. I think many corporations have thinned out middle management excessively, and taught the remaining managers to only present good news (or get fired). So top management is only hearing what they want to hear. And the middle managers are now just looking for their next job, with no longer any loyalty or long-term commitment to their company or concern about its long term future. Y2K may well expose the seriousness of this problem.

I think the SEC efforts to ensure stockholders are informed of companies preparation status are wise; companies will not want to admit they are in trouble; penalties for lying should be severe and personal, not just fines to a (bankrupt?) corporation. How do we hold the government as accountable?

Educational/7: Last week The International Emergency Management Society (TIEMS 98) [note two digits] held its annual conference in Washington, D.C. Y2K was not mentioned in the program. These are the people who help us recover from earthquakes, floods, hurricanes, etc. I was told that a spokesperson from FEMA mentioned Y2K as a problem that had to be solved. She said FEMA was not compliant now but had plans to become compliant. She did not mention any possible disruptions or disasters that might result from firms or systems not being compliant. Hence, Y2K was described as an IT problem with no connection to the subject matter of the conference. A "workshop" on Y2K was scheduled during a coffee break. Three people showed up. Judging from informal conversations during the conference my impression is that emergency management professionals from around the world do not yet regard Y2K as a matter of professional interest to them.

Government/7: I think this is going to be a major domino effect. Small feeder companies are not going to have the cash or manpower to convert systems, and buy new equipment, they will fail. This will then lead to larger companies being unable to provide services as a result of them not getting necessary supplies.

This coupled with an "electronic" based currency which will, in most cases, become nonexistent leads to a society with no real currency, and no method of exchanging goods and services. The hardest hit will necessarily be high population areas, because of their high reliance on an information based job structure, and their inability to provide basic living needs, food, electric, water.

Government/7: The Platte River study shows what can happen when infrastructure services are stopped. It causes all kinds of problems.

Government/7: I voted last week and entered what I thought was a slightly pessimistic "5." Then I read the ITAA Year 2000 Outlook for May 15. I thought the FAA and DOD were being more than optimistic in their projections for completing their conversions—much too little much too late. Loss of air traffic would be a major inconvenience to this country. The failure of our military to take an aggressive position in this unavoidable technology collision is unforgivable and chilling. But what sent my score spiraling downward is the failure of the utilities to respond to what is rapidly becoming a crisis. We used to talk in the seventies about sitting in the dark and cold because of the oil crisis. We may well be facing exactly that in 18 months because the power, oil, and gas companies don't seem to be responding to the looming disaster. Maybe the survivalists had it right. Maybe "7" is not low enough.

Military/7: The public and political awareness has been too little too late. Inaction of the Congress and White House has led to a far too casual attitude towards the Y2K crisis until recently. Even now, the attention is totally inadequate. Midrange corporations, state and local governments and major providers of basic services may face moderate to major failures in their individual systems. Current deregulation of the nation's power industry has diverted attention from the Y2K crisis to competition and corporate reorganization. I strongly feel that even if a few minor power companies experience failure on January 1, 2000 it would likely lead to a major power outage across large sections of the nation. Only by disconnecting the power grid infrastructure can individual power companies prevent the sudden surge of power demand caused by the local failures which will in turn cause a system overload and failure. Economically the world is a single market. The failures in Asia and Europe will create a severe strain on the US markets and an economic downturn. Health care industry is not ready with contingency plans to keep their basic systems in operation, little less to account for a sudden power loss. The lack of such plans may cause deaths of 100s of Americans.

Military/7: I believe that there will be failures of various systems for about a one month time frame; banks will have troubles; electric systems will have trouble; manufacturing will have troubles. It will take about a month to correct the various problems. People will be upset with the press and congress for not taking steps soon enough, and a third party might win the elections.

Military/7: We will likely experience regional failures in distribution systems (information, supply, etc.) where Y2K responsibilities were not clearly defined and "system of systems" testing was not adequately performed between organizations. Most organizations will probably not have adequate plans and resources on hand to immediately recover from system failures.

Military/7: Outages of services will likely occur. Many items will likely remain unidentified and will impact other systems leading to a larger outage. There will be attempts to ensure contingencies are enacted, some are actually being enacted now. The political crises will result from lack of proper planning and the general public will raise their voices to point their finger at administrations and leadership for not anticipating and taking enough action.

Some agencies and services have not yet become enlightened as to the Y2K issues. I have been visiting businesses (small and large) and have asked if they have taken any actions. Their responses, "What problem?" or, "That computer thing?" Considering these responses, we are in severe need for the media and the political leaders to start educating the public and helping to awaken action. I see little action in this area and it is mixed in its review—that there is a major problem to it is all hype and exaggerated!

Organization/7: It's extremely important that it be understood that any negative impacts we experience will—in fact—be temporary. There will be an end to it, and we will then rebuild and go on. We need to focus on how to whether "the storm," not cope with an apocalypse.

Organization/7: I fall somewhere between 7 and 8. I do think there will be significant infrastructure problems like power outages, bank failures, food shortages and so on...but I do not think that these will lead to violence or social unrest...just because I don't think that people in reality generally react that way to hardship. In the former Soviet Union, life goes on, even though most folks never get paid, the lights go out all the time, etc.

Organization/7: During the last of 1999 I expect considerable disruption as media driven panic sets in among the economic underclasses and Joe Sixpacks (AKA The Lumpenproletariat, The Great Unwashed) who live on maxed out credit and understand little or nothing of economics much less computer systems.

For most of the year 2000 I expect an economic replay of 1934 in terms of production, unemployment, and social distress. As more and more systems, and their linkages are jerry-rigged into operation, I expect a decent uplift in economic activity by the last quarter of Y2000. This may well be restricted by: (1) energy and transport problems; and (2) the lack of international trade caused by other countries and areas continuing to have significant Y2K infastructure problems.

Another impact—whose extent is unknown and unknowable—will come from the various levels of government. In particular this will focus on the ability (or inability) to collect revenue and dispense it. The real question, I guess, is whether the politicians, at all levels, can face the situation and work creatively to solve it; or will fall back into political bickering and fingerpointing (Nero fiddling while Rome burns comes to mind). The very thought of 2000 being an election year gives me the cold sweats.

Level 8: Depression; Infrastructure Crippled; Markets Collapse; Local Martial Law

March 1998 Survey

Consulting/8: I foresee the US government instituting a military style draft for IT professionals to assist in the software remediation process. Although it would be politically dangerous, Mr. Clinton, AT THIS TIME, should declare a state of national emergency. Al Gore, the father of the "Information Super Highway," will soon find that it will dead end on a very high cliff. He will ultimately inherit the blame for the chaos that will undoubtedly occur soon. Why wasn't he on top of Y2K back in 1992-1993?

Corporate/8: How do you declare martial law when the military systems also fail?

Corporate/8: I see this as worst case, but am leaning more and more this way as time goes on and not enough is being done by government to avert the inherent dangers. Additionally, the large majority of people in the United States are still completely unaware of the problem, and if aware, have no idea of the full impact on our lives—especially the effect of the failure of the utilities companies, etc. This will greatly exacerbate the situation and will result in panic and social incidents/disruptions (which I added to the # 8 list).

Organization/8: For want of two digit repairs well tested, the application was lost; for want of the application, the systems were lost; for want of the systems, the EDIs were lost; for want of the EDIs, the networked enterprises were lost; for want of many public and private enterprises, much of the cyber kingdom was lost.

Government/8: Fooling ourselves into believing a "magic bullet" exists only exacerbates the problem. I suspect we are going to be in denial until the end of this year when a lot of systems will start failing.

Government/8: At all levels and all enterprises, Y2K is pretty much a case of "too little, too late" that is going to affect everyone, even those who have completed their own Y2K projects. "Six Degrees Of Separation" is even more true now than when the play was first performed. Nothing the government can do at this point will completely resolve the expected downturn before it happens. I believe that at this point the best thing the Feds can do is encourage decentralized disaster recovery efforts (by decentralized, I mean at the neighborhood level, with the local firehouse or school as the rally point), with the full admission that outside help may be late in arriving if at all. Given the recent performance of FEMA, anything less will not be believed, and giving more money to FEMA is *not* the answer. This is definitely going to be a case where the "Six P's" apply, and the sooner we do the "Prior Planning" the lower the "Poor Performance" level will be.

I also feel that the real danger of Y2K is the strong probability that members of the executive branch will use it as an excuse to ignore the various restrictions placed on them by numerous legal documents. The Internet is rife with rumors that the executive branch has already implemented regulations declaring that anyone who prepares for disaster is a "hoarder" and by definition a criminal. True or not, this is exactly the kind of thing we don't need. People should not be punished for taking care of themselves without recourse to a government nanny.

Vendor/8: I do not think anybody is serious about fixing the problems. As long as we can charge on our plastic cards, we are happy. We think developing countries (Do NOT call them third world countries) have more problems. It is not so. People in those countries know how to write books and do simple arithmetic without much fuss. It is here where we depend on computers so much we face disasters. We have lawyers to make it worse.

MAY 1998 SURVEY

Consultant/8: I fully expect disruptions of up to 3-6 months within the manufacturing/transportation sectors and a 1-3 month disruption in the Utility sector, resulting in local disruptions and imposition of martial law. I also fully expect the impact to be much more severe in Asian economies where Y2K awareness/resolutions are lagging those in the US and Canada. This could create some radical changes in the balance of global and regional security structures particularly in Asia.

Consultant/8: Anyone trying to cover up the true state of their Y2K compliance progress will be exposed in the harshest light when Y2K hits. It behooves everyone to be as honest as possible now to avoid uncontrolled panic later.

Corporate/8: I have not seen, heard or read anything since the last survey that would lead me toward a more optimistic conclusion. There has been no visible increase in the level of activity in the government or private sector. Furthermore, in my own company's Y2K project, we have just come to appreciate how big the testing effort is going to be. It is huge—and we don't have mainframes or COBOL to deal with! We run packaged applications (such as Oracle Financials) on UNIX and NT and are still facing a huge resource drain as we enter testing. The deafening silence coming from other companies regarding this matter is not reassuring.

Corporate/8: It will be rough in the US, much worse elsewhere. I fear a multiplier effect, such as failure to move seed/fertilizer/pesticide in early 2000 leading to total loss of some crops in late 2000, and consequent devastating famine in some countries. I estimate from 10M to 300M deaths from this effect alone, and if wars start then all bets are off.

Educational/8: This selection is based on the following assumptions:

1. that the current thrust of Federal government efforts, as well as public and private efforts in general, continues on its current course;

2. that major initiatives continue to be based on an extremely limited definition of the nature and scope of

the set of problems facing us, a limited definition that principally involves information technology and cyberspace and ignores major environmental, economic, domestic welfare, societal, security, and global consequences; and

3. that near term steps fail to be taken to mandate, fund, and establish a Special Y2K Emergency Mitigation and Management Office (or Special Action Office) in the Executive Office of the President, or elsewhere in the government, a Special Action Office that would have a far more comprehensive mission than the present extraordinarily small White House-based effort, a Special Action Office that would have the authority, leadership, and resources to act to prevent, minimize, prepare for and ameliorate the possible melange of crises and the aftermath of the crises that can be expected if a worst case scenario were to evolve.

If such steps were undertaken and effectively initiated during the summer or early fall of 1998, then the disastrous consequences of Y2K problems could be significantly reduced.

Government/8: I think some of the optimism is fading when I hear that some of the most progressive organizations such as Social Security are hedging, and the increasing level of corporate complaints about the dismal response from vendors and suppliers concerning compliance status. It looks like two steps forward and three steps back. I previously voted a 7, but this time an 8.

Government/8: I'm Government, Federal. I voted 8 and still vote the same. At the time I cast my original vote I was leaning towards 9 because I felt that it was too late to avoid severe disruptions, but that crisis management, if it commences in time, could keep the situation at a level 8 or even 7. The type of crisis management I consider necessary is for both the utility firms and railroads to admit that they have serious problems and then plan together so that the tracks that are fixed first are the ones that feed coal to the generating plants that will be operational first. Similarly, the telecoms must tell the other key components of the infrastructure which types of communication links are most vulnerable so that reasonable contingency plans can be developed. At the time of the first vote, I hadn't seen any signs of this sort of process ever getting established. However, there are rumblings that indicate that some of Mr. Koskinen's actions may lead to this result. The sooner the better.

Also, more journalists are starting to write stories indicating that maybe there really is a problem after all. This erodes some of the denial and makes the subject more appropriate for serious discussion. The sooner each individual and firm accepts the problem and prepares for the consequences, the better we will all be in the end. I'm now a solid 8, instead of an 8 leaning toward 9.

Other/8: I have increased my rating since last time because I have heard it takes about 18 months for emergency measures organizations to prepare and practice contingency plans for disasters and my local EMO has not been aware of Y2K disasters. For example, they have no contingency plans for telephones being out of service. I will continue to try to alert my EMO that Y2K contains a risk of disruptions.

Other/8: Whether or not markets will "collapse," I don't know. It depends on your definition of "collapse" (as of its current highs, the Dow could fall to between 5800 and 6400, and still not kill the long-term bull market which began in August of 1982—that would be a decline of 31 to 37 percent. Using the same methods, I was able to correctly call the bottom in 1987, to within 10 points they would have worked in 1990 at the bottom, too, but I was otherwise occupied—these past predictions are not something that should be advertised, please) Also, a depression depends on definition as well, but I'd rate the chances of at least temporary 20%+ unemployment as certainly significant. How long this lasts, there's no way to know. In terms of relating the stock market to an economy like that, it depends on how investors (particularly the institutions) react. If they simply move money from non-Y2K compliant businesses into compliant ones, the averages themselves could hold up relatively well, until we start to come out of this. (Incidentally, those businesses, organizations, nations and individuals which go into this prepared will not only survive, they will thrive, and flourish in the post-Y2K world.) And if investors properly recognize that Y2K is an "artificial" depression or severe recession, the market will simply fly upwards as we begin to emerge from this. However, for the shorter term, experts seem to be overlooking very key areas in their analysis—i.e., the impact of a severe oil shortage or attempts to repair fossil fuel power utilities, for instance, among numerous other things.

Local martial law seems, at this point, to be just a given. Not to mentioning ration of all sorts—energy (definitely), perhaps food, even transportation and travel.

We *will* get through this—at this point, it's a matter of how well the triage is set up, and how well the contingency plans are both developed and executed. But because the US is ahead in preparation, we will also come out ahead of the rest of the world on the other side of this. In point of fact, I actually expect we will rebuild the rest of the world. We may well experience the greatest economic boom in history in the post-Y2K world. Unfortunately, the price we—and the world—will pay for that will be exceedingly high.

Vendor/8: Although I'd like to think on the positive side and say we'll only see a "6," I think things may slide downhill to an "8" possible "9" since the administration is still taking no positive actions. We still have the opportunity to take an active hand in minimizing the negative effects in the US if communities start taking the situation in hand and put in contingency plans to help its citizens. However, I think the greatest impact upon the US economy will be from global Y2K effects, such as Japan's economy failing further due to the fact that 80 percent of its power is from Nuclear reactors. If they're shut down for safety reasons, Japan's already weakened economy (which is strategically intertwined with our own) will have huge problems to cope with.

Level 9: Supply/Infrastructure Collapse; Widespread Social Disruptions and Martial Law

MARCH 1998 SURVEY

Corporate/9: Proper English aside, I cannot tell you how badly I want to be mistaken. FEMA or other gov't agency should be mobilized to begin contingency planning and disaster recovery for basic infrastructure, food and water distribution.

Other/9: Y2K will be a seminal event of the 20th century of the same importance as the two World Wars and the Great Depression. It will be the principal accelerate in the advent of the Information Age which will alter society and government in ways as profound as the American and French Revolutions. Y2K will be a wild ride.

Consultant/9: I think some areas will be infrastructure-wise intact with possible exceptions of petroleum based products might be rationed heavily and shortages there; those areas reliant upon wood generated and hydro-electric utilities that are prepared might be best off. I would have liked to have picked 8.5 or 8.75 as the number I feel is more likely the average. I hope I'm wrong. But available evidence points towards what I picked.

Government/9: I have seen many lies and half truths on this issue in the government agency that I worked as a contractor for until recently. Nobody is really working on the problem the way it needs to be worked on. This is going to be a disaster. Goodbye FDIC.

Consultant/9: Unless the president mobilizes the energies or this country then I believe there is not a chance for the above not happening. The Chief Executive Officer of this country must take responsibility to alert the populace NOW and then allocate resources to ensure that all basic services will work. I sent the President an e-mail saying "that there was no mention of the Y2K problem in the State of the Union message thereby giving a false impression that there IS NO PROBLEM. I strongly suggest that the Federal government make it the only priority of national importance that a clear and precise focus is applied to the testing of basic services in the United States." It is also clear that once the populace believes there is a problem there will be a problem. Think of the economic impact if everyone decides NOT to fly from December 1999 to February 2000. What will happen to the economies of Puerto Rico, Hawaii, and Alaska without air travel? Need we even ask the fail safe status of missiles? The fail safe status of our electrical distribution complex? etc. I have over 35 years of experience in the computer industry and would welcome the opportunity to be of assistance wherever and whenever the country mobilized to address the Y2K problem.

MAY 1998 SURVEY

Consultant/9: In my opinion the real problem is not the computer problem that may be identified and corrected but the problem that will occur from embedded systems and the computer problems that are not corrected. Planning for a contingency that includes lack of water and traffic lights not working (just to mention two items) which therefore dictates that employees will not be able to work in their respective buildings but also includes the possibility that they could not get there as well. The companies, especially the small ones, that rely on just in time inventory will not be able to receive new shipments in a timely manner. This will pyramid into chaos. The handling of the situation will depend on when it starts and when each important piece of the problem is solved. I would be glad to discuss this in more detail if it is appropriate.

Consultant/9: Although I realize that a "more detailed survey late this summer" will deal with Y2K impacts outside of the United States," my main concern for the past three years has been the fact that Nuclear Weapons Command and Control Systems (hardware and software) in China, India, Iran, Pakistan, Russia, and to a lesser extent in France, Israel, the United Kingdom, and the United States have not been completely debugged.

Russia has NOT even begun to address the problem. The military infrastructure refuses to believe that a problem exists, the government does not have the necessary funding available nor the qualified personal to address the tasks. Authorities in both Pakistan and Iran refuse to believe a problem exists. China and India currently are unknowns. Therefore, the probability of accidental explosions of nuclear weapons remains very high.

Consultant/9: I must admit that "disaster"-related threads in the various Y2K discussion forums are beginning to have an effect on me and my thinking. The major reason why I would now select the rating "9" over "8" is the persistent notion that food/fuel supply lines for major urban areas have perhaps 10 days to two weeks before they go "dry." I believe that Y2K disruptions will endure more than 2 weeks. Therefore, I have to select "9."

Consultant/9: My estimation remains steady, as a Federal Government contractor, I vote for a 9.

Consultant/9: Since the last survey I see very little additional ACTION but I do see additional awareness. Without a dramatic (exponential) increase in action on the part of business and government the outlook is not good.

It will be a shame if the legacy of the 20th Century is that when we needed statesmanship from our elected officials we got politics and scandal and when we needed leadership from the best and brightest business people we got avoidance, Mergers and Acquisitions or silence (Gates, Grove). The words, "not with a bang but with a whimper" come to mind.

I must also add that my anger is rising. The American people at large do not understand the implications on them, on their jobs and families. It is time for elected officials at all levels and senior business management to hear the message that THEY ARE ACCOUNTABLE. Perhaps we need a lobbyist and a PR firm to get this message across since that is the way things work! It would be interesting to know if the frustration level is rising and also what people are doing about it other than moving to the hills.

Corporate/9: There is rampant worry and confusion regarding how Year 2000 will affect public utilities! No one seems to know, and certainly no one is accepting any responsibility for providing answers!

Until we have a full UNDERSTANDING of what electric utility companies are doing (or not doing) about the Year 2000 problem, and the interdependencies of the so-called "power grid," we are just kidding ourselves if we think that we have ANY IDEA as to the magnitude of the Year 2000 problem.

I think that NOW is the time for the Federal Government to TAKE CHARGE of the utility companies, and ask the absolutely critical questions that need to be asked. And to then get ANSWERS, based on TESTING, as soon as possible, so at least contingency plans can be formulated, if needed. (Or, guarantee to everyone that there is no need to worry about it, as it is all under control.)

(A question: If ALL of the "power grid" went down, could ANY part of it come up? With the switch from analog to digital technology over the past years, does one need electricity to be able to generate electricity?)

Government/9: I fear there will be a supply/infrastructure collapse with widespread disruptions leading to martial law for at least a short period of time. I predict that there will be a period after January 1, 2000, that some services, "leading one: lack of electricity," will affect some of the people. Later, as supplies/services run out, we will have a recognition period where there will be an honest to goodness concentrated effort led by the Federal government to correct the problem, here and abroad. The recognition period will be followed by the crisis period. There will be unbelief that this is possible in the U.S., finger pointing by politicians. This will be followed by our "you don't need freedom now for the good of all" period under martial law. Once the supply infrastructure has been returned to "normal," we will have witnessed a giant shift in economic wealth to corporations that will become the leaders of tomorrow. This summation is based upon expert type articles that indicate a lack of serious effort to date at the government or corporate level.

Other/9: I have quit the Y2K business and have gotten active in the munions industry.

Other/9: One of the most important, long-reaching effects of Y2K will be to fundamentally alter the role of government in the world. The widespread failure of government computers will forcibly reduce reliance on government and increase the influence and state and local government entities. There will be a commensurate transfer of power from state to city and county governments. The centralized, large welfare model will be radically reengineered.

Vendor/9: I think WDCY2K is providing an incredible service in terms of raising public/private awareness of the horrific potential of Y2K problems. America will recover from the Y2K crises, with stronger IT systems and strategies in place, but the transition will be painful, and may bring out the worst in many people for the short term.

Vendor/9: Disasters will worsen over time due to our inability to prevent, stop, or reverse them. This snowball effect is similar to the Y2K problem itself—lack of understanding and inability to prevent or stop in time, allows snowballing failure.

Level 10: Collapse of U.S. Government;
Possible Famine

March 1998 Survey

Other/10: As one who spent an entire year working with Congress and the executive agencies on Y2K issues I have come face to face with complete irresponsibility and fecklessness in the US government. Federal agencies define "mission critical systems" as meeting their own payrolls, not the public's health, safety and well-being. Congress is unable to repair its own million+ lines of code, a direct indication of the paralysis of that institution which is unable to act even to preserve its own ADP capability. The so-called champions of Y2K in the Federal government agencies are mere sloganeers looking to surf on a wave. They believe that they can leap from this wave before it crashes like a tsunami on the beaches. In fact they can no more escape this on-rushing tide than the natives of Vesuvius could escape the volcano that covered their area in a matter of hours, burying it for 20 centuries under an ocean of lava. The Federal government seems poised to be buried as deeply and for as long as Pompeii and Hurrculeaneum. The waste of time during the last year by the Federals is as great a Folly as if the leaders detonated the nuclear weapons stock and unleashed the feared, horrific nuclear winter. Thanks to the Folly in 1997 millions of humans will suffer and die.

Other/10: We're just not ready, and we won't be. It's like "kinda pregnant." No, either you are or you're not. Same goes here, either the world will be ready or it won't.

May 1997 Survey

[No responses]

Other Responses

arch 1998 Survey

Consultant/11: "11" is a cop out perhaps, but it has a formal meaning: The data leads to conflicting conclusions. It's *not* "don't know" or "no opinion." It might be considered a subset of "insufficient data," but I think it's more like "This does not compute!" (But 0, it's *not*.)

Other/NA: 1. Significant widespread impact for some enterprises (particularly those doing business in Asia and Eastern Europe). 2. Local impact for many enterprises. 3. Some market adjustment (15 to 20 percent, dropping initially but rebounding when the actual scope becomes clear); the biggest hit will come from international markets. 4. Some economic slowdown but no recession; this will be due as much to the incipient need for another major "correction" as to the actual Year 2000 problem. (In other words, it may happen anyway.) 5. The US government will be embarrassed, but—in spite of the fantasies of certain parts of the political spectrum—will **not** collapse. 6. Maybe a comet will be spotted heading for Earth. That way, Peter de Jager will still be able to shout, "The sky is falling....!" (Sorry—couldn't resist.)

May 1998 Survey

Consultant/11: As in my response to the previous survey, 11 is a cheat, but I'll stick with it. It translates to "all bets are off." When significant factors are too close to call, and when they lead to seriously conflicting outcomes, I find putting things at any point on the scale to be unsupportable. The task is to develop a response that incorporates the conflicting possibilities.

Resources

A few weeks in the lab can often save you an afternoon in the library.
—Dennis Brothers

You're back here because you want to learn more about the Year 2000 problem and how to track it. An abundance of information exists out there; the challenge, as mentioned back in Chapter 6, is to sort and sift through it all. But chances are you can find an answer—or, at least, an opinion—for just about any question you have, ranging from basic issues to detailed instructions. Time spent doing a little research will save you lots of figuring things out on your own.

Web Sites

Web sites are your best source of information about Y2K. The challenge, though, is knowing where to go to find what you want to find. Here is a list of key sites for doing Y2K research. This section isn't exhaustive and doesn't have lots of links to specific topics; the sites below do a better job of keeping such lists up to date. Rest assured that the sites below will keep you plenty busy.

Also understand that much controversy and disagreements exist over Y2K. Just because a site is listed below doesn't mean that I necessarily agree with those who run the site (or vice versa). Take everything (including what I've written in this book) with a grain of salt.

A word of warning: Web sites, like books, go "out of print"; that is, they vanish, though sometimes a "ghost" version still exists on the Web. None of the sites below is guaranteed to be there still, but chances are that most of them will be.

Many sites offer documents to download instead of showing you a web page. These documents are usually in one of two formats: Adobe Acrobat (.PDF files) and Microsoft Word (.DOC files). You can download an Acrobat reader for your browser from `http://www.adobe.com/prodindex/acrobat` (all you need is the reader, not the full Acrobat product).

Finally, here are a few notes on typing URLs[1] into your web browser. Be sure that you use a forward slash (/), not a back slash (\) unless you're sure that's what's in the URL. Note that some files end with ".html" and some end with ".htm"; look carefully to see which is which. That funny squiggly character ("~") is called a tilde and is usually at one end of the keyboard or the other, and most often is a shifted character (i.e., you have to hold the SHIFT key down to type it). And most browsers will let you dispense with the "http://," which should make typing in these URLs a bit less tedious.

News clippings

There are several excellent sites for tracking news about Y2K.

- `http://www.year2000.com/y2karticles.html` (The Year 2000 Information Center—News Clippings)

This is the probably the oldest and probably the best. It has archives going back to 1996. These help give you an idea of how much coverage has grown; there are often more articles in a single day in 1998 than there were in an entire month in 1997.

- `http://www.techweb.com/wire/technews/year2000.html` (Year 2000 Approaches)

  TechWeb, a net news service owned by CMP, lists all its Y2K news articles here.

- `http://www.y2ktoday.com` (Y2K Today)

  This site allows you to set up a customized profile on Y2K articles that you want to have called to your attention. It also has articles and other resources.

- `http://www.cruxnet.com/~sanger/y2k` (Sanger's Review of Y2K News Reports)

  Not a lot of articles, but the ones there are selected with thought and summarized so that you can quickly review them.

- `http://www.zdnet.com/zdy2k` (ZDNet's Y2K Site)

  Ziff-Davis' on-line collection of its own Y2K articles. Does a good job of challenging the conventional wisdom on both sides.

- `http://www.y2knewswire.com` (Y2K Newswire)

You can sign up for this service, which will deliver Y2K news summaries to your e-mail address daily.

- http://www.fcw.com/ref/hottopics/ y2kcontents.htm (Federal Computer Weekly Y2K Hot Topics)

  This focuses largely on the government (as you might expect).

- http://www.y2knews.com (Y2K News Magazine)

  This is the home site for Y2K News Magazine; it lists current news articles with brief summaries.

- http://www.cbn.org/y2k/index.asp (CBN News Y2K Center)

  CBN News has provided some of the earliest and most balanced TV coverage of Y2K (and I'm not saying that just because they interviewed me).

Y2K Bookmark Sites

Many sites contain lists of links to relevant Y2K sites, documents, and so on. These are good places to start research on specific topics, such as utilities, embedded systems, and personal preparation. What's interesting is that these are almost always run by individuals. Here are a few of the more useful or complete ones; note that the "General Y2K" sites listed after these usually contain links as well.

- http://pw1.netcom.com/~ggirod/book-mark.html (Year 2000 Bookmarks)

George Girod's web page remains my favorite general Y2K bookmark site. It's where I usually start when I'm trying to track down a specific piece of information; indeed, I used it while writing this book.

- `http://ourworld.compuserve.com/homepages/roleigh_martin/y2klinks.htm` (Roleigh Martin's home page)

  Roleigh Martin was one of the earliest and most outspoken researchers into potential Y2K impacts on power utilities (with good reason: he lives in Minnesota). This is his list of "phenomenal Year 2000 links." He tends to be focused on infrastructure and embedded systems issues.

- `http://www.bluemarble.net/~storageu/y2k.htm` (Y2K Times)

  Run by Gary Eubanks, this site contains a list of Y2K links, as well as articles and papers on Y2K.

- `http://www.y2klinks.com` (Y2K Links)

  This site is smaller and a bit more eclectic, but helps to fill in some other gaps. It boasts an AI "bot" named Millie who will converse with you and try to dig out answers to questions you have about Y2K with regards to specific companies or products. The human counterpart, Natasha Flazynski, welcomes e-mail as well. This site is also part of the Year 2000 Millennium Resource Web Ring, that is, a series of Y2K web sites linked into a ring.

- `http://www.azstarnet.com/~tres/Y2K.html`
  (Y2K links)

  Yet another privately supported list of Y2K sites.

- `http://headlines.yahoo.com/Full_Coverage/`
  `Tech/Year_2000_Problem` (Yahoo! Y2K Coverage)

  Yahoo!'s Y2K site, with a list of recent news articles
  and links to other Y2K sites.

Y2K Commentary and Analysis

Some of these are specific to one person, others provide
papers and articles from a variety of sources.

- `http://www.year2000.com` (The Year 2000 Information Group)

  This is Peter de Jager's web site and one of the best
  places to start. It has the press clippings site mentioned above, a list of user groups, and an archive of
  white papers and articles that cover the spectrum of
  Y2K topics.

- `http://www.yourdon.com/index.htm` (Ed Yourdon)

  Ed has been well known in software engineering cir-
  cles for the past two decades. He and his daughter
  Jennifer wrote *Time Bomb 2000* (see the Books section below); this is his web site.

- `http://www.yardeni.com/cyber.html` (Dr. Ed Yardeni's CyberEconomics and Y2K site)

  Yardeni is Chief Economist of Deutsche Bank Securities and has developed a reputation on Wall Street for accurate economic forecasting during the 1990s. This site presents his views and analysis on Y2K, as well as links to other relevant web sites.

- `http://www.y2ktimebomb.com` (Westergaard Year 2000)

  Another one of the oldest Y2K sites. This contains news analysis, regular columns, and other resources on Y2K.

- `http://www.tmn.com/~doug` (Douglass Carmichael, Shakespeare & Tao Consulting)

- `http://www.tmn.com/~frautsch` (Dr. Mark Frautschi, Shakespeare & Tao Consulting)

  Doug (cited in Chapter 12) has been giving a lot of thought to the social ramifications of Y2K. His cohort Mark has written in detail on the Y2K embedded systems problem; he can be found What they have to say is worth reading.

- `http://www.isen.com` (David Isenberg Home for Stupid Networks and SMART People)

  David originated the diagram used in Chapter 12 and had other writings on Y2K. His real focus, though, is the need to make our networks less "smart" and more robust and reliable.

- http://www.comlinks.com (Communication Links, Inc.)

Alan Simpson has been very outspoken and visible on Y2K issues, particularly dealing with potential Y2K liability of corporations. This site contains various articles and editorials on different Y2K topics.

- http://www.garynorth.com/y2k/search_.cfm (Gary North's Y2K web site)

I have strong disagreements with Gary's approach and agenda, but he probably feels the same way about me. Here's his site; try to draw your own conclusions rather than accepting his at face value.

- http://www.kiyoinc.com/current.html (Cori Hamasaki's Weather Reports)

Cory is a mainframe consultant who has done Y2K work for various federal agencies in the DC area. (He's also a faithful attendee of the WDCY2K group.) I don't always agree with Cory's conclusions, either, but I do take what he says seriously; he has lots of contacts in D.C.

- http://www.gartner.com (The Gartner Group)

One of the IT research firms often quoted for Y2K
statistics. This will get you to their public web site;
some of their Y2K reports are available for reading.

- `http://www.usa.capgemini.com` (Cap Gemini
  America)

Another IT research firm commonly cited on Y2K
statistics.

- `http://www.softwaremanagement.com` (Software Management Network)

Nicholas Zvegintzov, President of SMN, has been the
most vocal critic of the entire Y2K issue, having
stated that "is not a huge problem of computer software, nor a unique problem, nor a difficult problem
to solve, but it is the focus of a huge and unique
racket." Having actually been involved in a Fortune
50 corporation's Y2K effort for 18 months, I strongly
disagree with most of his assertions.

- `http://www.russkelly.com/experts.html`
  (Russ Kelly Associates, Inc. Y2K Experts Site)

Russ Kelly has summarized where many of the best
known Y2K experts (including himself) stand with
regards to Y2K and has links to their web sites. A
good, brisk read.

- `http://www.bfwa.com/y2k` (BFWA—Year 2000
  issues)

Yep, this is my own web site. I'll post here further Y2K thoughts and reflections as I get time, though the truth is, I'd just as soon get back to software development, object technology, and enterprise architecture.

Government

Here are some sites to help determine just what the government is doing and how it thinks things are going.

- `http://www.itpolicy.gsa.gov/mks/yr2000/cioy2k.htm` (Year 2000 Federal CIO Council)

  The U.S. Government's official Y2K site, as much as one exists. Come here to find out what the different departments and agencies are doing on Y2K. It contains links to Y2K sites for many of those organizations. It has lots of other goodies hidden, if you are patient and search through it.

- `http://www.gao.gov/y2kr.htm` (U.S. General Accounting Office - Y2K reports)

  The GAO has been issuing reports since early 1997 on the Y2K problem in general and the U.S. government's problems and risk in particular. These provide a good counterbalance to the more optimistic reports that come out of the various government departments and agencies.

- `http://www.y2k.gov` (President's Council on Year 2000 Conversion)

This is the official web site for the Council headed up by John Koskinen, the President's Y2K "czar."

- `http://www.senate.gov/~y2k/index.html` (Senate Special Committee on the Year 2000)

The official web site of the Senate's special committee, chaired by Sen. Robert Bennett (R-UT), with Sen. Chris Dodd (D-CT) as vice-chair.

- `http://www.house.gov/reform/gmit/y2k/index.htm` (House Subcommittee on Government Management, Information, and Technology)

This subcommittee, chaired by Rep. Steve Horn (R-CA), with Rep. Dennis Kucinich (D-OH) as ranking member, forms half of the House's Y2K task force. Rep. Horn is best known for his Y2K "report cards" issued each quarter on how the government is doing in its Y2K repairs.

- `http://www.house.gov/science/y2k.htm` (House Subcommittee on Technology)

This is the other half of the House's Y2K task force. Rep. Connie Morella (R-MD) chairs this subcommittee, with Rep. James Barcia (D-MI) as the ranking minority member.

- `http://home.swbell.net/adheath/testimony.htm` (Heath's Exhaustive Y2K Testimony Links)

An absolutely invaluable service provided by Adrian Heath, this site lets you quickly track down testimony (if available) before any of the Congressional hearings on Y2K.

- http://www.stateside.com/y2k.html (Stateside Report: Special Y2K Report Highlights)

Stateside Associates issued a report on how each of the 50 states is doing on Y2K. The report out there as of this writing is dated June 1998; it's not clear if and when they'll update it.

- http://www.wdcy2k.org (Washington D.C. Year 2000 group)

The WDCY2K group is the largest (over 1600 members as of October 1998) and most active Y2K group in the world. Its monthly meetings regularly draw 250-350 attendees, more than many commercial Y2K conferences.

Specific Topics

Again, this section isn't meant to be exhaustive. Here are some representative sites that touch upon the areas of personal and family preparation covered in Part II; you can and should track down others.

EDUCATION

I frankly couldn't find any web sites that dealt with Y2K and educational institutions, be they grade schools, high schools, colleges, or universities. This is one search you may have to make on your own.

HEALTH AND FITNESS

- `http://www.rx2000.org` (Rx2000 Solutions Institute)

  Rx2000 is a nonprofit, member-supported organization dealing with Y2K issues in health care.

- `http://www.fda.gov/cdrh/yr2000/year2000.html` (U.S. Food & Drug Administration—Y2K)

  The FDA's Y2K web page; the main focus is on biomedical devices, but there are other issues touched upon as well.

HOME AND HEARTH (UTILITIES)

- `http://www.nerc.com/~y2k/y2k.html` (North American Electricity Reliability Council)

  The NERC was formed in the aftermath of the 1965 East Coast blackout and is the official coordinating agency of the power companies.

- `http://www.amwa-water.org/y2k/index.html` (Association of Metropolitan Water Agencies)

  The AMWA represents water agencies that serve 150,000 people or more; the total AMWA membership is responsible for water for about 100 million people.

- `http://ourworld.compuserve.com/homepages/ roleigh_martin` (Roleigh Martin)

  As noted above, Roleigh Martin has focused on Y2K impact on utilities: power, water, and so on. This site has several articles and many links to other sites.

- `http://www.euy2k.com` (Electric Utilities and Year 2000)

  Rick Cowles runs this web site. He attracts controversy, but comes across as knowledgeable about the power industry.

- `http://www.swrcb.ca.gov/html/ y2klinks.html` (California State Water Resources Control Board)

  This lets you see how a given state is approaching Y2K and water issues.

FOOD AND SUPPLIES

- `http://www.cassandraproject.org` (The Cassandra Project)

  This is probably the best known of the personal, family, and community preparedness sites. They operate from a presumption that there's a significant risk of infrastructure failure and detail how to prepare accordingly. The URL above was supposed to be active as of October 31, 1998; their old URL was `http://millennia-bcs.com`.

- `http://www.fema.gov/library` (FEMA—Reference Library)

  The U.S. Federal Emergency Management Agency has a series of web pages and documents dealing with virtually every aspect of emergency preparation and response for families. This URL will show you a "blueprint" of their on-line library; click on the room desired (particularly "Preparation and Training" and "Response and Recover") to see lists of documents available.

WORK

- `http://www.erols.com/steve451/impact.htm` (Dealing with the Year 2000 Problem)

  Steven Davis was a pioneer in Y2K contingency planning; his site could and should be listed in several places in this section. His site has a great section for small businesses, with information, instructions, and related links.

- `http://www2.prudential.com/corporate/technology/prutech.nsf/webpgs/yr2ksbs` (Prudential's Small Business Y2K Guide)

  This site has a brochure and a set of worksheets for doing Y2K remediation in a small business.

- `http://www.jrothermel.com` (JKR Associates)

  JKR Associates is putting together a consortium of Y2K service and tool providers to offer a "low tech/

low cost" Y2K solution center for groups of small enterprises (e.g., churches). This site isn't up as of press time; check it out to see if it is of use.

MONEY AND LAW

* http://www.year2000.com/y2klawcenter.html (The Year 2000 Law Center)

    This is part of the Year 2000 Information Center web site. It contains a series of papers on different legal aspect of Y2K, as well as recent news articles on the same subject.

* http://www.2000legal.com (2000 Legal Com)

    Many other web sites discuss legal issues surrounding Y2K; this is a representative one.

* http://www.sec.gov/consumer/y2kaskit.htm (Questions to Ask about the Year 2000)

    This is checklist from the Securities and Exchange Commission (SEC) on what you as an investor should be asking your broker or money manager about Y2K.

FAMILY, COMMUNITY, NATION

Many of the sites above, such as those for the Cassandra Project and for Steven Davis, deal with setting up community Y2K efforts. In particular, the Cassandra Project maintains a list of Y2K community groups and has instructions on how to set up one of your own.

Humor

Here is at least one web site to keep the lighter side of the whole thing:

- `http://www.duh-2000.com` (Duh-2000: The Contest)

   This site runs a monthly contest for the dumbest thing said about Y2K; submissions welcomed. It keeps track of all the past entries, so there's plenty of, ah, shortsightedness to browse. My personal favorite to date was Tom Clancy (yes, *that* Tom Clancy) telling CNN, "Actually, I think somebody just made that up, and if the Y2K problem, you know, the Year 2000 computer problem is real, nobody's proven it to me yet."[2]

Books

Many books on Y2K exist, including now this one, and many more will probably come out. The first wave of books focused largely on the corporate and organizational issues; the second wave sought to explain the problem to the general public and, in many cases, how to prepare for it.

This book was designed specifically to fit in with Prentice Hall's other Y2K offerings. These include:

- **Time Bomb 2000** by Edward and Jennifer Yourdon (Yourdon Press, 1997). The first Y2K book to reach a mass audience, it explains sector-by-sector what the possibilities are for Y2K problems. It is probably the single best-selling book on Y2K.

- **The Year 2000 Software Crisis: Challenge of the Century** by William M. Ulrich and Ian S. Hayes (Yourdon Press, 1997, ISBN 0-13-655664-7). An instant standard in the field, this gives a detailed exposition of just what an organization (corporation, government agency, educational institution) needs to go through for Y2K remediation. If you think that Chapter 3 overstated how hard Y2K remediation is, then read this book.

- **The Year 2000 Software Crisis: The Continuing Challenge** by William M. Ulrich and Ian S. Hayes (Yourdon Press, 1998, 0-13-960154-6). The follow-up to their previous work, Ulrich and Hayes cover legal, testing, and contingency planning issues in more detail.

- **Year 2000: Best Practices for Y2K Millennium Computing** by Dick Lefkon, ed. (Prentice-Hall PTR, 1998, ISBN 0-13-646506-4). This compilation brings together over 100 separate articles covering different topics in organizational Y2K remediation.

Obviously, the last three books aren't intended for the general public, though if you have to deal with Y2K at work, you may want to check them out.

I won't include here a complete survey of other Y2K and related books; look for recommendations on the Web. But here's a personal selection out of the dozens of books available.

- **Year 2000: Personal Protection Guide** by J. R. Morris (Sterlingmoor Publishing Company, 1998, ISBN 0-9663988-3-1) gives a very detailed set of checklists for all the various commitments, obligations, assets, debts, accounts, records, and other aspects of your life that you might want to document prior to Y2K.

- **A business guide to the Year 2000** by Lynn Craig and Mike Kusmirak (Cambridge Publishers, Ltd., 1997, ISBN 1-901572-072). Published in England, this remains one of the best Y2K books for small businesses.

- **The Year 2000 Software Problem: Quantifying the Costs and Assessing the Consequences** by Capers Jones (Addison-Wesley, 1998, ISBN 0-201-30964-5). If you are anxious to put numbers on the Y2K problem, this book will give them to you. Jones acknowledges the high margin of error, but does a very credible job of attempting to count the uncountable: how much software is really out there and how much of that will have to be fixed.

- **Teaching Chipmunks to Dance** by Chris Jesse (Kendall/Hunt Publishing Company, 1997/1998, ISBN 0-7872-4613-1). Subtitled "The Business Leaders' Guide to Making the Distributed Enterprise Year 2000 Compliant," this slim volume focuses less on the technical details and more on the human issues in getting the job done.

- **Out of the Blue: Wild Cards and Other Big Future Surprises** by John L. Petersen (The Arlington Institute, 1997, ISBN 0-9659027-2-2). Petersen's book isn't about Y2K per se, but instead about unexpected "wild card" events and the type of impact they could have. It presents 77 such wild cards, including one ("Major Information Systems Disruptions") that matches Y2K closely.

- **The Mythical Man-Month** (20th Anniversary Edition) by Frederick P. Brooks (Addison-Wesley, 1995, ISBN 0-201-83595-9). After watching the whole Y2K debacle unfold, I've come to the conclusion that this book should be required reading, not just for anyone who works in information technology (IT) but for anyone who works for an organization that uses IT. In fact, we should simplify things and just make it a requirement for high school graduation. Our lives are inexorably entwined with IT, and this book touches on all the risks, trials, and tribulations in trying to design that IT to work correctly. As an IT consultant, I am discouraged by how often I encounter the same problems detailed by Brooks nearly 25 years ago.

Closing Thoughts

This section could have included dozens of additional books and hundreds of additional web sites. The list above isn't exhaustive or even definitive; it's just a sampling, a good place to start. The real resource, though, is you: your willingness to become informed and take action.

Endnotes

Chapter 1

1 Capers Jones, *The Year 2000 Software Problem* (Addison-Wesley, 1998), p. 80; Capers Jones, "Contingency Planning: Damage Control for Euro and Year 2000 Software Problems", electronic presentation sent in private communication with the author.

2 Ibid.

3 "Horn releasesY2K grades: Executive Branch merits an overall," press release, Committee on Government Reform and Oversight, September 9, 1998.

4 Ibid.

5 Testimony of Steven Hock before the Committee on Banking, Housing, and Urban Affairs, U.S. Senate, June 10, 1998.

6 Opening statement by Sen. Robert F. Bennett, Chairman, Senate Special Committee on the Year 2000 Technology Problem, U.S. Senate, June 12, 1998.

7 As reported in *ITAA Year 2000 Outlook* electronic newsletter, September 11, 1998 (Vol. 3, No. 33).

8 Jones, *see endnote 2.*

9 As originally and thoroughly explained in *The Mythical Man-Month*, Frederick P. Brooks, Jr. (Addison-Wesley, 1975).

10 "Y2K Impact Report: Economic Sectors," The Cutter Consortium, May 1998.

Chapter 2

1   Complete text of this testimony can be found in Appendix A.

2   One byte (8 bits) can represent either −128 to 127 or 0 to 255; 2 bytes can represent either −32768...32767 or 0...65535. Software developers tend to count starting with 0, not wanting to waste a perfectly good value; note the range of values associated with the scenarios in Part III.

3   Note to you Macintosh, Amiga, Atari ST, NeXT, and Sun loyalists: I'm not neglecting your systems, I'm just trying to keep the comparisons as direct as possible, tracing the Intel platform with CP/M->MS-DOS->Windows software. Besides, you can comfort yourselves with the observation that any comparison with contemporary WinTel platforms would be unfair anyway.

4   OK, after the discussion about "kilo" in Chapter 1, you need to know that it means a slightly different value when applied to computer memory, storage, and other addressing issues. Computers use base-2 in addressing; 1024 is the number closest to 1000; so a kilobyte is 2^{10} bytes, that is, 1024 bytes

5   The next step above is the terabyte (TB) = 2^{40} bytes = 1024 GB, or just over one trillion bytes (1,099,511,627,776 bytes, to be exact). Or, to use another measure, that's storage equivalent to nearly 1600 CD-ROM disks. There are terabyte storage devices available today for large computers. If Moore's law holds up, you should be able to get 1-TB hard drives for your personal computer by 2008. Note that we should likewise have 1-gigahertz (GHz = 1 billion cycles/second) CPUs in personal computers by the end of the year 2000.

6   Note to those of you in the computer industry: Yes, this section is a tremendously simplified outline of a complex marketplace over a 50-year period. On the other hand, as it stands, it's likely more than 90 percent of the readers of this book care to know on the subject. After all, the topic here is Y2K, not the evolution of modern information technology.

7   Every personal computer I have bought has cost about $3000—as a complete system—at the time that I bought it. That benchmark of PCs costing around $2500 plus or minus a few hundred has held for nearly 20 years. The rapid drop of actual complete system prices in the past few years has been remarkable, though the manufacturers haven't been too happy about it.

8   There is an even simpler level: **microcode**, which is embedded within the chip itself and which helps tell the chip how to behave. There are

some cases of microcode with Y2K problems, but that has little bearing on our story here.

9   After converting it into assembly language, an assembler is then invoked to finish the translation into executable machine language instructions, that is, executable code.

10 Capers Jones, *The Year 2000 Software Problem*, pp. 45-49.

11 Talk given by Larry DeBoever of the META Group at the Enterprise Architecture Conference, September 1, 1998, Boston, MA.

12 "Doomsday 2000?", *Computerworld*, September 6, 1993.

13 "The Problem You May Not Know You Have," Paul Gillin, <u>*Computerworld*</u>, February 13, 1984.

14 Some writers have argued that the savings in database and memory cost even since 1985 outweigh the Y2K costs being incurred by most organizations. Such analysis does not, in my opinion, properly take into account both the costs and damages likely to be wreaked by Y2K problems in embedded systems—and, when all is said, done, and repaired, probably won't even hold up for regular computer systems as well.

15 "Doomsday 2000?" *Computerworld*, [date], 1993.

Chapter 3

1   See "The Real Software Crisis," Bruce F. Webster, *BYTE Magazine*, January 1996.

2   The classic work on this is *The Mythical Man-Month* by Frederick P. Brooks, originally written in 1975 and reissued in a twentieth anniversary edition in 1995 (Addison-Wesley, 1995).

Chapter 4

1   Besides, engineers like to start counting at "0," due largely to having to work with a limited number of bits. For example, if you've got just 1 byte—8 bits—to work with, you can have 256 items, numbered 0 through 255. If an engineer had been in charge of creating the Julian or Gregorian calendars, they would likely have started out with A.D. 0, which would have made 100, 200, …, 1900, and 2000 all the first years of a century, rather than the last. By the same logic, the years A.D. 0…99 would have been the "0th" century; right now, we'd be in the

nineteenth century (hey, it makes sense—all the years start with "19," don't they?); and we'd be on the verge of entering the twentieth century. It's all very rational and efficient, but it also goes a long ways to explaining why we don't put engineers in charge of things more often.

2   An amazing number were concentrated into a single letter to the editor written by Jeff Carlock and published in the May 21, 1998, issue of the *Wall Street Journal*. I submitted an op-ed piece debunking all of them. The Journal didn't run it. I've extracted a few for this chapter.

3   These reports are all available on-line at http://www.gao.gov/y2kr.htm.

4   These surveys are available at http://www.wdcy2k.org.

5   Jeff Carlock's letter to the *Wall Street Journal*, May 21, 1998.

6   "FAA Systems: Serious Challenges Remain in Resolving Year 2000 and Computer Security Problems" (GAO/T-AIMD-98-251), U.S. General Accounting Office, August 6, 1998.

7   "Industry wakes up to the Year 2000 menace", *Fortune*, April 27, 1998.

8   A twentieth-anniversary edition, with the complete text of the original and several more essays by Brooks, including an analysis of his various assertions, is available from Addison-Wesley (1995, ISBN 0-201-83595-9). Incidentally, Brooks was also the one who coined the phrase "silver bullet" as referring to some miraculous solution for IT projects; his essay "No silver bullet—essence and accident in software engineering" is found in this special edition as well.

9   See Ed Yourdon, *Decline and Fall of the American Programmer* (Prentice-Hall, 1992), which he then followed with *Rise and Resurrection of the American Programmer* (Prentice-Hall, 1998).

10 For a general introduction to complex adaptive systems, see John Holland, *Hidden Order: How Adaptation Builds Complexity* (Perseus Press, 1996) and Kevin Kelly, *Out of Control: The New Biology of Machines, Social Systems, and the Economic World* (Perseus Press, 1995), among others.

11 Capers Jones, *The Year 2000 Software Problem,* p. 80; "Contingency Planning: Damage Control for Euro and Year 2000 Software Problems," presentation.

12 Actually, many people argue—with, I fear, validity—that we no longer have the technology and expertise to send people to the moon, that we have actually lost ground in many areas.

13 A twentieth anniversary edition, with the complete text of the original and several more essays by Brooks, including an analysis of his various assertions, is available from Addison-Wesley (1995, ISBN xxxxxxxxx). Incidentally, Brooks was also the one who coined the phrase "silver bul-

let" as referring to some miraculous solution for IT projects; his essay "No silver bullets" is found in this special edition as well.

14 You may want to check out the Web site at http://www.duh-2000.com, which runs a monthly contest for the most stupid thing said publicly about Y2K.

15 See Ed Yourdon, *The Decline and Fall of the American Programmer* (Prentice Hall, 199x), which he then followed with *The Rise and Resurrection of the American Programmer* (Prentice Hall).

16 For information on complex adaptive systems, see John Holland, *Hidden Order* (publisher) and Kevin Kelly, *Out of Control* (publisher), among other books.

17 The resolution of the current deliberations of the House Judiciary Panel and the possible vote of the House of Representatives on articles of impeachment could have a large impact on such an effort, though one could argue that Clinton should use Y2K as a reason to mobilize the country and put all this behind him. On the other hand, by early 1999, we could be looking at President Gore.

Chapter 5

1 But see the discussion at the start of Chapter 4 on when the transition actually occurs.

2 One of the better known proponents of this is Gary North (http://www.garynorth.com). Though North doesn't discuss it as such on his site, he has stated in other writings his belief in Christian Reconstruction, which states that Christians will help rebuild civilization in accordance with their beliefs after Y2K causes it to collapse.

3 This may seem like an extreme scenario, but I ran into a real-world version of this back in July 1996, when I first started working in Washington, DC. The DC Public Health Commissioner had issued a warning a few weeks earlier about high levels of bacteria in the water supply and then abruptly cancelled it. However, many residents and workers within the District weren't taking any chances; restaurants were serving bottled water, and people at work cautioned me about drinking from the water fountains. Truth was, the water *did* taste funny, and a glass of tap water that sat at my desk during one of my first weekends there had *something* growing in it on Monday. It was quite a while before I drank water out of the tap again.

4 From an article in *Parade Magazine* (November 9, 1997) written by Thomas E. Ricks and based on his book, *Making The Corps* (Scribner,

1997). The list details what Ricks felt were the fundamental lessons
learned by recruits at the U.S. Marine Corps boot camp at Parris Island,
South Carolina.

Chapter 6

1   See Appendix A for the rest of my testimony.

2   Were I to do it over again, I would drop the reference to martial law—
    which predicts a specific response by government officials—and instead
    make reference to what could be the driving consequences, that is, sig-
    nificant disruption in services, followed by possible civil unrest. While
    I didn't agree with all that Mr. Kucinich had to say, I felt that he was
    right in this point.

3   Posted by Paul Milne, as cited by Tom Benjamin in an unpublished pa-
    per on Y2K sent to me via e-mail.

4   "2000 is Too Soon, DC Officials Say," Eric Lipton, *The Washington
    Post*, October 3, 1998.

5   I could go into a long discourse here on the evils of social promotion
    and some of the other educational malpractice committed in the name
    of "self-esteem," but his is neither the place or the time.

Chapter 7

1   Testimony of Michael A. Friedman, M.D., Acting Commissioner,
    Food And Drug Administration, U.S. Department of Health And Hu-
    man Services before the Senate Special Committee on the Year 2000
    Technology Problem on July 23, 1998.

2   Testimony of Kenneth W. Kizer, M.D., M.P.H., Under Secretary For
    Health, Department of Veterans Affairs before the Senate Special Com-
    mittee on the Year 2000 Technology Problem on July 23, 1998.

3   These estimates and other information in this paragraph come from
    "Medicare Computer Systems: Year 2000 Challenges Put Benefits and
    Services in Jeopardy," GAO/AIMD-98-284, September 1998.

4   Comment made at the March 1998 meeting of the Washington DC
    Year 2000 group, among other settings. The other two places he cited:
    in a plane or in an elevator. Of the three, the hospital worries me the
    most.

5 You, too, eh? The sad thing was that I actually did this successfully several years ago—got myself into great shape and got a great insurance policy. I'd like to switch to another one now, but I'm not quite as svelte and active as I was then.

6 About 1500 calories and nearly 100 grams of fat in a whole pie, as I recall. I don't want to think about how many of those I ate before the labeling went into effect.

7 You can find it lots of places; an official on-line source is http://www.nal.usda.gov:8001/py/pmap.htm.

8 The things you discover helping your children do their homework. We found this in the Reuters Health News Service, but the study was done by Dr. Joseph Feldman and others at SUNY. It noted that cigarette smoking "...is associated with an increased incidence of genital warts" in both HIV-positive and HIV-negative women. The Web link I found looking for it again was http://www.reutershealth.com/news/doc/199703/19970318epc.html, but you'll now need to pay to get access to it.

9 On the other hand, when I was a child, it was often worse than this when my mom would take me to Balboa Naval Hospital in San Diego. I fell off my bike in 4th grade on the way to school; it literally took them all day to (a) examine me, (b) take an X-ray of my arm, (c) decide I had a greenstick fracture, and (d) put a cast on it. Even just a regular doctor's visit took hours.

10 A great Web source for information on this is at the FDA's Y2K biomedical device site, http://www.fda.gov/cdrh/yr2000/year2000.html.

11 Shamelessly adapted from a magnetic graffiti refrigerator magnet we own that says, "Nothing tastes as good as being thin feels!" Guess what one of my guiding principles is?

Chapter 8

1 There are actually four power grids, each semi-independent of the other. See the Statement for the Record of the Special Committee on the Year 2000 Technology Problem of the United States Senate Hearing, June 12, 1998, on Computers and the Electric Power Grid submitted by the National Rural Electric Cooperative Association. Available on-line at http://www.nreca.org/leg_reg/6-12TestimonyFinal.html.

2 Opening Statement, Sen. Bob Bennett (R-UT), Special Committee on the Year 2000 Technology Problem, Hearing on the Risks of Y2K on the Nation's Power Grid, June 12, 1998. Available on-line at http://www.senate.gov/~bennett/pr0612b98.html.

3 As reported in several news stories. See, for example, the ABC News report at http://www.abcnews.com/sections/tech/DailyNews/ y2k_utilities980611.html.

4 For information about hooking up a generator at home, as well as getting a sense of how much power you may need, see the article "Selecting the Right Portable Generator After a Disaster" by the Virginia Cooperative Extension at http://www.ext.vt.edu/pubs/disaster/490-303/490-303.html.

5 While doing missionary work in Central America back in the 1970s, I transferred to Panama City, Panama, just in time for a massive water outage in the part of town where our apartment was. After four days of no water (in Panama in July) except for a few buckets we got each day from a water truck—and used primarily to flush the toilet—we were all pretty ripe. We finally went into another part of the city just to use someone else's shower.

6 Opening Statement of FCC Commissioner Michael K. Powell before the Senate Special Committee on the Year 2000 Technology Problem, July 31, 1998 (http://www.fcc.gov/Speeches/Powell/Statements/ stmkp819.html)

7 To spare me a lot of e-mail messages, the phone is a Nokia 6160. The service provider will remain nameless, but it's hard to miss their billboards and other promotions.

8 Art Gross, former CIO of the IRS, said at a Y2K breakfast (which I attended) in November 1997 that the IRS had over 7000 PBXs, and that they were not Y2K compliant. His concern: That they could not buy and install new, compliant PBXs in time, and that the manufacturer might not even be able to build that many compliant systems in time.

9 See the testimony of Kathleen Hirning, Chief Information Officer, Federal Energy Regulatory Commission, before the House Subcommittee on Technology Committee on Science, May 14, 1998 (found at http://www.ferc.fed.us/y2k/tes_katie51498.html, among other places).

10 The San Andreas fault, which runs from the Gulf of Cortez up through the San Francisco peninsula, was responsible for the San Francisco earthquake of 1906. It is now is overdue for another large earthquake, likely to be 8.0 or higher on the Richter scale (Loma Prieta was 7.1). Californians know this and await what is simply known as the Big One with a perverse mixture of fear and pride.

11 California went through a prolonged drought from 1987 to 1992, and so many such water conservation practices were promoted. To this day, my wife cannot bear to see a TV show or movie where someone turns on a tap and lets it run while standing there, talking.

12 See, for example, the *Washington Post* article, "Postal Service Emerging as Key Year 2000 Backup," Stephen Barr, October 7, 1998.

13 "Testing your PC for the millennium bug," found at http://www.y2ktimebomb.com/Tip/Lord/lord9819.htm.

14 As an example, see "Metro Stops Payment on Troubled Computer; Officials Predict Delays if Problems Continue," Alice Reid, the *Washington Post*, April 29, 1998. The District of Columbia had a $20 million contract with BDM International to put in a new computer system to control its Metro subway system and was withholding payment due to continuing problems with the new system. The District's CIO has stated publicly that the District will not have all its Y2K problems solved in time; the Metro appears to be a good candidate, though one would hope the new systems put in by BDM did not have Y2K problems.

15 A concise summary of all this can be found at http://magic.hofstra.edu/~cgordon1/energy.htm.

16 Tolstoi's actual quote, from *The Kreutzer Sonata*, involved beauty, not simplicity.

17 From the novella "Shadrack in the Furnace" by Robert Silverberg. One of those mottos I've picked up and quoted for years.

18 I discovered this in the aftermath of the Loma Prieta quake. Within 12 hours, there was scarcely a D- or AA-cell battery to be found in the Santa Cruz area, but the stores literally had piles of C-cells. That's because most battery-powered devices you see these days use D- or AA-cells.

19 This was the one thing we lacked in the aftermath of the Loma Prieta quake: we had no way of cooking food. Dumb.

Chapter 9

1 A brief summary of the Church's welfare program, which includes global humanitarian aid, can be found at http://www.lds.org/en/4_Global_Media_Guide/Welfare_and_Humanitarian.html.

2 If you need a refresher course on it, check it out at } http://www.nal.usda.gov:8001/py/pmap.html

3 For the complete story—as well as more than you probably wanted to know about alternatives to toilet paper, past and present—see the Bay Paper Company's chronicle of the 1973 toilet paper shortage at http://baypaper.com/toiletpaper.html.

4 That is, Chapter 11 of the book, not Chapter 11 bankruptcy. No pun intended.

5 You can contact your local Red Cross chapter and ask for the brochure
   "Your Family Disaster Supplies Kit" (ACR 4463) or read it on their Web
   site at URL is http://www.redcross.org/disaster/safety/displan.html
6 After getting the kids off the roof and taking them with us, of course.
7 Warning: Children have been known to sneak into these kits and eat all
   the good stuff.
8 You can reach Ms. Tate at (435) 835-8283 or write to her at 302 E 200
   N, Manti, UT 84642.
9 The full article can be found, among other places, at http://walton-
   feed.com/grain/cooking.

Chapter 10

1 "Merrill cuts 3,400 jobs, reports weaker results," Patrick McGeehan,
   The *Wall Street Journal*, October 14, 1998.
2 As stated in various news reports. See, for example, http://www.spo-
   kane.net/stories/1998/Jul/29/S427490.asp. If you'd like the Communist Party (USA) perspective, see http://ww.hartford-hwp.com/cp-usa/
   archives98/98-08-01.html.
3 "Fifty Years of Social Security," Martha A. McSteen, then-Acting Commissioner of Social Security, 1995; posted on the SSA History Web site
   at http://199.173.225.3/history/50mm2.html.
4 Dr. Ed Yardeni, chief economist of Deutsche Bank Securities, runs it at
   http://www.progsys.com/yardeni/y2kfind.asp. Here, for example, is the
   Y2K disclosure for Merrill Lynch's 10Q filing for August 10, 1998:

   *The modifications for Year 2000 systems compliance are
   proceeding according to plan and are expected to be completed in early 1999. Merrill Lynch's recent acquisitions, continued global expansion, and higher-than-expected systems
   consulting costs have increased the total projected expense
   from $300 million to approximately $375 million. Based on
   information currently available, the remaining costs are estimated at $200 million and will cover hardware and soft-
   ware upgrades, systems consulting, and computer
   maintenance. These expenditures are not expected to have a
   material adverse impact on Merrill Lynch's financial position, results of operations, or cash flows in future periods.
   However, the failure of securities exchanges, clearing organizations, vendors, clients, or regulators to resolve their own*

processing issues in a timely manner could result in a material financial risk to the company. Merrill Lynch is devoting necessary resources, including contacting vendors, to address all Year 2000 issues in a timely manner.

5 You can find these reports and related U.S. Government Y2K documents on-line at http://www.itpolicy.gsa.gov/mks/yr2000/cio.htm.

6 This is a good reality check. Let's say a firm has, say, 500 Information Technology (IT) personnel and typically spends $100 million per year on them (salaries, benefits, infrastructure, etc.). This same firm then says that it expects to spend $200 million on Y2K in 1999. That's the equivalent of having 1000 IT personnel working on the project. Just what is that money being spent on? Does the firm think that it can get together 1000 IT personnel in short order to work on Y2K? The lesson is: Be wary of any organization that is scheduled to spend the bulk of its Y2K money in 1999.

Chapter 11

1 For Yardeni's ever-growing list of Y2K issues and their potential economic impact, see his on-line book, "Year 2000 Recession?" at http://www.yardeni.com/y2kbook.html.

2 The stock market—at least, the major indices—continued to climb for another year and a half after Greenspan's remark before starting the down-and-up seesaw that has been going on since mid-1998.

3 "Will the Bug Bite the Bull?", Steven Levy, *Newsweek*, May 4, 1998, p. 62.

4 Central processing unit (CPU) chips in computers and embedded control systems execute instructions in an orderly sequence, based on how those instructions are arranged in memory and the directions they contain. However, these processors typically have an **interrupt** signal that other devices connected to it (such as input/output devices) can send. When that happens, the processor stops, saves what it's working on, handles the interrupt request, restores what it has saved, and then picks up where it left off. It's possible for another, higher-priority interrupt to come in while the CPU is handling the first one, in which case it goes through the same process (save state, handle, restore state), and so on, up through several levels of nested interrupts.

This approach to processing is known as *interrupt-driven*. Many of us are like this in real life, especially at work. So the phrase as applied to

514   The Y2K Survivial Guide

people gained currency among software and hardware engineers: "If you need that from Webster soon, you'd better go ask him—he's largely interrupt-driven and may not get around to it if you don't say anything."

5   Actually, this is a twice-adopted term. It comes originally from physics, where it describes a span of frequencies of electromagnetic signals—radio waves, light, and so forth. That frequency determines the amount of information that can be carried per unit of time by that signal, so the greater the bandwidth, the more information that can be sent. The phrase was adopted in computer architecture to describe the ability to transfer information between components of a system for example, "The network doesn't have the bandwidth to move those large images around in real time." Technogeeks adopted it to describe how much more work someone could get done: "Well, you could ask Webster for that report, but with that book he's writing, he doesn't have much bandwidth left."

6   For comments on Social Security vs. the FMS, see the interview with Jack Brock of the U.S. General Accounting Office by Ed Yardeni as part of Yardeni's Y2K Action Conference, August 19, 1998, at http://www.yardeni.com/transcripts/broc1.pdf. For Rep. Steve Horn's grading of government agencies, see http://wwww.house.gov/reform/gmit/y2k/y2kcharts.pdf. Both of these will require that you have the Adobe Acrobat PDF reader; you can download it from http://www.adobe.com/prodindex/acrobat/readstep.html.

7   *Iatrogenic* is a medical term that refers to illnesses or injuries caused by medical professionals and facilities while attempting to handling an existing condition, for example, having a surgeon leave a surgical instrument inside a patient, or picking up a staph infection while staying in a hospital. A 1994 report in the *Journal of the American Medical Association* indicated that 180,000 people die each year in the United States due to iatrogenic causes; JAMA 1994;272:1851-7 cited at http://home.cio.net/chiro/topics/drugs.html

8   Statistics taken from the *Economic Digest* of A&A Contract Custom Brokers Ltd., found at http://www.aacb.com/Edigest/edmar98.htm.

9   For a lot of information on identify theft, see the Privacy Rights Clearinghouse Web site on it at http://www.privacyrights.og/identity.html.

10 As reported at http://wwww.privacyrights.org/cases/case9697.html#identity.

11 As cited in a review of the book at http://www.scottburns.com/970316SU.htm.

12 See http://www.yardeni.com/y2kconfl.html. for conference proceedings.

Chapter 12

1 Adapted with permission from the on-line article "Year 2000: Who Will Do What and When Will They Do It? Towards Actions," found at http://www.tmn.com/~doug. Doug adapted the diagram from "SMART Letter #7—Scenarios Facing Year 2000—May 15, 1998" copyright © 1998 by David S. Isenberg and found at http://www.is-en.com. Both sites are well worth visiting.

2 The End Of The World As We Know It, in case you don't remember from earlier in the book.

3 The administration made that announcement on February 4, 1998, just a day or so after it sought (and received) substantial media coverage for announcing the White House Millennium Project, headed by Hillary Rodham Clinton (http://www.whitehouse.gov/Initiatives/Millennium/main-ie.shtml). Yet Koskinen's appointment got so little coverage that I didn't find out about it until several days after it happened, even though I was living in Washington, DC at the time and was neck-deep in Year 2000 issues.

4 As noted in Chapter 4, the most common is that the administration is waiting until after the November 1998 elections at the very least, because it doesn't want to cause anxieties in and about the economy. Don't be surprised if the issue receives a sudden burst of public attention by the Administration sometime in the November 1998 to January 1999 timeframe; certainly no later than the president's 1999 State of the Union address, though that's a year later than most Y2K analysts and leaders had hoped for.

As also noted, an even more cynical scenario has President Clinton setting up Vice-President Gore as the "white knight" in charge of Y2K toward the end of 1999. Should things go smoothly, then the vice-president has a feather in his cap for the 2000 election. If things don't go smoothly, then the vice-president will campaign on the them of "Let's keep a steady hand on the tiller; let him finish the job he's begun."

Lest this seem partisan, let me point out that I am a lifelong registered Democrat, albeit a profoundly disgusted and disappointed one.

5 Incidentally, the same question could be asked of Bill Gates, CEO of Microsoft and the single most-widely recognized technology leader. Gates

initially dismissed the Y2K problem altogether; Microsoft then belatedly put up a Web site devoted to Y2K "issues" in Microsoft products.

6   The title of this book, notwithstanding, this is not a survivalist text. The publisher chose the title.

7   A good Web site about the Cuban Missile Crisis is at http://www.hyperion.advanced.org/11046/.

8   Even as recently as 1984 we had the TV miniseries "The Day After" depicting a limited nuclear exchange between the United States and the USSR, along with its aftermath. Far more graphic and despairing was the BBC production "Threads," which came out at about the same time. But the collapse of the Soviet Union has diminished the theme in either serious or popular treatment. Probably the last major film to portray a nuclear exchange and aftermath was 1992's *Terminator 2: Judgment Day,* which offered what is probably the most dramatic portrayal on film of a nuclear blast over a major city.

9   Located at http://www.garynorth.com/y2k/search.cfm.

10 See, for example, http://www.chetday.com/musing3.html.

11 At which point, you would have a lot of roving, starving, cranky people with guns—which sounds pretty much like what survivalists are fleeing in the first place.

12 Here's a thought that has never occurred to me before. We've long talked about nuclear missiles targeted at military installations and metropolitan areas; I wonder if any were ever deliberately targeted at crop producing or other agricultural regions.

13 I'm not sure I'm so much anti-social as a-social; frankly, I have barely enough time to spend with my wife and kids, so I'm leery about starting up new friendships that I won't have time to maintain. It may not make much sense, but there you have it.

14 If you haven't had teenagers of your own, especially girls, you probably won't fully appreciate what a gracious act it was for a senior to ask a sophomore she doesn't even know to go shopping with her. Those of you who do are probably picking your jaws up off the floor and trying to track down my e-mail address to ask me where we live.

15 Actually, at my old software firm, the phrase was "Start out stupid and work up from there."

16 But carefully. I fully recognize that there are apartment buildings and neighborhoods where going and knocking on ten doors at random stands a good chance of ending in very unpleasant encounters, if not actual violence.

Chapter 13

1   Long before then, though, the already-popped kernels would start to burn, creating that distinctive odor that can fill an office or a home in an amazingly short time. It also tends to leave dark scorch marks on the microwave floor or rotating tray. So don't try this to completion unless you're prepared to deal with that

2   See the ITAA Year 2000 User Demand survey results at http://www.itaa.org/survey.htm.

3   See, for example, the apologies and explanations about a six-month backlog of food storage products from Walton Feed at http://www.waltonfeed.com/portela1.html.

4   Dave's account, with photos, can be found at http://www.rideau-info.com/local/brownstory.html.

5   Lorie's account is at http://www.rideau-info.com/local/stormdiet.html.

6   Again, from http://www.rideau-info.com/local/brownstory.html.

Chapter 14

1   Hence, if you go back and read works such as The Limits to Growth, The Population Bomb, The Coming Dark Age, and similar works of 20-30 years ago, you'll find that they are consistently wrong in their predictions of future trends and events.

2   The End Of The World As We Know It, in case you skipped ahead to this chapter and missed the earlier references to this acronym.

3   These scenarios are modeled after those used for the March/May 1998 WDCY2K surveys documented in Appendix B. As noted in that survey, the scale of damages was based in part on a list of possible Y2K effects tied to the percentage of unrepaired Y2K defects given in "How serious is the Year 2000 problem?" Capers Jones, paper dated November 29, 1997.

4   For actual statistics on past economic contractions, I am indebted to two papers: "Is the US Economy More Recession Proof Than It Used To Be?", Edward Renshaw, Professor of Economics, State University of New York at Albany (http://www.albany.edu/~renshaw/leading/ess13.html); and "<title>", <author> (http://www.scruz.net/~kangaroo/L-presidentsresponsible.htm).

5   For the phrase and the concept, I am indebted to John L. Petersen's excellent book Out of the Blue: Wild Cards and Other Big Future Surprises

(The Arlington Institute, Arlington, VA, 1997, ISBN 0-9659027-2-2). Incidentally, Petersen has a Y2K equivalent in his long list of "wild cards" in the book; see "Major Information Systems Disruptions" on pp. 108-109.

6   Yes, I know I'm using just two digits here. Anyone who gets confused about what date being discussed has more problems than this book can handle.

7   Serious concern about a new strain of flu, known as "swine flu," led President Gerald Ford to initiate a massive national vaccination effort. The strain never really showed up in any significant amount, even among those unvaccinated.

8   Comet Kohoutek, spotted on its way in toward the sun late in 1973, was expected to be the "comet of the century." It was a dud.

9   As per Johnny Carson with toilet paper in 1973.

10 A directed graph, for those of you who understand the mathematical reference.

Chapter 16

1   As in "snowball's chance." The ratings are 0 to 5 snowballs, with 5 representing the highest chances of success.

2   Sometimes known as the WISCY ("whiskey") question: Why isn't someone coding yet?

3   Capers Jones, The Year 2000 Software Problem: Quantifying the Costs and Assessing the Consequences, p. 23.

4   You can find details at http://impact.arc.nasa.gov/news/1998/mar/16.html.

5   You can reach the forum archives at http://catless.ncl.ac.uk/Risks/. As a recent example: A file generated with information for 50,000 direct-deposit social assistance (welfare) payment was discovered to have an error before the payments were actually sent. So the erroneous file was deleted, and a new file was created and transmitted over to the bank generating the payments. However, an operator at that bank failed to let the computer know about the new file, and so those 50,000 people didn't get their direct-deposit payments on the expected day. (ACM Risks Digest, Vol. 20, Issue 2, Oct. 3, 1998; reported by Mark Brader) Small cause, big effect.

6   "No Silver Bullet—Essence and Accidents of Software Engineering," IFIPS, 1986; reprinted in The Mythical Man-Month (twentieth Anniversary Edition), Frederick P. Brooks, 1995.

7 Some of the standard works include: The Psychology of Computer Programming (Gerald Weinberg, 1971); The Mythical Man-Month (Frederick P. Brooks, 1975); Peopleware (Tom DeMarco and Timothy Lister, 1987); *Principles of Software Engineering Management* (Tom Gilb, 1988); *Assessment and Control of Software Risks* (Capers Jones, 1994); *Journey of the Software Professional* (Luke Hohmann, 1997).

8 Bruce F. Webster, Statement Submitted to the Subcommittee on Government Management, Information, and Technology Hearing on "Year 2000: Biggest Problems, Proposed Solutions," U.S. House of Representatives, June 22, 1998.

9 "Y2K Not Only Problem Looming," *USA Today*, October 9, 1998; posted at http://www.millecon.com/releases/98a09nr1.htm.

Appendix B

1 Complete text of the original survey is given later in Appendix B.

2 Impact scale derived from possible Y2K consequences outlined in "How Serious Is the Year 2000 Software Problem", Capers Jones, November 29, 1998

3 "Social incidents" and "disruptions" have to do with demonstrations, work stoppages, strikes, organized vandalism, looting, and riots.

4 "Supply/infrastructure problems" have to do with food shortages, fuel/heating oil shortages, disruptions in public utilities (power, gas, telecom), disruptions in transportation (airlines, trucking), and so on.

5 "Will the Bug Bite the Bull?", Steven Levy, *Newsweek*, May 5, 1998, p. 62.

Resources

1 Uniform Resource Locator, in case you were wondering what URL stands for. And while you're at it: "http" means "hypertext transfer protocol" and "html" means "hypertext markup language".

2 Still on-line for you're own browsing as of this writing at http://cnn.com/books/dialogue/9808/tom.clancy.cnn/index.html.

About the Author

Bruce F. Webster

Bruce F. Webster has become an internationally recognized authority on the Year 2000 crisis. He organized from scratch the corporate wide Y2K contingency planning effort for a Fortune 50 company, with the goal of protecting billions in daily transactions and over half a trillion dollars in assets. He has provided analysis and documents on the Y2K issue to Senate and House committees and has testified several times before Congress. He has presented information on Y2K contingency planning to U.S. intelligence agencies; he was the keynote speaker for a private Y2K conference held at the World Bank; and he was an invited speaker at the Middle East Year 2000 Conference held in Lebanon. He has also spoken on Y2K issues and risks in a wide variety of other conferences and settings, including the Center for Strategic and International Studies, the University of Chicago Graduate School of Business, and the Hackers' Conference. He has been written about in *Newsweek*, interviewed for NBC and CBN News, televised on C-SPAN and *The 700 Club*, and cited in *Barron's*, *National*

Journal, Datamation, American Banker, the Chicago *Tribune,* and various other news reports.

Most notably, Webster is founder (under Fannie Mae's direction) and co-chair of the Washington D.C. Year 2000 Group (www.wdcy2k.org). The WDCY2K group is the largest—over 1600 members—and most active Y2K organization in the world. It brings together each month two to three hundred leaders, managers, and technologists from industry, finance, government, and the military to discuss Y2K issues, share solutions, and coordinate efforts.

Webster has been involved in software engineering for over 20 years and has provided consulting to a wide variety of firms, including Fannie Mae, Sprint, Capital One, USF&G, Global One, ARINC, Motorola, and MCI. His achievements include: helping to start up two different software companies; contributing to nearly a dozen commercial software products; writing over 160 articles on technology industry analysis, software development, and product evaluation including two popular and influential columns ("According to Webster," *BYTE,* 1985-87; "State of the Mac," *Macworld,* 1989-91); authoring **Pitfalls of Object-Oriented Development** (M&T Books, 1995), **The Art of 'Ware** (M&T Books, 1995), and **The NeXT Book** (Addison-Wesley, 1989); giving presentations and seminars on software development in such places as Tokyo, Costa Rica, New York City, San Francisco, Boston, Dallas, and Kansas City; and teaching computer science for two years at Brigham Young University.

Webster is Chief Technical Officer for Object Systems Group (www.osgcorp.com), a consulting firm working to help Fortune 500 companies successfully develop and deploy information technology. He is based out of Dallas, TX, where he does high-level consulting on Year 2000 contingency planning, complexity issues in technology, enterprise architecture, software development management and organization, information technology infrastructure, object-oriented development, reuse, and quality assurance.

Webster (www.bfwa.com) can be reached via his own e-mail address (bwebster@bfwa.com) or

c/o Object Systems Group:
e-mail: bwebster@osgcorp.com
p-mail: Object Systems Group,
               122 W. Carpenter Fwy, Suite 550
               Irving, TX 75039
phone: 972.650.2026 (fax: 972.650.9020)

Index